GMAT®

All the
Quant

This guide provides an in-depth look at the variety of GMAT questions that test
your knowledge of fractions, decimals, and percents. Learn to see the connections
among these part–whole relationships and practice implementing strategic shortcuts.

Acknowledgements

A great number of people were involved in the creation of the book you are holding.

Our Manhattan Prep resources are based on the continuing experiences of our instructors and students. The overall vision for this edition was developed by Stacey Koprince, who determined what strategies to cover and how to weave them into a cohesive whole.

Stacey Koprince was also the primary author and she was supported by a number of content experts. Chelsey Cooley, Daniel Fogel, Mario Gambino, Whitney Garner, David Mahler, Andrea Pawliczek, and Helen Tan served as a sounding board during the writing phase, vetting ideas and editing new content. Chelsey Cooley also wrote a number of new problems for the guide and David Mahler proofed them all. The handwritten solutions were all the work of Helen Tan. Mario Gambino managed production for all images, handwritten and otherwise, with Derek Frankhouser and Israt Pasha lending their design expertise.

Matthew Callan coordinated the production work for this guide. Once the manuscript was done, Naomi Beesen and Emily Meredith Sledge edited and Cheryl Duckler proofread the entire guide from start to finish. Carly Schnur designed the covers.

Retail ISBNs: 978-1-5062-4854-7, 978-1-5062-6254-3
Retail eISBN: 978-1-5062-4855-4
Course ISBN: 978-1-5062-4859-2
Course eISBN: 978-1-5062-4860-8

GMAT® Strategy Guides

GMAT All the Quant

GMAT All the Verbal

GMAT Integrated Reasoning & Essay

Strategy Guide Supplements

Math

GMAT Foundations of Math

GMAT Advanced Quant

Verbal

GMAT Foundations of Verbal

September 3, 2019

Dear Student,

Thank you for picking up a copy of *All the Quant*. I hope this book provides just the guidance you need to get the most out of your GMAT studies.

At Manhattan Prep, we continually aspire to provide the best instructors and resources possible. If you have any questions or feedback, please do not hesitate to contact us.

Email our Student Services team at gmat@manhattanprep.com or give us a shout at 212-721-7400 (or 800-576-4628 in the United States or Canada). We try to keep all our books free of errors, but if you think we've goofed, please visit manhattanprep.com/GMAT/errata.

Our Manhattan Prep Strategy Guides are based on the continuing experiences of both our instructors and our students. The primary author of the 7th Edition All the Quant guide was Stacey Koprince. Project management and design were led by Matthew Callan, Mario Gambino, and Helen Tan. I'd like to send particular thanks to instructors Chelsey Cooley, Daniel Fogel, Whitney Garner, David Mahler, Andrea Pawliczek, and Emily Meredith Sledge for their content contributions.

Finally, we are indebted to all of the Manhattan Prep students who have given us excellent feedback over the years. This book wouldn't be half of what it is without their voice.

And now that *you* are one of our students too, please chime in! I look forward to hearing from you. Thanks again and best of luck preparing for the GMAT!

Sincerely,

Chris Ryan
Executive Director
Product Strategy

TABLE OF CONTENTS

UNIT TWO: Algebra

UNIT FIVE: Geometry

The GMAT Mindset

The GMAT is a complex exam. It feels like an academic test—math, grammar, logical reasoning—but it's really not! At heart, the GMAT is a test of your *executive reasoning skills.*

Executive reasoning is the official term for your ability to make all kinds of decisions in the face of complex and changing information. It makes sense, then, that graduate management programs would want to test these skills. It's crucial for you to understand *how* they do so because that understanding will impact both how you study for the GMAT and how you take the test.

You do need to know various math and grammar facts, rules, and concepts in order to do well on the GMAT—and this makes the test feel similar to tests that you took in school. There's one critical difference though: When your teachers gave you tests in school, they tested you on material they expected you to know how to handle. Your teachers wouldn't put something on the test that they *expected* you to get wrong. That would be cruel!

Well, it would be cruel if the main point of the exam was to test your mastery of those facts, rules, and concepts. But that isn't the main point of the GMAT. Rather, the GMAT wants to know how well you make decisions regarding when to invest your limited time and mental energy—and when *not* to.

In other words, the GMAT wants to know how you make business decisions. And no good businessperson invests in every single opportunity placed in front of them, just because it's there. A good businessperson evaluates each opportunity, saying yes to some and no to others. That's what you're going to do on the GMAT, too. You'll invest in a majority of the problems presented to you, but you *will* say no to some—the ones that look too hard or seem like they'll take too long to solve. These are literally bad investments.

So the GMAT will offer you questions that it thinks you will not be able to do. How does it accomplish this? The GMAT is an adaptive test; that is, it adapts to you as you take it, offering easier or harder questions based on how you're doing on the test. Ideally, you'll do well on the material that you know how to answer in a reasonable amount of time. Your reward? You'll earn questions that are too hard for you to do—either they'll take too long to answer or they'll be so hard that you wouldn't be able to do them even if you had unlimited time.

Then what? If you try to use a "school mindset" on the test, you'll keep trying to answer the questions even though you really can't do them. You'll waste a bunch of time and then, later, you'll have to rush on other questions. As a result, you'll start to miss questions that you actually do know how to answer and your score will go down. This is the business equivalent of spending most of your annual budget by August. . .and then not having enough money left to run the business well from September through December.

Instead, use your "business mindset" to carry you through the exam. When the test finds your limit, acknowledge that! Call it a bad investment and let that problem go (ideally before you've spent very much time on it). Choose an answer, any answer, and move on.

Extend the business mindset to your studies as well. If there are certain topics that you really hate, decide that you're not going to study them in the first place. You're just going to bail (guess quickly and move on) when one of those "opportunities" comes up. (One caveat: You can't bail on huge swaths of content. For example, don't bail on all of algebra; that represents too great a portion of the Quant section. You can, though, bail on a subset—say, absolute values and sequences.)

Start orienting yourself around your business mindset today. You aren't going to do it all. You're going to choose the best opportunities as you see them throughout the test. When you decide not to pursue a particular "investment," you're going to say no as quickly as you can and forget about it—don't waste precious resources on a poor investment opportunity! Move on to the next opportunity, feeling good about the fact that you're doing what you're supposed to do on the GMAT: making sound investment decisions about what to do and what *not* to do.

Quantitative Reasoning on the GMAT

The Quantitative Reasoning (or Quant) section of the GMAT consists of two different question types: Problem Solving and Data Sufficiency.

Problem Solving (PS) problems are standard, multiple-choice math questions with five answer choices. Data Sufficiency (DS) problems are unique to the GMAT. These also have five multiple-choice answers; you'll learn how DS works in this guide.

You'll need to average approximately two minutes per question in the Quant section, though your timing for individual questions will likely range from almost no time at all to approximately three minutes. The "almost no time at all" questions will be your *bail* questions: questions that look way too hard or that you know are a big weakness of yours (in other words, bad investment opportunities!). On other questions, you'll choose to invest some extra time—perhaps on a harder question in an area of strength.

You'll learn more about time management, as well as other test details, both in this guide and in the online resources associated with this guide. You can also test your skills using official GMAT problems that are published by the test makers in The GMAT Official Guide (also known as "the big OG" or "the OG"). These problems appeared on the official GMAT in the past, so they're a fantastic resource to help you get ready for the real test. (Note: The OG is sold separately from the Manhattan Prep strategy guides.)

Fractions, Decimals, Percents, and Ratios

In this unit, you will learn about the relationships between fractions, decimals, percents, and ratios and how to manipulate and solve for all forms. This unit also includes the basics of the Data Sufficiency question type, as well as an introduction to two important strategies for the GMAT: when and how you can use real numbers rather than algebra to solve (via three methods: Test Cases, Choose Smart Numbers, and Work Backwards) and when and how you can estimate.

In This Unit

FDPs

In This Chapter

- Common FDP Equivalents

- Converting among Fractions, Decimals, and Percents

- When to Use Which Form

In this chapter, you will learn the basic usage of fractions, decimals, and percents, as well as how to move back and forth quickly among the three. You'll also learn what kinds of calculations are most easily performed in which form.

CHAPTER 1 **FDPs**

FDPs stands for fractions, decimals, and percents. These three forms are grouped together because they are different ways to represent the same number. For example:

A **fraction** consists of a numerator and a denominator: $\dfrac{1}{2}$

A **decimal** uses place values: 0.5

A **percent** expresses a relationship between a number and 100: 50%

All three are equal to each other and represent the same number: $\dfrac{1}{2} = 0.5 = 50\%$.

Ratios are closely related to fractions but not quite the same; you'll learn more about ratios in a couple of chapters.

The GMAT often mixes fractions, decimals, and percents in a single problem, and certain kinds of math operations are easier to perform on one form compared to the others. In order to achieve success with FDP problems, you need to shift amongst the three accurately and quickly. Try this problem:

A sum of money is divided among three sisters. The first sister receives $\dfrac{1}{2}$ of the total, the second receives $\dfrac{1}{4}$ of the total, and the third receives the remaining $10. How many dollars do the three sisters split?

(A) $10
(B) $20
(C) $30
(D) $40
(E) $50

To solve, you have to figure out what proportion of the money the first two sisters get so that you know what proportion the third sister's $10 represents. The information is provided in fractions, and it's not too difficult to add up the relatively simple fractions $\dfrac{1}{2}$ and $\dfrac{1}{4}$. However, harder fractions would make the work a lot more cumbersome. In general, adding fractions is annoying because you have to find a common denominator.

Decimals and fractions are much easier to add. Because the problem talks about parts of a whole, convert to percentages. The first sister receives 50% of the money and the second receives 25%, leaving 25% for the third sister. That 25% represents $10, so 100% of the money is 4 times as much, or $40. The correct answer is (D).

In order to do this kind of math quickly and easily, you'll need to know how to convert among fractions, decimals, and percents. Luckily, certain common conversions are used repeatedly throughout the GMAT. If you memorize these conversions, you'll get to skip the calculations. The next two sections of this chapter cover these topics.

Common FDP Equivalents

Save yourself time and trouble by memorizing the following common equivalents:

Fraction	Decimal	Percent
$\frac{1}{1}$	1	100%
$\frac{1}{2} = \frac{2}{4} = \frac{3}{6} = \frac{4}{8} = \frac{5}{10}$	0.5	50%
$\frac{3}{2}$	1.5	150%

Fraction	Decimal	Percent
$\frac{1}{4} = \frac{2}{8}$	0.25	25%
$\frac{3}{4} = \frac{6}{8}$	0.75	75%
$\frac{5}{4}$	1.25	125%
$\frac{7}{4}$	1.75	175%

Fraction	Decimal	Percent
$\frac{1}{8}$	0.125	12.5%
$\frac{3}{8}$	0.375	37.5%
$\frac{5}{8}$	0.625	62.5%
$\frac{7}{8}$	0.875	87.5%

Fraction	Decimal	Percent
$\frac{1}{5} = \frac{2}{10}$	0.2	20%
$\frac{2}{5} = \frac{4}{10}$	0.4	40%
$\frac{3}{5} = \frac{6}{10}$	0.6	60%
$\frac{4}{5} = \frac{8}{10}$	0.8	80%

Fraction	Decimal	Percent
$\frac{1}{10}$	0.1	10%
$\frac{3}{10}$	0.3	30%
$\frac{7}{10}$	0.7	70%
$\frac{9}{10}$	0.9	90%

Fraction	Decimal	Percent
$\frac{1}{3} = \frac{2}{6}$	$0.\overline{3} \approx 0.333$	$\approx 33.3\%$
$\frac{2}{3} = \frac{4}{6}$	$0.\overline{6} \approx 0.666$	$\approx 66.7\%$
$\frac{4}{3}$	$1.\overline{3} \approx 1.333$	$\approx 133.3\%$

Fraction	Decimal	Percent
$\frac{1}{6}$	$0.1\overline{6} \approx 0.167$	$\approx 16.7\%$
$\frac{5}{6}$	$0.8\overline{3} \approx 0.833$	$\approx 83.3\%$
$\frac{1}{9}$	$0.1\overline{1} \approx 0.111$	$\approx 11.1\%$

Fraction	Decimal	Percent
$\frac{1}{100}$	0.01	1%
$\frac{1}{50}$	0.02	2%
$\frac{1}{25}$	0.04	4%
$\frac{1}{20}$	0.05	5%

Converting among Fractions, Decimals, and Percents

If you see a number that isn't on the Common Equivalents list to memorize, you can convert among fractions, decimals, and percents. The table below shows how:

FROM ↓ TO→	Fraction	Decimal	Percent
Fraction $\frac{1}{4}$		Divide the numerator by the denominator: $1 \div 4 = 0.25$ Alternatively, multiply the top and bottom to get the denominator to equal 100: $\frac{1}{4} \times \frac{25}{25} = \frac{25}{100} = 0.25$ Note: These operations are hard if the fraction is annoying; in that case, see whether you can estimate.	Divide the numerator by the denominator and move the decimal two places to the right: $1 \div 4 = 0.25 \rightarrow 25\%$
Decimal 0.375	Use the place value of the last digit in the decimal as the denominator and put the decimal's digits in the numerator. Then, simplify: $\frac{375}{1,000} = \frac{3}{8}$		Move the decimal point two places to the right: $0.375 \rightarrow 37.5\%$
Percent 65%	Use the digits of the percent for the numerator and 100 for the denominator. Then, simplify: $\frac{65}{100} = \frac{13}{20}$	Find the percent's decimal point and move it two places to the left: $65.0\% \rightarrow 0.65$	

Think before you convert, though. If the conversion is annoying—you have to do long division or similar—don't do it. Instead, see whether you can estimate or use some other approach. For example, converting 0.65 to a percent or fraction isn't too bad. But converting $\frac{7}{13}$ to a decimal or percent would be very annoying.

Instead, can you estimate? The fraction is almost $\frac{7}{14}$, or 0.5.

Pop quiz: Is $\frac{7}{13}$ a little larger or a little smaller than $\frac{7}{14}$? Play around with that a little bit. Later in this guide, you'll learn how to estimate this quickly.

You'll get plenty of practice with these skills throughout this book, but if you'd like some more, see Manhattan Prep's *GMAT Foundations of Math*.

When to Use Which Form

As you saw in the "three sisters" problem, when you have to add or subtract, percentages (or decimals) tend to be easier. By contrast, fractions work very well with multiplication and division.

If you have already memorized the given fraction, decimal, and percent conversions, you can move among the forms quickly. If not, you may have to decide between taking the time to convert from one form to the other and working the problem using the less convenient form (e.g., in order to add, you could convert fractions to decimals or you could leave them in fraction form and find a common denominator).

Try this problem:

> What is 37.5% of 240 ?

If you convert the percent to a decimal and multiply, you will have to do a fair bit of arithmetic, as shown on the left:

$$
\begin{array}{r}
0.375 \\
\times\ 240 \\
\hline
0 \\
15000 \\
75000 \\
\hline
90.000
\end{array}
\Bigg\}
$$

Alternatively, recognize that $0.375 = \dfrac{3}{8}$.

$$(0.375)(240) = \dfrac{3}{\cancel{8}}\ \cancel{240}^{\,30} = 3(30) = 90$$

This is much faster!

Try something a bit harder:

> A dress is marked up $16\frac{2}{3}$% to a final price of $140. What was the original price of the dress?

$16\frac{2}{3}$% is on the memorization list; it is equal to $\dfrac{1}{6}$. In order to increase a number by $\dfrac{1}{6}$, add a sixth of the number to itself: $1 + \dfrac{1}{6} = \dfrac{7}{6}$. Call the original price x and set up an equation to find x:

$$x + \dfrac{1}{6}x = 140$$

$$\dfrac{7}{6}x = 140$$

$$x = \left(\dfrac{6}{7}\right)140 = \dfrac{6}{\cancel{7}}\ \cancel{140}^{\,20} = 120$$

Therefore, the original price was $120.

Decimals and percents work very well with addition and subtraction because you don't have to find common denominators. For this same reason, decimals and percents are often preferred when you want to compare numbers or perform certain estimations. For example, which is larger, $\dfrac{3}{5}$ or $\dfrac{5}{8}$?

You could find common denominators, but both fractions are on the "conversions to memorize" list:

$$\dfrac{3}{5} = 60\% \qquad\qquad\qquad \dfrac{5}{8} = 62.5\%$$

The larger fraction is $\dfrac{5}{8}$.

In some cases, you may decide to stick with the given form rather than convert. If you do have numbers that are easy to convert, though, then use fractions for multiplication and division and use percents or decimals for addition and subtraction as well as for estimating or comparing numbers.

Advanced material for the FDPRs unit (primarily covering additional strategies for decimals and digits) can be found in Atlas, Manhattan Prep's online learning platform. Use the online material only if you feel that you have mastered everything in the FDPR unit of this strategy guide and only if you are aiming for a Quant section score of 48 or higher.

Problem Set

Now that you've finished the chapter, try these problems. On the GMAT, quant problems will always provide five answer choices. In this guide, you will sometimes have fewer than five answer choices (and sometimes none at all).

1. Express the following as fractions and simplify: 0.4   0.008

2. Express the following as fractions and simplify: 420%   8%

3. Express the following as decimals: $\dfrac{9}{2}$ $\dfrac{3,000}{10,000}$

4. Express the following as percents: $\dfrac{83}{1,000}$ $\dfrac{25}{8}$

5. Express the following as percents: 80.4   0.0007

6. Order from least to greatest: $\dfrac{8}{18}$ 0.8   40%

7. 20 is 16% of what number?

8. What number is 62.5% of 96 ?

Solutions

1. $\frac{2}{5}$ and $\frac{1}{125}$: To convert a decimal to a fraction, write it over the appropriate power of 10 and simplify:

$$0.4 = \frac{4}{10} = \frac{2}{5}$$
$$0.008 = \frac{8}{1000} = \frac{1}{125}$$

2. $\frac{21}{5}$ or $4\frac{1}{5}$ and $\frac{2}{25}$: To convert a percent to a fraction, write it over a denominator of 100 and simplify:

$$420\% = \frac{420}{100} = \frac{21}{1} \text{ (improper)} \quad \text{OR} \quad 4\frac{1}{5} \text{ (mixed)}$$
$$8\% = \frac{8}{100} = \frac{2}{25}$$

3. **4.5 and 0.3:** To convert a fraction to a decimal, divide the numerator by the denominator:

$$\frac{9}{2} = 9 \div 2 = 4.5$$

It often helps to simplify the fraction *before* you divide:

$$\frac{3,000}{10,000} = \frac{3}{10} = 0.3$$

4. **8.3% and 312.5%:** To convert a fraction to a percent, rewrite the fraction with a denominator of 100:

$$\frac{83}{1,000} = \frac{8.3}{100} = 8.3\%$$

Alternatively, convert the fraction to a decimal and shift the decimal point two places to the right:

$$\frac{25}{8} = 25 \div 8 = 3\frac{1}{8} = 3.125 = 312.5\%$$

5. **8,040% and 0.07%:** To convert a decimal to a percent, shift the decimal point two places to the right:

$$80.4 = 8,040\%$$
$$0.0007 = 0.07\%$$

6. $40\% < \frac{8}{18} < 0.8$: To order from least to greatest, express all the terms in the same form (your choice as to which form!):

$$\frac{8}{18} = \frac{4}{9} = 0.4444... = 0.\overline{4}$$
$$0.8 = 0.8$$
$$40\% = 0.4$$
$$0.4 < 0.\overline{4} < 0.8$$

7. **125:** The sentence translates as $20 = (16\%)x$. Fraction form is better for multiplication or division, so convert 16% into a fraction first: $16\% = \dfrac{16}{100} = \dfrac{4}{25}$. Then solve for x:

$$20 = \frac{4}{25}x$$
$$20\left(\frac{25}{4}\right) = x$$
$$(5)(25) = x$$
$$x = 125$$

8. **60:** The sentence translates as $x = (62.5\%)(96)$. 62.5% is one of the common FDP equivalents to memorize; the fraction form is $\dfrac{5}{8}$. Solve for x:

$$x = \left(\frac{5}{8}\right)96$$
$$x = (5)(12)$$
$$x = 60$$

Data Sufficiency 101

In This Chapter

- How Data Sufficiency Works
- The Answer Choices
- Starting with Statement (2)
- Value vs. Yes/No Questions
- The DS Process
- Testing Cases

In this chapter, you will learn how to tackle Data Sufficiency (DS) problems, including an overall process to help you solve the problems efficiently. You'll also learn how to test cases on DS; this strategy will help you handle more complicated problems as you advance in your studies.

CHAPTER 2 Data Sufficiency 101

The GMAT invented its own type of math problem, **Data Sufficiency** (DS), that tests how you think logically about mathematical concepts. DS problems are a cross between math and logic. Imagine that your boss just dumped a bunch of papers on your desk, saying, "I'm wondering whether we should raise the price on this product. Can you answer that question from this data? If so, which pieces do we need to prove whether we should or should not raise the price?" What would you do?

Your boss has asked a specific question: Should you raise the price? You have to decide which pieces of information will allow you to answer that question—or, possibly, that you don't have enough information to answer the question at all.

This kind of logical reasoning is exactly what you use when you answer DS questions.

How Data Sufficiency Works

You will certainly need to know math in order to answer Data Sufficiency questions, but you also need to know how DS works in the first place. And you need to know certain strategies that will help you to work through DS problems efficiently and effectively.

Consider this question: How old is Farai?

Obviously, you can't answer that question right now—you have no information about Farai or Farai's age. Imagine that you're also told a fact: Farai is 10 years older than Dmitry.

But you don't know anything about Dmitry's age either! The GMAT would say that this fact—Farai is 10 years older than Dmitry—is *not sufficient* (i.e., not enough) to answer the question. If you do know this fact, though, then what additional information would allow you to be able to answer the question?

Well, if you knew how old Dmitry was, then you could figure out how old Farai was. For example, if Dmitry is 10, then Farai would have to be 20.

So if you know *both* that Farai is 10 years older than Dmitry *and* that Dmitry is 10 years old, then you have *sufficient* (i.e., enough) information to answer the question: How old is Farai?

Every DS problem has the same basic form. It will ask you a question. It will provide you with some facts. And it will ask you to figure out what combination of facts is *sufficient* to answer the question.

Take a look at another example, in full DS form:

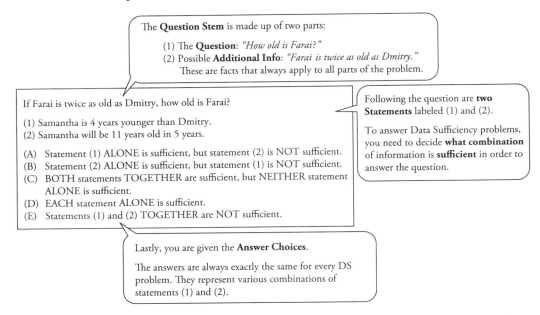

The **Question Stem** always contains the **Question** you need to answer. It may also contain **Additional Info** (also known as *givens*) that you can use to help answer the question.

Below the question stem, the two **Statements** provide additional facts or given information—and you are specifically asked to determine what combination of those two statements would be sufficient to answer the question.

The **Answer Choices** describe various combinations of the two statements: For example, statement (1) is sufficient, but statement (2) is not. Note that the answer choices don't contain any possible ages for Farai. DS questions aren't asking you *to* solve; they're asking *whether* you *can* solve. (No need to try to figure out what all of those answer choices mean right now; you'll learn as you work through this chapter.)

DS questions look strange but you can think of them as deconstructed Problem Solving (PS) questions— the "regular" type of multiple-choice math problem. Compare the DS-format problem shown earlier to the PS-format problem below:

> Samantha is 4 years younger than Dmitry, and Samantha will be 11 years old in 5 years. If Farai is twice as old as Dmitry, how old is Farai?

The two questions contain exactly the same information; that information is just presented in a different order. The PS form puts all of the givens as well as the question into the question stem. The DS problem moves some of the givens down to statement (1) and statement (2).

As is true for the given information in PS problems, the DS statements are always true. In addition, the two statements won't contradict each other. In the same way that a PS question wouldn't tell you that $x > 0$ and $x < 0$ (that's impossible!), the two DS statements won't do that either.

In the PS format, you would need to calculate Farai's age. In the DS format, you typically will *not* need to solve all the way to the end; you only need to go far enough to know whether Farai's age can be calculated. Since every DS problem works in this same way, it is critical to learn how to work through all DS questions using a systematic, consistent process. Take a look at how this plays out:

If Farai is twice as old as Dmitry, how old is Farai?

(1)   Samantha is 4 years younger than Dmitry.

(2)   Samantha will be 11 years old in 5 years.

(A)   Statement (1) ALONE is sufficient, but statement (2) is NOT sufficient.
(B)   Statement (2) ALONE is sufficient, but statement (1) is NOT sufficient.
(C)   BOTH statements TOGETHER are sufficient, but NEITHER statement ALONE is sufficient.
(D)   EACH statement ALONE is sufficient.
(E)   Statements (1) and (2) TOGETHER are NOT sufficient.

The goal: Figure out which pieces of information *would* allow you to answer the question (How old is Farai?).

Your first task is to understand what the problem is saying and jot down the information in math form. Draw a T on your page to help keep the information organized; write information from the question stem above the horizontal line. Make sure to include a question mark to indicate the question itself (later, you'll learn why this is important):

$$\boxed{?} \quad F = \underline{\quad} \, ?$$

$$F = 2D$$

(1)   (2)

Hmm. Reflect for a moment. If they tell you Dmitry's age, then you could just plug it into the given equation to find Farai's age. Remember that!

Take a look at the first statement. Also, write down $\frac{AD}{BCE}$ off to the right of your scratch paper, above the line (you'll learn what this is as you work through this chapter):

(1)   Samantha is 4 years younger than Dmitry.

$$\boxed{?} \quad F = \underline{\quad} \, ?$$

$$F = 2D$$

AD
BCE

(1)   S = D − 4   (2)

2

Translate the first statement and jot down the information below the horizontal line, to the left of the T. (Not confident about how to translate that statement into math? Use Manhattan Prep's *GMAT Foundations of Math* to practice translating.)

The first statement doesn't allow you to solve for either Samantha or Dmitry's real age. Statement (1), then, is *not sufficient*. Cross off the top row of answers, (A) and (D).

Why? Here's the text for answers (A) and (D):

> (A)   Statement (1) ALONE is sufficient, but statement (2) is NOT sufficient.
>
> (D)   EACH statement ALONE is sufficient.

These two answers indicate that statement (1) *is* sufficient to answer the question. But statement (1) is *not* sufficient to find Farai's age, so both (A) and (D) are wrong.

The answer choices will always appear in the order shown for the above problem, so any time you decide that statement (1) is not sufficient, you will always cross off answers (A) and (D) at the same time. That's why the $\frac{AD}{BCE}$ answer grid groups these two answers together on the top row.

Next, consider statement (2), but wait! First, forget what statement (1) told you. Because of the way the DS answers are constructed, you must evaluate the two statements *separately* before you look at them together. So here's just statement (2) by itself:

> (2)   Samantha will be 11 years old in 5 years.

$$\boxed{?} \quad F = \underline{\quad} ?$$

$$F = 2D$$

$$\frac{\cancel{AD}}{BCE}$$

(1) S = D − 4	(2) S + 5 = 11
(NS)	

In your T diagram, write the information about statement (2) below the horizontal line and to the right. It's useful to separate the information this way in order to help remember that statement (2) is separate from statement (1) and has to be considered completely by itself first. (You'll always organize the information in this way: The question stem goes above the T, statement (1) goes below and to the left of the T, and statement (2) goes below and to the right.)

Back to statement (2). This one allows you to figure out how old Samantha is now, but *alone* the info doesn't connect back to Farai or Dmitry. By itself, statement (2) is *not* sufficient. Of the remaining answers (BCE), answer (B) says that statement (2) is sufficient by itself. This isn't the case, so cross off answer (B).

When you've evaluated each statement by itself and haven't found sufficient information, you must look at the two statements together. Statement (2) allows you to figure out Samantha's age. Statement (1) allows you to calculate Dmitry's age if you know Samantha's age. Finally, the question stem allows you to calculate Farai's age if you know Dmitry's age!

$$F = \_\_\_?$$

$$F = 2D$$

$$\cancel{AD}$$
$$\cancel{B}C\cancel{E}$$

(1) $S = D - 4$ (NS)   (2) $S + 5 = 11$ (NS)

(1 + 2) (S)

As soon as you can tell that you *can* find Farai's age, write an S with a circle around it to indicate *sufficient*. Don't actually calculate Farai's age; you only need to know that you *can* calculate it. Save that time and mental energy for other things on the test.

The correct answer is (C): both statements together are sufficient to answer the question but neither statement alone is sufficient.

The Answer Choices

The five Data Sufficiency answer choices will always be exactly the same (and presented in the same order), so you won't even need to read them on the real test. By then, you'll have done enough DS problems to have them memorized. (In fact, to help you memorize, this book won't even show the DS answer choices in end-of-chapter problem sets.)

Here are the five answers written in an easier way to understand:

  (A) Statement (1) *does* allow you to answer the question, but statement (2) *does not.*
  (B) Statement (2) *does* allow you to answer the question, but statement (1) *does not.*
  (C) Neither statement works on its own, but you can use them *together* to answer the question.
  (D) Statement (1) works by itself *and* statement (2) works by itself.
  (E) Nothing works. Even if you use both statements together, you still can't answer the question.

Answer (C) specifically says that neither statement works on its own. For this reason, you are required to look at each statement by itself first *and decide that neither one works alone* before you are allowed to evaluate the two statements together.

Here's an even shorter way to remember the five answer choices, the "12-TEN" mnemonic (memory aid):

1	only statement 1
2	only statement 2
T	together
E	either one
N	nothing works

2

As you practice DS over the next couple of weeks, make an effort to memorize the five answers. If you do a couple of practice DS problems every day in that time frame, you'll likely memorize the answers without conscious effort—and you'll solidify the DS lessons you're learning right now.

Speaking of solidifying the lessons you're learning, set a timer for 2 minutes and try this problem:

What is the value of 20% of x?

(1)   30 is $\frac{1}{2}$ of x.

(2) x is 0.25 of 240.

(A)   Statement (1) ALONE is sufficient, but statement (2) alone is not sufficient to answer the question asked.

(B)   Statement (2) ALONE is sufficient, but statement (1) alone is not sufficient to answer the question asked.

(C)   BOTH statements (1) and (2) TOGETHER are sufficient to answer the question asked, but NEITHER statement ALONE is sufficient.

(D)   EACH statement ALONE is sufficient to answer the question asked.

(E)   Statements (1) and (2) TOGETHER are NOT sufficient to answer the question asked.

Ready? What did you get? (If you got stuck and didn't get to an answer, pick one anyway. That's what you'll have to do on the real test, so you might as well practice that now.)

Start with the question stem: What is 20% of x? Pause. Your first goal is to understand the significance of the question. This is DS—you don't have to find the actual value. What would you need to know in order to be confident that you *could* calculate that value?

If you can find a single value for x, then you can find 20% of that value, so the real question is a bit simpler: What is x?

$$\boxed{?}\quad x = \underline{\qquad}\ ?$$

Congratulations! You've just rephrased a DS question. Rephrasing a question allows you to get right down to the heart of the question—and save yourself time and mental energy as you solve.

Now, you can dive into the statements with a simpler plan: Will this statement allow you to find a single value for x? Jot down your answer grid $\begin{smallmatrix}AD\\BCE\end{smallmatrix}$ and look at the first statement:

(1)   30 is $\frac{1}{2}$ of x.

Some people may be able to evaluate this statement without writing anything down. Others will want to jot it down in "real math" terms—as an equation, not a sentence.

$$\boxed{?} \quad x = \underline{\quad\quad} ?$$

$$\text{AD}$$
$$\text{BCE}$$

(1) $30 = \dfrac{1}{2}x$	(2)

Statement (1) is a linear equation with just one variable. This equation can indeed be solved for a single value of x, so this statement is sufficient to answer the question. Which row should you cross off in the grid, AD or BCE?

Think of statement (1) as associated with answer choice (A). If statement (1) is sufficient, then answer (A) needs to stay in the mix; cross off the bottom row, BCE.

What's next? Pause and try to remind yourself before you keep reading.

Now, forget about statement (1) and take a look at statement (2):

   (2) x is 0.25 of 240.

If you feel confident that this statement will also translate into a linear equation with just one variable, then you may choose not to write anything down. If you're not sure, though, write it down to confirm.

This equation will also allow you to solve for a single value for x, so statement (2) is sufficient to answer the question.

Since statement (2) is also sufficient, cross off answer (A) and circle answer (D): Either statement alone is sufficient to answer the question. Do actually take the time to do this on your scratch paper before you select your answer on screen. It won't take you more than a second and this action will help to minimize careless mistakes on the test.

$$\boxed{?} \quad x = \underline{\quad\quad} ?$$

$$\cancel{A}\,\textcircled{D}$$
$$\cancel{BCE}$$

(1) $30 = \dfrac{1}{2}x$	(2) $x = (0.25)240$
$\textcircled{S}$	$\textcircled{S}$

2

Here's a summary of the answer choice process when starting with statement (1):

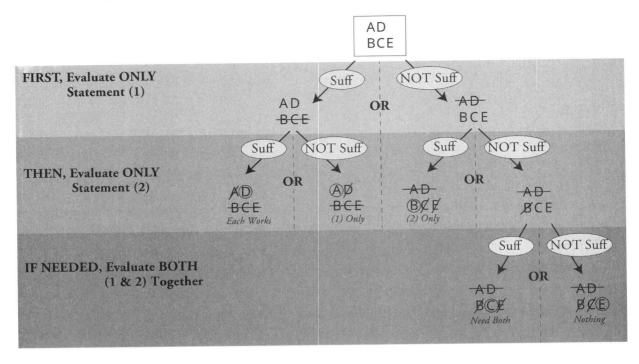

Starting with Statement (2)

If statement (1) looks hard or annoying, you can start with statement (2) instead. Your process will be the same; you'll just make one small change in your answer grid.

Try this problem:

> If Farai is twice as old as Dmitry, how old is Farai?
>
> (1)   Two years ago, Dmitry was twice as old as Samantha.
>
> (2)   Samantha is 6 years old.

> 1
> 2
> T
> E
> N

(From now on, the full answer choices won't be shown. Start memorizing! You can also glance back at earlier pages until you know the answers by heart.)

First, what to do with that question stem? You can write it down the same way you did before, but now that you've learned about rephrasing, add one more thing. If you found D's age, you could find F's age, so the question can be rephrased as "$D = ?$"

Next, statement (1) is definitely more complicated than statement (2), so start with statement (2) this time. Lay out your scratch paper in the same way—statement (1) on the left and statement (2) on the right—but this time write $\frac{BD}{ACE}$ for your answer grid (you'll learn why in a minute):

(2)   Samantha is 6 years old.

$$F = 2D \qquad \boxed{?} \begin{array}{l} F = \underline{\quad} ? \\ D = \underline{\quad} ? \end{array} \quad \begin{array}{l} BD \\ ACE \end{array}$$

(1)	(2) $S = 6$

Statement (2) is not sufficient to determine Farai's age. Think of this statement as associated with answer (B). Since the statement is *not* sufficient, you *don't* want to keep (B), so cross off the row that contains that answer: the top row (BD).

Whenever you decide to start with statement (2), you'll always use the $\begin{smallmatrix}BD\\ACE\end{smallmatrix}$ answer grid, and you'll always cross off either the entire top row or the entire bottom row, depending on whether statement (2) is sufficient.

Now, forget about statement (2) and assess statement (1):

(1)   Two years ago, Dmitry was twice as old as Samantha.

$$F = 2D \qquad \boxed{?} \begin{array}{l} F = \underline{\quad} ? \\ D = \underline{\quad} ? \end{array} \quad \begin{array}{l} \cancel{BD} \\ ACE \end{array}$$

(1) $D - 2 = 2(S-2)$	(2) $S = 6$
	(NS)

That translation is tricky. Since it's talking about the time period 2 years ago, subtract 2 from each of D and S. Then translate and write the rest of the equation. By itself, is statement (1) sufficient?

Nope! This isn't enough to find a specific age for Farai, Dmitry, or Samantha. Cross off (A), the first of the remaining answers in the bottom row, and now assess the two statements together:

$$F = 2D \qquad \boxed{?} \begin{array}{l} F = \underline{\quad} ? \\ D = \underline{\quad} ? \end{array} \quad \begin{array}{l} \cancel{BD} \\ \cancel{A}CE \end{array}$$

(1) $D - 2 = 2(S-2)$	(2) $S = 6$
(NS)	(NS)

(1 + 2) $D = \#$ (S)

2

You can plug Samantha's age (from the second statement) into the formula from statement (1) to find Dmitry's age, and Dmitry's age is sufficient to answer the question. Together, the statements are sufficient.

The correct answer is (C): Neither statement works alone, but *together* the information is sufficient to answer the question.

Here's a summary of the answer grid process when starting with statement (2):

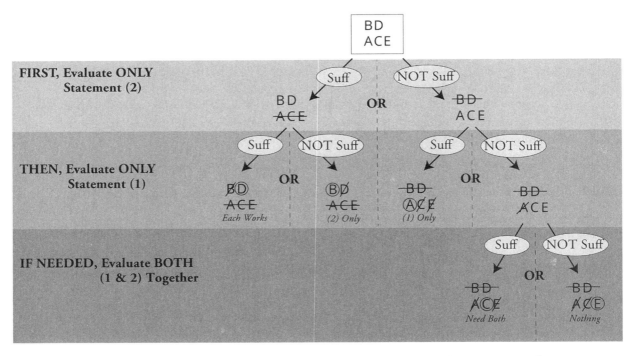

The two answer grids work the same way, regardless of which one you use. When starting with statement (1), always use the AD/BCE grid. Think of statement (1) as associated with the first answer letter in that grid, (A).

When starting with statement (2), always use the BD/ACE grid and think of this statement as associated with the first answer letter, (B).

In either case, when assessing your starting statement, you will get to cross off an entire row:

- If the first statement you try *is* sufficient, cross off the *bottom row* (the row that does *not* contain the letter associated with that statement).
- If the first statement you try is *not* sufficient, cross off the *top row* (the row containing the letter associated with that statement).

Once you've crossed off an entire row and have just one row left, assess the answers in the remaining row, one answer at a time.

Finally, you must assess the statements separately before you can try them together—and you'll only try them together if neither one is sufficient on its own. In other words, you will only consider answers (C) and (E) if you have already crossed off answers (A), (B), and (D).

Value vs. Yes/No Questions

Data Sufficiency questions come in two "flavors": Value or Yes/No.

So far, you've done Value questions. On these, it is necessary to find a single value in order to answer the question. If you can't find any value or you can find two or more values, then the information is not sufficient.

Here's an example of a Value question with one accompanying statement:

> How old is Farai?
>
> (1) Farai's age is a multiple of 4.

Farai could be 4 or 8 or 12 or any multiple of 4. Because it's impossible to determine one particular value for Farai's age, the statement is not sufficient to answer the Value question: How old is Farai?

Now, consider this question:

> Is Farai's age an even number?
>
> (1) Farai's age is a multiple of 4.
> (2) Farai is between 19 and 22 years old.

This question is fundamentally different. It's not asking for a value; it's asking *whether* something is true. These are called Yes/No questions and there are three possible answers to this type of question:

1. Always Yes: Sufficient!

2. Always No: Sufficient!

3. Maybe (or Sometimes Yes, Sometimes No): Not Sufficient

It may be a surprise that Always No is sufficient to answer the question. Imagine that you ask a friend to go to the movies with you. If she says, "No, I'm sorry, I can't," then you did receive an answer to your question (even though the answer is negative). You know she can't go to the movies with you.

Apply this reasoning to the Farai question. Is statement (1) sufficient to answer the question: Is Farai's age an even number?

> (1) Farai's age is a multiple of 4.

2

If Farai's age is a multiple of 4, Farai could be 4, 8, 12, ... but in *every* case, the answer to the question is Yes. Even though you don't know how old Farai is, the information is sufficient to answer the specific question asked: Yes, Farai must be an even number of years old.

Because statement (1) is sufficient, keep answer (A) in the mix. Cross off the bottom row of answers (BCE).

In the sample notes above, notice that the question is jotted down with the question mark included: *Is F even?* It's crucial to include both the starting "question word" (*Is*) and the question mark; if you omit these, then later you might mistakenly think that the problem is telling you that *F is even*—and, if that happens, you're much more likely to get this question wrong.

You might not make that mistake on this particular problem, but this is a potential source of error on *any* Yes/No problem (and sometimes on Value problems), so get into the habit of writing that question mark every time. Always distinguish between *facts* (things you know to be true) and *questions*.

Okay, back to the problem. Next, check statement (2):

(2)   Farai is between 19 and 22 years old.

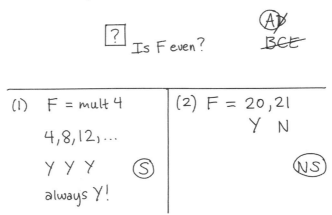

Farai could be 20, in which case the age is even. However, Farai could also be 21, in which case the age is odd. The result here is Sometimes Yes, Sometimes No, so the information in statement (2) is *not* sufficient to answer the question. Cross off answer (D).

The correct answer is (A): The first statement is sufficient but the second is not.

Note two common traps. First, for statement (2), someone might think that Farai must be 20, not 21, because the age is even. But the problem doesn't *tell* you that Farai's age is even; it asks *whether* Farai's age is even.

Answer (C) is also a trap answer on this problem. If you think that you need to find one specific value for Farai's age, then you'll think that you need both pieces of information: If Farai is *between* 19 and 22 *and* the age is a multiple of 4, then Farai must be 20 years old.

But the problem doesn't ask how old Farai is. It asks only whether the age is an even number—and the first statement is sufficient to answer that question.

The DS Process

This section summarizes each step that you've learned in one consistent DS process. You can use this on every DS problem on the test. (You can even use the overall framework on regular Problem Solving problems!)

Your process consists of three distinct stages: Understand, Plan, and Solve. Most people dive straight into the third step, Solve, but this can create all kinds of issues. You may find yourself halfway through a solution and it then falls apart on you. Or you'll realize most of the way through that there was some easier, faster way you could have approached this.

The Understand and Plan steps help you to make sure that you actually want to do this problem in the first place (business mindset—don't do them all!) and they help you to settle on a solution process that is efficient and effective.

Step 1: Understand

First, just *glance* at the problem to note the overall type—in this case, it's a DS. Where does it look messy or complex? Include the question stem and both statements in your glance.

Next, *read* the problem and decide: Is this a Value or a Yes/No?

Value: The question asks for the value of an unknown (e.g., What is x?).

A statement is **Sufficient** if it provides **exactly one possible value**.

A statement is **Not Sufficient** if it provides **more than one possible value**.

Yes/No: The question asks whether a given piece of information is true (e.g., Is x even?). Most of the time, these will be in the form of Yes/No questions.

A statement is **Sufficient** when the answer is **Always Yes** or **Always No**.

A statement is **Not Sufficient** when the answer is **Sometimes Yes, Sometimes No**.

Jot down both the given information and the question itself. If the information is straightforward, it's fine to jot as you read. If the information is at all complex (especially if it's a story!), you may want to read the whole thing before you jot anything down.

Finally, *given* information—that is, any information in the question stem other than the question itself—is true information that you must consider or use when answering the question. Write this information separately from the question itself. It's important to distinguish between what you were *told* is true and what you were *asked* to find.

Step 2: Plan

Reflect on the question and the givens, and rephrase the question if you can. If you have a lot of information, you may also need to decide how to *organize* your work.

At the least, you'll usually be able to simplify what is written on screen. For example, if the question stem asks, "What is the value of x?" then you might write down something like $x = ?$

For more complicated question stems, you will likely have more work to do to rephrase the question—but rephrasing will make your job easier when you get to the next step. Ideally, before you go to the statements, you will be able to articulate a fairly clear and straightforward question (or, at least, one that's a little more clear than the original question).

2

Consider this problem:

Is $\frac{3x}{2} + y = \frac{x}{2} + y + 1$?

(1) $x = 1$

(2) $x + y = 1$

Do you need to know the individual values of x and y in order to answer the question? Or is there some simpler thing you could find? It's tough to tell when the equation is that annoying.

If you're given an equation, the first task is to put the "like" variables together. Also, when working with the question stem, make sure to carry the *Is* and the question mark through your work:

Is $\frac{3x}{2} + y = \frac{x}{2} + y + 1$?

Hmm. There are x variables on both sides of the equation. Ditto for the y variables. Get them together on one side and keep simplifying:

Is $\left(\frac{3x}{2} - \frac{x}{2}\right) + y + (-y) = 1$?

Is $\frac{2x}{2} = 1$?

Is $x = 1$?

Check it out: The variable y drops out completely! That whole thing is really just asking whether $x = 1$. The rephrased question is a lot better than the original one. (Note: You may need to write out more steps of math to simplify. Write it out—don't do math in your head and open yourself up to careless mistakes!)

It might seem silly to keep writing *Is* and the question mark on each line, but don't skip that step or you'll be opening yourself up to a careless error (you'll see how later in this book). By the time you get to the end, you don't want to forget that this is still a *question*, not a statement or a given. You don't actually know whether $x = 1$.

Step 3: Solve

Now that you've got the question you want to answer, use the answer grid to evaluate the statements.

If you start with statement (1), then write the AD/BCE grid on your scrap paper. If you start with statement (2), then write BD/ACE instead.

Here is the rephrased problem:

Is $x = 1$?

(1) $x = 1$

(2) $x + y = 1$

Statement (1) is sufficient to answer the question: Yes, $x = 1$. Keep answer (A) in the mix, so cross off the bottom row of answers:

AD

~~BCE~~

Statement (2) might have looked more promising before you rephrased the question. Now, though, you know that the value of y doesn't matter. Can you tell whether $x = 1$ from this statement?

If $x = 1$ and $y = 0$, then $x + y = 1$ and the answer is Yes, $x = 1$.

However! If $x = 0$ and $y = 1$, then $x + y = 1$ and the answer is No, $x \neq 1$.

Since this is a Sometimes Yes, Sometimes No answer, statement (2) is not sufficient to answer the question.

Cross off answer (D) and circle correct answer (A) on your grid:

(A) D̸

B̶C̶E̶

If you decide to start with statement (2), your overall process is almost identical, but you'll use the BD/ACE grid instead.

Whether you use AD/BCE or BD/ACE, you will always:

- Cross off the *top* row if the first statement you try is *not* sufficient
- Cross off the *bottom* row if the first statement you try *is* sufficient

Finally, remember to forget the first statement you try when moving to the next statement! Try each statement by itself first. Only evaluate the two statements together if you've already crossed off answers (A), (B), and (D), so that only answers (C) and (E) are left.

Here's a summary of the 3-step process:

Step 1: Understand

Glance at the problem. Note that it's DS and also notice which parts look annoying or complex. (Don't think about this yet. Just notice.)

Read the problem. Don't rush it. Your goal right now is just to understand what it's asking. Is it Value or Yes/No?

Jot down information. Don't do anything with this info yet.

Step 2: Plan

Reflect on what you know so far. Any ideas about how to rephrase (simplify) the complex parts in the question stem or even in the statements, if applicable?

Organize your information, if needed, and organize your thoughts. Do you have a decent idea for how to solve in a reasonable amount of time?

If so, proceed. If not, make the call to bail: Pick a random answer and move on.

Step 3: Solve

If you make it to this stage, go ahead and do whatever work is needed to solve this problem. Note that even the best laid plans sometimes fail. If things aren't working the way you thought they would or you're realizing that this is taking a lot more time than you'd planned, get out of the problem. Have a business mindset—don't use up too many of your resources on any one business opportunity!

Testing Cases

Data Sufficiency problems often allow for multiple possible scenarios, or cases—in fact, this occurred on statement (2) of the last problem. There are an infinite number of possible values for *x* and *y*, as long as $x + y = 1$.

When a statement is set up to allow multiple cases, you can use the **Test Cases** strategy to determine whether a statement is sufficient or not sufficient. This process can feel a little different for Yes/No vs. Value questions, so you'll get a chance to try both in this section.

2

When you're doing this, your goal is to try to prove the statement *insufficient*, if possible. Why? As soon as you find both one Yes answer and one No answer, you're done! Then it's Sometimes Yes/Sometimes No, which is not sufficient to answer the question. Think of this as trying to find contradictory answers.

If you keep getting a Yes answer every time, even when you're actively trying hard to find a No answer (or vice versa), then you can feel pretty confident that this statement is giving you a definitive answer—that is, that the statement is sufficient to answer the question.

Consider this problem:

> If x and y are positive integers, is the sum of x and y between 50 and 60, inclusive?
>
> (1) $x - y = 6$

First, **Understand**. This is a DS Yes/No problem. It tells you that x and y are positive integers and asks whether $x + y$ is between 50 and 60, inclusive. (*Inclusive is math-speak for include the endpoints—50 and 60—in the range.*)

Glance at the statement. You aren't given enough information to be able to solve definitively for specific values of x and y; there are many possible values. So you can test cases on this problem. You'll need to pick positive integers (given by the question stem) and you'll be trying to prove or disprove a sum in the 50–60 range.

Use that understanding to **Plan**. You also need to follow any constraints given in the statement. In this case, the two numbers have to be positive integers and $x - y$ must equal 6. Go ahead and try any two numbers that fit these constraints, then see what happens.

Solve. Case 1: $x = 10$ and $y = 4$.

These numbers are both positive integers and are valid based on the constraint from the first statement $(10 - 4 = 6)$. Now, try to answer the Yes/No question: $10 + 6 = 16$, so in this case No, the sum is not between 50 and 60, inclusive.

You now have a No answer. Go back to the Plan step for a second. Can you think of another set of numbers that will give you the opposite, a Yes answer? What kind of numbers would you need?

Think about what a Yes answer means. The sum would have to be in the 50–60 range, so you'll need larger starting numbers. You might have to play with the numbers a bit to find a good pairing.

Solve. Case 2: $x = 30$ and $y = 24$.

These numbers are both positive integers and valid for the first statement $(30 - 24 = 6)$. Now, answer the Yes/No question: $30 + 24 = 54$, so in this case, Yes, the sum is between 50 and 60, inclusive.

Because you have found both a Yes case and a No case, you have proved that this statement is not sufficient to answer the question.

Here's a summary of the process:

1. In the Understand phase of the DS process, notice that you *can* test cases on a particular problem. You can do this when the problem and the statement allow for multiple possible values. Also think to yourself, "What would contradictory answers look like on this problem?" For instance, in the above problem, a sum between 50 and 60 (inclusive) would be a Yes, while any other sum would be a No.

2. Come up with a Plan. Consider two things:

   • First, what kinds of numbers are you *allowed* to pick? Any numbers you use must fit the facts given in the question stem and in the statement that you're testing right now.

   • Second, what kinds of numbers would be likely to give you a *different* or contradictory answer?

3. Solve. Process your first case:

   • Choose your first set of numbers.

   • Double-check that the numbers work with all of the given facts. If your chosen numbers "break" any of the facts—that is, make any fact in the question stem or the statement on which you're working right now false—*discard* that case. Cross that case out on your scratch paper and start again.

   • Solve and find the specific answer for this case. On a Yes/No problem, you'll get either Yes or No. On a Value problem, you'll get a numerical value.

4. Solve again! Try to find a second case that gives you a *different* answer. Before you choose numbers, remind yourself of what a contradictory answer looks like for this problem. On a Yes/No problem, you'll be looking for the opposite of what you found for the first case (if you found a Yes the first time, you're looking for a No, or vice versa). For a Value problem, you'll be looking for a different numerical answer (if you found a value of 3 the first time, then the second time you're looking for any number other than 3).

If you can find two contradictory answers, you're done! That statement is not sufficient to provide one consistent answer, so you can cross off the relevant answer(s) on your grid and move to the next step in your DS process.

What if you try to find a different answer but keep finding the same answer? Try this problem:

   If x and y are positive integers, is the product of x and y greater than 20 ?

   (1) x is a multiple of 11 and y is divisible by 2.

Math vocab alert: *Product* means *multiply*. A *multiple* of a number is that number multiplied by a series of integers. For example, the positive multiples of 4 are 4, 8, 12, 16, and so on. And *divisible by 2* means that you'll get an integer when you divide that number by 2.

Understand. The two variables are positive integers and the question is a Yes/No: Is $xy > 20$?

Plan. Many possible values are allowed, so test cases. Look for contradictory answers.

Solve. Case 1: Test $x = 11$ and $y = 2$. The product is $(11)(2) = 22$, which is greater than 20. The answer to the question in this case is Yes. Now, can you find a No answer?

Solve. Case 2: How about $x = 11$ and $y = 4$? Then xy will be 44…hmm. Increasing the value of either variable just makes the product even greater. Can you go smaller?

It's not possible. The smallest multiple of 11 is 11 and the smallest positive integer divisible by 2 is the number 2, so the smallest product of the two is 22.

You've just proved the statement sufficient. The given information leads to an Always Yes answer; it is impossible to find a No case, no matter what you try. The Test Cases strategy can help you figure out the "theory" behind the answer, or the mathematical reasoning that proves the statement is sufficient.

2

This won't always work so cleanly. Sometimes, you'll keep getting all Yes (or all No) answers but you won't be able to figure out the theory behind it all. If you test three or four different cases, and you're actively seeking out a contradictory answer but never find it, then go ahead and assume that the statement is sufficient, even if you're not completely sure why.

Here's how testing cases would work on a Value problem:

> If x and y are prime numbers, what is the product of x and y?
>
> (1)   The product xy is even.

Math vocab alert: *Prime* numbers are numbers that are divisible by exactly two numbers: themselves and 1. The number 2 is the smallest prime number (and the only even prime!). Other examples include 3, 5, 7, 11, 13, and 17.

Understand. Theory problem—no real numbers given. Can only choose primes for x and y. What is the value of xy? The statement contains the word *even*…

Plan. Think about even and odd—*and* prime. The only even prime number is 2. All other prime numbers are odd. Whenever you multiply anything by 2, the result is even, so if the product xy is even and those numbers are both prime, one of those numbers has to be 2.

Solve. Case 1: $x = 2$ and $y = 3$. Both numbers are prime numbers and their product is even, so these are legal numbers to try. In this case, the product is 6. Are you allowed to choose numbers that will give a different product?

Solve. Case 2: $x = 2$ and $y = 5$. Both numbers are prime numbers and their product is even, so these are legal numbers to try. In this case, the product is 10.

The statement is not sufficient because there are at least two different values for the product of x and y.

When you're testing cases on DS, take an "I'm going to try to find different answers" mindset:

- After you try your first case, think about how that math worked. What kind of number would be a good one to try for your second case in order to try to get a different answer?
- If you do find two different answers (Yes and No, or two different numbers), then immediately declare that statement not sufficient.
- If, after several tries, you keep finding the same answer despite actively trying to use numbers that will give a different answer, that statement is likely sufficient. By now, you may even be able to say why (because you've seen why different kinds of numbers keep giving the same result). Even if you can't articulate why, go ahead and assume that the statement is sufficient.

Now, you're ready to test your DS skills in this chapter's problem set. As a reminder, the problem sets in this book will not include the DS answer choices; if you forget what they are, you can look them up in this chapter.

As you continue to work through the chapters in this book, you can also continue practicing DS via *Official Guide* problems (if you have that book). Start with lower-numbered problems first, in order to practice the process, and work your way up to more difficult problems as you gain expertise.

Problem Set

As you solve each problem, focus on solidifying your DS process. Before you check your answers, review your work. Did you write down (and use) your answer grid? Did you look at each statement separately before looking at them together? Did you mix up or skip any of the steps of the process? You may want to rewrite your work before you review the answers.

The five answer choices for every problem are as follows. (Note: In future problem sets, the answer choices for DS problems will *not* be given.)

(A) Statement (1) ALONE is sufficient, but statement (2) alone is NOT sufficient to answer the question asked.

(B) Statement (2) ALONE is sufficient, but statement (1) alone is NOT sufficient to answer the question asked.

(C) BOTH statements (1) and (2) TOGETHER are sufficient to answer the question asked, but NEITHER statement ALONE is sufficient.

(D) EACH statement ALONE is sufficient to answer the question asked.

(E) Statements (1) and (2) TOGETHER are NOT sufficient to answer the question asked, and additional data are needed.

1. If $2x + y = 7$, what is the value of x ?

(1) $y = 3$

(2) $3x + y = 9$

2. If x is a positive integer, is x less than 10 ?

(1) x is a multiple of 8.

(2) $x < 15$

3. A certain bag contains only red and blue marbles. Are there at least 25 red marbles in the bag?

(1) Fewer than 40% of the marbles in the bag are red.

(2) There are at least 90 marbles in the bag.

Now that you've practiced the DS process, test out your skills on a couple of lower-numbered *Official Guide* problems. When you review, ask yourself what you need to do to make the process smoother (including how you set up your scratch paper).

Solutions

2

1. **(D):** First, understand. This is a DS Value problem. The question stem provides a given equation and asks for the value of x. What would you need to know in order to be able to find the one and only value for x ?

    Plan. Since the question stem also provides an equation, $2x + y = 7$, you could find x if you know the value for y. Jot that down on your scratch paper. Also, statement (1) looks easier, so start there.

    (1) SUFFICIENT: If you know the value of y, then you can plug it into the equation given in the question stem to find the value of x. Eliminate answers (B), (C), and (E).

    (2) SUFFICIENT: The question stem provides one linear equation (no squares or similar complications). The statement provides a different linear equation. You can use the two equations to solve for the individual values of the two variables. Eliminate answer (A).

    The correct answer is **(D)**: Each statement works alone.

2. **(C):** First, understand. The question stem indicates that x is a positive integer; jot that down. Yes/No question: Is $x < 10$? If x is between 1 and 9 inclusive, the answer is Yes. If x is 10 or greater, the answer is No. If you can't place x definitively into one of those two categories, the answer is Maybe/Who Knows?/Not Sufficient. And since the problem allows many possible values, test cases.

    Plan. You're only allowed to use positive integers for x. The "change point" is whether x is <10 or ≥ 10, so think about both groups of values when testing cases.

    (1) INSUFFICIENT: x could be 8, in which case the answer is Yes. But x could also be 16, in which case the answer is No. Since there are two different answers, this statement is not sufficient; cross off answers (A) and (D).

    (2) INSUFFICIENT: x could be 14, in which case the answer is No. But x could also be 8, in which case the answer is Yes. Since there are two different answers, this statement is not sufficient; cross off answer (B).

    (1) AND (2) SUFFICIENT: Return to the Plan step and remind yourself of the combined constraints. Positive integers only. Multiple of 8. Less than 15. What cases can you test?

    x could be 8, in which case the answer is Yes. The next multiple of 8 is 16…but this fails the constraint that $x < 15$. There's no other case to test; the only answer is Yes, so together, the two statements work.

    The correct answer is **(C)**: The two statements work together but neither one works alone.

3. **(E):** First, understand. There are only red and blue marbles in the bag—but there's no indication in the question stem as to the number of each color or the total number of marbles. The question is Yes/No: Is red ≥ 25 ?

    Glance at the statements. One contains a percent sign and one has a real number.

    Plan. Remind yourself of an important point on the GMAT when dealing with percents vs. real numbers. If you only know information about a percentage of something, you can't figure anything out about the real numbers associated with that something.

(1) INSUFFICIENT: This statement provides information about the percentage of red marbles. Percentages alone cannot give you the real number. Eliminate answers (A) and (D).

(2) INSUFFICIENT: This statement does provide a real number: There are 90 marbles total. But there could be just 1 red marble or 89 red marbles. This isn't enough to know whether at least 25 are red. Eliminate answer (B).

(1) AND (2) INSUFFICIENT: The combined information is complicated; time to do a little calculation. Fewer than 40% of the marbles are red. There are at least 90 marbles total. To simplify testing cases, use 90 as the total for now. To find 40% of 90, take 10% and multiply by 4; 10% is 9, so 40% is $(9)(4) = 36$.

Fewer than 36 marbles are red. There could be 35 red marbles, in which case the answer is Yes. But there could also be 20 red marbles, in which case the answer is No. Even together, the two statements aren't enough to solve.

The correct answer is **(E)**: Even together, the two statements aren't sufficient to answer the question.

Fractions and Ratios

In This Chapter

In this chapter, you will learn the relationship between fractions and ratios and how to use either form to solve problems. You'll also learn all of the needed computation skills to manipulate fractions and ratios.

CHAPTER 3 Fractions and Ratios

Fractions are most often used to express numbers that fall in between integers. For example, the fraction $\frac{13}{2}$, which equals 6.5, falls between the integers 6 and 7:

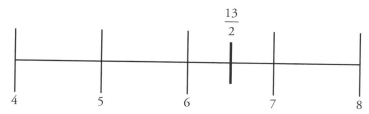

All fractions express what's called a **part-to-whole relationship**. The top number (the numerator) is the *part* and the bottom number (the denominator) is the *whole*. For example, if you eat 5 of the 8 slices in a pizza, you have eaten 5 parts out of 8 (the whole pizza), or $\frac{5}{8}$ of the pizza. You left $\frac{3}{8}$ of the pizza for your friend Sam.

Ratios, on the other hand, express what's called a **part-to-part relationship**. In the pizza example, you ate 5 parts and Sam ate 3 parts. The ratio of pizza that you ate to pizza that Sam ate is 5 to 3.

Something interesting happens here: Notice that the 5 and the 3 are the numerators of the two fractions from the prior paragraph. A ratio consists of all of the parts of a whole—and you can actually create the whole by adding up the parts! In this case, $5 + 3 = 8$, which is the whole, or the denominator, of the fractions. When talking about ratios, this *whole* is called the **ratio total**.

You can convert any fraction to a ratio and vice versa. If a bouquet of flowers has 1 rose for every 3 tulips, then the ratio of roses to tulips is 1 : 3. The *whole* is $1 + 3 = 4$. Therefore, $\frac{1}{4}$ of the bouquet consists of roses and $\frac{3}{4}$ consists of tulips.

Ratios can be written in three different ways:

1. 1 to 3

2. 1 : 3

3. $\frac{1}{3}$

In the third case, you'll need to learn how to read the sentence to know whether it's talking about a fraction or a ratio. The following are examples of ratios:

- The ratio of dogs to cats is $\frac{3}{4}$.

- This bouquet contains $\frac{3}{4}$ as many roses as daisies. (For every 3 roses, there are 4 daisies.)

- For every 3 blue cars sold, there are 4 red cars sold. (The ratio of blue cars sold to red cars sold is 3 : 4.

3

In the first example, the sentence outright tells you that the number that looks like a fraction is really a ratio. The second and third, though, make you interpret the information. In each case, the information conveyed is part-to-part. If you can write a sentence that fits the pattern "For every *X* of the first thing, there are *Y* of the second thing," then you know you have a ratio.

Fractions will always have two portions (with the *part* on top and the *whole* on the bottom), but ratios can have two or more portions. For example, you could have 2 horses to 3 rabbits to 7 llamas, or a ratio of 2 : 3 : 7.

Finally, fractions and ratios both express a *relationship* between two (or more, for ratios) items, but by themselves they do not tell you the exact quantities in question—knowing that someone ate $\frac{1}{2}$ of a pizza does not indicate how many slices that person ate. If the pizza had 8 slices, then that person ate 4 of them, but if the pizza had 10 slices, then that person ate 5.

Similarly, knowing that the ratio of dogs to cats is 2 to 3 does *not* indicate the actual number of dogs and cats. There could be 2 dogs and 3 cats, or 6 dogs and 9 cats, or any other combination that works out to 2 dogs for every 3 cats. (Note: If the problem is talking about something that can't reasonably come in non-integer quantities, such as dogs and cats, then the problem is assuming what's called an *integer constraint*: Only integer values are allowed for the real number of dogs and cats.)

Ratio Labels

It's vital to jot down the order in which the ratio information is given. After all, "the ratio of dogs to cats is 2 : 3" is very different from "the ratio of dogs to cats is 3 : 2."

It is very easy to accidentally reverse the order of a ratio—especially on a timed test like the GMAT. In order to avoid these reversals, write units on either the ratio itself or on the variables you create, or on both.

Thus, if the ratio of dogs to cats is 2 : 3, you might write any of the below:

D : C 2 : 3	$\dfrac{D}{C} = \dfrac{2}{3}$	$\dfrac{2 \text{ dogs}}{3 \text{ cats}}$

However you choose to jot down this information, label the ratio on your scratch paper carefully—every time.

Types of Fractions

It's useful to know certain terms in order to study for the GMAT, but you don't need to memorize these names for the test. You just need to know that these different categories exist.

Proper fractions are those that fall between 0 and 1. In proper fractions, the numerator is always smaller than the denominator. For example:

$$\frac{1}{4}, \frac{1}{2}, \frac{2}{3}, \frac{7}{10}$$

Improper fractions are greater than or equal to 1. In improper fractions, the numerator is always greater than or equal to the denominator. For example:

$$\frac{5}{4}, \frac{13}{2}, \frac{11}{3}, \frac{101}{10}$$

An improper fraction can be rewritten as a mixed number (an integer and a proper fraction together). For example:

$$\frac{5}{4} = \frac{4}{4} + \frac{1}{4} = 1\frac{1}{4} \qquad\qquad \frac{11}{3} = \frac{9}{3} + \frac{2}{3} = 3\frac{2}{3}$$

Most of the time, you'd only need to convert to a mixed number at the end of the problem, in order to match the format of the answers. If you are still in the middle of the problem, don't convert to a mixed number unless you absolutely have to, because you can't use mixed numbers easily in normal math operations (e.g., multiplying by another number).

Numerator and Denominator Rules

In fractions, certain key rules govern the relationship between the **numerator** (the top number) and the **denominator** (the bottom number) of proper fractions. The following rules apply only to positive numbers.

If you increase the numerator of a fraction, while holding the denominator constant, the value increases:

$$\frac{1}{8} < \frac{2}{8} < \frac{3}{8} < \frac{4}{8} < \cdots$$

You are increasing the *part* while keeping the *whole* constant. Increasing only the numerator is like eating more slices of the same pizza: You eat 1 out of 8 slices, then 2 out of 8 slices, and so on.

If you increase the denominator of a fraction, while holding the numerator constant, the value gets smaller and smaller as it approaches 0:

$$\frac{1}{2} > \frac{1}{3} > \frac{1}{4} > \frac{1}{5} \cdots > \frac{1}{1,000} \cdots \to 0$$

This time, you're increasing the *whole* but leaving the *part* constant. Imagine that you have one slice of a whole pizza and, magically, the rest of the pizza (but not your slice!) keeps getting bigger and bigger. Your one part (one slice) becomes a smaller and smaller portion of the entire pizza.

Pop quiz: Is $\frac{7}{13}$ a little greater or a little less than $\frac{7}{14}$, or 0.5 ? The denominator gets a little *smaller* in this example, not larger.

When you *increase* the denominator, the fraction gets *smaller*. So when you *decrease* the denominator, the opposite happens: The value of the fraction *increases* a little. Therefore, $\frac{7}{13}$ is a little greater than 0.5.

Finally, consider this lesser-known rule that the GMAT likes to employ (still for positive numbers only): Adding the exact same number to *both* the numerator and the denominator brings the fraction *closer* to 1, regardless of the fraction's value.

If the starting fraction is *less* than 1, the fraction gets closer to 1 (it *increases*) as you add the same number to the top and bottom:

$$\frac{1}{2} < \frac{1+1}{2+1}, \text{ or } \frac{1}{2} < \frac{2}{3}$$

$$\frac{2}{3} < \frac{2+9}{3+9}, \text{ or } \frac{2}{3} < \frac{11}{12}$$

$$\frac{11}{12} < \frac{11+988}{12+988}, \text{ or } \frac{11}{12} < \frac{999}{1,000}$$

$$\text{Thus: } \frac{1}{2} < \frac{2}{3} < \frac{11}{12} < \frac{999}{1,000} \cdots \to 1$$

And if the starting fraction is *greater* than 1, the fraction gets closer to 1 (it *decreases*) as you add the same number to the top and bottom:

$$\frac{3}{2} > \frac{3+1}{2+1}, \text{ or } \frac{3}{2} > \frac{4}{3}$$

$$\frac{4}{3} > \frac{4+9}{3+9}, \text{ or } \frac{4}{3} > \frac{13}{12}$$

$$\frac{13}{12} > \frac{13+988}{12+988}, \text{ or } \frac{13}{12} > \frac{1{,}001}{1{,}000}$$

Thus: $\frac{3}{2} > \frac{4}{3} > \frac{13}{12} > \frac{1{,}001}{1{,}000} \cdots \rightarrow 1$

Simplifying Fractions and Ratios

Simplifying a fraction is a way to express a fraction or ratio in its lowest terms. Answers in fraction or ratio form on the GMAT will always be presented in fully simplified terms. If you multiply or divide both the numerator and the denominator by the same number, you don't actually change the value of the fraction because you're actually multiplying or dividing by 1. You're always allowed to do this as long as you do the same thing to the top and bottom of the fraction or all parts of the ratio. For example:

Fraction:

$$\frac{24}{30} = \frac{24 \div 6}{30 \div 6} = \frac{4}{5}$$

Ratio:

$$4 : 12 : 16$$
$$\frac{4}{4} : \frac{12}{4} : \frac{16}{4}$$
$$1 : 3 : 4$$

You can simplify (or reduce) a fraction or ratio by dividing both the numerator and the denominator by any common factors until no common factors remain (either one at a time, or in a single step):

Two steps: $\quad \frac{75}{45} = \frac{75 \div 5}{45 \div 5} = \frac{15}{9} = \frac{15 \div 3}{9 \div 3} = \frac{5}{3}$

One step: $\quad \frac{75}{45} = \frac{75 \div 15}{45 \div 15} = \frac{5}{3}$

Simplify before You Multiply

When multiplying fractions, you could first multiply the numerators together, then multiply the denominators together, and finally simplify the resulting product. For example:

$$\frac{8}{15} \times \frac{35}{72} = \frac{8(35)}{15(72)}$$

Next step? You don't have a calculator on the GMAT, so time to do long multiplication...

$$\frac{8(35)}{15(72)} = \frac{280}{\cdots}$$

Wait! Stop! Don't even do that first step. If the math is that annoying, pause and think about what else you could do. In this case, you'd eventually have to simplify that fraction, so why not do that first?

In general, always try to simplify before you multiply: Cancel common factors from the top and bottom of the fractions.

For example, the **8** in the numerator and the **72** in the denominator both have 8 as a factor. Thus, the 8 can be simplified to 1 and the 72 can be simplified to 9:

$$\frac{\overset{1}{\cancel{8}}}{15} \times \frac{35}{\underset{9}{\cancel{72}}}$$

It doesn't matter that the numbers appear in two different fractions. When multiplying fractions together, you can treat all of the numerators as one group and all of the denominators as another. You can cancel anything in the top group with anything in the bottom. (You can't do this when you're adding or subtracting two fractions—just when you're multiplying.)

What next? The **35** and **15** both have 5 as a factor, so simplify those two numbers as well:

$$\frac{\overset{1}{\cancel{8}}}{\underset{3}{\cancel{15}}} \times \frac{\overset{7}{\cancel{35}}}{\underset{9}{\cancel{72}}} = \frac{1(7)}{3(9)} = \frac{7}{27}$$

Make your life easier: Always simplify before you multiply! These numbers are a lot nicer than what you would have gotten by multiplying first.

Add and Subtract Fractions: Use a Common Denominator

If you're asked to add or subtract fractions, first consider whether it would be better to convert to percents or decimals instead. If you see common conversions that you have memorized, it's likely going to be easier to convert from fractions to percents or decimals first.

If you do decide to add or subtract in fraction form, follow these steps:

1. Find a common denominator.

2. Rewrite each fraction so that it is expressed using this common denominator.

3. Add up the numerators only.

Here's an example:

$$\frac{3}{8} + \frac{7}{12}$$

$$\frac{9}{24} + \frac{14}{24} \qquad \text{A common denominator is 24. Thus, } \frac{3}{8} = \frac{9}{24} \text{ and } \frac{7}{12} = \frac{14}{24}.$$

$$\frac{9}{24} + \frac{14}{24} = \frac{23}{24} \qquad \text{Finally, add the numerators to find the answer.}$$

Why don't you also add up the denominators? Think back to the pizza you shared with your friend Sam at the beginning of this chapter. You ate 5 of the 8 slices, or $\frac{5}{8}$ of the pizza, and Sam ate 3 of the 8 slices, or $\frac{3}{8}$ of the pizza. Together, you ate $\frac{8}{8}$ of the pizza—that is, the whole thing!—not $\frac{8}{16}$, or half of the pizza.

In this example, you have to simplify the fraction at the end:

$$\frac{11}{15} - \frac{7}{30}$$

$$\frac{22}{30} - \frac{7}{30}$$ A common denominator is 30: $\frac{11}{15} = \frac{22}{30}$. Leave $\frac{7}{30}$ the same.

$$\frac{22}{30} - \frac{7}{30} = \frac{15}{30}$$ Subtract the numerators.

$$\frac{15}{30} = \frac{1}{2}$$ Simplify $\frac{15}{30}$ to find the answer: $\frac{1}{2}$.

3 Dividing Fractions: Use the Reciprocal

What if you're asked to do the following math?

$$\frac{1}{2} \div \frac{3}{4}$$

If you're asked to divide by a fraction (in this case, you're asked to divide by $\frac{3}{4}$), instead multiply by the reciprocal. The reciprocal of a fraction is the *flip* of that fraction. For example:

The reciprocal of $\frac{3}{4}$ is $\frac{4}{3}$.   The reciprocal of $\frac{2}{9}$ is $\frac{9}{2}$.

What is the reciprocal of an integer? Think of an integer as a fraction with a denominator of 1. For example, the integer 5 is the fraction $\frac{5}{1}$. To find the reciprocal, flip it:

The reciprocal of 5, or $\frac{5}{1}$, is $\frac{1}{5}$.   The reciprocal of 8 is $\frac{1}{8}$.

In order to divide by a fraction, follow these steps:

1. Change the divisor (the second number) into its reciprocal.

2. Multiply the fractions.

For example:

$$\frac{1}{2} \div \frac{3}{4}$$ First, change the divisor $\frac{3}{4}$ into its reciprocal $\frac{4}{3}$.

$$\frac{1}{2} \times \frac{4}{3}$$ Rewrite the problem as multiplication.

$$\frac{1}{\cancel{2}_1} \times \frac{\cancel{4}^2}{3} = \frac{2}{3}$$ Solve. Simplify before you multiply!

Split Up Double-Decker Fractions

The division of fractions can be shown by putting the fractions themselves into a **double-decker fraction**. Consider one of the previous examples:

$$\frac{1}{2} \div \frac{3}{4} \text{ can also be written as a double-decker fraction this way: } \frac{\frac{1}{2}}{\frac{3}{4}}$$

You can rewrite this as the top fraction divided by the bottom fraction. Then, solve normally by using the reciprocal of the second fraction and then multiplying:

$$\frac{\frac{1}{2}}{\frac{3}{4}} = \frac{1}{2} \div \frac{3}{4} = \frac{1}{\cancel{2}} \times \frac{\cancel{4}}{3} = \frac{2}{3}$$

In addition, you can often simplify more quickly by multiplying both top and bottom by a common denominator of the "fractions within the fraction":

$$\frac{\frac{1}{2}}{\frac{3}{4}} = \frac{\frac{1}{2} \times 4}{\frac{3}{4} \times 4} = \frac{2}{3}$$

In this case, the common denominator of 2 and 4 is 4, so multiply both the top and bottom by 4 to make the fractions within the fraction drop out.

The Unknown Multiplier

You've already learned that if you multiply the top and the bottom of a fraction by the same number, you will end up with an equivalent fraction. For example:

$$\frac{4}{7} = \frac{8}{14} = \frac{12}{21}$$

A ratio is equivalent to the most-reduced fraction, $\frac{4}{7}$, in the above example. For example, you might be told that there are 4 dogs for every 7 cats. That ratio doesn't (necessarily) tell you the actual number of dogs and cats, though. You could have exactly 4 dogs and 7 cats, but you could also have 8 dogs and 14 cats, or 12 dogs and 21 cats, and so on.

The $\frac{8}{14}$ fraction is the result of multiplying the top and bottom of the base ratio, $\frac{4}{7}$, by 2.

The $\frac{12}{21}$ fraction is the result of multiplying the base ratio by 3.

The number by which you multiply the ratio to find the actual number of things is called the **unknown multiplier**. Every ratio has an unknown multiplier, and that multiplier is the same for every part of the ratio.

Recall from earlier in this chapter that every ratio has a ratio total, calculated by adding up the parts of the ratio.

If the ratio of dogs to cats is 4 to 7 and there are 8 actual dogs, what else can you figure out? Lay out the information in a table—and always include the ratio total as one column in the table:

	Part	Part	Whole
	Dogs	**Cats**	**Total**
Ratio	4	7	
Multiplier			
Actual	8		

The multiplier for dogs must be $\frac{8}{4} = 2$. Since the multiplier is always the same for all parts of a ratio, write 2 in all of the multiplier boxes. (Note: The multiplier must be an integer for this problem, because you must have whole numbers of dogs and cats.)

	Dogs		**Cats**		**Total**
Ratio	4	+	7	=	11
	×		×		
Multiplier	**2**	=	**2**	=	**2**
	=		=		
Actual	8	+		=	

Now, you can determine that there are 14 cats. You can even calculate the total number of animals, either by adding dogs and cats ($8 + 14 = 22$) or by multiplying the ratio total ($4 + 7 = 11$) by the multiplier, 2.

If you know the ratio and you know any one of the actual values, then you can calculate everything in the table.

Try this problem:

> A display holds 56 devices, all of which are either phones or tablets. If the ratio of phones to tablets is 3 : 4, how many of the devices in the display are phones?

Draw a table and begin to fill it in:

	Phones	**Tablets**	**Total**
Ratio	3	4	
Multiplier			
Actual	⬭		56

Add the top row to obtain a total of 7. The ratio of phones to tablets to total is $3 : 4 : 7$. The multiplier for the total is $\frac{56}{7} = 8$, so 8 is the multiplier across the board.

	Phones	Tablets	Total
Ratio	3	4	7
Multiplier	8	8	8
Actual	(24)		56

There are $3 \times 8 = 24$ phones in the display. (Again, the multiplier must be an integer for this problem.)

If you prefer, you can also solve algebraically. Call the unknown multiplier x. The ratio is $3 : 4$ and the actual numbers of phones and tablets are $3x$ and $4x$, respectively.

The problem indicates that the total number of devices equals 56:

$$\text{Phones} + \text{Tablets} = \text{Total}$$
$$3x + 4x = 56$$
$$7x = 56$$
$$x = 8$$

Plug the multiplier into the expression for phones ($3x$) to determine how many phones are in the display: $(3)(8) = 24$. There are 24 phones in the display.

The unknown multiplier is particularly useful with three-part ratios. For example:

> A recipe calls for amounts of lemon juice, orange juice, and water in the ratio of $2 : 5 : 7$. If the mixture yields 35 milliliters of liquid, how much orange juice was included?

First, set up the given information, including the total for the base ratio:

	L	O	W	Tot
R	2	5	7	14
M				
A		( )		35

Next, begin calculating what you need in order to find the value for the Orange-Actual cell. Compare the actual total to the ratio total to find the multiplier.

	L	O	W	Tot
R	2	5	7	14
M		2.5		2.5
A		(12.5)		35

In this problem, the unknown multiplier turns out not to be an integer. This result is fine, because the problem deals with continuous quantities (milliliters of liquids).

Here's how to set up the problem algebraically:

$$\text{Lemon} + \text{Orange} + \text{Water} = \text{Total}$$
$$2x \quad + \quad 5x \quad + \quad 7x \quad = \quad 14x$$

Now, solve: $14x = 35$, or $x = 2.5$. Thus, the amount of orange juice is $5x = 5(2.5) = 12.5$ milliliters.

Comparing Fractions: The Double-Cross

Which fraction is greater, $\frac{7}{9}$ or $\frac{4}{5}$?

The traditional method of comparing fractions involves finding a common denominator and comparing the two fractions. The common denominator of 9 and 5 is 45.

Thus, $\frac{7}{9} = \frac{35}{45}$ and $\frac{4}{5} = \frac{36}{45}$. In this case, $\frac{4}{5}$ is slightly greater than $\frac{7}{9}$.

Why? Because the numerator 36 is greater than the numerator 35. Once you find a common denominator, the only thing you need to compare is the numerator—so take advantage of that fact to make the work go faster:

$(7 \times 5) = 35 \quad (4 \times 9) = 36$

$\frac{7}{9} \quad \frac{4}{5}$

Set up the fractions next to each other. Multiply the numbers across the arrows and put each answer by the corresponding numerator (*not* the denominator!).

$$35 < 36$$
$$\frac{7}{9} < \frac{4}{5}$$

Since 35 is less than 36, the first fraction must be less than the second one.

Essentially, you have done the same thing as before—you just didn't bother to write down the common denominator of 45. This process can save you time when comparing fractions on the GMAT.

You can even use the double-cross method to add or subtract fractions, with one more step: Draw a third arrow straight across the bottom. All three arrows mean *multiply*. For example:

$$\frac{7}{9} + \frac{4}{5}$$

$(7)(5) = 35 \quad \frac{7}{9} \,{}_+\, \frac{4}{5} \quad (9)(4) = 36$

$(9)(5) = 45$

$^{35}\frac{7}{9} \,{}_+\, \frac{4}{5}^{36} = \frac{71}{45}$

Essentially, multiply across all three arrows, as shown. Add the two results for the numerators (or subtract, if the problem asks you to subtract). For the denominator, just use the single number from the bottom multiplication.

Since this method involves multiplying, check the numbers before you start. If they're large enough to annoy you, you might want to use the traditional method of finding a common denominator.

Multiple Ratios: Make a Common Term

You may encounter two separate ratios containing a common element (e.g., dogs to cats and cats to birds). To combine the ratios, you can use a process remarkably similar to creating a common denominator for fractions.

Consider the following problem:

> In a box containing action figures from Game of Thrones, there are 3 figures of Arya for every 2 figures of Brienne, and 5 figures of Arya for every 4 figures of Daenerys. What is the ratio of Daenerys figures to Brienne figures?

Jot down the given info as you try to understand the story:

$$A : B \qquad\qquad A : D$$
$$3 : 2 \qquad\qquad 5 : 4$$

The question asks for the ratio of D to B, but neither of the given ratios contains both of these variables. What now?

Just as you can change *fractions* to have common *denominators*, you can change ratios so that the common *terms* correspond to the same quantity. Once you do this, you can put everything together in one big three-part ratio.

The two ratios have Arya in common, but the two values for Arya are different. In order to combine the two ratios, the values for Arya must be the same.

$$\underline{A : B : D}\qquad\qquad\qquad\qquad \underline{A : B : D}$$
$$3 : 2 : ? \qquad \rightarrow \text{Multiply by 5} \rightarrow \qquad 15 : 10 : ?$$
$$5 : ? : 4 \qquad \rightarrow \text{Multiply by 3} \rightarrow \qquad 15 : ? : 12$$

This is the combined ratio: $\boxed{15 : 10 : 12}$

Once the A's are the same (15), combine the two ratios into one big three-part ratio. Note: Do not add the two A's together. Just use the base number, 15.

Now, answer the question. Pull out just the parts that you are asked for: D and B. The ratio D to B is 12 to 10, which simplifies to 6 to 5.

Try this same problem but with a different question:

> In a box containing action figures from Game of Thrones, there are 3 figures of Arya for every 2 figures of Brienne, and 5 figures of Arya for every 4 figures of Daenerys. What is the least number of action figures that could be in the box?

First, you still want to combine the two separate ratios into one big ratio, as you did for the first version of the problem. So $A : B : D$ is $15 : 10 : 12$.

Next, what could the *actual* number of action figures be, not just the ratio? The actual values for the action figures are the ratio numbers multiplied by an unknown multiplier (which must be a positive integer, since you need whole action figures). The question asks for the *least* number of action figures, so use the least possible multiplier, 1. In other words, the ratio itself represents the least number of action figures.

Therefore, the least possible number of action figures is $15 + 10 + 12 = 37$.

Complex Fractions: Don't Split the Denominator

A complex fraction is a fraction in which there is a sum or a difference in the numerator or the denominator. For example:

$$\frac{x + y}{z}$$

When simplifying fractions that incorporate sums or differences, remember this rule: You may split up the terms of the numerator, but you may *never* split the terms of the denominator.

For example, you can add up the two terms in the numerator in this example, but you may decide it's easier to split it into two fractions first and add after:

$$\frac{480 + 165}{10} = \frac{480}{10} + \frac{165}{10} = 48 + 16.5 = 64.5$$

By contrast, the terms in this example may *not* be split:

$$\frac{5}{15 + 10} \neq \frac{5}{15} + \frac{5}{10} \quad \text{NO!}$$

Instead, simplify the denominator first:

$$\frac{5}{15 + 10} = \frac{5}{25} = \frac{1}{5}$$

Often, GMAT problems will involve complex fractions with variables. On these problems, it is tempting to split the denominator. Do not fall for it!

$$\frac{5x - 2y}{x - y} \neq \frac{5x}{x} - \frac{2y}{y} \quad \text{NO!}$$

Unfortunately, $\frac{5x - 2y}{x - y}$ cannot be simplified further, because neither of the terms in the numerator shares a factor with the entire denominator.

On the other hand, the expression $\frac{6x - 10}{10}$ can be simplified by splitting the numerator. Both terms in the numerator share a factor with the denominator, and by splitting into two fractions, you can write each part in simplified form:

$$\frac{6x - 10}{10} = \frac{6x}{10} - \frac{10}{10} = \frac{3}{5}x - 1$$

Relative Values and Data Sufficiency

Some problems will give you concrete values while others will provide only relative values:

Concrete values are actual amounts (# of tickets sold, liters of water, etc.).

Relative values relate two quantities using fractions, ratios, percents, or decimals (twice as many, ratio of 2 : 3, 60% less, etc.).

Try this Data Sufficiency problem:

A company sells only two kinds of pie: apple pie and cherry pie. What fraction of the total pies sold last month were apple pies?

(1) The company sold 460 pies last month.

(2) The company sold 30% more cherry pies than apple pies last month.

When a question asks for a relative value, not a concrete or actual value, you don't need as much information in order to solve.

The question asks what fraction of the total pies sold were apple pies:

$$\frac{\text{apple pies}}{\text{total pies}} = ? \quad \text{or} \quad \frac{a}{a + c} = ?$$

Statement (1) indicates that the total number of pies sold was 460, so $a + c = 460$:

$$\frac{a}{460} = ?$$

The value of a is still unknown, so this statement is not sufficient. Eliminate answer choices (A) and (D).

Statement (2) indicates that the company sold 30% more cherry pies than apple pies; in other words, the number of cherry pies sold was 130% of the number of apple pies sold:

$$1.3a = c$$

On the surface, this may not seem like enough information. But watch what happens when you replace c with $1.3a$ in the rephrased question.

$$\frac{a}{a + c} = ?$$
$$\frac{a}{a + 1.3a} = ?$$
$$\frac{\cancel{a}}{2.3\cancel{a}} = \frac{1}{2.3}$$

The a variables drop out. Statement (2) actually does provide enough information to find the value of the fraction. The correct answer is (B).

How could you recognize that statement (2) is sufficient without having to do that algebra?

This DS question stem was asking for a relative value (*What* fraction *of the total pies…*). Relative values are really just ratios in disguise. The ratio in this question is as follows:

apple pies sold : cherry pies sold : total pies sold

The question asks for the ratio of apple pies sold to total pies sold, or apple : total. Statement (2) provides the ratio of apple pies sold to cherry pies sold. You could write it this way:

$$a : c$$
$$10 : 13$$

The number 13 is 30% greater than the number 10, so this ratio fits the given information. And, if you know the two parts of the ratio, then you can find the ratio total:

$$a : c : t$$
$$10 : 13 : 23$$

As a result, the ratio of apple pies to total pies ($a : t$) is 10 : 23. Statement (2) is sufficient to answer the question.

If you know a ratio, you can find a fraction based on using the ratio total. For example, 10 out of 23 total pies are apple, so the fraction of apple pies is $\frac{10}{23}$.

Also note that, although statement (2) allows you to determine the *relative* value, it does not provide enough information to calculate the *actual* number of pies. If the question had asked for a concrete number, such as the number of apple pies, you would have needed to use both statements to solve.

Problem Set

Note: On quant problems, the GMAT will always provide exactly five answer choices. In this guide, you will sometimes encounter multiple-choice problems with fewer than five answer choices.

For problems 1–5, decide whether the given operation will cause the original value to **increase**, **decrease**, or **stay the same**.

1. Multiply the numerator of a positive fraction by $\frac{3}{2}$.

2. Add 1 to the numerator of a positive fraction and subtract 1 from its denominator.

3. Multiply both the numerator and denominator of a positive fraction by $3\frac{1}{2}$.

4. Multiply a positive fraction by $\frac{3}{8}$.

5. Divide a positive fraction by $\frac{3}{13}$.

6. If $48 : 2x$ is equivalent to $144 : 600$, what is x?

7. Simplify: $\dfrac{8(3)(x)^2(3)}{6x}$

8. Simplify: $\dfrac{\frac{3}{5} + \frac{1}{3}}{\frac{2}{3} + \frac{2}{5}}$

9. Simplify: $\dfrac{12ab^3 - 5a^2b}{3ab}$

10. Initially, the markers and pens in a drawer were in the ratio of 5 : 7. Then, 6 pens were removed. If there are 35 markers in the drawer, how many pens are left?

    (A) 29

    (B) 43

    (C) 49

Save the problem set below for review after you finish this entire guide.

11. Which of the following fractions has a value between $\frac{3}{5}$ and $\frac{2}{3}$?

   (A) $\frac{9}{14}$

   (B) $\frac{8}{18}$

   (C) $\frac{16}{21}$

12. A cleaning solution mixture calls for a ratio of 1 part bleach for every 4 parts water. When mixing the solution, Aki made a mistake and mixed in half as much bleach as was required by the ratio. The total solution consisted of 27 milliliters. How much bleach did Aki put into the solution, in milliliters?

   (A) 3

   (B) 4

   (C) 6

13. The amount of time that three people worked on a certain project was in the ratio of 2 : 3 : 5. If the project took 110 hours, what is the difference between the number of hours worked by the person who worked for the longest time and the person who worked for the shortest time?

   (A) 22

   (B) 33

   (C) 55

14. Challenge! Every game of chess that Artem played this month resulted in a win, a loss, or a tie. What fraction of the chess games that Artem played this month did he win?

   (1) The number of games that resulted in a tie was $\frac{1}{4}$ of the number of games that Artem won.

   (2) Artem lost $\frac{2}{5}$ of the games.

Solutions

1. **Increase:** Multiplying the numerator of a positive fraction by a number greater than 1 increases the numerator. As the numerator of a positive fraction increases, its value increases.

2. **Increase:** As the numerator of a positive fraction increases, the value of the fraction increases. As the denominator of a positive fraction decreases, the value of the fraction also increases. Both actions will work to increase the value of the fraction.

3. **Stay the same:** Multiplying or dividing the numerator and denominator of a fraction by the same number is equivalent to multiplying by 1, so doing this will not change the value of the fraction.

4. **Decrease:** Multiplying any positive number by a positive, proper fraction (a fraction between 0 and 1) decreases the number.

5. **Increase:** Dividing a positive number by a positive, proper fraction (a fraction between 0 and 1) increases the number.

6. **100:** Consider the first given, $48 : 2x$, the ratio, and the second given, $144 : 600$, the actual. Put the info in a ratio table and find the multiplier:

	Part 1	Part 2
R	48	2x
M		
A	144	600

Try some numbers to see what you'd need to multiply 48 by to get to 144. How about 48×2? Not enough; that's only 96. What about 48×3? $50 \times 3 = 150$, so 48×3 has to be 6 less. . .Yes, that's 144! Plug the info into the table and solve for x:

	Part 1	Part 2
R	48	2x
M	3	3
A	144	600

For the second part, the ratio number times the multiplier gives the actual value: $(2x)(3) = 600$, so $x = 100$.

7. **12x:** First, cancel terms in both the numerator and the denominator. Then, combine terms:

$$\frac{8(3)(x)^2(3)}{6x}$$

$$= \frac{8(\cancel{3})(x)^2(3)}{_2\cancel{6}\,x}$$

$$= \frac{^4\cancel{8}(x)^2(3)}{\cancel{2}x}$$

$$= \frac{4(x)\cancel{x}(3)}{\cancel{x}}$$

$$= 4(x)(3)$$

$$= 12x$$

8. $\dfrac{7}{8}$: To get rid of the fractions within fractions, first find the common denominator of all the fractions-within-fractions. The denominators are all 5 or 3, so the common denominator is 15. Next, multiply everything by the fraction $\dfrac{15}{15}$:

$$\left(\frac{\frac{3}{5}+\frac{1}{3}}{\frac{2}{3}+\frac{2}{5}}\right)\left(\frac{15}{15}\right) = \frac{9+5}{10+6} = \frac{14}{16} = \frac{7}{8}$$

Alternatively, add the fractions in the numerator and denominator:

$$\frac{\frac{14}{15}}{\frac{16}{15}} = \frac{^7\cancel{14}}{_1\cancel{15}} \times \frac{^1\cancel{15}}{_8\cancel{16}} = \frac{7}{8}$$

9. $4b^2 - \dfrac{5}{3}a$: Split the numerator. Then, cancel terms in both the numerator and denominator:

$$\frac{12ab^3 - 5a^2b}{3ab} = \frac{12ab^3}{3ab} - \frac{5a^2b}{3ab} = 4b^2 - \frac{5}{3}a$$

10. **(B) 43:** Find the unknown multiplier, then use it to calculate the initial number of pens in the drawer. Include the Total column when you make the table, but only use it if the problem requires you to. (Note: The given information is shown in bold; the calculated information is not bold.)

	M	P	Tot
R	5	7	
M	7	7	
A	35	49	

There were initially 49 pens in the drawer but 6 were removed, so 43 pens remain.

11. **(A) $\frac{9}{14}$:** The two starting fractions are both on the "common conversions" list, so consider converting to percentages or decimals:

$$\frac{3}{5} = 0.6 = 60\% \text{ and } \frac{2}{3} = 0.6\overline{6} = 66\frac{2}{3}\%$$

Take a look at the answers. Are there any that are well below or above that range?

Answer (B), $\frac{8}{18}$, is less than 0.5 (since $\frac{9}{18}$ is 0.5), so eliminate this answer. What about the other two? Answer (C), $\frac{16}{21}$, is close to $\frac{15}{20}$, which is 0.75. But is $\frac{16}{21}$ greater than or less than 0.75? In order to go from $\frac{15}{20}$ to $\frac{16}{21}$, you have to add 1 to both the numerator and denominator. If you start with a positive fraction less than 1 and add the same positive number to both the top and bottom, the fraction will get closer to 1—that is, it will increase. Therefore, $\frac{16}{21}$ must be greater than 0.75. It cannot be correct; the only answer remaining is **(A)**.

12. **(A) 3 mL:** The proper ratio of bleach to water is 1 : 4. However, Aki accidentally put in half as much bleach as the ratio called for. Sketch out the given info in a ratio box and think about how to proceed:

	B	W	Total
R	orig: 1 oops: 0.5	4	
M			
A	?		27

The actual ratio Aki used was 0.5 : 4, and the total volume of the mixture was 27 milliliters. This would be a lot easier to solve if you knew the unknown multiplier or if you knew how much bleach or water Aki actually used. In fact, you (sort of) do: The answer choices represent three possible values for the amount of bleach used. Work backwards!

If Aki used 4 milliliters of bleach, then the mixture would have had 23 milliliters of water (since the whole thing is 27 mL). The ratio, then, would be 4 : 23. Does that reduce to a ratio of 0.5 : 4?

$$4 : 23 \rightarrow 0.5 : \frac{23}{8}$$

Divide 4 by 8 to get 0.5. Do the same thing to the 23. Nope, that value is not 4. Eliminate answer (B).

Is that answer too big or too small? $\frac{23}{8}$ is just a bit smaller than $\frac{24}{8}$, or 3. But the water part of the ratio is supposed to be 4, not 3, so there isn't enough water in this mixture. In order for more of the 27 milliliters of mixture to be water, you need less bleach, so the answer must be the smaller number, 3 milliliters.

If you're not sure, you can check (but don't do more math than you need to do!). If Aki used 3 milliliters of bleach, then the mixture contained $27 - 3 = 24$ milliliters of water. The ratio 3 : 24 does reduce to the ratio 0.5 : 4.

13. **(B) 33:** The ratio is 2 : 3 : 5. Call x the unknown multiplier, so the actual number of hours for each person are $2x$, $3x$, and $5x$. Use this to set up an equation and solve for x:

$$2x + 3x + 5x = 110$$
$$10x = 110$$
$$x = 11$$

Therefore, the person who worked for the longest time put in $5(11) = 55$ hours, and the person who worked for the shortest time put in $2(11) = 22$ hours. This represents a difference of $55 - 22 = 33$ hours.

14. **(C):** There are three possible outcomes for each game: W, L, or T. The question asks for the fraction of games won, or $\frac{W}{W + L + T}$. Note that the question is asking for a relative value, not the actual numbers involved; it may be possible to find this fraction without knowing the actual number of wins and the total number of games.

The first statement mentions both ties and wins, while the second mentions only losses. Since the second statement is less complex, start there and write $\frac{BD}{ACE}$ on your scratch paper.

(2) INSUFFICIENT: Artem lost 2 out of every 5 games. At most, then, Artem won 3 out of every 5 games, but he could have won fewer. All you can tell for sure is that Artem won or tied 3 out of 5 games. Eliminate answers (B) and (D).

(1) INSUFFICIENT: This statement can be interpreted as a ratio. For every 1 game tied, Artem won 4 games. The ratio of ties to wins is 1 : 4. No information is given about losses, however, so this information is not enough to determine the fraction of games won out of the total number of games. Eliminate answer (A).

(1) AND (2) SUFFICIENT: Set up a partial ratio box. Since the question asks for a fraction and never provides real numbers, you only need the first row (the Ratio row). The ratio of $T : W$ is 1 : 4.

	T	*W*	*L*	**Total**
R	1	4	*L*	$5 + L$

The second statement indicates that L represents 2 parts out of a total of 5 parts. That information is the equivalent of providing a second equation so that you can solve for the two unknowns (L and the ratio total). If you like, you can just memorize the idea that if there is only one unknown part of the ratio (L in this case) *and* you're also told the relationship between that unknown and the ratio total, then you can always find the relationship between any of the three individual parts and the total. If you want to understand why this is true, read on (understanding why may help you to remember this fact).

Statement (2) can be written algebraically as $\frac{L}{Total} = \frac{2}{5}$. The ratio box indicates that the total is $5 + L$. You can substitute that into the statement (2) equation to solve for the L part of the ratio. (This is DS, so don't actually solve. Just know that you can.) If you know the ratio value of L, you know all three parts of the ratio, so you can find $\frac{W}{W + L + T}$.

The correct answer is **(C):** Both statements together are sufficient, but neither one works alone.

Strategy: Arithmetic vs. Algebra 1

In This Chapter

- Test Cases
- Choose Smart Numbers
- Work Backwards

In this chapter, you will learn three strategies for avoiding algebra and using real numbers (arithmetic) instead. You can use these strategies on both the Quantitative and Integrated Reasoning sections of the GMAT.

CHAPTER 4 Strategy: Arithemetic vs. Algebra 1

When you first learned how to do math, you started with arithmetic—that is, you did math stuff with real numbers. Later on sometime, you learned about variables (or unknowns) and started to do algebra.

Which of these problems is easier for you to solve?

What percent of a number is 50% of 10% of that number?	What percent of 100 is 50% of 10% of 100 ?
(A) 1%	(A) 1%
(B) 5%	(B) 5%
(C) 10%	(C) 10%

The setup of the two problems is identical—one just has real numbers rather than unknowns. In the first problem, you would assign a variable to the unknown *number* mentioned, and then you would use algebra to solve. You may think that this version is not particularly difficult, but no matter how easy you think it is, it's still easier to work with the real numbers given in the second problem.

In general, arithmetic is easier than algebra—for everyone. Our brains just work better with real numbers.

So take this mantra into the test with you: Don't just do the math presented to you, in the form it is presented. Pause to evaluate—make a conscious choice! If the algebra on a particular problem is really easy for you, go for it. Often, though, using real numbers will be faster and easier—and that means more time and mental energy to spend elsewhere on the test.

Here's the exciting thing: There are a number of ways to turn GMAT algebra into arithmetic. You've already learned about one strategy in the Data Sufficiency chapter: Test Cases.

In those DS problems, some theoretical question was asked, and multiple possible values were allowed to be used in the problem. . .in other words, the question involved some algebra. But algebra is annoying—so, where possible, try some real numbers (test cases) to see whether you can get different answers (not sufficient!) or whether you keep getting the same answer (sufficient!).

This general principle (try some real numbers/do arithmetic instead of algebra) can apply to Problem Solving (PS) problems as well. The details just change a bit in terms of how you execute.

There are three main main strategies that you can use to turn algebra into arithmetic on PS problems:

1. Test Cases (TC)

2. Choose Smart Numbers (SN)

3. Work Backwards (WB)

In this chapter, you'll learn the basics for each question type. As you continue your studies, you'll continue to learn more about these strategies until you're an expert for the real test.

Test Cases

You can actually **Test Cases** (TC) on Problem Solving problems, too—in one specific circumstance. When the problem asks which answer choice *must be* or *could be* something (true or false or have some certain characteristic), you can use this strategy.

Consider this problem:

If x and y are integers and $xy = 6$, which of the following must be true?

(A) x is even.
(B) x equals either 2 or 3.
(C) Either x or y is even.

Understand. Both are integers. The product xy equals 6. *Must be* signals that you could test cases. According to this question stem, one (and only one) of the answers *must be true* all the time.

Plan. If the numbers are both integers and multiply to 6, then they could be 2 and 3, or 1 and 6, or... anything else? They could also be negative, such as -2 and -3. Feel free to start with a positive case, but see how the math plays out; you may want to try a negative later.

Solve. Case 1: $x = 2$ and $y = 3$. In this case...hmm, all of the answers are true. Can you think of a case to test that would give you a different response for answer (A)? In other words, can you choose a value for x that is *not* even?

Case 2: Swap the two numbers. If $x = 3$ and $y = 2$, then you can eliminate answer (A). Answers (B) and (C) are still in. Take a look at the text of those two answers; what do you want to try next?

Case 3: Try something other than 2 and 3. If $x = 1$ and $y = 6$, then you can eliminate answer (B).

The correct answer is **(C)**, the only remaining answer.

These *must be* questions aren't super common on the GMAT, so more often, you'll test cases on DS problems—but it's good to know that you can use this strategy on certain PS problems, too.

Let's summarize that process.

U: First, during the Understand step, **recognize** that you can test cases on a PS problem. The question will ask what *must* or *could be* a certain thing (true, false, or a certain characteristic).

P: During the Plan step, **think about** any **constraints** you're given; this determines what kinds of numbers you are allowed to try. Also think about what kinds of numbers might give you a different answer. You'll learn more strategies for this step later in this guide.

S: Then, **choose one set of numbers**, following any constraints given in the problem, and test the answers. Cross off any answers that fail the test. **Decide what to test next:** Look at the remaining answer choices and think about what kind of case might help you to knock out one (or more) of the choices. Repeat until you're down to one answer (or you get stuck; in that case, guess from the remaining answers and move on).

Choose Smart Numbers

The next two strategies, **Choose Smart Numbers** (SN) and **Work Backwards** (WB) apply only to PS problems. On the real test, expect to see one to three PS problems for *each* of these two strategies. (And you can use all three of these strategies on the Integrated Reasoning section, too!)

When the problem asks you to find either a variable expression or a relative number (such as a percentage, a fraction, or a ratio), you can choose smart numbers. This strategy is similar to testing cases, but not quite the same.

Remember this problem?

> What percent of a number is 50% of 10% of that number?

(A) 1%

(B) 5%

(C) 10%

Understand. It keeps talking about *a number* but never offers a real value for that number. Even the answer choices aren't actual values—they're just percentages, or relative values. In this case, you can pick your own value for the problem.

So far, this probably feels similar to testing cases. Here's the great part: Unlike DS, this problem type has specific answer choices, so you only need to try one case when you use SN. That one case will lead to one of the answers and then you're done! (The only exception to this on PS is the *must be* or *could be* problem type shown in the prior section, for which you may need to test multiple cases.)

Plan. Since the problem deals with percentages, 100 is a nice number to pick.

$$\boxed{\# = 100}$$

Jot this down and put a big box around it—you may need to use it multiple times, so you want to find it again easily.

Now, anywhere the problem talks about *that number*, you're going to use 100. Let's see how that works:

> What percent of a number is 50% of 10% of that number?

Solve. Start with the concrete numbers in the question:

Note: Since it's all multiplication, you can do that math in either order. It's your choice whether to take 10% first or 50% first. Either way, 50% of 10% of 100 equals 5.

The starting number is 100 and the *50% of 10% of that number* portion of the question now equals 5. Plug this information into the original question:

> **Original:** What percent of a number is *50% of 10% of that number*?
>
> **Rephrased:** What percent of 100 is 5 ?

Since it asks for the percent and gives you the two real numbers, put the *of* number on the bottom of a fraction and the other number on top: $\frac{5}{100} = 5\%$. You can also think it through logically if you prefer: 5 is 5% of 100. Go find a match in the answers.

The correct answer is (B).

Let's summarize that process.

U: During the Understand step, **recognize** that you can use smart numbers. It's a PS problem. The problem will keep talking about a certain thing but will never give a real number for that thing, in the question stem or in the answer choices. The answers will contain variables or relative values, such as fractions, percents, or ratios.

P: During the Plan step, think about **what kind of number will work nicely** in the problem. You'll learn more strategies for this step later in this guide.

S: Finally, **use your chosen number to work through the math** until you find a numerical answer, then find the choice that matches your numerical answer.

Work Backwards

On certain problems, you can also work backwards from the answer choices. Some problems do give you real numbers for everything; in this case, you can't choose your own numbers to try as you did for the first two strategies.

Consider this problem:

> Flannery is 28 years old and Harumi is 11 years old. In how many years will Flannery's age be twice Harumi's age?
>
> (A) 3
> (B) 4
> (C) 6
> (D) 8
> (E) 9

There are ways to solve this problem algebraically, but that's a lot more annoying than doing some arithmetic. But this problem has real numbers already…so now what?

The problem is asking you to solve for one of the numbers in the answer choices. The numbers in the answer choices are "nice" numbers—they look pretty easy to work with. So you could just do the problem backwards, trying each answer choice till you find the one that works.

That might seem like it could take a long time. What if you have to try all five answers?

The good news: You won't have to. The GMAT will put numerical answers in increasing order or decreasing order (so, in this case, either 3, 4, 6, 8, 9 or 9, 8, 6, 4, 3). This little feature means that you'll likely never have to try more than two answer choices when working backwards.

Understand. $F = 28$ and $H = 11$. In how many years will $F = 2H$? The answer choices represent that actual number of years and they're "nice" numbers, so work backwards.

Plan. When working backwards, start with answer (B) or (D). In this case, answer (B) is smaller, so start there. (Why not answer (C)? You'll learn a little later.) Start a chart on your scratch paper showing answer (B) and what it represents. You're going to keep adding new columns to this chart as you perform each step.

Solve. Work through the problem, using answer (B). When you get to the last piece of information given in the question stem, check whether your math matches what the problem says:

> Flannery is 28 years old and Harumi is 11 years old. In how many years will Flannery's age be twice Harumi's age?

$$F = 28 \text{ now}$$
$$H = 11 \text{ now}$$

Yrs from now:	F will be:	H will be:	F is 2H ?
(B) 4	32	15	No

The very last piece of given information is that F will be twice H's age. But this isn't what happens with answer (B)—15 times 2 is 30, not 32. So this answer cannot be correct. Cross it off.

Next, look at the way that math played out. Do you need a larger value for "years from now" or a smaller one? How can you tell?

If you aren't sure (it's not easy to tell on this problem!), try answer (D)—by comparing the results from testing (B) and (D), a pattern in the answer choices will emerge:

Yrs from now:	F will be:	H will be:	F is 2H ?
(B) 4	32	15	No $H < \frac{1}{2}$
(D) 8	36	19	No $H > \frac{1}{2}$

In 8 years, H will be 19 and F will be 36. Once again, F is not double H's age. This answer is still not the right one. But something's different this time. Using choice (B), H was *less* than half of F. That is, answer (B) was too small. But using answer (D), H is now *more* than half of F. Answer (D) goes too far! What does that mean?

You need a number that's greater than 4 and less than 8. Only answer choice (C) qualifies. You can check the math if you're not sure—but the GMAT is a timed test, so don't do work that you don't need to do.

The correct answer is (**C**).

Here's how you *can* figure out directly that you needed a larger number on this problem (though it's not easy—so feel free not to go this far with it!). In the original scenario, twice H's age is 22, which is 6 years less than F at 28. Jot down what you know:

Using answer (B): In 4 years, F will be 32 and H will be 15. Double 15 to get 30, which is 2 years less than 32. So the 2H value has gotten *closer* to half of F's age but is still *less* than half of F's age.

In other words, more time needs to pass before H will be half of F, so you'd need to try a larger number. Your test for (D) would show that it was too large, and so again, you'd choose (C).

The fact that the answers are in order is exactly what allows you to "follow the pattern" when working backwards. You'll always start with either answer (B) or answer (D).

Imagine you have the same problem but the five answers are (A) 6, (B) 8, (C) 9, (D) 10, and (E) 12. You'd try (B), 8, first and, as above, you'd figure out that 8 was incorrect. What would that mean?

If you were able to analyze the math, you'd realize that (B) was *too large*, so the correct answer must be (A), the only smaller choice. You'd never have to try answer (D).

Don't spend a ton of time trying to figure that out though. If you don't see a quick way to tell whether you need to go larger or smaller, just test (D) and compare it to (B) to find the pattern. Here's what would happen for the new answer choices:

> (B): In 8 years, F will be 36 and H will be 19. Double H is 38, not 36. This is too big and off by 2 ears.

> (D): In 10 years, F will be 38 and H will be 21. Double H is 42, not 38. This is too big and off by 4 years.

Both (B) and (D) are wrong in the same direction, but (D) is even farther off. Choosing a bigger answer choice made things worse! So you now know that (A) is the correct answer.

Consider these three possible patterns of answers; what does each one mean? For each example, assume you've tried answers (B) and (D) and determined that they're incorrect.

Example 1	Example 2	Example 3
(A) 1	(A) 1	(A) 5
(B) 2 too small	(B) 2 too small	(B) 4 not right; can't tell which way to go
(C) 3	(C) 3	(C) 3
(D) 4 too big	(D) 4 too small, but closer	(D) 2 still wrong in the same direction as (B), but closer
(E) 5	(E) 5	(E) 1

In the first example, answer (B) is too small but (D) is too big. The correct answer must be in between, so the only possible choice is answer (C).

In the second example, answers (B) and (D) are both too small, but answer (D) gets *closer* to the right answer. The pattern is sending you to answer (E).

The third example is more complex. You can tell answer (B) is wrong but you're not sure which way to go, so you try answer (D) next. Once you've tried (D), you can see the pattern: Answer (D) is still "off" in the same way as (B) but is getting closer. In this case, the pattern is pointing you to go further to answer (E).

This pattern idea is why you want to try answers (B) and (D) vs. answer (C). Starting with answers (B) and (D) will show you the "spaced-out" pattern among all five answers.

Here's a summary of the working backwards process.

U: First, **recognize** that you can work backwards. It's a PS problem and the answers represent a single variable in the problem (for example, they represent one person's age, not the difference between the ages of two people). The answers will contain actual values—no variables or relative values—and those values should be pretty "nice" to work with for that type of problem, whatever it is.

P: Second, glance at the answers; do they increase or decrease? **Start with answer (B) or (D).** Note: This summary will assume that the answers increase and that you start with answer (B).

Set up a little table on your scratch paper. **Organize to make it easier** to run through the math again with another answer, just in case.

S: Do the math from the beginning of the problem to the last fact given in the problem. **If the answer you started with, (B), is correct, the last fact will match,** so this will be the correct answer. If it doesn't match, cross off answer (B).

Is there an easy way to tell whether to go larger or smaller? If not, try answer (D).

If you can tell that you need a *smaller* number, then the answer must be (A). Pick it and move on. If you can tell that you need a *larger* number, cross off answer (A) and try answer (D).

If you try (D) and it's correct, you're done. If not, cross it off. Then, **examine the pattern created by answers (B) and (D)** and make your choice among the remaining answers accordingly.

Note: As you practice working backwards, you will get better at being able to decipher the pattern shown by answers (B) and (D). But if you aren't sure, you'll have to decide between trying more answers and just guessing and moving on. If you've already spent 2+ minutes, it's probably best just to guess and move on unless the math is very fast. You've eliminated two answers, so your chances of guessing correctly are pretty good.

You'll continue to learn more advanced techniques for each of these three strategies as you work your way through this guide. Now, practice what you just learned in the following problem set.

Problem Set

Practice your test-taking strategies: Smart Numbers, Test Cases, Work Backwards. Try the algebraic/ textbook way as well to compare methods. When you're done, ask yourself which way you prefer to solve *this* problem and why.

On the real test, you won't have time to try both methods; you'll have to make a decision and go with it. Learn *how* to make that decision while studying; then, the next time a new problem pops up in front of you, you'll be able to make a quick (and good!) decision about what to do.

1. If $a < 0$ and $b < c$, which of the following must be true?

    (A) $ab < c$

    (B) $ac > b$

    (C) $ab > 0$

    (D) $ac < 0$

    (E) $ab > ac$

2. At the beginning of the day, the ratio of $5 bills to $10 bills in Thom's wallet was 2 to 3. Thom then paid for a purchase with one $5 bill and four $10 bills, and did not receive change. Afterwards, Thom observed that the ratio of $5 bills to $10 bills in the wallet was 3 to 2. How many $5 bills were in Thom's wallet at the beginning of the day?

    (A) 4

    (B) 6

    (C) 8

    (D) 10

    (E) 12

3. Two libraries are planning to combine a portion of their collections in one new space. The new space will house $\frac{1}{3}$ of the books from Library A, along with $\frac{1}{4}$ of the books from Library B. If there are twice as many books in Library B as in Library A, what proportion of the books in the new space will have come from Library A?

    (A) $\frac{1}{3}$

    (B) $\frac{2}{5}$

    (C) $\frac{1}{2}$

    (D) $\frac{7}{12}$

    (E) $\frac{3}{5}$

4

Answers and explanations follow on the next page. ▶ ▶ ▶

Solutions

1. **(E)** $ab > ac$: The question stem asks a *must be* question, so test cases on this problem. The stem also indicates that a is negative and that b is less than c. Since the first piece of information makes a distinction between positive and negative, think about the second piece of information in that same context. If b is less than c, then they could both be positive or both be negative, or b could be negative while c is positive.

    Glance at the answers. They all involve multiplication of various combinations of the variables. Answers (C) and (D) also include > 0 or < 0, which are shorthand for positive and negative, respectively. What do you know about rules around positive and negative when multiplying two numbers together? If you're not sure, try a couple of small numbers to see what happens.

    If the two numbers have the same sign, such as $(1)(2) = 2$ or $(-1)(-2) = 2$, then the product will be positive. If the two numbers have the opposite sign, such as $(1)(-2) = -2$, then the product will be negative.

    Given that, test answers (C) and (D) first.

    (C) $ab > 0$. The variable a is negative, but b could be negative or positive. If b is positive, then this choice is false; that is, it is not always true. Eliminate.

    (D) $ac < 0$. The variable a is negative, but c could be negative or positive. If c is negative, then this choice is false; that is, it is not always true. Eliminate.

    For the other three choices, try real values. Remember: a must be negative and $b < c$. Try whatever comes to mind first for your first test, then think about how to alter the first test in order to get another answer to drop out.

	Test 1 $a = -1$ $b = -2$ $c = 3$	Test 2 $a = -1$ $b = -2$ $c = -1$
(A) $ab < c$	$(-1)(-2) < 3$ $2 < 3$ True	$(-1)(-2) < -1$ $2 < -1$ False
(B) $ac > b$	$(-1)(3) > -2$ $-3 > -2$ False	(already eliminated)
(E) $ab > ac$	$(-1)(-2) > (-1)(3)$ $2 > -3$ True	$(-1)(-2) > (-1)(-1)$ $2 > 1$ True

    Answer (B) drops out in the first test. For the second, look at how the math worked. You can make the value for c negative, so it cannot be greater than the positive ab product, making choice (A) false.

2. **(A) 4:** Thom started with a certain ratio of bills, used some of those bills, and then finished with a different ratio of bills. Annoyingly, the problem doesn't offer any real numbers as a starting point. You could solve algebraically—but you could also just use the answer choices as your starting point and work backwards. Start with answer (B):

$5 at start	Start ratio	Pay	New ratio
	$5 : $10	−1 $5	$5 : $10
	2 : 3	−4 $10	= 3 : 2?
(B) 6	Actual 6 : 9	New 5 : 5	No

If Thom started with six $5 bills, and the starting ratio was 2 : 3, then the unknown multiplier is 3 and there were nine $10 bills to start. After paying out the given amounts, Thom would be left with a new ratio of 5 : 5, or 1 : 1, but the problem specifies that the new ratio should be 3 : 2, so (B) is not correct. Try (D) next:

$5 at start	Start ratio	Pay	New ratio
	$5 : $10	−1 $5	$5 : $10
	2 : 3	−4 $10	= 3 : 2?
(B) 6	Actual 6 : 9	New 5 : 5	No
(D) 10	Actual 10 : 15	New 9 : 11	No

This time, the new ratio would be 9 : 11, which still doesn't match the given ratio of 3 : 2, so answer (D) is also incorrect.

Now, what's the pattern between the two choices? It might help to view the ratios as fractions (you can always "read" ratios as fractions without literally rewriting them):

Answer (B) ratio	Answer (D) ratio	Desired new ratio
$\frac{5}{5}$ or $\frac{1}{1}$	$\frac{9}{11}$	$\frac{3}{2}$

The ratio given by answer (B) is 1. Answer (D) got smaller. But the desired ratio, $\frac{3}{2}$, is larger than both, so moving from answer (B) to answer (D) was the wrong direction. The answer must be **(A)**.

If you don't feel confident in that reasoning, go ahead and try answer (A). It will work!

3. **(B)** $\frac{2}{5}$: The answers are in relative form, so you can use smart numbers. When working with fraction problems, choose a common denominator of the fractions given in the problem, in case you have to divide by either of those denominators. In this case, the problem contains the fractions $\frac{1}{3}$ and $\frac{1}{4}$, so use the common denominator of 12. Any multiple of 12 will work, but keep things simple and use 12 itself.

Assign the value 12 to the total for the *smaller* library—in this case, Library A—because the other library has twice as many books. As a result, Library B's capacity, 24, is also a multiple of the denominators 3 and 4:

$$(12)\left(\frac{1}{3}\right) = 4 \text{ of Library A's books will move to the new space.}$$

$$(24)\left(\frac{1}{4}\right) = 6 \text{ of Library B's books will move to the new space.}$$

The new space will therefore contain 10 books total. Because 4 out of 10 of those books came from Library A, 40%, or $\frac{2}{5}$, of the books in the new space will have come from Library A.

The correct answer is **(B)**.

Bonus Exercise: Take a look at the wrong answers. Can you figure out how someone would have gotten to any of them?

Answer (A), $\frac{1}{3}$, is one of the numbers given in the question. Also, it's the proportion of the books in the combined original libraries that are Library A's (that is, all books, not just the moved books).

Answer (D), $\frac{7}{12}$, represents the sum of $\frac{1}{3}$ and $\frac{1}{4}$, which is a simple—too simple!—arithmetic combination of two of the given numbers.

Answer (E), $\frac{3}{5}$, represents the proportion of Library B's books in the new space. If you calculated this answer, then you may have solved correctly, but for the wrong thing. How can you avoid making that kind of mistake in future?

Percents

In This Chapter

In this chapter, you will learn how to translate and solve percent problems, as well as how to approach more advanced percent topics such as percent increase and decrease. You'll also learn how to benchmark percents—a strategy that will allow you to perform computations much more quickly.

CHAPTER 5 Percents

Percent literally means "per one hundred." You can think of a percent as a special type of fraction (or decimal) that involves the number 100:

> Of the students, 75% like chocolate ice cream.

This means that, out of every 100 total students, 75 like chocolate ice cream.

In fraction form, this is written as $\frac{75}{100}$, which simplifies to $\frac{3}{4}$.

In decimal form, this is written as 0.75.

One common mistake is the belief that 100% equals 100. In fact, 100% means $\frac{100}{100}$. Therefore, 100% = 1.

A multiplier greater than 1, in percent terms, is greater than 100%. For example, if your salary this year is 1.2 times your salary last year, then your salary is now 120% of what it was last year. (Nice!)

A multiplier less than 1 is less than 100%. For example, if your expenses this year are 0.78 of last year's expenses, then your current expenses are 78% of your previous expenses.

Percents as Decimals: Move the Decimal

You can convert percents into decimals by moving the decimal point two spaces to the left:

$$525\% = 5.25 \qquad 52.5\% = 0.525 \qquad 5.25\% = 0.0525 \qquad 0.525\% = 0.00525$$

A decimal can be converted into a percent by moving the decimal point two spaces to the right:

$$0.6 = 60\% \qquad 0.28 = 28\% \qquad 0.459 = 45.9\% \qquad 1.3 = 130\%$$

> **Strategy Tip:** Remember, the percent always looks "bigger" than the decimal!

Percent, Of, Is, What

These four words are by far the most important when translating percent questions. In fact, many percent word problems can be rephrased in terms of these four words:

Percent	=	divide by 100	$\overline{100}$
Of	=	multiply	$\times$
Is	=	equals	=
What	=	unknown value	x, y, or any variable

For example, try this problem:

> What is 70 percent of 120 ?

First, as you read left to right, translate the question into an equation:

x	$=$	70	$\overline{100}$	$\times$	120
What	is	70	percent	of	120 ?

Now, solve the equation:

$$x = \frac{70}{100} \times 120$$

$$x = \frac{7}{10} \times 120$$

$$x = 7 \times 12$$

$$x = 84$$

This translation works no matter what order the words appear in. Try another example:

> 30 is what percent of 50 ?

This statement can be translated directly into an equation:

30	$=$	x	$\overline{100}$	$\times$	50
30	is	what	percent	of	50 ?

In the examples above, x represents the unknown value that you have been asked to find. If you have a Data Sufficiency problem, you might be done already; because the equation has only one variable, and that variable is not a square or in any kind of weird form, you can find a single value for x. That would be sufficient if, for example, the problem asked you to find x.

If you are doing a Problem Solving problem, you may need to solve for x, which means "get x by itself on one side." For example:

$$30 = \frac{x}{100} \times 50$$

$$30 = \frac{x}{2}$$

$$60 = x$$

Look for *percent, of, is*, and *what* as you translate percent problems into equations; those four words should provide the necessary structure for each equation.

As you get better with translation, you may eventually feel comfortable using a shortcut. Take a look at this example:

> Thirty is what percent of 50 ?

First, note that this problem *gives* you two real numbers and asks you to *find* a percent. When this is the setup, you can use the following shortcut.

Think of the *what percent of 50* portion as saying *what percent **out of** 50*. Put the *out of* number in the denominator. Put the other number in the numerator. The *what percent* part goes by itself on the other side of the equation as shown here:

$$\frac{30}{50} \times 100 = x\%$$

Whenever you see *what percent of a number*, you can think of this as "percent out of" that number and go straight to writing a fraction for the left side of the equation. Put the *out of* number on the bottom and the other number on the top. Then, multiply by 100 to go from the decimal form of the number to the percent form.

Fast Math: Percent Benchmarks

You can calculate most percentages quickly using some combination of 50%, 10%, 5%, and 1% of the original number. These percentages are **benchmark** percentages, or common building blocks for other numbers.

For example, the previous section asked you to find 70% of 120. Note that 70% is the equivalent of 50% + 10% + 10%. Calculate 50% and 10% of the number and add up the building blocks:

100% (original number)	50%	10%	50% + 10% + 10% = 70%
120	60	12	60 + 12 + 12 = 84

Here's another way: 70% is equivalent to 10% × 7, as shown here:

100% (original number)	10%	10% × 7 = 70%
120	12	12 × 7 = 84

There are typically multiple ways to compute an ugly percent from a combination of benchmark percents. The numbers you're dealing with may mean that, one time, you'd rather do the 50% + 10% + 10% version but, another time, you'd rather to the 10% × 7 version. Pause and think about the numbers involved before rushing to do the calculation.

Try this problem:

What is 15% of 90 ?

100% = 90
10% = 9
5% = 4.5
15% = 9 + 4.5 = 13.5

Now, try this one:

What is 6% of 50 ?

$$100\% = 50$$
$$1\% = 0.5$$
$$6\% = (1\%)(6) = (0.5)(6) = 3$$

You can also find 5% and 1% and add them up—whatever seems easier to you. Just take a moment to think about your approach and make the best choice for you.

Test your skills on these drills:

1. What is 18% of 50 ?

2. What is 40% of 30 ?

3. What is 75% of 20 ?

Here are the answers:

1. $100\% = 50$
   $$20\% = (10\%)(2) = (5)(2) = 10$$
   $$2\% = \text{move the decimal from } 20\% = 1$$
   $$18\% = 20\% - 2\% = 10 - 1 = 9$$

2. $100\% = 30$
   $$10\% = 3$$
   $$40\% = (4)(10\%) = (4)(3) = 12$$

3. Don't forget about your fraction-conversion skills! Sometimes, it's easier to convert to fractions and cancel. $75\% = \frac{3}{4}$, so:

$$\frac{3}{\cancel{4}_1}\left(\cancel{20}^{5}\right) = (3)(5) = 15$$

Why is it (arguably) easier to use the benchmark method on the first two problems, but easier to use fractions on the third problem?

Most people don't memorize the fraction conversion for 18%, so converting to fractions for the first problem would be annoying.

The second problem could go either way, but because 40% is a multiple of 10%, and 10% is very easy to find, building the answer is still quick.

In the third problem, 75% would take multiple steps to build via the percent method, plus 75% also converts to a very nice fraction: $\frac{3}{4}$. In this case, it will probably be easier to use the fraction here (especially because the starting number, 20, is a multiple of 4, so the denominator will cancel entirely).

Percent Increase and Decrease

Consider this example:

> The price of a cup of coffee increased from 80 cents to 84 cents. By what percent did the price change?

If you want to find a change, whether in terms of percent or of actual value, use the following equation:

$$\textbf{Percent Change} = \frac{\textbf{Change in Value}}{\textbf{Original Value}}$$

In the coffee example, you want to find the *change* in terms of percent. Write $\frac{x}{100}$ to represent an unknown percent:

$$\text{Percent Change} = \frac{\text{Change}}{\text{Original}}$$

$$\frac{x}{100} = \frac{4}{80} = \frac{1}{20}$$

Cross-multiply to get rid of the fractions and solve:

$$\frac{x}{100} = \frac{1}{20}$$
$$20x = 100$$
$$x = 5$$

Therefore, the price increased by 5%.

If you feel comfortable thinking in percents, you can also use the benchmark approach to answer that question. The price went from 80 cents to 84 cents, an increase of 4 cents. That additional 4 cents represents what percentage of the original price, 80 cents?

Ten percent of 80 cents is 8 cents. Halve the 8 cents to get 4 cents. And this figure is half of 10%, or 5%. The percent increase is equivalent to 5%.

Alternatively, a question might ask:

> If the price of a $30 shirt is decreased by 20%, what is the final price of the shirt?

In this case, the question didn't tell you the new percent; rather, it gave the percent decrease. If the price decreases by 20%, then the new price is 100% − 20% = 80% of the original. Use the new percent, not the decrease in percent, to solve for the new price directly. You can use this equation:

$$\text{New Percent} = \frac{\text{New Value}}{\text{Original Value}}$$

Once again, use x to represent the value you want, the new price:

$$\frac{80}{100} = \frac{x}{30}$$
$$\frac{4}{5}(30) = x$$
$$24 = x$$

The new price of the shirt is $24.

Alternatively, you can solve directly without setting up a proportion. The starting price is $30 and this price is decreased by 20%. Find 20% of $30 and subtract:

$$\$30 - (20\%)(\$30) \qquad 20\% \text{ of } 30 \text{ is } 6$$

$$\$30 - \$6 = \$24$$

Increasing or Decreasing from the Original

When dealing with percent change, how you calculate depends on what is considered the "original" number, or starting point. For example, if a problem asks how much *smaller* the population was in 1980 than in 1990, which is the original number—the population in 1980 or that in 1990?

Don't try to do math yet. Just think. The question says the number gets smaller, with the population in 1990 as the high point. In this case, the 1990 population is the starting point, or original number—it's the starting point of the story.

Next, when talking about a percent change made to a number, always think of the original number as 100%, or your baseline for future calculations.

For example, if you increase the number 100 by 10%, you'll get $100 + 10 = 110$. The new number will be 110% of the original number, regardless of your starting number. Here are some common language cues for this concept:

> 10% increase = 110% of the original
>
> 10% greater than = 110% of the original

If you decrease a number, then you subtract from 100%:

> 45% decrease = 55% of the original
>
> 45% less than = 55% of the original

Use this conversion to save steps on percent problems. For example:

> What number is 50% greater than 60 ?

Fifty percent greater than is the same as *150% of*. So one path is to rewrite the question:

> What number is 150% of 60 ?

Translate into an equation, using 1.5 or $\frac{3}{2}$ to represent 150%:

$$x = \frac{3}{2} \times 60$$
$$x = 90$$

Another path is to use benchmarks. What number is 50% greater than 60 ? Well, 50% of 60 is 30. So 50% greater than 60 is $60 + 30 = 90$.

Successive Percent Change

Some problems will ask you to calculate successive percents. For example:

> If a ticket increased in price by 20%, and then increased again by 5%, by what percent did the ticket price increase in total?

Although it may seem counterintuitive, the answer is *not 25%*. When you have *successive* percent changes, the answer will never be to just add or subtract the percentages.

Walk through this with real numbers. If the ticket originally cost $100, then the first increase would bring the ticket price up to 100 plus 20% of 100 (or $20) for a total of $120.

The second increase of 5% is now based on this *new* ticket price, $120:

$$120 + (0.05)(120) = \$126$$

The price increased from $100 to $126, so the percent increase is the change divided by the original, or $\dfrac{26}{100} = 26\%$.

Why is it 26% and not 25%? Because the second calculation is based on a larger starting number—you're taking 5% of 120, not 100. This will always be true when you are doing two percent increases in a row, so the total percent increase will always be more than the number you'd get if you just added the two percentages together.

In short, successive percents *cannot* simply be added together; instead, you have to calculate each piece separately. This holds for successive increases, successive decreases, and for combinations of increases and decreases.

Try this problem:

> The cost of a plane ticket is increased by 25%. Later, the ticket goes on sale and the price is reduced 20%. What is the overall percent change in the price of the ticket?

You can *multiply* these changes together; you can't just add or subtract them. A 25% increase followed by a 20% decrease is the same as 125% of 80% of the original number:

$$\left(\frac{125}{100}\right)\left(\frac{80}{100}\right)x = \,?$$
$$\left(\frac{5}{4}\right)\left(\frac{4}{5}\right)x = x$$

The 20% decrease entirely offsets the 25% increase. The new price is exactly the same as the original price. You can also work through the math using a real number, as shown in the previous problem:

$$\$100 + (25\% \text{ of } \$100) = \$125$$
$$\$125 - (20\% \text{ of } \$125) = \$100$$

Finally, remember how two successive percent increases will result in a percent change that is greater than the number you'd get if you added the two numbers together? (In that problem, the answer was 26%, not 25%.)

If you have two successive percent decreases, the overall percent decrease will be less than the number you'd get if you just added the two together. For example, if the price of a TV decreased by 10% and then decreased by another 10%, look what happens:

$$\$100 - (10\% \text{ of } \$100) = 100 - 10 = \$90$$
$$\$90 - (10\% \text{ of } \$90) = 90 - 9 = \$81$$

Why does it work that way? By definition, the second number in the calculation, $90, is smaller than the original number, $100. So 10% of that number is going to be smaller. Instead of a total decrease of 10% + 10% = 20%, the total decrease is actually 10% + 9% = 19%.

5

Problem Set

1.   A stereo was marked down by 30% and sold for $84. What was the presale price of the stereo?

   (A) $100

   (B) $120

2.   A car loan is offered at 8% annual interest, compounded annually. After the first year, the interest due is $24. What is the principal on the loan?

3.   If x is 40% of y and 50% of y is 40, then 16 is what percent of x ?

4.   A bowl is half full of water. Four cups of water are then added to the bowl, filling the bowl to 70% of its capacity. How many cups of water are now in the bowl?

5.   Challenge problem! (Data Sufficiency answers not given; check the DS chapter if needed.)

   Company X has exactly two product lines and no other sources of revenue. If the consumer product line experiences a k% increase in revenue (where k is a positive integer) in 2015 from 2014 levels and the machine parts line experiences a k% decrease in revenue in 2015 from 2014 levels, did Company X's overall revenue increase or decrease in 2015 ?

   (1) In 2014, the consumer products line generated more revenue than the machine parts line.

   (2) $k = 8$

6.   If 800 is increased by 50% and then decreased by 30%, what is the resulting number?

7.   If 1,500 is increased by 20% and then reduced by y%, yielding 1,080, what is y ?

   (A) 20

   (B) 30

   (C) 40

8.   A bottle is 80% full. The liquid in the bottle consists of 60% guava juice and 40% pineapple juice. The remainder of the bottle is then filled with 200 milliliters of rum. How much guava juice is in the bottle?

   (A) 360 ml

   (B) 480 mL

   (C) 600 mL

   (D) 720 mL

   (E) 900 mL

9.   Challenge problem! Company Z sells only chairs and tables. What percent of its revenue in 2008 did Company Z derive from its sales of chairs?

   (1) In 2008, the price of tables sold by Company Z was 10% higher than the price of chairs sold by Company Z.

   (2) In 2008, Company Z sold 20% fewer tables than chairs.

Solutions

1. **(B) $120:** Understand and Plan before you try to Solve. This problem is worded in a very annoying way: It provides the answer after 30% is taken, but not the original or starting number. The original number is what you want to take 30% of though. What to do?

   Luckily, the GMAT is a multiple-choice test. The answers represent the starting number—so just try them to see which one matches the information given in the problem.

   (A) $100. Take 30%: $30. In this case, the new price would be $100 - 30 = 70$, but the problem says the new price is $84. This one's incorrect and (B) is the only remaining answer, so that one must be correct.

   Here's how to do the math, but note that on the GMAT, if you have only one answer left, stop solving. Go ahead and pick it.

   (B) $120. Take 30%: $(10\%)(3) = (12)(3) = 36$.

   $120 - 36 = 84$. Bingo! Answer **(B)** is indeed correct.

   Alternatively, you could rephrase the given information to say the following:

   $84 is 70% of the original price of the stereo.

   You could then translate this statement into an equation and solve:

   $$84 = \left(\frac{70}{100}\right)x$$
   $$84 = \left(\frac{7}{10}\right)x$$
   $$840 = 7x$$
   $$120 = x$$

2. **$300:** Although this looks like an interest problem, you can think of it as a percent change problem. The percent change is 8%, and the change in value is $24:

   $$\text{Percent Change} = \frac{\text{Change in Value}}{\text{Original Value}}$$
   $$\frac{8}{100} = \frac{24}{x}$$
   $$\frac{2}{25} = \frac{24}{x}$$
   $$2x = (24)(25)$$
   $$x = (12)(25) = 300$$

   The principal amount of the loan is $300.

   Alternatively, you could use benchmarks. $24 represents a change of 8%:

   $$8\% = 24$$
   $$1\% = \frac{24}{8} = 3$$
   $$10\% = 30$$
   $$100\% = 300$$

Examine those two solution methods. Which one works better for you? If you would have naturally thought of the first one, but you like the second better, what do you need to practice in order to get comfortable enough with benchmarks that you think of that solution method first next time?

3. **50%:** You can translate the first two sentences directly into equations. Just slow down and reflect/Plan for a moment. Use the simplest versions of the equivalent fractions:

$$x \text{ is } 40\% \text{ of } y \rightarrow x = \left(\frac{2}{5}\right) y$$

$$50\% \text{ of } y \text{ is } 40 \rightarrow \left(\frac{1}{2}\right) y = 40$$

Reflect again. The second equation has only one variable, so solve for y:

$$\left(\frac{1}{2}\right) y = 40$$

$$y = 80$$

Now, replace y with 80 in the first equation to solve for x:

$$x = \left(\frac{40}{100}\right)(80)$$

$$x = \frac{4}{10} \times 80$$

$$x = 4 \times 8 = 32$$

Be careful now. The question asks, *16 is what percent of* x *?* You figured out that $x = 32$, so this question is really asking, *16 is what percent of 32 ?*

Create a new variable (z) to represent the unknown value in the question and solve:

$$16 = \frac{z}{100} \times 32$$

$$\frac{100}{32} \times 16 = z$$

$$\frac{100}{2} \times 1 = z$$

$$50 = z$$

Alternatively, use the translation shortcut. Place the "percent of" number on the bottom of the fraction and the other number on the top:

$$\frac{16}{32} \times 100 = 0.5 \times 100 = 50\%$$

Or, if you feel *really* comfortable with percents, think logically. What percent of 32 is 16 ? Sixteen is half of 32, so 16 is 50% of 32.

4. **14 cups of water:** Understand and Plan before you Solve. If the bowl was already half full of water, then it was originally 50% full. Adding 4 cups of water increased the percentage by 20% of the total capacity of the bowl.

    Use benchmarks to solve. The measurement 4 cups is equivalent to 20%. What else can you figure out?

    $$20\% = 4 \text{ cups}$$
    $$10\% = 2 \text{ cups}$$
    $$70\% = (2)(7) = 14 \text{ cups}$$

    There are 14 cups of water in the bowl.

    Alternatively, you can set up a proportion. You know 4 represents 20% of the capacity. Let x represent 70% of the capacity. Set up the proportion and solve for x:

    $$\frac{4}{x} = \frac{20}{70}$$
    $$\frac{4}{x} = \frac{2}{7}$$
    $$28 = 2x$$
    $$14 = x$$

5. **(A):** This question requires you to employ logic about percents. No calculation is required, or even possible, since no real numbers are given.

    Here's what you know so far (use new variables c and m to keep track of your information):

    2014:

    > Consumer products makes c dollars
    >
    > Machine parts makes m dollars
    >
    > Total revenue $= c + m$

    2015:

    > Consumer products makes c dollars increased by k%
    >
    > Machine parts makes m dollars decreased by k%
    >
    > Total revenue $= ?$

    What would you need to answer the question *did Company X's overall revenue increase or decrease in 2015?* Certainly, if you knew the values of c, m, and k, you could achieve sufficiency, but the GMAT would never write such an easy problem. What is the *minimum* you would need to know to answer definitively?

    Since both changes involve the same percent (k), you know that c increases *by the same percent* by which m decreases. As a result, whichever number is greater (c or m) will constitute a bigger change to the overall revenue. Why?

    If c started off greater, then a k% increase in c means more new dollars coming in than you would lose due to a k% decrease in the smaller number, m. On the other hand, if c is smaller, then the k% increase would be smaller than what you would lose due to a k% decrease in the larger number, m.

    So you really need to know whether c or m is greater. You don't actually need to know k at all!

5

The question can be rephrased, *Which is greater,* c *or* m *?*

(1) SUFFICIENT: This statement indicates that *c* is greater than *m*. Thus, a *k*% increase in *c* is greater than a *k*% decrease in *m*, so the overall revenue went up.

(2) INSUFFICIENT: Knowing the percent change doesn't help, since you don't know whether *c* or *m* is bigger.

Note that you could try some real numbers, although this problem is probably faster with logic. Using statement (1) only:

2014:

> Consumer products makes $200
>
> Machine parts makes $100
>
> Total revenue = $300

2015: If *k* = 50

> Consumer products makes $300
>
> Machine parts makes $50
>
> Total revenue = $350

This one case yields an answer of Yes—the overall revenue did increase. However, you might have to test several sets of numbers to establish that this will always be true. (That's the main reason that logic is faster here!) You can experiment with different values for *c* and *m*, and you can change *k* to any positive integer (you don't need to know what *k* is). As long as *c* is greater than *m*, you will get the same result. The increase to the larger *c* will always be greater than the decrease to the smaller *m*.

The correct answer is **(A)**: Statement (1) is sufficient to answer the question, but statement (2) is not.

6. **840:** This is a successive percent question. Since the numbers in the problem are fairly nice, one approach is to calculate step-by-step.

Start with 800. Increase by 50%, or 400. Now, you have $800 + 400 = 1,200$.

From 1,200, decrease by 30%. Benchmark: 10% is 120, so 30% is 360. Subtract: $1,200 - 360 = 840$.

Alternatively, set up the math as follows. Increasing by 50% is the same as *150% of* something. Decreasing by 30% is the same as *70% of* something. So the full problem translates to *What is 150% of 70% of 800?*

$$\frac{150}{100} \times \frac{70}{100} \times 800 = ?$$

$$\frac{3}{2} \times \frac{7}{10} \times 800 = ?$$

$$\frac{21}{20} \times 800 = ?$$

$$21 \times 40 = 840$$

7. **(C) 40:** Break the question into two parts. First, 1,500 is increased by 20%. Find 20% percent of 1,500.

If 10% of 1,500 is 150, then 20% is 300. The new number is $1,500 + 300 = 1,800$.

Next, 1,800 is reduced by y% to get to 1,080. The answer choices represent y, so try them to see which one works. Start with the middle of the three answers.

(B) 30%. Find 30% of 1,800: 10% of 1,800 is 180, so 30% is $(180)(3) = 540$. Next, $1,800 - 540 = 1,260$. The answer is supposed to be 1,080, not 1,260, so answer (B) is incorrect.

The other two possibilities for y are 20% and 40%. Think about what happened with the math when trying 30%. Do you need a larger or smaller percentage?

When using 30%, the number to subtract was 540, yielding an answer of 1,260. In order to get down to 1,080, you'd need to subtract a larger number. So you're looking for a larger percentage decrease than 30%.

Only answer **(C)** is larger than 30%, so it must be correct. (You can try the math to make sure—but the GMAT is a timed test. If you feel confident in the logic, don't try the math; just select the answer and move on.)

8. **(B) 480 mL:** If the bottle was 80% full, and adding 200 milliliters of rum filled it to capacity, then 200 milliliters is equal to 20% of the bottle's total capacity.

The figure 80% is 4 times 20%, so the other 80% of the bottle represents $(200\text{mL})(4) = 800$ mL.

The guava juice represents 60% of that 800 milliliters. Use benchmarks to figure out how much guava juice there is:

$$100\% = 800 \text{ mL}$$
$$10\% = 80 \text{ mL}$$
$$60\% = (80 \text{ mL})(6) = 480 \text{ mL}$$

The bottle contains 480 milliliters of guava juice.

Alternatively, you could work backwards to solve this problem. The answer choices represent the amount of guava juice in the mixture; also the answers are relatively "clean" numbers, making working backwards less cumbersome.

Start with answer (B) or (D), your choice. This solution will start with (B) since that number is smaller.

(B) 480 mL. This represents 60% of the liquid currently in the bottle. This problem has some intricate details. The answers represent the guava juice, which is 60% of the liquid that's currently in the bottle—but that liquid only fills 80% of the bottle. Lay out separate steps for each of these circumstances.

First, find the amount of liquid in the bottle. That represents 80% of the bottle's capacity, so find the value for the 20% that's empty and see whether it matches the figure given in the problem:

Guava = 60% of liquid	100% of liquid	Liquid = 80% of capacity	20% of capacity = 200 ?
(B) 480	60% = 480 10% = 80 100% = (80)(10) = 800	80% = 800 divide both by 4 20% = 200	Yes!

It's a match so this is the correct answer. If you had started with answer (D) and done the same math, you'd get the following:

Guava = 60% of liquid	100% of liquid	Liquid = 80% of capacity	20% of capacity = 200 ?
(D) 720	60% = 720 10% = 120 100% = (120)(10) = 1,200	80% = 1,200 10% = 150 20% = (150)(2) = 300	No!

Using answer (D), 20% of the capacity is 300 milliliters, but the problem said that it was 200 milliliters, so this is not the correct answer. Further, 300 is too much, so the answer has to be smaller. At this point, you'd cross off answers (D) and (E), then try answer (B) next.

9. **(C):** First, notice that the question is asking only for the *percent* of its revenue the company derived from chairs. The question is asking for a relative value, so you may not need to know any actual values in order to solve.

    The question asks for the revenue from chairs as a fraction of the total. Also, total revenue is made up of the revenue from chairs and the revenue from tables:

    $$\frac{R_C}{\text{Total Rev}} \qquad\qquad \text{Total Rev} = R_C + R_T$$

    If you know the ratio of chair revenue to total revenue, you can find the requested percentage. But note also that, if you're given relationships involving table revenue, you might also be able to find the requested percentage, since that second equation is true, too.

    Also, note that the GMAT will expect you to know that Revenue = Price × Quantity Sold.

    The revenue derived from tables is the price per table multiplied by the number of tables sold. The revenue derived from chairs is the price per chair multiplied by the number of chairs sold. You can create some variables to represent these unknown values:

    $$R_T = P_T \times Q_T$$
    $$R_C = P_C \times Q_C$$

    (1) INSUFFICIENT: This statement provides the relative value of the price of tables to the price of chairs. If the price of tables was 10% higher than the price of chairs, then the price of tables was 110% of the price of chairs:

    $$\frac{P_T}{P_C} = 1.1$$

    However, no information is given on quantity sold, so it's not possible to determine anything about the relative value of their revenues.

    (2) INSUFFICIENT: If the company sold 20% fewer tables than chairs, then the number of tables sold is 80% of the number of chairs sold:

    $$\frac{N_T}{N_C} = 0.8$$

    However, no information is given about price, so it's not possible to determine anything about the relative value of their revenues.

5

(1) AND (2) SUFFICIENT: Hmm. The first statement was about price, but not quantity. The second statement was about quantity, but not price. Could they work together to find a consistent *relative* value?

$$R_T = P_T \times N_T$$

The formula above is for revenue of tables. The first statement provided info about how the price of tables relates to the price of chairs (or how P_T relates to P_C). The second statement provided information about how the number of tables relates to the number of chairs (or how N_T relates to N_C).

When you know those relative relationships for the right side of the equation, then it's possible to calculate the relative relationship for the left side of the equation—that is, how table revenue relates to chair revenue.

If you know how table revenue relates to chair revenue, then you can always figure out what percentage each represents out of total revenue. For example, if you knew that table revenue was three times as much as chair revenue, then table revenue would have to be 75% of total revenue and chair revenue would have to be 25% of total revenue, because 75% is three times as much as 25%.

In other words, you don't have to calculate anything further (since this is Data Sufficiency). You can just know that, if you know the relative relationship between price and the relative relationship between quantity, then you can find the relative relationship between revenue.

The correct answer is **(C)**: The two statements together are sufficient but neither one alone is sufficient.

If you really want to see how this works from a textbook math perspective, read on. But it's strongly recommended to stop right here!

Replace P_T with $1.1P_C$ and replace N_T with $0.8N_C$:

$$R_T = P_T \times N_T$$
$$R_T = 1.1P_C \times 0.8N_C$$
$$R_T = (0.88)(P_C \times N_C)$$

On the right-hand side, $P_C \times N_C = R_C$, so substitute that in:

$$R_T = 0.88R_C$$

Taken together, the two statements provide the relative value of the revenues for tables and chairs.

You can use that to find the relative value of chair revenue to total revenue. Rearrange the equation so that you can write a ratio:

$$\frac{R_T}{R_C} = \frac{0.88}{1}$$

RevChair : RevTable : RevTotal

1 : 0.88 : 1.88

Finally, use the needed parts of the ratio to solve:

$$\frac{R_C}{\text{Total Revenue}} = \frac{1}{1.88} \approx 53\%$$

Save time on DS problems by avoiding unnecessary computation. Once you know you can find the needed figure, choose your answer and move on to the next problem.

CHAPTER 6

Digits and Decimals

In This Chapter

- Digits
- Decimals
- Place Value
- Rounding to the Nearest Place Value
- Powers of 10: Shifting the Decimal
- Decimal Operations

In this chapter, you will learn how digits, decimals, and place value are tested on the GMAT, as well as how to perform the needed computations on numbers in decimal form, including rounding.

CHAPTER 6 Digits and Decimals

Digits

Every number is composed of digits. There are only 10 digits in our number system: 0, 1, 2, 3, 4, 5, 6, 7, 8, 9. The term **digit** refers to one "building block" of a number; it does not refer to the entire number. For example, 356 is a number composed of three digits: 3, 5, and 6.

Integers can be classified by the number of digits they contain. For example:

2, 7, and -8 are each single-digit numbers (they are each composed of one digit).

43, 63, and -14 are each double-digit numbers (composed of two digits).

500,000 and $-468,024$ are each six-digit numbers (composed of six digits).

789,526,622 is a nine-digit number (composed of nine digits).

Integers such as the above always have a nonzero digit as the first number. For instance, 2 is a single-digit number, but you can't write 02 and call that a two-digit integer. If a problem specifies a two-digit integer, then the first digit has to be some value from 1 to 9.

Non-integers are not generally classified by the number of digits they contain, since you can always add any number of zeros at the end, on the right side of the decimal point:

$$9.1 = 9.10 = 9.100$$

Decimals

Decimals are yet another way to write numbers that fall between integers. For example, the decimal 6.3 falls between the integers 6 and 7:

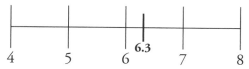

Some useful groupings of decimals include the following:

Group	Examples
Decimals less than -1:	$-3.6, -12.01$
Decimals between -1 and 0:	$-0.65, -0.5$
Decimals between 0 and 1:	0.2, 0.45
Decimals greater than 1:	2.9, 42.42

Note that an integer can be expressed as a decimal by adding the decimal point and the digit 0. For example:

$$8 = 8.0 \qquad -123 = -123.0 \qquad 400 = 400.0$$

Place Value

Every digit in a number has a particular **place value** depending on its location within the number. For example, in the number 452, the digit 2 is in the ones (or units) place, the digit 5 is in the tens place, and the digit 4 is in the hundreds place. The name of each location corresponds to the value of that place. Thus:

The 2 is worth two ones (i.e., $2 \times 1 = 2$).

The 5 is worth five tens (i.e., $5 \times 10 = 50$).

The 4 is worth four hundreds (i.e., $4 \times 100 = 400$).

You can write the number 452 as the *sum* of these products:

$$452 = (4 \times 100) + (5 \times 10) + (2 \times 1)$$

The chart to the left analyzes the place value of all the digits in the number **7,891,023.8347**.

Notice that all of the place values that end in "ths" are to the right of the decimal; these are all fractional values.

Millions	Hundred Thousands	Ten Thousands	Thousands	Hundreds	Tens	Units Or Ones	.	Tenths	Hundredths	Thousandths	Ten Thousandths
7	8	9	1	0	2	3	.	8	3	4	7

Analyze just the decimal portion of the number **0.8347**:

8 is in the tenths place, giving it a value of 8 tenths, or $\frac{8}{10}$.

3 is in the hundredths place, giving it a value of 3 hundredths, or $\frac{3}{100}$.

4 is in the thousandths place, giving it a value of 4 thousandths, or $\frac{4}{1,000}$.

7 is in the ten-thousandths place, giving it a value of 7 ten thousandths, or $\frac{7}{10,000}$.

To use a concrete example, 0.8 might mean eight tenths of one dollar, which would be 80 cents. Additionally, 0.03 might mean three hundredths of one dollar, or 3 cents.

Rounding to the Nearest Place Value

The GMAT occasionally requires you to round a number to a specific place value. For example:

What is 3.681 rounded to the nearest tenth?

First, find the digit located in the specified place value. The digit 6 is in the tenths place.

Second, look at the right-digit neighbor (the digit immediately to the right) of the digit in question. In this case, 8 is the right-digit neighbor of 6. If the right-digit neighbor is 5 or greater, round the digit in question *up*. Otherwise, leave the digit alone. In this case, the hundredths-digit number, 8, is greater than 5, so you're going to have to round up. Go back to the digit in question, 6, and round up to 7. Thus, 3.681 rounded to the nearest tenth equals 3.7. Note that all the digits to the right of the right-digit neighbor are irrelevant when rounding.

Rounding appears on the GMAT in the form of questions such as this:

> If x is the decimal 8.1d5, with d as an unknown digit, and x rounded to the nearest tenth is equal to 8.1, which digits could NOT be the value of d?

In order for x to be 8.1 when rounded to the nearest tenth, the right-digit neighbor, d, must be less than 5. Therefore, d cannot be 5, 6, 7, 8, or 9.

Powers of 10: Shifting the Decimal

What are the patterns in this table?

In words	Thousands	Hundreds	Tens	Ones	Tenths	Hundredths	Thousandths
In numbers	1,000	100	10	1	0.1	0.01	0.001
In powers of ten	10^3	10^2	10^1	10^0	10^{-1}	10^{-2}	10^{-3}

The place values continually decrease from left to right by powers of 10. Understanding this can help you understand the following shortcuts for multiplication and division.

When you multiply any number by a positive power of 10, move the decimal to the right of the specified number of places. This makes positive numbers larger:

$89.507 \times 10 = 895.07$ 10 is the same as 10^1, so move the decimal to the right 1 space.

$3.9742 \times 10^3 = 3,974.2$ The exponent is 3, so move the decimal to the right 3 spaces.

When you divide any number by a positive power of 10, move the decimal to the left of the specified number of places. This makes positive numbers smaller:

$89.507 \div 10 = 8.9507$ Move the decimal to the left 1 space.

$4,169.2 \div 10^2 = 41.692$ Move the decimal to the left 2 spaces.

Sometimes, you will need to add zeros in order to shift a decimal:

$2.57 \times 10^6 = 2,570,000$ Add 4 zeros at the end.

$14.29 \div 10^5 = 0.0001429$ Add 3 zeros at the beginning.

Finally, note that negative powers of 10 reverse the regular process: Move the decimal in the opposite direction that you'd have used for a positive power. Now, multiplication makes the number smaller and division makes the number larger:

$$6{,}782.01 \times 10^{-3} = 6.78201 \qquad 53.0447 \div 10^{-2} = 5{,}304.47$$

You can think about these processes as trading decimal places for powers of 10.

For instance, all of the following numbers equal 110,700:

$$110.7 \times 10^3$$
$$11.07 \times 10^4$$
$$1.107 \times 10^5$$
$$0.1107 \times 10^6$$
$$0.01107 \times 10^7$$

The number in the first column gets smaller by a factor of 10 as you move the decimal one place to the left, but the number in the second column gets bigger by a factor of 10 to compensate, so the overall number still equals 110,700.

Decimal Operations

Addition and Subtraction

To add or subtract decimals, first, check the answers to see whether you can just estimate instead. If not, line up the decimal points. Then, add zeros to make the right sides of the decimals the same length:

$4.319 + 221.8$		$10 - 0.063$	
Line up the decimal points and add zeros.	4.319 + 221.800 —————— 226.119	Line up the decimal points and add zeros.	10.000 − 0.063 —————— 9.937

> **Addition and subtraction:** Line up the decimal points!

Multiplication

To multiply decimals, ignore the decimal point until the end. Just multiply the numbers as you would if they were whole numbers. Then count the total number of digits to the right of the decimal point in the starting numbers. The product should have the same number of digits to the right of the decimal point:

	Count the digits to the right of the decimal:	Multiply normally:	Move the decimal 3 places to the left:
0.02×1.4	3	14 $\times$ 2 —— 28	$28 \rightarrow 0.028$

If the product ends with 0, that 0 still counts as a place value. For example: $0.8 \times 0.5 = 0.40$, since $8 \times 5 = 40$.

Multiplication: Count all the digits to the right of the decimal point—then multiply normally, ignoring the decimals. Finally, put the same number of decimal places in the product.

If you are multiplying a very large number and a very small number, the following trick works to simplify the calculation: Move the decimals the same number of places, but *in the opposite direction*. For example:

$0.0003 \times 40,000 = ?$

Move the decimal point *right* four places on the $0.0003 \rightarrow 3$

Move the decimal point *left* four places on the $40,000 \rightarrow 4$

$0.0003 \times 40,000 = 3 \times 4 = 12$

This technique works because you are multiplying and then dividing by the same power of 10. In other words, you are trading decimal places in one number for decimal places in another number. This is just like trading decimal places for powers of 10, as you saw earlier.

Division

If you ever need to do long division, first...stop. Make sure you can't estimate or do something else that is less annoying. Here's one less annoying way: You can always simplify division problems that involve decials by shifting the decimal point *in the same direction* in both the divisor and the dividend, even when the division problem is expressed as a fraction:

$$\frac{0.0045}{0.09} = \frac{45}{900}$$

Move the decimal 4 spaces to the right in both the numerator and the denominator to make whole numbers. Always move the same number of places in the top and bottom.

Note that this is essentially the same process as simplifying a fraction. You multiply the numerator and denominator of the fraction by the same number—in this case, 10^4, or 10,000.

Division: Use whole numbers! To dump the decimals, move the decimal the same number of places in the top and the bottom of the fraction.

If you absolutely must do long division with decimals and there is a decimal point in the dividend (the number under the division sign), you can bring the decimal point straight up to the answer and divide normally:

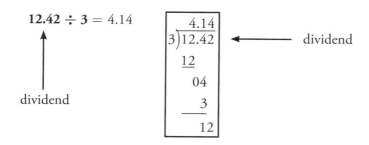

6

However, if there is a decimal point in the divisor (the outer number), shift the decimal point the same number of times to the right in both the divisor and the dividend to make the *divisor* (the outer number) a whole number. Then, bring the decimal point up and divide:

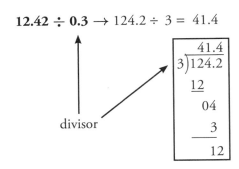

$$12.42 \div 0.3 \rightarrow 124.2 \div 3 = 41.4$$

Move the decimal 1 space to the right to make 0.3 a whole number. Then, move the decimal 1 space to the right in 12.42 to make it 124.2.

> **Keep track of the decimal:** To simplify multiplication, you can move decimals in *opposite* directions. But to simplify division, move decimals in the *same* direction. Either way, make sure you're moving the decimal the same number of places to trade off equally.

Advanced material for the Fractions, Decimals, Percents, and Ratios (FDPR) unit (primarily covering additional strategies for decimals and digits) can be found in Atlas, Manhattan Prep's online learning platform. Use the online material only if you feel that you have mastered everything in the FDPR unit of this strategy guide and only if you are aiming for a Quant section score of 48 or higher.

6

Problem Set

Solve each problem, applying the concepts and rules you learned in this section.

1. In the decimal 2.4*d*7, *d* represents a digit from 0 to 9. If the value of the decimal rounded to the nearest tenth is less than 2.5, what are the possible values of *d* ?

2. Simplify: $\dfrac{0.00081}{0.09}$

3. Which integer values of *b* would give the number $2002 \div 10^b$ a value between 1 and 100 ?

    (A) $\{-1, -2\}$

    (B) $\{-2, -3\}$

    (C) $\{1, 2\}$

    (D) $\{2, 3\}$

4. Simplify: $(4 \times 10^{-2}) - (2.5 \times 10^{-3})$

5. If *k* is an integer and 0.02468×10^k is greater than 10,000, what is the least possible value of *k* ?

6. What is $4{,}563{,}021 \div 10^5$, rounded to the nearest whole number?

Solutions

1. **{0, 1, 2, 3, 4}:** The rounded decimal is less than 2.5, so it must round to 2.4. This represents rounding down, so the value of d must be 0, 1, 2, 3, or 4.

2. **0.009:** Shift the decimal point five spaces to eliminate the decimal points (note that this means adding zeros to the number in the denominator), then simplify:

    $$\frac{0.00081}{0.09} = \frac{81}{9,000} = \frac{9}{1,000} = 0.009$$

3. **(D) {2, 3}:** Understand before you try to solve (and if you don't understand, guess and move on). Some of the answers contain positive numbers and some contain negative numbers, so should that exponent be positive or negative? The starting value is 2,002, but the ending value is between 1 and 100, so 2,002 needs to get smaller. Specifically, it will have to be either 2.002 or 20.02 in order to fall between 1 and 100. If you start from 2,002 and divide by a power of 10 to get to 20.02 or 2.002, you'd want to divide by 10 or 100 or 1,000—in other words, you want that exponent to be positive to make the divisor larger. Eliminate choices (A) and (B).

    Of the two remaining answers, both contain the value 2, so apparently 2 must be one value for b. Is the other value 1 or 3? $2,002 \div 10^1 = 200.2$. Too big! The answer must be 2 and 3.

    If you're not sure of the logic, check. $2,002 \div 10^3 = 2,002 \div 1,000 = 2.002$. Perfect!

    The correct answer is **(D) {2, 3}**.

4. **0.0375:** First, rewrite the numbers in standard notation by shifting the decimal point. Then, add zeros, line up the decimal points, and subtract:

    $$\begin{array}{r} 0.0400 \\ - \ 0.0025 \\ \hline 0.0375 \end{array}$$

5. **6:** Understand and Plan before you Solve. Understand: Multiplying 0.02468 by a positive power of 10 will shift the decimal point to the right. Your goal is to make the number greater than 10,000.

    Plan: Shift the decimal point to the right until the result is greater than 10,000, keeping track of how many times you shift the decimal point.

    Solve: Shifting the decimal point five times results in 2,468. This is still less than 10,000. Shifting one more place yields 24,680, which is greater than 10,000.

6. **46:** To divide by a positive power of 10, shift the decimal point to the left. This yields 45.63021. To round to the nearest whole number, look at the tenths place. The digit in the tenths place, 6, is more than 5. Therefore, round up: The number is closest to 46.

Strategy: Estimation

In This Chapter

- How to Estimate
- When to Estimate
- Using Benchmarks to Estimate

In this chapter, you will learn how to identify when to estimate on the GMAT, as well as how to stay within reasonable bounds and minimize errors in your estimations.

CHAPTER 7 Strategy: Estimation

You can estimate your way to an answer on problems with certain characteristics. Try these two problems:

1. $\frac{7}{13} + \frac{5}{11}$ is approximately equal to

   (A) 0
   (B) 1
   (C) 2

2. Of 450 employees at a company, 20% are managers and the rest are not managers. If 60% of the managers work in the engineering department, how many managers do not work in the engineering department?

   (A) 36
   (B) 54
   (C) 90
   (D) 180
   (E) 216

Before you look at the solutions in the next section, try to figure out how you would recognize that you *can* estimate on these two problems.

How to Estimate

Before we dive in, remember that Understand, Plan, and Solve process from Data Sufficiency? This is called the UPS process and you can use it on Problem Solving problems as well.

Here's a little graphic that helps you to know what kinds of steps to take at each stage in that process:

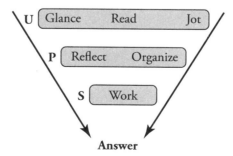

Step 1: Understand. Glance at the problem. First, notice whether it's PS or DS. If it's PS (as in this case), glance at the answers. The first one has whole, "easy" numbers.

1. $\frac{7}{13} + \frac{5}{11}$ is approximately equal to

    (A) 0
    (B) 1
    (C) 2

Then, read the problem. This problem contains the word *approximately*. It's literally telling you to estimate! When you see this kind of language, do not even try to do exact calculations. Take the problem at its word and estimate. Also, jot down the given expression.

Step 2: Plan. First, converting to common denominators here would be pretty annoying, as would converting the fractions to decimals or percents. Second, it's telling you to estimate and the answers are 0, 1, and 2. Round those annoying fractions to easier ones and estimate whether the sum is closest to 0, 1, or 2.

Step 3: Solve. $\frac{7}{13}$ is very close to $\frac{7}{14}$, or $\frac{1}{2}$, so call that first fraction 0.5.

Note that $\frac{7}{13}$ is a little *larger* than $\frac{7}{14}$ because increasing only the denominator makes a positive fraction smaller. In other words, you rounded down so your answer will be a little too small. The next time you need to estimate, if possible, round up so that you are minimizing the amount of error that you introduce.

Since $\frac{5}{11}$ is a little bit less than $\frac{1}{2}$, you can round up this time. Call the second fraction 0.5 as well.
The approximate sum is $0.5 + 0.5 = 1$, so the answer is (B).

2. Of 450 employees at a company, 20% are managers and the rest are not managers. If 60% of the managers work in the engineering department, how many managers do not work in the engineering department?

    (A)   36
    (B)   54
    (C)   90
    (D)   180
    (E)   216

The second problem doesn't tell you that you can estimate; nevertheless, it contains an important clue that points toward estimation.

In the Understand step, your first task is to glance at the problem:

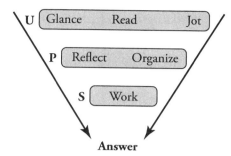

On all PS problems, get in the habit of glancing at the answers, too. In this case, the answers are pretty far apart. When that's true, you can often estimate. (Note that sometimes the numbers only need to be far apart in relative terms—in the first problem, the numbers are only 1 apart, but 2 is twice as big as 1, and there's a big relative difference between 1 and 0.)

Step 1: Understand. The answers are decently far apart, so plan to estimate wherever it makes sense in the process. Also, the question asks for the number of *managers* who do *not* work in engineering. Jot that down on your scrap paper.

Step 2: Plan. The problem provides information about certain categories of employees by percentages, as well as the total number of employees, so your task is going to be to take percentages of that 450 figure. But save yourself some time by using the answers to estimate as you go.

Step 3: Solve. First, find the number of managers, which is 20% of 450. Use benchmarks: 10% of 450 is 45, so 20% is twice as many, or 90.

There are 90 *total* managers, so a fraction of that group will be smaller. None of the answers that are 90 or greater can be the correct answer; cross off (C), (D), and (E).

Next, what percentage of these 90 managers do *not* work in engineering? If 60% of those managers *do* work in engineering, then 40% do not. You could take 40% of 90…but you don't have to. Half of 90 is 45, so the number of managers not in engineering must be less than 45. The only possible answer is (A).

The four wrong answers are all traps built into the problem. The value for managers, 90, is there. The value 54 represents 60% of the managers (instead of 40%). The value 180 represents 40% of the entire 450 employees rather than 40% of just the managers. And the value 216 represents mistakenly taking 80% and then 60% of the total number of employees, rather than 20% and then 40%.

When to Estimate

Estimate whenever the problem explicitly asks for an approximate answer. In addition, consider estimating when the answers are far apart or when they cover certain "divided" characteristics (more on this below).

In many cases, this estimation will get you all the way to the correct answer. In others, you may be able to eliminate some answers before guessing on a hard problem.

Consider these possible answers:

    (A) −6
    (B) −3
    (C) −2
    (D)   1
    (E)   2

These answers can be divided into two groups: positive and negative. If you are running out of time or are not sure how to answer the question in the normal way, you may be able to tell whether the answer should be positive or negative. If so, you'll be able to eliminate two or three answers before making a guess.

Other examples of a divided characteristic: A fraction problem might have some answers greater than 1 and others less than 1. A probability problem may have some answers greater than 0.5 and some answers less than 0.5 (or greater or less than half).

Whenever you run into these divided characteristics, you may be able to estimate, so train yourself to look for these opportunities during the Understand phase.

Using Benchmarks to Estimate

The Benchmark method for calculating percents was first introduced in the Percents chapter. You can also use benchmarks to estimate.

The easiest percent benchmarks are 50%, 10%, and 1%. You can also use easy fraction benchmarks to estimate. The easiest fraction benchmarks are $\frac{1}{2}$, the quarters $\left(\frac{1}{4}, \frac{3}{4}\right)$, and the thirds $\left(\frac{1}{3}, \frac{2}{3}\right)$.

Try this problem:

> A television originally priced at $700 was offered at a 12% discount. What was the sale price of the television?
>
>   (A) $650
>   (B) $616
>   (C) $560

Because 10% of 700 is 70, the discount is something more than $70. The new price, then, must be somewhat less than $700 - 70 = 630$. Answer (A) can't be correct.

Next, the answer does need to be somewhat smaller than 630, but not very much smaller—the difference between 10% and 12% is not that much. So answer (B) looks better than answer (C).

And, indeed, a 20% discount would result in another $70 off, for a total $140 discount, or a sale price of $560. Answer (C) is definitely too small. The correct answer must be (B).

(If you check the math: $10\% + 1\% + 1\% = 70 + 7 + 7 = \$84$, and $700 - 84 = \$616$. But don't do this math on the test unless it's necessary!)

You can also use benchmark values to compare fractions:

$$\text{Which is greater: } \frac{127}{261} \text{ or } \frac{162}{320} \text{ ?}$$

Don't try to solve yet. First, Understand and Plan. It would be seriously annoying to use the double-cross method here without a calculator. It would be even more annoying to find common denominators. And there's your clue! When they give you math that clearly won't be done in 2 minutes without a calculator, there must be another way to approach it.

Each one is smaller than 1. Hmm. How does each fraction compare to $\frac{1}{2}$? It turns out that 127 is less than half of 261 and 162 is more than half of 320, so $\frac{162}{320}$ must be the greater fraction.

You can also use benchmark values to estimate computations involving fractions:

$$\text{What is } \frac{10}{22} \text{ of } \frac{5}{18} \text{ of 2,000 ?}$$

Again, that math is annoying, so estimate. What nicer fractions are these fractions close to?

The fraction $\frac{10}{22}$ is a little bit less than $\frac{1}{2}$ and $\frac{5}{18}$ is a little bit more than $\frac{1}{4}$. Use these to estimate:

$$\frac{1}{2} \text{ of } \frac{1}{4} \text{ of } 2,000 = 250$$

Therefore, $\frac{10}{22}$ of $\frac{5}{18}$ of $2,000 \approx 250$.

Notice that the rounding errors compensated for each other:

$\dfrac{10}{22} \approx \dfrac{10}{20} = \dfrac{1}{2}$ You decreased the denominator, so you rounded up: $\dfrac{10}{22} < \dfrac{1}{2}$.

$\dfrac{5}{18} \approx \dfrac{5}{20} = \dfrac{1}{4}$ You increased the denominator, so you rounded down: $\dfrac{5}{18} > \dfrac{1}{4}$.

If you had rounded $\frac{5}{18}$ to $\frac{6}{18} = \frac{1}{3}$ instead, then you would have rounded both fractions up. This would lead to a slight but systematic overestimation:

$$\frac{1}{2} \times \frac{1}{3} \times 2,000 \approx 333$$

That might be good enough, depending on how far apart the answer choices are, but it's a little risky. If possible, try to make your rounding errors cancel out. If you round up in one part of the calculation, try to round down in another (or vice versa).

Problem Set

Directions: On some, try doing the official math *and* estimating to see how much time and effort estimation can save you. When you're done, analyze your work. How did you know you could estimate? At which point in the problem did the estimation come into play? Could you have streamlined the process or made better estimates at any step along the way? Finally, continue to look for opportunities to estimate on every GMAT problem you do from now on!

1. At a particular school, 65% of the students have taken language classes. Of those students, 40% have studied more than one language. If there are 300 students at the school, how many have studied more than one language?

    (A)   78

    (B)   102

    (C)   120

    (D)   150

    (E)   195

2. A total of 9,180 people participated in a research study on the genetics of eye color. Of the participants, $\frac{4}{9}$ had two parents with blue eyes, and of the remaining participants, $\frac{8}{17}$ had one parent with blue eyes. How many participants, in total, had at least one blue-eyed parent?

    (A)   780

    (B)   2,700

    (C)   4,320

    (D)   6,480

    (E)   8,400

3. Every elementary school student in a certain town attends one of two schools, and at both schools, each student is assigned to a specific classroom. Broad River Academy has 29 classrooms with an average of 17 students per classroom, and Lakeside School has 19 classrooms with an average of 18 students per classroom. Approximately what percent of the town's elementary school students attend Broad River Academy?

    (A)   29%

    (B)   41%

    (C)   48%

    (D)   59%

    (E)   82%

Answers and explanations are on next page

Solutions

1. **(A) 78:** First, Understand. Glance at the problem: Problem Solving. Percentages in the question. Numerical answers. Not very close together. Jot:

    $$65\% = L \qquad \rightarrow 40\% \text{ OF } L > 1 \text{ lang}$$
    $$300 = T$$

    Next, Plan. Reflect on the info. The starting point is 300, but 65% is a bit annoying. You *can* figure out that number. Do you want to take the time to do so?

    If you've noticed that the answers are decently far apart, you know you can estimate. Since 65% is very close to $\frac{2}{3}$, that's the way to go (especially with 300 as the starting point!).

    Finally, Solve:

    $$\frac{2}{3} \text{ of } 300 \text{ is } 200.$$

    Note that you rounded up, so your estimate will be a little higher than the official number.

    Benchmark to calculate 40% of that number. Find 10% of the number, then multiply by 4 to get 40%:

    $$10\% \text{ of } 200 = 20, \text{ so } 40\% = 20 \times 4 = 80$$

    Approximately 80 students have studied more than one language. The closest answer is 78.

2. **(D) 6,480:** The ugly fractions jump out. The first fraction isn't too bad, but $\frac{8}{17}$ is really annoying. Couple that with the starting number of 9,180 people and no calculator and this looks like a terrible problem.

    But wait! During your Understand phase, when you did your first glance, did you glance at the answer choices? If not, start making that a part of your glance on PS problems and notice this: The answers are spread very far apart. What does that mean?

    Estimate your way to the answer. Both fractions are near 50%, so you might round to that benchmark, but aim to make your rounding errors balance across all of the steps.

    Of the 9,180 people, $\frac{4}{9}$ had two parents with blue eyes. If you round the number of people down to 9,000, you don't need to approximate the $\frac{4}{9}$ fraction at all: $\frac{4}{9}$ of 9,000 is 4,000. This is a slight underestimation of the number of people who had two parents with blue eyes.

    Next, how many people remain? About $9,000 - 4,000 = 5,000$. Of these people, $\frac{8}{17}$ or approximately 50% had one parent with blue eyes. Half of 5,000 is 2,500, which is a slight overestimation of the number of people who had one parent with blue eyes.

    In total, about $4,000 + 2,500 = 6,500$ people had at least one parent with blue eyes. The only close answer is 6,480.

3. **(D) 59%:** Glance at those answers. They contain pretty annoying percentages. If only they'd given nicer numbers—they wouldn't even have had to change them very much.

That's your big clue! The answers are basically 30%, 40%, 50%, 60%, and 80%—so estimate on this problem.

The question asks for B students as a percentage of all students. The number of B students is $(29)(17) = $ yuck. And the number of L students is $(19)(18)$. It's easy to round 29 up to 30 and 19 up to 20, but what about that 17 and 18? Can you just round everything up? Write out the math that needs to happen but don't do anything; just examine it:

$$\frac{(29)(17)}{(29)(17) + (18)(19)}$$

The 17 on the top can cancel with the one 17 on the bottom, but it also has to cancel with something in the $(18)(19)$ term. Why not have it cancel the 18? That's close enough:

$$\frac{(29)\cancel{(17)}}{(29)\cancel{(17)} + \cancel{(18)}(19)} \approx \frac{29}{29 + 19} \approx \frac{30}{30 + 20} = \frac{30}{50} = \frac{60}{100}$$

And estimate once again at the middle step. On a fraction, estimate in the *same* direction to balance out your estimations: If you estimate up on the top, also estimate up on the bottom. The closest match is 59%.

Algebra

In this unit, you'll learn how to process all of the algebra found on the GMAT, including exponents, roots, linear and quadratic equations, inequalities, and formulas of various kinds. You'll also learn additional strategies for the Data Sufficiency problem type, as well as for Test Cases and Choose Smart Numbers. Finally, you'll learn how to solve combo and max/min problems.

In This Unit

PEMDAS

In This Chapter

- Subtraction of Expressions
- Fraction Bars as Grouping Symbols

In this chapter, you will learn the **order of operations**—the rules for simplifying equations.

CHAPTER 8 PEMDAS

When simplifying an algebraic expression, you have to follow a specific order of operations: Parentheses Exponents (Multiplication/Division) (Addition/Subtraction), or **PEMDAS** as it's referred to in the United States. If you learned math in other English-speaking countries, you may have memorized slightly different acronyms; however, the rules are still the same. Multiplication and division are in parentheses because they are on the *same* level of priority. The same is true of addition and subtraction. When two or more operations are at the same level of priority, work from left to right. For example:

Simplify: $5 + (2 \times 4 + 2)^2 - |7(-4)| + 18 \div 3 \times 5 - 8$

P = PARENTHESES. First, perform all of the operations that are *inside* parentheses. Note that in terms of order of operations, absolute value signs are equivalent to parentheses. In this expression, there are two groups of parentheses:

$(2 \times 4 + 2)$ and $|7(-4)|$

In the first group, there are two operations to perform, multiplication and addition. According to PEMDAS, multiplication must come before addition:

$(2 \times 4 + 2) = (8 + 2) = 10$

In the second group, perform the operation inside first (multiplication), then take the absolute value of that number:

$|7(-4)| = |-28| = 28$

Now the original expression looks like this:

$$5 + 10^2 - 28 + 18 \div 3 \times 5 - 8$$

E = EXPONENTS. Second, take care of any exponents in the expression:

$$10^2 = 100$$

Now, the expression looks like this:

$$5 + 100 - 28 + 18 \div 3 \times 5 - 8$$

M&D = MULTIPLICATION & DIVISION. Next, perform all the multiplication and division. When only multiplication and division are involved, you can do the work in any order. If that seems complicated, keep it simpler by working left to right:

$$\underline{18 \div 3} \times 5$$
$$6 \times 5 = 30$$

Now the expression reads:

$$5 + 100 - 28 + 30 - 8$$

A&S = ADDITION & SUBTRACTION. Lastly, perform all the addition and subtraction. Always work from left to right when doing a mix of addition and subtraction:

$5 + 100 - 28 + 30 - 8$

$105 - 28 + 30 - 8$

$77 + 30 - 8$

$107 - 8$

The answer:

99

Subtraction of Expressions

One of the most common errors involving the order of operations occurs when an expression with multiple terms is subtracted. The subtraction must occur across *every* term within the expression. Each term in the subtracted part must have its sign reversed. For example:

$x - (y - z) = x - y + z$ The signs of both y and $-z$ have been reversed. Note that "minus a negative" turns into a positive.

$x - (y + z) = x - y - z$ The signs of both y and z have been reversed.

$x - 2(y - 3z) = x - 2y + 6z$ The signs of both y and $-3z$ have been reversed.

Now, try another example:

What is $5x - [y - (3x - 4y)]$?

Both expressions in parentheses must be subtracted, so the signs of each term must be reversed for *each* subtraction, working from the inside out. Note that the square brackets are just fancy parentheses, used so that you avoid having double parentheses right next to each other:

$$5x - \left[y - (3x - 4y)\right] =$$
$$5x - (y - 3x + 4y) =$$
$$5x - (5y - 3x) =$$
$$5x - 5y + 3x = \mathbf{8x - 5y}$$

Fraction Bars as Grouping Symbols

In any expression with a fraction bar, pretend that there are parentheses around the numerator and denominator of the fraction. This may be obvious as long as the fraction bar remains in the expression, but it is easy to forget if you eliminate the fraction bar or add or subtract fractions. For example:

Simplify: $\dfrac{x-1}{2} - \dfrac{2x-1}{3}$

The common denominator for the two fractions is 6, so multiply the numerator and denominator of the first fraction by 3 and those of the second fraction by 2:

$$\frac{x-1}{2}\left(\frac{3}{3}\right) - \frac{2x-1}{3}\left(\frac{2}{2}\right) = \frac{3x-3}{6} - \frac{4x-2}{6}$$

For the next step, treat the expressions $3x - 3$ and $4x - 2$ as though they were enclosed in parentheses. Once you combine them, actually put in parentheses for these numerators. Then, reverse the signs of both terms in the second numerator when you distribute the subtraction:

$$\frac{(3x-3) - (4x-2)}{6} = \frac{3x-3-4x+2}{6} = \frac{-x-1}{6} = -\frac{x+1}{6}$$

The last two forms are both acceptable as the answer. You can leave the negative sign in each of the two terms in the top of the fraction. You can also pull a negative out of both terms and put that negative sign out front.

8

Problem Set

1. Evaluate: $(4 + 12 \div 3 - 18) - [-11 - (-4)]$

2. Evaluate: $-|-13 - (-17)|$

3. Evaluate: $\left(\dfrac{4+32}{2-(-6)}\right) - (4 + 8 \div 2 - (-6))$

4. Simplify: $x - (3 - x)$

5. Simplify: $(4 - y) - 2(2y - 3)$

8

Solutions

1. **−3:**

$$(4 + 12 \div 3 - 18) - (-11 - (-4)) = \qquad \text{Division before addition/subtraction}$$
$$(4 + 4 - 18) - (-11 + 4) =$$
$$(-10) - (-7) = \qquad \text{Subtraction of negative} = \text{addition}$$
$$-10 + 7 = -3 \qquad \text{Arithmetic—watch the signs!}$$

2. **−4:**

$$-|-13 - (-17)| =$$
$$-|-13 + 17| = \qquad \text{Subtraction of negative} = \text{addition}$$
$$-|4| = -4$$

Note that the absolute value *cannot* be made into $13 + 17$. You must perform the arithmetic inside grouping symbols *first*, whether inside parentheses or inside absolute value bars, *then* remove the grouping symbols.

3. **−9:**

$$\left| \frac{4 + 32}{2 - (-6)} \right| - [4 + 8 \div 2 - (-6)] =$$
$$\left(\frac{4 + 32}{2 + 6} \right) - (4 + 8 \div 2 + 6) =$$
$$\left(\frac{40}{8} \right) - \left| 4 + 4 + 6 \right| =$$
$$5 - 14 = -9$$

4. **$2x - 3$:** Reverse the signs of every term in the parentheses:

$$x - (3 - x) = x - 3 + x = 2x - 3$$

5. **$-5y + 10$ (or $10 - 5y$):** Reverse the signs of every term in the subtracted parentheses:

$$(4 - y) - 2(2y - 3) = 4 - y - 4y + 6 = -5y + 10 \ (\text{or } 10 - 5y)$$

Linear Equations and Combos

In This Chapter

- Expressions vs. Equations
- Solving One-Variable Equations
- Two Variables: Solving by Substitution
- Two Variables: Solving by Elimination
- Two Variables: Solving for the Combo
- Absolute Value Equations

In this chapter, you will learn the difference between expressions and equations, as well as how to simplify and solve linear equations via various methods, including one strategy often used on the GMAT: the combo. You'll also learn how to solve equations containing absolute values.

CHAPTER 9 Linear Equations and Combos

Here's an example of a linear equation: $x - 13y = 24$.

Linear equations are equations in which all variables have an exponent of 1. In the equation above, the variable x can be written x^1. (This is always true when a variable doesn't have a "visible" exponent: The exponent is in fact 1.)

In addition, in linear equations, no variables are multiplied together.

The term **combo** is short for *combination of variables*. This is a test-taking term referring to questions such as "What is $x + y$?" The expression $x + y$ is a combo.

Expressions vs. Equations

Equations (such as $x + y = 6$) contain an equals sign, while expressions (such as $x + y$) do not.

An expression, even one that contains variables, represents a value. When manipulating or simplifying expressions, you have to follow certain rules to ensure that you don't change the value of the expression.

There are several methods for simplifying expressions. You can:

1. Combine like terms: $6z + 5z \rightarrow 11z$

2. Find a common denominator: $\frac{1}{12} + \frac{3x^3}{4} \times \left(\frac{3}{3}\right) \rightarrow \frac{1}{12} + \frac{9x^3}{12} = \frac{9x^3 + 1}{12}$

3. Pull out a common factor: $2ab + 4b \rightarrow 2b(a + 2)$

4. Cancel common factors: given $y \neq 0$, simplify $\frac{5y^3}{25y} \rightarrow \frac{y^2}{5}$

These moves are all valid because they do not change the value of the expression. In other words, if you plug numbers into both the original and simplified forms, the value stays the same. For example, replace z in the first expression with 3:

Original form	Simplified form
$6z + 5z$	$11z$
$6(3) + 5(3)$	$11(3)$
$18 + 15$	33
33	

Thus, $6z + 5z$ is equivalent to $11z$.

Since equations contain an equals sign, they behave differently. In order to keep the two sides of the equation equal, any change made to one side must also be made to the other side. Also, the change may alter the values on both sides of the equation—though the two sides will still be equal to each other. For example:

$$3 = 3$$ This is a valid equation: 3 equals 3.

$$(2)3 = 3(2)$$ Multiply both sides by 2.

$$5 + 6 = 6 + 5$$ Add 5 to both sides.

$$11 = 11$$ The two sides are still equal, but have different values.

In general, there are six operations you can perform to both sides of an equation. Remember to perform the action on the *entire* side of the equation. For example, if you were to square both sides of the equation $\sqrt{x} + 1 = x$, you would have to square the entire expression $\left(\sqrt{x} + 1\right)$, as opposed to squaring each term individually.

You can:

1. Add the same thing to both sides:

$$\begin{array}{rcl} z - 13 &=& -14 \\ +13 && +13 \\ \hline z &=& -1 \end{array}$$

2. Subtract the same thing from both sides:

$$\begin{array}{rcl} x + 8 &=& 34 \\ -8 && -8 \\ \hline x &=& 26 \end{array}$$

3. Multiply both sides by the same thing:

$$\frac{4}{a} = a + b$$
$$a \times \left(\frac{4}{a}\right) = (a + b) \times a$$
$$4 = a^2 + ab$$

4. Divide both sides by the same thing:

$$3x = 6y + 12$$
$$\frac{3x}{3} = \frac{6y + 12}{3}$$
$$x = 2y + 4$$

5. Raise both sides to the same power:

$$\sqrt{y} = y + 2$$
$$\left(\sqrt{y}\right)^2 = (y + 2)^2$$
$$y = (y + 2)^2$$

6. Take the same root of both sides:

$$x^3 = 125$$
$$\sqrt[3]{x^3} = \sqrt[3]{125}$$
$$x = 5$$

9

Solving One-Variable Equations

In order to solve one-variable equations, isolate the variable on one side of the equation (isolate = get the variable by itself). In doing so, make sure you perform identical operations on both sides of the equation.

Also, generally speaking, follow PEMDAS *in reverse*. Where possible, try to make moves that keep values positive, since people usually make fewer math mistakes with positive values versus negative values. Try these examples:

$3x + 5 = 26$	Subtract 5 from both sides.
$3x = 21$	Divide both sides by 3.
$x = 7$	

$w = 17w - 1$	Subtract w from both sides.
$0 = 16w - 1$	Add 1 to both sides.
$1 = 16w$	Divide both sides by 16.
$\frac{1}{16} = w$	

$\frac{p}{9} + 3 = 5$	Subtract 3 from both sides.
$\frac{p}{9} = 2$	Multiply both sides by 9.
$p = 18$	

When simplifying an *expression* (not like the examples just given), you'd follow PEMDAS, in which case multiplication and division would come before addition and subtraction. When simplifying an *equation*, by contrast, follow PEMDAS in reverse: Add and subtract first, to get the plain numbers over to the other side of the equation, then multiply or divide to move the numbers that are "attached" to the variable.

Two Variables: Solving by Substitution

Sometimes the GMAT asks you to solve a system of equations with more than one variable. You might be given two equations with two variables, or perhaps three equations with three variables. In either case, there are two primary textbook ways of solving simultaneous equations—substitution or elimination—and a third way that occurs on the GMAT, the combo. This section deals with the first method, substitution. For example:

Use substitution to solve for *y*.
$x + y = 9$
$2x = 5y + 4$

First, isolate the variable you *don't* want to solve for—in this case, you don't want *x*. Choose the equation in which it is easier to isolate *x*:

$x + y = 9$
$x = 9 - y$

Next, substitute the right-hand side of that equation into the other equation. In this case, substitute $9 - y$ wherever you see x:

$$2x = 5y + 4$$
$$2(9 - y) = 5y + 4$$

Now you've got an equation with just y, the variable that you want. Solve for y:

$$2(9 - y) = 5y + 4$$
$$18 - 2y = 5y + 4$$
$$14 = 7y$$
$$2 = y$$

You can also substitute your solution for y into either of the original equations in order to solve for x—but first check whether you need to do that. Most of the time, the GMAT will ask for just one variable. Here's how to solve for the second variable, just in case:

$$x + y = 9$$
$$x + 2 = 9$$
$$x = 7$$

If the problem had asked you to solve for x, you would start by isolating y in one of the equations and then substituting into the second equation. You can choose which equation to do first versus second—and if you do have to solve for both variables, you can also choose in which order you solve. But if, as will usually be the case, you're asked to solve only for one variable, first isolate the variable you *don't* want, and then substitute to solve for the variable you do want.

Two Variables: Solving by Elimination

Alternatively, you can solve simultaneous equations by elimination. In this method, you can add or subtract the two equations to eliminate one of the variables—though you'll minimize mistakes if you plan on adding whenever you do this, not subtracting. For example:

Solve the following for y.

$x + y = 9$
$2x = 5y + 4$

To start, line up the terms of the equations:

$$x + y = 9$$
$$2x - 5y = 4$$

The goal is to get the coefficient (or number) in front of the variable you *don't* want (in this case, x) to be the same *number* but the opposite sign (positive or negative). You accomplish this by multiplying one of the equations by some number. For example, multiply the first equation by -2:

$$-2(x + y = 9) \rightarrow -2x - 2y = -18$$

Now, the x coefficient in both equations is the same number (2) but opposite in sign. Next, add the equations to eliminate the undesired variable:

$$-2x - 2y = -18$$
$$+2x - 5y = 4$$
$$\overline{-7y = -14}$$

Finally, solve the resulting equation for the unknown variable:

$$-7y = -14$$
$$y = 2$$

The GMAT will usually ask you to solve for just one of the two variables, but if you do have to find both, then substitute the value for the known variable into either of the starting equations to find the value for the other variable. Use whichever equation looks easier to you:

$$x + y = 9$$
$$x + 2 = 9$$
$$x = 7$$

Two Variables: Solving for the Combo

Combo questions might look, at first glance, much like certain algebra questions you were asked in school. Try this Data Sufficiency problem:

What is the value of $\frac{x}{y}$?

(1) $\frac{x + y}{y} = 3$

(2) $y = 4$

It wasn't unusual to be asked, in school, to solve for $\frac{x}{y}$, or $x + y$, or any similar combination of variables. Find x, find y, and voilà! You can calculate any desired combination of the variables, too.

GMAT combo problems, however, have one key difference: Your goal is to solve directly for the *combination* of variables, not for each individual variable. There are two steps in a combo problem: noticing the combo and manipulating to match it.

First: Notice that the question asks for a combo.

When a question asks directly for a combination of variables, you have a combo problem. (There are ways to disguise a combo—you'll learn about this later.)

Second: Manipulate any given information to try to match the combo.

In this case, the question stem doesn't contain any additional given information and the question itself is already simplified: $\frac{x}{y} = ?$

Jump into the statements:

(1) $\frac{x + y}{y} = 3$

If you weren't looking for the combo, you might start to simplify the equation by multiplying both sides by y, getting $x + y = 3y$. However, the combo contains a fraction $\left(\dfrac{x}{y}\right)$, so keep that denominator right where it is. How else can you manipulate the equation while preserving the fraction? Split the numerator and simplify:

$$\frac{x}{y} + \frac{y}{y} = 3$$

$$\frac{x}{y} + 1 = 3$$

$$\frac{x}{y} = 2$$

Statement (1) is sufficient!

AD

~~BCE~~

Here's statement (2):

(2) $y = 4$

The statement provides no information about x, so it is not sufficient.

(A) ~~D~~

~~BCE~~

The correct answer is (A).

When you solve for a combo in Data Sufficiency (DS), your ultimate goal is to try to find a single match for the desired combo. If you can, then the statement is sufficient.

The problem above also contains a common DS trap called the C-Trap. Problems with this trap appear to work only when both statements are used together—that is, the answer appears to be (C). In actuality, one of the two statements works by itself and (C) is incorrect. Take a look at the two statements again:

(1) $\dfrac{x + y}{y} = 3$

(2) $y = 4$

If you are trying to solve for both x and y individually, you will realize pretty quickly that neither statement alone will get you there. Put the two statements together, however, and it is possible to find the individual values of both x and y.

9

There's just one hitch: The problem didn't ask for the values of x and y. It asked for the value of $\frac{x}{y}$, and statement (1) is sufficient all by itself to find that combo. Since answer (C) specifically says that you have to use both statements together and that *neither one alone is sufficient*, it cannot be correct.

Keep an eye out for the C-Trap on DS problems. If it is obvious that the two statements do work together, reexamine each one individually; one might work all by itself. Combo problems are a very common place for C-Traps to occur.

Try another combo problem:

> What is the value of $x + y$?
>
> (1) $x - y = 1$
> (2) $x = 3 - y$

Notice that the question asks for a combo. The question stem asks directly for a combo: $x + y$.

Manipulate any given information to try to match the combo. Jot down $x + y = ?$ on your scratch paper. Now look at statement (1):

> (1) $x - y = 1$

Hmm. How can you turn this into $x + y$? How about $x = y + 1$. Good, now there's an addition sign—but it's not between the x and y. What next?

It turns out that, no matter how you manipulate the equation, you can't change the original subtraction relationship between x and y into addition. As a general rule, if the relationship between the two variables starts out as addition, you cannot switch it to subtraction, or vice versa, without some additional information to add to the equation. Ditto if the relationship begins as multiplication—you cannot switch it to division, or vice versa, without additional information.

Statement (1) is not sufficient; cross off answers (A) and (D):

~~AD~~
BCE

Now, look at statement (2):

> (2) $x = 3 - y$

This one also doesn't have $x + y$. At least, not right now. But put x and y on the same side:

> $x + y = 3$

Although you can't find the individual values for x and y, you do have the value for the combo $x + y$. And that's all you need!

This statement is sufficient to answer the question. The correct answer is (B).

~~AD~~
ⒷCE

A question stem may also try to disguise the combo. Consider this question:

If $a + b = c$, what is the value of c?

The question itself asks for a single variable, but it also provides given information in the form of an equation that contains three variables total. Given that equation, if you are able to find the value of the combo $a + b$, then you could also find the value of c. So the real question is this:

What is c? Or, what is $a + b$?

Finally, while combos show up more often on DS, you may also see them on Problem Solving problems. Here's an example:

If $2x + y = 18$ and $x + 2y = 12$, what is the value of $x + y$?

(A)   2
(B)   6
(C)   8
(D)   10
(E)   12

Since you're given two equations and two variables, you could solve for the individual values of x and y—but when the question asks for a combo, it's usually faster to solve for the combo!

Note two characteristics about the combo: the R&R. First, the desired *relationship* between the variables is addition ($+$). Second, the desired *ratio* of the coefficients—the values in front of the variables—is 1 : 1 (you have one x and one y).

Take a look at the two equations. Do you see any way to combine them that would give you an addition relationship and a 1 : 1 ratio between the variables?

$$
\begin{array}{r}
2x + y = 18 \\
+ \quad x + 2y = 12 \\
\hline
3x + 3y = 30
\end{array}
$$

Add them up! Divide by 3 to solve for the combo: $x + y = 10$. The correct answer is (D).

You can also solve for x and y individually and then add them up; that will just take longer. A little time investment up front can often save you more time later on in the problem. (And if you don't see how to solve directly for the combo, you can always go ahead and solve individually.)

Notice that the question asks for a combo.

A question stem may ask for the combo directly or it may try to disguise the combo. You may have to do a little rephrasing in order to find the combo. Start training yourself to look for this feature.

Manipulate any given information to try to match the combo.

Your goal is to try to match the combination of variables (look for the R&R: relationship and ratio). Most of the time, if you try to solve for each variable individually, it will take longer and, on DS, you risk falling into a trap answer. Go for the combo!

Absolute Value Equations

Absolute value refers to the *positive* value of the expression within the absolute value brackets. For instance, if you know that $|x| = 5$, then x could be either 5 or -5 and the equation would still be true. There's exactly one circumstance in which the value isn't positive: when it's zero. In this case, $|x| = 0$, so $x = 0$.

Unless the answer is zero, equations that involve absolute value generally have two solutions. In other words, there are *two* numbers that the variable could equal in order to make the equation true, because the value of the expression inside the absolute value brackets could be *positive or negative*.

Here's how to solve an absolute value equation:

Solve for w, given that $12 + |w - 4| = 30$.

First, isolate the absolute value expression:

$$12 + |w - 4| = 30$$
$$|w - 4| = 18$$

Second, once you have an equation of the form |variable expression| = a with $a > 0$, you know that the variable expression *without* the absolute value symbols could be ±. Remove the absolute value brackets and solve the equation for two different solutions:

CASE 1: When w is positive, $w = a$.

$$w - 4 = 18$$
$$w = 22$$

CASE 2: When w is negative, $-w = a$.

$$-(w - 4) = 18$$
$$w - 4 = -18$$
$$w = -14$$

Advanced material for the Algebra unit (primarily covering additional strategies for equations, formulas, and inequalities) can be found in Atlas, Manhattan Prep's online learning platform. Use the online material only if you feel that you have mastered everything in the Algebra unit of this strategy guide and only if you are aiming for a Quant section score of 48 or higher.

Problem Set

Now that you've finished the chapter, try the following problems.

1. Solve for x: $2(2 - 3x) - (4 + x) = 7$

2. Given $z \neq \frac{3}{2}$, solve for z: $\frac{4z - 7}{3 - 2z} = -5$

3. What is the sum of x, y, and z ?

    $x + y = 8$
    $x + z = 11$
    $y + z = 7$

    (A)   1

    (B)   13

    (C)   26

4. Solve for y: $22 - |y + 14| = 20$

5. If $y = 2x + 9$ and $7x + 3y = -51$, what is the value of x ?

    (A)   –6

    (B)   –3

    (C)   0

6. If $a = 3bc$ and $abc \neq 0$, what is the value of c ?

    (1) $a = 10 - b$

    (2) $3a = 4b$

7. Every attendee at a monster truck rally paid the same admission fee. How many people attended the rally?

    (1)   If the admission fee had been raised to $15 and twice as many people had attended, the total admission fees collected would have been three times the amount actually collected.

    (2)   If the admission fee had been raised to $22.50 and two-thirds as many people had attended, the total admission fees collected would have been 150% of the actual admission fees collected.

8. If $A = \dfrac{\frac{x}{3}}{\frac{2}{y}}$, what is A ?

    (1) $xy = 8$

    (2) $\dfrac{x}{y} = 2$

9

9. If $x \neq 0$ and $x\left(x - \frac{5x + 6}{x}\right) = 0$, what are all of the possible values of x ?

10. At a certain coffee shop, a mocha sells for $3.00 and a cappuccino sells for $2.25. In total, the shop sold $180 worth of mochas and cappuccinos over the course of a day. How many mochas did the shop sell?

    (1) The shop sold 10 more cappuccinos than it did mochas.

    (2) The combined price of all of the cappuccinos sold was equal to the combined price of all of the mochas sold.

Solutions

1. **−1:**

$$2(2 - 3x) - (4 + x) = 7$$
$$4 - 6x - 4 - x = 7$$
$$-7x = 7$$
$$x = -1$$

2. $\frac{4}{3}$:

$$\frac{4z - 7}{3 - 2z} = -5$$
$$4z - 7 = -5(3 - 2z)$$
$$4z - 7 = -15 + 10z$$
$$8 = 6z$$
$$z = \frac{8}{6} = \frac{4}{3}$$

3. **(B) 13:** It is possible to solve for x, y, and z individually, but you can save a significant amount of time by solving for the combo: What is $x + y + z$? The equations collectively contain exactly two "copies" of each variable and these variables are always added. Add the three equations together:

$$
\begin{aligned}
x + y \quad\quad &= 8 \\
x \quad\quad + z &= 11 \\
+ \quad\quad y + z &= 7 \\
\hline
2x + 2y + 2z &= 26
\end{aligned}
$$

Divide the equation by 2: the combo $x + y + z = 13$.

4. $y = \{-16, -12\}$: First, isolate the expression within the absolute value brackets. Then, solve for two cases, one in which the expression is positive and one in which it is negative:

$$22 - |y + 14| = 20$$
$$2 = |y + 14|$$

Case 1: $y + 14 = 2$
$$y = -12$$

Case 2: $-(y + 14) = 2$
$$y + 14 = -2$$
$$y = -16$$

5. **(A) −6:** The question asks for x, so you need to figure out how to eliminate y. Since the first equation already has y isolated, substitute the first equation into the second equation:

$$y = 2x + 9 \qquad 7x + 3y = -51$$

$$7x + 3(2x + 9) = -51$$
$$7x + 6x + 27 = -51$$
$$13x + 27 = -51$$
$$13x = -78$$
$$x = -6$$

Note that answer (B) is a trap. The value for y is −3, but the question asked for x, not y.

6. **(B):** Since the question asks about c and provides a given equation that contains c, solve the given equation for c:

$$c = \frac{a}{3b}$$

What would you need to know in order to calculate c? Take a look at the equation this way:

$$c = \left(\frac{1}{3}\right)\left(\frac{a}{b}\right)$$

If you can find a value for the combination $\frac{a}{b}$, then you can calculate c. This problem is a combo problem in disguise! Try to solve for the combo.

(1) INSUFFICIENT: $a = 10 - b$. Can this be manipulated into the desired combo? If you add b to both sides ($a + b = 10$), you get a combo, but not the desired one. If you divide everything by b, you partially get the desired combo: $\frac{a}{b} = \frac{10}{b} - 1$. The problem is that there's another b associated with the 10. There isn't a way to get just $\frac{a}{b}$ by itself on one side and only a numerical value (no variables) on the other side. Statement (1) is not sufficient, so cross off answers (A) and (D).

(2) SUFFICIENT: This time, the desired combo can be created: $3a = 4b \rightarrow \frac{a}{b} = \frac{4}{3}$ This statement is sufficient.

The correct answer is **(B):** Statement (2) is sufficient, but statement (1) is not.

7. **(E):** This question asks how many people attended a monster truck rally. The total amount collected equals the number of attendees times the admission fee, or $T = A \times P$. The question asks for A.

(1) INSUFFICIENT: If the price had been $15 and twice as many people had attended, the total would be three times greater. Therefore:

$$3T = 2A \times 15$$
$$3T = 30A$$

The value of A depends on the unknown value of T, so more than one answer is possible, and this statement is not sufficient.

(2) INSUFFICIENT: If the price had been \$22.50 and two-thirds as many people had attended, the total would be 150% of the actual total. Therefore:

$$1.5T = \frac{2}{3}A \times 22.50$$
$$1.5T = 15A$$

The value of A depends on the unknown value of T, so more than one answer is possible, and this statement is not sufficient.

(1) AND (2) INSUFFICIENT: In order to be able to solve for the value of A, you would need two different equations. Take a look at the two equations: If you multiply the second one by 2, the two equations will be identical. In other words, they are the same; you have only one equation. Combining the two statements is therefore no more sufficient than either statement alone.

The correct answer is **(E)**: Using the two statements together is still not sufficient.

8. **(A):** This question is a combo problem in disguise. The question asks for A, but the value of A depends on x and y. Before diving into the statements, simplify the given equation:

$$A = \frac{\frac{x}{3}}{\frac{2}{y}}$$
$$A = \frac{x}{3} \times \frac{y}{2}$$
$$A = \frac{xy}{6}$$

If you can find the value of the combo xy, you can answer the question.

(1) SUFFICIENT: Statement (1) matches the rephrased question, so it is sufficient to answer the question.

(2) INSUFFICIENT: In general, it's not possible to find the value for the multiplication combo xy from the value for the division combo $\frac{x}{y}$. This is always the case, so you can memorize this rule. (Why is this the case? When given $\frac{x}{y} = 2$, the x could be 2 and the y could be 1, in which case xy is 2. Alternatively, x could be 4 and y could be 2, in which case xy is 8. There will be an infinite number of values that could work.)

The correct answer is **(A)**: Statement (1) alone is sufficient, but statement (2) is not.

9. **{6, −1}:** Distribute the multiplication by x. Note that, when you cancel the x in the denominator, the quantity $5x + 6$ is implicitly enclosed in parentheses:

$$x\left(x - \frac{5x + 6}{x}\right) = 0$$
$$x^2 - (5x + 6) = 0$$
$$x^2 - 5x - 6 = 0$$
$$(x - 6)(x + 1) = 0$$
$$x = 6 \text{ or } -1$$

10. **(D):** Call the number of mochas m and the number of lattes c. The total revenue can be expressed as the equation $3m + 2.25c = 180$. The question asks for the value of m. If you can find the value of c, then you can find the value of m, so the question can be rephrased as this: What is the value of m or c?

    (1) SUFFICIENT: This statement can be translated into the equation $m + 10 = c$. This can be substituted into the first equation: $3m + 2.25(m + 10) = 180$. This can be solved for m (though don't actually solve!).

    (2) SUFFICIENT: This statement can be translated into the equation $3m = 2.25c$. Again, this can be substituted into the equation given in the question stem: $3m + 3m = 180$. This can be solved for m.

    The correct answer is **(D):** Each statement alone is sufficient.

Data Sufficiency 201

In This Chapter

- Test Cases Redux
- The C-Trap
- Avoid Statement Carryover
- Guessing Strategies

In this chapter, you will learn more about Data Sufficiency strategies, including how to avoid certain traps and common mistakes on DS and how to eliminate wrong answers and make an educated guess.

CHAPTER 10 Data Sufficiency 201

You're ready for your next level of Data Sufficiency studies. First, refresh your DS skills.

Step 1: Understand

First, just *glance* at the problem to note the overall type—in this case, it's DS. Where does it look messy or complex? Include the question stem and both statements in your glance.

Next, *read* the problem and decide: Is this a Value or a Yes/No?

Value: The question asks for the value of an unknown (e.g., What is x?).

A statement is **Sufficient** if it provides **exactly one possible value**.

A statement is **Not Sufficient** if it provides **more than one possible value**.

Yes/No: The question asks whether a given piece of information is true (e.g., Is x even?). Most of the time, these will be in the form of Yes/No questions.

A statement is **Sufficient** when the answer is **Always Yes** or **Always No**.

A statement is **Not Sufficient** when the answer is **Sometimes Yes, Sometimes No**.

Jot down both the given information and the question itself. If the information is straightforward, it's fine to jot as you read. If the information is at all complex (especially if it's a story!), you may want to read the whole thing before you jot anything down. When you are ready to jot, draw a T-diagram on your paper; write information from the question stem above the horizontal line of the T.

Given information—that is, any information in the question stem other than the question itself—is true information that you must consider or use when answering the question. Write this information separately from the question itself. It's important to distinguish between what you were *told* is true and what you were *asked* to find. For the question stem, write facts to the left and the question more to the right, both above the line.

Step 2: Plan

Reflect on the question and the given, and rephrase the question if you can. If you have a lot of information, you may also need to decide how to *organize* your work.

Step 3: Solve

If you understand the problem and have a decent plan to solve (it doesn't need to be perfect!), go ahead and follow your plan. If, on the other hand, you realize that you don't understand the problem or you don't have a decent plan, this is an excellent time to pick any answer and move on. Save that time and mental energy for a problem that has a better chance of paying off.

Test Cases Redux

You also learned how to test cases—one of the strategies for avoiding algebra by using real numbers instead. Try this problem:

Is $b < 0$?

(1) $b^3 < b$

(2) $b^2 > b$

Step 1: Understand. DS. Yes/No. The problem is a theory problem and it's asking whether b is less than 0, so you can test some real numbers.

Asking whether b is less than 0 is the same as asking whether b is negative, so you'll almost certainly want to try some negative numbers.

Also, rephrase the question: Is b negative?

Step 2: Plan. What kind of numbers would be good to try on this problem? Where possible, try 0 or 1. Also, the statements contain exponents, so that's another vote for considering negative values. (There's also one other type of number to consider when you see exponents—did you spot it when you tried the problem? If not, feel free to play around with the statements a little before you keep reading.)

Step 3: Solve. Dive into the statements.

(1) $b^3 < b$

Reflect on this statement for a moment. You cube a number…and the cube is *smaller* than the starting number. That's a little weird! For what kinds of numbers does that happen?

Case 1: Negatives work! If $b = -2$, then $-8 < -2$. Therefore, -2 is a possible value for b. In this case, Yes, b is negative. Next, can you get a No answer?

Cases 2 and 3 (attempts): Try a positive to see whether that makes a difference. If $b = 1$, then it is not true that $1 < 1$. Discard this case. What about a larger positive value, like $b = 2$? It's not true that $8 < 2$. Any number greater than 1 would make the statement $b^3 < b$ false, so you can't use those numbers in your cases.

Are there any other kinds of numbers that can be used? As you'll learn in the next chapter, negative numbers and fractions between 0 and 1 do funny things when raised to an exponent. You've already tried a negative; maybe it's time to try a fraction?

Case 4: Fractions between 0 and 1 also get smaller when you raise them to a power. If $b = \frac{1}{2}$, then $\frac{1}{8} < \frac{1}{2}$. Therefore, $\frac{1}{2}$ is a valid case to test for b. In this case, No, b is not a negative number.

Since there is a Yes and a No, statement (1) is not sufficient. Cross off answers (A) and (D).

(2) $b^2 > b$

Hmm. You square something, and it gets bigger. What kinds of numbers do that?

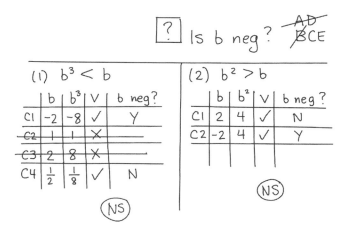

Case 1: If $b = 2$, then $4 > 2$. Therefore, 2 is a valid case and, in this case, No, b is not a negative number. Next, can you get a Yes answer?

To get a Yes answer, b has to be negative, so try a negative value next.

Case 2: If $b = -2$, then $4 > -2$. Therefore, -2 is a possible value and, in this case, Yes, b is negative.

Since there is a Yes and a No, statement (2) is not sufficient. Cross off answer (B).

Finally, try the two statements together:

(1) $b^3 < b$

(2) $b^2 > b$

The goal now is to find cases that are valid for *both* of the statements simultaneously. That's a lot of work! Rather than start from scratch, first examine the cases that you already tested; are any valid for both statements? If so, you can reuse your work.

You've already tested $b = -2$ for both. That test gave a Yes answer, so your Yes case is done. Now, can you find a case that is valid for both statements and that gives a No answer? Examine the No cases that you tried before.

10

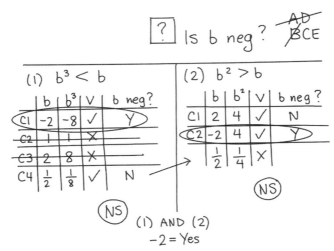

For statement (1), you tried $\frac{1}{2}$. Are you allowed to try that value for statement (2)? That would give $\frac{1}{4} > \frac{1}{2}$, which is false, so cross off this case entirely. Statement (2) doesn't allow values between 0 and 1.

$$(1) \text{ AND } (2)$$

$$-2 = \text{Yes}$$

$$\frac{1}{2}? \quad \text{inv} \qquad \text{must be neg}$$

$$2? \quad \text{inv} \qquad \text{\textcircled{S}}$$

$$0? \quad \text{inv}$$

You tried $b = 2$ for statement (2), but during statement (1), you already figured out that any value greater than 1 won't be valid.

What about 0? No, that doesn't work either. The only values that work for both statements are negative, so b must be a negative number. Together, the statements are sufficient.

The correct answer is (C): Both statements together are sufficient, but neither one is sufficient by itself.

Think back over how the math played out. When you see exponents on future Test Cases problems, what kinds of numbers do you want to consider?

Start with 0 and 1, if possible. Consider whether you may want a negative. And think about fractions between 0 and 1 (or, maybe, fractions between 0 and -1). All of these characteristics can result in weird outcomes with exponents—outcomes that might serve to give you a different answer when testing cases.

Here's a summary of the Test Cases strategy for DS problems:

Understand: First, **recognize** that you can test cases. The question stem and the statement will allow for multiple possible values; it doesn't lock you into using one set of values.

Articulate the *facts* given in the problem and separate them from the *question* that is being asked. Remind yourself of your goal when testing cases on DS: Try to find two different answers so that you can call that statement Not Sufficient and move on.

10

Plan: First, **think about** any **constraints** you're given. The constraints are the facts given in the problem and can be found in *two* places: (1) the question stem and (2) the two statements. You are only allowed to try numbers that fit the given facts. (As you work on one statement alone, ignore any facts given in the *other* statement.)

Next, use the given facts as clues to figure out what kinds of numbers you *do* want to try. These clues will help you to find the kinds of numbers that can give you different answers.

Solve: Then, **test one set of numbers**. Choose your values, write them down, then check your numbers against the facts in the problem to make sure that you have chosen a valid case. If your chosen numbers "break" any of the facts—that is, make any fact in the question stem or the statement on which you're working right now false—*discard* that case. All of the given facts must be true, so any numbers you choose must go along with those facts. Cross an invalid case off on your scratch paper and start again.

If you have a valid case, solve to find an answer to the question. On a Yes/No question, you will get either a Yes or a No. On a Value question, you will get a particular value.

Then, try to find a second case that gives you a *different* answer. Remind yourself of what a different answer looks like for this problem. For example, if the question is "Is $b > 5$?" and your first answer is Yes, then you would want to find a No case. For this particular question, a No case would only occur when b is equal to or less than 5, so choose such a value for your second case.

If you can find two different answers, you're done! That statement has a Sometimes Yes/Sometimes No answer, so you can cross off the relevant answer(s) on your grid and move to the next step in your DS process.

If you keep getting the same answer, try to to articulate *why* this is happening. If you are trying the same kind of number each time, then you may need to try a different kind of number to find that opposite case—so trying to articulate what's happening can lead you to realize that you need to try a specific kind of number that will get you to a different answer.

Alternatively, articulating what's happening with the math may allow you to realize that you will always get that same answer—in other words, that this statement is sufficient.

At times, you may get the same answer after a few cases but not be able to articulate what's happening. If you're not sure why but you also don't see how to get a different answer after trying a few different kinds of numbers, don't keep sitting on this problem. Go ahead and call this statement sufficient and move on.

The C-Trap

Set a timer for 4 minutes and try these two DS problems.

What is the value of x ?

(1) $12x + 4y = 4(21 + y)$

(2) $y = 12$

If $a + b = c$, what is the value of c ?

(1) $b = 5$

(2) $2(a + c) = 22 + 2(c - b)$

What did you get for the first one?

What is the value of x ?

(1) $12x + 4y = 4(21 + y)$

(2) $y = 12$

Step 1: **Understand.** It's a DS that asks for the value of x; it provides no additional information. Glance at the statements. Statement (1) is a lot messier. (For a reason, it turns out. It's setting a trap!)

Step 2: **Plan.** Since statement (2) is easier, start there. Make a mental note that, when you get to statement (1), you're going to want to simplify it.

Step 3: **Solve.** Statement (2) provides no information about x, so it's not sufficient. Eliminate answers (B) and (D). So far, so good (you haven't hit the trap yet).

Here's where the trap closes: You know that statement (2) gives you y. Look at statement (1): It contains an equation with both x and y. That equation doesn't look like it could possibly work by itself because it contains two variables. So you get rid of answer (A), choose answer (C), and move on...but you just fell into the C-Trap (first introduced in the prior chapter). Answer (C) is *not* the correct answer!

When you see a messy equation, first try to simplify the information. For instance, you can divide everything by 4. What else?

$$\overset{3}{\cancel{12}}\, x + \cancel{4}\, y = \cancel{4}\,(21 + y)$$
$$3x + y = 21 + y$$
$$3x = 21$$
$$x = 7$$

Interesting. The variable y drops completely out of the equation. This statement is enough all by itself to get a definitive value for x.

The correct answer is (A): Statement (1) alone is sufficient to answer the question, but statement (2) alone is not.

The C-Trap occurs when you (mistakenly) think that you need *both* statements to answer the question, but it turns out that *just one* of those statements is enough all by itself. The text for answer (C) states that you have to use both pieces of information and that *neither one alone is sufficient.*

It is certainly true that, if you have both pieces of information, you can find x—but you don't *need* both pieces together. Statement (1) will do the job by itself.

If you ever find yourself thinking, "Oh, it's *completely* obvious that using the two pieces of information together will get you to the answer," pause for a moment! This test isn't often super-obvious—so double-check. Ask yourself whether you might be falling for the C-Trap. It may be the case that one of the pieces of information is sufficient on its own.

10

Here's the second problem. Did you get (C) as your answer? If so, try it again right now:

If $a + b = c$, what is the value of c ?

(1) $b = 5$

(2) $2(a + c) = 22 + 2(c - b)$

Step 1: **Understand.** It's a DS Value. It asks for the value of c, but it also gives the equation $a + b = c$. This is a combo question in disguise! If you can solve for the combo $a + b$, that will give you the value of c. So the rephrased question is this: What is c *or* what is the combo $a + b$?

Step 2: **Plan.** Statement (1) is straightforward, but statement (2) is complicated. That complexity signals that there may be some way to simplify.

Step 3: **Solve**, starting with the easier statement (1). Knowing that $b = 5$ is not enough to get to the value of the combo $a + b$. Statement (1) is not sufficient, so cross off answers (A) and (D).

Statement (2) is a lot messier, so simplify. Before you start, remind yourself of what would be sufficient: Can you find c, or can you find the combo $a + b$?

$$2(a + c) = 22 + 2(c - b)$$
$$a + c = 11 + (c - b)$$
$$a = 11 - b$$

The variable c drops out completely. Now, can you get the combo $a + b$? Yes!

$$a = 11 - b$$
$$a + b = 11$$

Statement (2) is sufficient all by itself. The correct answer is (B).

This problem sets up a C-Trap that many people will fall for even if they do figure out that the question is a combo. When the test gives you something messy, it's probably trying to hide something from you. Whenever you see an "ugly" equation (or, really, any equation!), take some time to try to simplify the messiness so that you can understand what the test is really asking or telling you.

Avoid Statement Carryover

When you first learned how to do Data Sufficiency, you learned one very important step: Evaluate each statement individually before evaluating the two statements together.

The GMAT likes to set a certain trap that plays off of this step (and you may have already fallen for this trap in the past). Take a look at this problem (you may remember seeing a similar one earlier in this guide):

If Farai is twice as old as Dmitry, how old is Farai?

(1)   Samantha will be 11 years old in 5 years.

(2)   Samantha is 4 years younger than Dmitry.

The question asks how old F is and provides a relationship: $F = 2D$. The rephrased question is "What is F or D ?" since the equation provides a direct relationship between the two variables.

10

Here's how the trap works. You can find S's age from statement (1), but that's not enough to get to D or F, so you cross off answers (A) and (D).

In evaluating the second statement, you realize that, since you know how old S is, you can find D, and knowing D is sufficient to answer! So the answer is (B).

The answer is actually *not* (B). What happened?

When working on statement (2), you used the information about S's age, but that's from statement (1)—at this stage, you're supposed to be evaluating each statement individually! You're not allowed to carry over information from one statement to the other right now; this is literally called the **Statement Carryover** trap. In the heat of the test, it's very easy to do this, even when you know that you're not supposed to—especially as the math becomes more complicated (and therefore distracting).

To help avoid this trap, use the T-diagram consistently when solving DS problems. When you are working on each statement, you are not allowed to "cross the vertical line" of the T. Keep the two statements completely separate. You can only look "up the T" and use the information from the question stem:

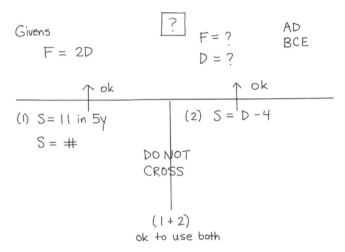

If you have eliminated answers (A), (B), and (D), you will then evaluate the two statements together. In this circumstance, go ahead and work below the two prior statements—and below the "Do Not Cross" line. Now, you're allowed to use the information from both statements.

Guessing Strategies

There are several strategies that can help you guess effectively. Even when you know how to solve and don't need to guess, you can avoid certain traps or careless mistakes by practicing these strategies.

Situation 1: The Identical Twins. Two statements provide *exactly* the same information.

Here is an example:

(1) $4y + 3x = 9$
(2) $6x - 18 = -8y$

Each statement provides an equation that contains x and y, but the variables are in a different order. When you see this, be suspicious; they are probably trying to hide something. Rearrange one of the two equations to match.

10

For instance, rearrange the second equation to match the placement of the variables in the first: $8y + 6x = 18$. Now, compare the two equations:

(1) $4y + 3x = 9$

(2) $8y + 6x = 18$

The second equation is exactly twice the first equation. Divide the second equation by 2 and you have the first equation. In other words, there are not two *different* equations here; there is just one equation. The statements are identical.

When the statements are identical, only two answers are possible. If the information in one statement is sufficient to answer the question, then it's sufficient in *either* statement, so the correct answer is (D).

Alternatively, if the information in one statement is *not* sufficient to answer the question, then the second statement also won't be sufficient. Further, that second statement adds no new information, so even together, the statements are insufficient, so the answer is (E).

If you see that the two statements are identical twins, immediately cross off answers (A), (B), and (C)—even if you are still working on the problem. That will forestall any careless mistakes. The answer must be either (D) or (E).

Situation 2: The Cannibal. One statement completely includes or incorporates the information given by the other.

Here is an example:

(1) $x > 20$

(2) $80 < x < 142$

The first statement indicates that x is greater than 20. The second statement indicates that x is between 80 and 142.

If x is between 80 and 142, then x must be greater than 20. Statement (2) tells you everything that statement (1) told you (x is greater than 20), plus additional information (x is between 80 and 142). Think of the second statement as the Cannibal; it cannibalized statement (1), plus it gives you additional information.

In this case, the answer cannot be (A), statement (1) alone, because statement (2) also provides that same piece of information. If the fact that x is greater than 20 is sufficient, then the answer must be (D): Each statement works alone.

The answer also cannot be (C). In order for answer (C) to be correct, each statement must contribute a *separate* piece of useful information (since you have to use them together). In the example above, statement (1) doesn't provide any *new* information relative to statement (2), so the answer cannot be (C).

The answer has to be (B), (D), or (E).

Here is another example:

(1) $x = 10$

(2) x is even.

This time, statement (1) is the Cannibal: if you know that $x = 10$, then you also know that x is even. Statement (2) gets cannibalized, so the answer cannot be (B) or (C).

10

If, at any point, you become aware that the information given in one statement is already 100% covered by the other statement, immediately cross off two answers: answer (C) and the answer that "goes with" the statement that was cannibalized:

- If statement (1) gets cannibalized, cross off answers (A) and (C).
- If statement (2) gets cannibalized, cross off answers (B) and (C).

If you end up having to guess, you'll be down to just three answers. Of the three remaining answers, the best guess is the one associated with the Cannibal—either (A) or (B)—since that statement provides at least two pieces of relevant information.

Situation 3: You suspect a C-Trap.

If it seems very clear to you that using the two statements together would be sufficient—it would have been obvious when you were 12 and first learning this math!—then be on the lookout for a possible C-Trap. If you suspect there may be a C-Trap even though you can't figure out why or which statement does work alone, then don't guess answers (C) or (E).

Next, decide which of the two statements contains the more complicated information. This one is the one more likely to work on its own (similar to the Cannibal), so choose the corresponding answer. For example, if statement (1) has the more complicated info, choose answer (A). If, on the other hand, statement (2) looks more complex, choose choice (B).

10

Problem Set

It's time to practice your Data Sufficiency skills.

1. If $y > 0$, what is the value of y ?

    (1) $y^2 \leq y$

    (2) y is an integer.

2. If $a \neq bc$, what is the value of $\dfrac{(a + bc)}{(a - bc)}$?

    (1) $abc = 32$

    (2) $a + b + c = 12$

3. If n is a one-digit positive integer, what is n ?

    (1) The units digit of 4^n is 4.

    (2) The units digit of n^4 is n.

4. If $x = 300 - y - z$, what is the value of x ?

    (1) $y = \dfrac{(x + z)}{2}$

    (2) $x = \dfrac{(y + z)}{2}$

5.

    If points p, q, and r appear on a number line as shown above, is $p < -5$?

    (1) The distance between p and r on the number line is at least 5.

    (2) The distance between p and q on the number line is at least 5.

Save the next problems for review after you finish this entire guide.

6. If x and y are integers, what is $x + y$?

    (1) $3^x = 81$

    (2) $5^x = \dfrac{25}{5^y}$

7. If x is a positive integer, what is the units digit of x ?

    (1) The units digit of $\dfrac{x}{10}$ is 4.

    (2) The tens digit of $10x$ is 5.

8. If x and y are integers, what is the value of $x^2 + 2xy + y^2$?

    (1) $x + y = 7$

    (2) $2x = \dfrac{28 - 4y}{2}$

10

Solutions

1. **(C):** The question stem allows any positive values for y, including fractions. The second statement is considerably easier than the first, so you might choose to start there.

    (2) INSUFFICIENT: The statement indicates that y is an integer. The value of y could be 1, 2, 14, 192, or any other positive integer.

    (1) INSUFFICIENT: What numbers make $y^2 \leq y$ true?

    > Case 1: If $y = 1$, then $1 \leq 1$. Therefore, 1 is a possible value for y.

    > Case 2: If $y = \frac{1}{2}$, then $\frac{1}{4} \leq \frac{1}{2}$. Therefore, $\frac{1}{2}$ is a possible value for y.

    There are at least two possible values for y.

    (1) AND (2) SUFFICIENT: Together, the two statements eliminate the fraction case $y = \frac{1}{2}$, but $y = 1$ is still a valid case. In order for $y^2 \leq y$ to be true, y must equal 0, 1, or a fraction between 0 and 1. Because y is a positive integer, it cannot be 0 or a fraction. The two statements together, then, are sufficient to answer the question: The value of y is 1.

    The correct answer is **(C):** The two statements together are sufficient, but neither one works alone.

2. **(E):** Why does the problem indicate that a doesn't equal bc? If that were true, then the bottom of the fraction could be 0—and the GMAT doesn't divide by 0. So you don't need to write that piece of information down. Do write down the question stem, and just note that it's a big combo. If you can find the value of a and bc, then you can solve. Or if you can find the whole combo $\frac{(a + bc)}{(a - bc)}$, then you can solve.

    (1) INSUFFICIENT: This statement doesn't allow you to re-create the whole big combo or to find a separately from bc.

    (2) INSUFFICIENT: This statement doesn't allow you to re-create the whole big combo or to find a separately from bc.

    (1) AND (2) INSUFFICIENT: You've got two equations with three variables, so you can't find each individual variable, and that means you can't find a separately from bc. Can you find the whole big combo? Try finding just $a + bc$ first.

    Rearrange the first equation: $a = \frac{32}{bc}$. Plug that into the second equation: $\frac{32}{bc} + b + c = 12$. Hmm. The variable a has disappeared now and there isn't a way to find the combo bc or the individual values b and c from this. There isn't a way to rearrange the information to get a by itself, bc, $a + bc$, or $a - bc$, so even using the two statement together, there's no way to solve.

    The correct answer is **(E):** Both statements together are still not sufficient.

10

3. **(E):** If n is a one-digit positive integer, it has to be 1, 2, 3, 4, 5, 6, 7, 8, or 9.

    (1) INSUFFICIENT: The units digit of 4^n is 4.

Case	n	The units digit of 4^n is 4.	What is n ?
#1	1	$4^1 = 4$ ✓	1
#2	2	$4^2 = 16$ ✗	invalid case
#3	3	$4^3 = 64$ ✓	3

Since n could be 1 or 3, statement (1) is not sufficient. (You might notice a pattern. It turns out that every $n =$ odd will return a units digit of 4. Every $n =$ even will return a units digit of 6.)

(2) INSUFFICIENT: The units digit of n^4 is n.

Case	n	The units digit of n^4 is n.	What is n ?
#1	1	$1^4 = 1$ ✓	1
#2	2	$2^4 = 16$ ✗	invalid case
#3	3	$3^4 = 81$ ✗	invalid case

You can continue to test each possible value for n in order, or you can think about any patterns you know for raising a number to a power.

For example, raising 5 to any power will always return a number that ends in 5. Therefore, 5^4 will end in 5, so 5 is a valid number for n:

n	The units digit of n^4 is n.	What is n ?
5	$5^4 = 625$ ✓	5

Because there are at least two possible values for n, statement (2) is not sufficient.

(1) AND (2) INSUFFICIENT: Both statements allow $n = 1$. Statement (2) does not allow 3, but does allow 5. Does $n = 5$ work for statement (1)?

n	The units digit of 4^n is 4.	What is n ?
5	$4^5 =$ (ends in 4) ✓	4

Note that you do *not* actually multiply out 4^5. Instead, note the pattern:

4^n	Units digit
4^1	4
4^2	6
4^3	4
4^4	6

This pattern repeats to infinity: 4 to any positive odd integer has a units digit of 4.

Because both 1 and 5 work for each statement, even the two statements together are not sufficient to answer the question.

The correct answer is **(E)**: Both statements together are still not sufficient.

4. **(B):** The question asks for the value of x but gives an equation that contains two other variables, y and z. Rephrase the question in terms of y and z.

This is a little tricky. If you place parentheses around the y and z, be careful with the signs: $x = 300 - (y + z)$. The negative sign outside applies to both the y and the z inside. So the rephrased question is: What is x, or what is the combo $y + z$?

(1) INSUFFICIENT: There are two equations and three variables, so you can't solve for each individual variable—but rearrange to see whether you can solve for the combo.

$$y = \frac{(x + z)}{2}$$
$$2y = x + z$$
$$2y - z = x$$

This isn't the right combo, so this statement is not sufficient.

(2) SUFFICIENT: Rearrange to see whether you can solve for the combo:

$$x = \frac{(y + z)}{2}$$
$$2x = y + z$$

The right side matches the combo, so plug this into the equation given in the question stem to see what happens:

$$x = 300 - (y + z)$$
$$x = 300 - (2x)$$
$$x + 2x = 300$$

That can be solved for a single value of x, so the correct answer is **(B)**: Statement (2) is sufficient, but statement (1) is not.

5. **(B):** When the GMAT provides a number line with a specific ordering of variables, you can assume that the variables do appear in that order on the line. In this case, the p and the q are both negative, and $p < q$. And r is positive. It's a Yes/No question: Is p less than -5 ?

Note a few things. The problem does not specify that the variables are integers, so anything is possible, as long as you follow the constraints noted in the previous paragraph. Also, you can test cases on this problem; specifically, try to find a case in which the value for p is less than -5 and a case in which the value for p is equal to or greater than -5.

(1) INSUFFICIENT: If p and r are at least 5 apart, then p could be -10 and r could be 10; in this case, Yes, p is less than -5. Alternatively, p could be -2 and r could be 10; in this case, No, p is not less than -5. Eliminate answers (A) and (D).

(2) SUFFICIENT: This statement is almost identical to the first one—so although you still generally want to ignore statement (1) at this point, do pay attention to the similarity. Statement (2) changes just one thing: The variable r becomes the variable p. Look at the number line and compare what the two statements indicate: (1) says that the p-to-r distance is at least 5 and (2) says that the p-to-q distance is at least 5.

The distance from p to r is greater, so if the p-to-q distance is at least 5, then the p-to-r distance must be at least 5 as well. In other words, statement (2) is a Cannibal: It already fully incorporates statement (1). As a result, the answer cannot be either (A) or (C). Cross those off on your answer grid. (Answer (A) is already crossed off, but (C) isn't crossed off yet.)

Now, process statement (2). If p and q are at least 5 apart, then p could be -10 and q could be -4; in this case, Yes, p is less than -5.

Alternatively, p could be -4 and q could be...no, that would make q positive and that's not allowed. If q is -0.01, then p would be -5.01. No matter how close to 0 you make q, it's still the case that subtracting 5 will make p less than -5, so Yes, p must be less than -5.

The correct answer is **(B)**: Statement (2) is sufficient, but statement (1) is not.

6. **(B):** The question asks for the combo $x + y$ and specifies that x and y are integers.

    (1) INSUFFICIENT: $3^x = 81$

    You could solve for the value of x, but the statement does not provide any information about the value of y, so this statement is not sufficient. Don't solve for x now; check statement (2) first:

    (2) SUFFICIENT:

$$5^x = \frac{25}{5^y}$$
$$\left(5^x\right)\left(5^y\right) = 25$$
$$5^{x+y} = 5^2$$
$$x + y = 2$$

    Note that, if you do not do the math (or you do it incorrectly), you may think that this statement is not enough to answer the question. In that case, you may have fallen into a C-Trap: The two statements together are definitely enough, but the answer cannot be (C) because one of the statements works by itself.

    The correct answer is **(B)**: Statement (2) is sufficient, but statement (1) is not.

7. **(B):** The question stem establishes that x is a positive integer and asks for the units digit of x. The units digit can consist of only a single digit: 0, 1, 2, 3, 4, 5, 6, 7, 8, or 9. Glance at the statements. This is a theory problem, so you can test cases to solve. Your goal will be to try to find cases that can give you different units digits for x.

10

(1) INSUFFICIENT: First, note that x is a positive integer but $\frac{x}{10}$ doesn't have to be an integer. The only requirement is that the units digit of $\frac{x}{10}$ is 4. For example, if $\frac{x}{10} = 4.5$, then x would be $(4.5)(10) = 45$. What happened? When dividing by 10, the digits each move one place to the right. In order for the 4 to be in the units digit after the division, the 4 must have started out in the tens digit of x. So any integer you try for x must have a 4 in the tens digit.

Case 1: $x = 45$. First, check that this makes the statement true: x does have a 4 as the tens digit, so $x = 45$ is a valid case to test.

Next, answer the question: What is the units digit of x? It's 5.

Case 2: What can you try that fits the facts in the problem but gives a different units digit as the answer? Try $x = 46$. This is valid because there is a 4 in the tens digit of x. What's the units digit? This time it's 6—a different value. Since there are at least two different values for the units digit of x, statement (1) is not sufficient. Cross off answers (A) and (D).

(2) SUFFICIENT: First, figure out what kinds of values for x are acceptable, given that the tens digit of $10x$ is 5. For example, if $x = 35$, then $10x$ is 350. If you multiply by 10, then all of the digits move one to the left. In order for the tens digit to be 5 after that multiplication, the 5 must have started out in the units digit. So any value you try for x must have a 5 in the units digit.

Wait! Don't try any cases yet. Go back and read that last sentence again.

If any acceptable case must have 5 in the units digit, you have your answer. The units digit of x is always 5.

The correct answer is **(B)**: Statement (2) is sufficient, but statement (1) is not.

8. **(D):** The question stem specifies that x and y are integers and asks what is the value of $x^2 + 2xy + y^2$? Since the expression is one of the common quadratic identities, write down the other form of this question: What is the value of $(x + y)^2$?

(1) SUFFICIENT: The work is made much easier if you recognized the quadratic identity and wrote down both forms. Knowing the value of $x + y$ is enough to find the value of $(x + y)^2$.

(2) SUFFICIENT: Glance at the equation. It contains an x and a y, but it's written in a much more confusing form than statement (1). Be suspicious when they do this; simplify:

$$2x = \frac{28 - 4y}{2}$$
$$4x = 28 - 4y$$
$$4x + 4y = 28$$
$$x + y = 7$$

Note that, after rearranging the second statement, the equation is identical to the equation given in the first statement: These are Identical Twins! In this circumstance, the answer must be either (D) or (E).

The correct answer is **(D)**: Each statement is sufficient by itself.

Exponents

In This Chapter

In this chapter, you will learn all about how to work with exponents—including when dealing with integers, fractions, positives and negatives, and so on. You'll also learn steps to simplify equations with exponents.

CHAPTER 11 Exponents

The mathematical expression 4^3 consists of a **base** (4) and an **exponent** (3).

The base (4) is multiplied by itself as many times as the power indicates (3):

$$4^3 = 4 \times 4 \times 4 = 64$$

In other words, exponents are actually shorthand for repeated multiplication.

Two exponents have special names: The exponent 2 is called the square, and the exponent 3 is called the cube:

5^2 can be read as five squared ($5^2 = 5 \times 5 = 25$).

5^3 can be read as five cubed ($5^3 = 5 \times 5 \times 5 = 125$).

All about the Base

A Variable Base

Variables can also be raised to an exponent, and they behave the same as numbers:

$$y^4 = y \times y \times y \times y$$

Base of 0 or 1

0 raised to *any* power equals 0.
1 raised to *any* power equals 1.

For example, $0^3 = 0 \times 0 \times 0 = 0$ and $0^4 = 0 \times 0 \times 0 \times 0 = 0$.

Similarly, $1^3 = 1 \times 1 \times 1 = 1$ and $1^4 = 1 \times 1 \times 1 \times 1 = 1$.

If you are told that $x = x^2$, then x must be either 0 or 1.

A Base of −1

$$(-1)^1 = -1 \qquad (-1)^2 = -1 \times -1 = 1 \qquad (-1)^3 = -1 \times -1 \times -1 = -1$$

This pattern repeats indefinitely. In fact:

$$(-1)^{\text{ODD}} = -1 \qquad (-1)^{\text{EVEN}} = 1$$

A Fractional Base

Squaring a fraction is the equivalent of multiplying the fraction by itself. You can also distribute the exponent before multiplying. For example:

$$\left(\frac{3}{4}\right)^2 = \frac{3}{4} \times \frac{3}{4} = \frac{9}{16} \qquad \left(\frac{3}{4}\right)^2 = \frac{3^2}{4^2} = \frac{9}{16}$$

When a fraction between 0 and 1 is raised to a power, an interesting thing occurs: The value gets smaller, not larger! For example:

$$\left(\frac{3}{4}\right)^1 = \frac{3}{4}$$

$$\left(\frac{3}{4}\right)^2 = \frac{3}{4} \times \frac{3}{4} = \frac{9}{16}$$

$$\left(\frac{3}{4}\right)^3 = \frac{3}{4} \times \frac{3}{4} \times \frac{3}{4} = \frac{27}{64}$$

Notice that $\frac{3}{4} > \frac{9}{16} > \frac{27}{64}$. If the fractional base is positive, as you continue to increase the value of the power, the value of the fraction continues to decrease.

If the base fraction is negative, then raising it to either an even or odd power makes the fraction *larger*, but for slightly different reasons. Raising to an even power turns the fraction positive, and a positive fraction is larger than a negative one:

$$\left(-\frac{3}{4}\right)^2 = -\frac{3}{4} \times -\frac{3}{4} = \frac{9}{16}$$

But when you raise a negative base to an odd power, it actually becomes *less* negative, or closer to 0. Because of that, the new fraction is actually larger than the original:

$$\left(-\frac{3}{4}\right)^3 = -\frac{3}{4} \times -\frac{3}{4} \times -\frac{3}{4} = -\frac{27}{64}$$

In general, remember that raising any proper fraction (fractions between -1 and 1) to any power will result in a new fraction that is *closer* to 0. This is still true for negative fractions raised to even powers. They are still closer to 0; they just happen to be closer on the positive end of the number line.

A Decimal Base

Like proper fractions, decimals between 0 and 1 decrease as their exponent increases, while negative decimals increase as the exponents increase by becoming either positive or less negative:

$$(0.6)^2 = 0.36 \qquad (0.5)^4 = 0.0625 \qquad (0.1)^5 = 0.00001$$

$$(-0.6)^2 = 0.36 \qquad (-0.5)^4 = 0.0625 \qquad (-0.1)^5 = -0.00001$$

A Compound Base

Just as an exponent can be distributed to a fraction, it can also be distributed to a product:

$$10^3 = (2 \times 5)^3 = (2)^3 \times (5)^3 = 8 \times 125 = 1,000$$

This also works if the base includes variables:

$$(3x)^4 = 3^4 \times x^4 = 81x^4$$

More on Negative Bases

When dealing with negative bases, pay particular attention to PEMDAS. Unless the negative sign is inside parentheses, the exponent does not distribute. For example:

$$-2^4 \qquad \neq \qquad (-2)^4$$
$$-2^4 = -1 \times 2^4 = -16 \qquad (-2)^4 = (-1)^4 \times (2)^4 = 1 \times 16 = 16$$

As with a base of -1, any negative bases raised to an odd exponent will be negative, and any negative bases raised to an even exponent will be positive.

Combining Exponential Terms with Common Bases

The rules in this section *only* apply when the terms have the *same* base. All of these rules are related to the fact that exponents are shorthand for repeated multiplication.

Multiply Terms: Add Exponents

When *multiplying* two exponential terms with the same base, *add the exponents*. This rule is true no matter what the base is:

$$z^2 \times z^3 = (z \times z) \times (z \times z \times z) = z \times z \times z \times z \times z = z^5$$
$$4 \times 4^2 = (4) \times (4 \times 4) = 4 \times 4 \times 4 = 4^3$$

Fortunately, once you know the rule, you can simplify the computation greatly:

$$z^2 \times z^3 = z^{2+3} = z^5$$

Divide Terms: Subtract Exponents

When *dividing* two exponential terms with the same base, *subtract the exponents*. This rule is true no matter what the base is:

$$\frac{5^6}{5^2} = \frac{5 \times 5 \times 5 \times 5 \times \cancel{5} \times \cancel{5}}{\cancel{5} \times \cancel{5}} = 5 \times 5 \times 5 \times 5 = 5^4$$

Fortunately, once you know the rule, you can simplify the computation greatly:

$$\frac{x^6}{x^2} = x^{6-2} = x^4$$

Anything Raised to the Zero Power is Equal to 1

This rule is an extension of the previous rule. If you divide something by itself, the quotient is 1:

$$\frac{a^3}{a^3} = \frac{\cancel{a} \times \cancel{a} \times \cancel{a}}{\cancel{a} \times \cancel{a} \times \cancel{a}} = 1$$

Look at this division by subtracting exponents:

$$\frac{a^3}{a^3} = a^{3-3} = a^0$$

Therefore, $a^0 = 1$.

Any base raised to the 0 power equals 1. The one exception is a base of 0.

Note that you cannot raise 0 to the 0 power. $0^0 = \frac{0}{0}$, which is *undefined* (but the GMAT does not test undefined numbers, so you don't need to memorize this). Although the GMAT doesn't test undefined numbers directly, you may need to use the knowledge that you cannot divide by 0 when considering values for variables in a denominator.

Negative Exponents

The behavior of negative exponents is also an extension of the rules for dividing exponential terms. For example:

$$\frac{y^2}{y^5} = \frac{\cancel{y} \times \cancel{y}}{y \times y \times y \times \cancel{y} \times \cancel{y}} = \frac{1}{y^3}$$

Look at this division by subtracting exponents:

$$\frac{y^2}{y^5} = y^{2-5} = y^{-3}$$

Therefore, $y^{-3} = \frac{1}{y^3}$.

This is the general rule: *Something with a negative exponent is just "one over" that same thing with a positive exponent.* You can rewrite y^{-3} by taking the reciprocal of y and dropping the negative sign from the exponent:

$$y^{-3} \rightarrow \left(\frac{1}{y}\right)^3 \rightarrow \frac{1}{y^3}$$

Here are some additional examples of how to take the reciprocal and drop the negative sign:

$$\frac{1}{3^{-3}} = 3^3 \qquad \left(\frac{x}{4}\right)^{-2} = \left(\frac{4}{x}\right)^2$$

Note that 0 to a negative power is undefined for the same reason that 0 to the power of 0 is undefined; both result in division by 0:

$$0^{-2} = \frac{1}{(0)^2} = \frac{1}{0} = \text{undefined}$$

Nested Exponents: Multiply Exponents

How can you simplify $(z^2)^3$? Expand this term to show the repeated multiplication:

$$\left(z^2\right)^3 = \left(z^2\right) \times \left(z^2\right) \times \left(z^2\right) = z^{2+2+2} = z^6$$

When you raise an exponential term to an exponent, multiply the exponents:

$$\left(a^2\right)^3 = a^{2\times3} = a^6$$

Fractions and Exponents

There are four broad categories of fractions that all behave differently when raised to a power. The result depends on the size and the sign of the fraction, as well as on the power. While it is not necessary to memorize all of the cases below, it is important to understand how each case works so that you know what numbers to try when testing cases, if necessary.

Divide fractions up into these four categories: less than -1, between -1 and 0, between 0 and 1, and greater than 1:

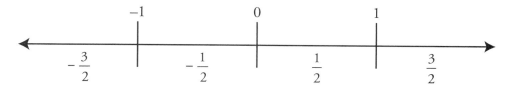

As you examine the math below, think about why the result is what it is.

Even Exponents (such as 2):

Less than -1	Between -1 and 0	Between 0 and 1	Greater than 1
$\left(-\dfrac{3}{2}\right)^2 = \dfrac{9}{4}$	$\left(-\dfrac{1}{2}\right)^2 = \dfrac{1}{4}$	$\left(\dfrac{1}{2}\right)^2 = \dfrac{1}{4}$	$\left(\dfrac{3}{2}\right)^2 = \dfrac{9}{4}$
$-\dfrac{3}{2} < \dfrac{9}{4}$	$-\dfrac{1}{2} < \dfrac{1}{4}$	$\dfrac{1}{2} > \dfrac{1}{4}$	$\dfrac{3}{2} < \dfrac{9}{4}$
Result is bigger.	Result is bigger.	Result is *smaller*.	Result is bigger.

If the exponent is even, then the fraction will get bigger in all circumstances except for one: when the fraction is between 0 and 1.

Odd Exponents (such as 3):

Less than -1	Between -1 and 0	Between 0 and 1	Greater than 1
$\left(-\dfrac{3}{2}\right)^3 = -\dfrac{27}{8}$	$\left(-\dfrac{1}{2}\right)^3 = -\dfrac{1}{8}$	$\left(\dfrac{1}{2}\right)^3 = \dfrac{1}{8}$	$\left(\dfrac{3}{2}\right)^3 = \dfrac{27}{8}$
$-\dfrac{3}{2} > \dfrac{27}{8}$	$-\dfrac{1}{2} < -\dfrac{1}{8}$	$\dfrac{1}{2} > \dfrac{1}{8}$	$\dfrac{3}{2} < \dfrac{27}{8}$
Result is *smaller*.	Result is bigger.	Result is *smaller*.	Result is bigger.

If the exponent is odd, on the other hand, then there are two circumstances in which the fraction gets smaller: when the number is between 0 and 1 (as before) *and* when the number is less than -1.

Negative Exponents (such as -2):

To raise a fraction to a negative power, raise the reciprocal to the equivalent positive power:

$$\left(\frac{3}{7}\right)^{-2} = \left(\frac{7}{3}\right)^{2} = \frac{7^2}{3^2} = \frac{49}{9} \qquad \left(\frac{x}{y}\right)^{-w} = \left(\frac{y}{x}\right)^{w} = \frac{y^w}{x^w}$$

Factoring Out a Common Term

In most cases, exponential terms that are added or subtracted cannot be combined; for example, you can't combine these two terms: $2^3 + 3^4$. However, if two terms with the same base are added or subtracted, you can factor out a common term. In the following example, factor out 11^3:

$$11^3 + 11^4$$
$$11^3 \left(11^0 + 11^1\right)$$
$$11^3 \left(1 + 11\right)$$
$$11^3 \left(12\right)$$

For any term that matches what you pulled out, an exponent of 0 is left behind; in this example, factoring 11^3 out of 11^3 leaves 11^0 behind. For all terms, the exponent becomes whatever is left behind. In the example above, 11^3 was pulled to the front, so the 11^4 term has 11^1 left over.

On the GMAT, it generally pays to factor exponential terms that have bases in common, and when doing so, factor out the smallest power. If the exponents are negative, factor out the term with the most negative exponent. Try this example:

If $x = 4^{20} + 4^{21} + 4^{22}$, what is the greatest prime factor of x ?

To find the prime factors of x, express x as a product (terms multiplied together). Factor 4^{20} out of the expression on the right side of the equation:

$$x = 4^{20} + 4^{21} + 4^{22}$$
$$x = 4^{20}\left(4^0 + 4^1 + 4^2\right)$$
$$x = 4^{20}\left(1 + 4 + 16\right)$$
$$x = 4^{20}\left(21\right)$$
$$x = \left(2^2\right)^{20}\left(3 \times 7\right)$$
$$x = \left(2^{40}\right)(3)(7)$$

Now that x has been expressed as a product, you can see all of its prime factors: 2, 3, and 7. The greatest prime factor is 7.

If the terms are all identical, you can use a great shortcut. For example:

$$11^4 + 11^4 + 11^4$$

The official math works this way:

$$11^4 + 11^4 + 11^4$$
$$11^4 \left(11^0 + 11^0 + 11^0\right)$$
$$11^4 \left(1 + 1 + 1\right)$$
$$11^4 \left(3\right)$$

Here's the shortcut: Count up the number of terms. In this case, there are three 11^4 terms. Multiply the term, 11^4, by the number of terms, 3: The answer is $11^3(3)$.

Equations with Exponents

Exponents can also appear in equations. In fact, the GMAT often complicates equations by including exponents or roots with unknown variables. Here are a few situations to look out for when equations contain exponents.

Even Exponents Hide the Sign of the Base

Any number raised to an even exponent becomes positive. For example:

$$3^2 = 9 \qquad \text{AND} \qquad (-3)^2 = 9$$

Another way of saying this is that an even exponent hides the sign of its base. Compare the following two equations:

$$x^2 = 25 \qquad\qquad |x| = 5$$

Do you see what they have in common? In both cases, $x = \pm 5$. The equations share the same two solutions. In fact, there is an important relationship: **For any x, $\sqrt{x^2} = |x|$.**

Here is another example:

$a^2 - 5 = 12$ By adding 5 to both sides, you can rewrite this equation as $a^2 = 17$. This equation has two solutions: $\sqrt{17}$ and $-\sqrt{17}$.

You can also say that the equation $a^2 = 17$ has two roots (the word *root* is a synonym for the word *solution*). The GMAT will sometimes use the word *root*, so if this term is new to you, make yourself a flash card to help remember.

Also note that not all equations with even exponents have two solutions. For example:

$x^2 + 3 = 3$ By subtracting 3 from both sides, you can rewrite this equation as $x^2 = 0$, which has only one solution: 0.

Odd Exponents Keep the Sign of the Base

Equations that involve only cube roots or other odd exponents have only one solution:

$x^3 = -125$ Here, x has only one solution, -5, because $(-5)(-5)(-5) = -125$. This will not work with positive 5.

$243 = y^5$ Here, y has only one solution, 3, because $(3)(3)(3)(3)(3) = 243$. This will not work with -3.

If an equation includes some variables with odd exponents and some variables with even exponents, treat it as dangerous, as it is likely to have two solutions. Any even exponents in an equation signal two potential solutions.

Same Base or Same Exponent

In problems that involve exponential expressions on *both* sides of the equation, it is imperative to rewrite the bases so that either the same base or the same exponent appears on both sides of the equation. Once you do this, you can usually eliminate the bases or the exponents and rewrite the rest as an equation. Consider this example:

If $(4^w)^3 = 32^{w-1}$, what is the value of w?

To start, rewrite the bases so that the same base appears on both sides of the equation. Right now, the left side has a base of 4 and the right side has a base of 32. Both 4 and 32 can be expressed as powers of 2, so you can rewrite 4 as 2^2 and you can rewrite 32 as 2^5.

Next, plug the rewritten bases into the original equation:

$$\left(4^w\right)^3 = 32^{w-1}$$
$$\left(\left(2^2\right)^w\right)^3 = \left(2^5\right)^{w-1}$$

Now, simplify the equation using the rules of exponents:

$$\left(\left(2^2\right)^w\right)^3 = \left(2^5\right)^{w-1}$$
$$2^{6w} = 2^{5w-5}$$

When the bases are identical (and no other bases exist), you can drop the bases, rewrite the exponents as an equation, and solve:

$$6w = 5w - 5$$
$$w = -5$$

Be very careful if 0, 1, or -1 is the base (or could be the base), since the outcome of raising those bases to powers is not unique. For instance, $0^2 = 0^3 = 0^{29} = 0$. So if $0^x = 0^y$, you cannot claim that $x = y$.

Likewise, $1^2 = 1^3 = 1^{29} = 1$, and $(-1)^2 = (-1)^4 = (-1)^{\text{even}} = 1$, while $(-1)^3 = (-1)^5 = (-1)^{\text{odd}} = -1$. Fortunately, the GMAT rarely tries to trick you this way.

Problem Set

Now that you've finished the chapter, try the following problems.

For problems 1 and 2, determine whether the inequality is TRUE or FALSE.

1. $\left(-\frac{3}{4}\right)^3 > -\frac{3}{4}$

2. $\left(\frac{x+1}{x}\right)^{-2} > \frac{x+1}{x}$, if $x > 0$.

3. $x^3 < x^2$. Describe the possible values of x.

4. Simplify: $\frac{m^8 p^7 r^{12}}{m^3 r^9 p} \times p^2 r^3 m^4$

5. If $p = \frac{x^{a+b}}{x^b}$, what is the value of positive integer p ?

   (1) $x = 5$

   (2) $a = 0$

6. Which of the following expressions has the greatest value?

   (A) $(3^4)^{12}$

   (B) $\left[\left(3^{30}\right)^{12}\right]^{\frac{1}{10}}$

   (C) $3^{30} + 3^{30} + 3^{30}$

   (D) $4(3^{47})$

   (E) $\left(3^{90}\right)^{\frac{1}{2}}$

7. Simplify: $(4^y + 4^y + 4^y + 4^y)(3^y + 3^y + 3^y)$

   (A) $4^{4y} \times 3^{3y}$

   (B) 12^{y+1}

   (C) $16^y \times 9^y$

   (D) 12^y

   (E) $4^y \times 12^y$

8. If x and y are integers, what is $x + y$?

   (1) $3^x = 81$

   (2) $5^x = \frac{25}{5^y}$

9. If m and n are positive integers and $(2^{18})(5^m) = (20^n)$, what is the value of m ?

10. If $B^3A < 0$ and $A > 0$, which of the following must be negative?

(A) AB

(B) B^2A

(C) B^4

(D) $\dfrac{A}{B^2}$

(E) $-\dfrac{B}{A}$

11

Solutions

1. **TRUE:** Cubing a negative number will maintain the negative sign, so the left-hand side of the inequality will stay negative. Raising a fraction between 1 and -1 to a power causes that fraction to move closer to 0 on a number line. If the starting number is between 0 and 1, the fraction will get smaller as it moves closer to 0. However, if the starting number is between -1 and 0, as it is in this problem, then the number will get larger as it moves closer to 0.

    The value $\left(-\frac{3}{4}\right)^3$, therefore, will be to the right of $-\frac{3}{4}$ on the number line, or closer to 0. It is true that $\left(-\frac{3}{4}\right)^3$ is greater than $-\frac{3}{4}$.

2. **FALSE:** Test a case (a real number!) to understand what the problem is asking. Note that the problem states that x is positive. Any number $\frac{x+1}{x}$, where x is positive, will be greater than 1. Therefore, raising that number to a negative exponent will result in a number smaller than 1:

    If $x = 1$, then:

    $$\text{Is } \left(\frac{1+1}{1}\right)^{-2} > \frac{1+1}{1} \text{ ?}$$

    $$\text{Is } (2)^{-2} > 2 \text{ ?}$$

    $$\text{Is } \left(\frac{1}{2}\right)^2 > 2 \text{ ?}$$

    You can solve that last line, but you don't need to if you've learned how numbers work. A fraction between 0 and 1 raised to a positive exponent will always get smaller, so the left side of that inequality cannot be greater than the 2. The statement is false.

3. **Any non-zero number less than 1:** First, consider possible positive values. As positive fractions between 0 and 1 are raised to a power (multiplied together), their value decreases. For example, $\left(\frac{1}{2}\right)^3 < \left(\frac{1}{2}\right)^2$. So these types of fractions are possible values for x. The number 1 makes the inequality false, though, as does any positive number greater than 1.

    The number 0 does not work in this inequality as 0 raised to any power equals 0 (ignoring the case of 0 raised to the 0 power).

    Now consider negative numbers. A negative number cubed is negative. Any negative number squared is positive. For example, $(-3)^3 < (-3)^2$. By definition, any negative number is smaller than any positive number, so this inequality is true for all negative values.

4. $m^9 p^8 r^6$: First, multiply the term on the right into the numerator of the fraction:

    $$\frac{m^8 p^7 r^{12}}{m^3 r^9 p} \times p^2 r^3 m^4 = \frac{m^{12} p^9 r^{15}}{m^3 r^9 p}$$

    Then, simplify the top and bottom of the fraction:

    $$\frac{m^{12} p^9 r^{15}}{m^3 r^9 p} = m^{(12-3)} p^{(9-1)} r^{(15-9)} = m^9 p^8 r^6$$

5. **(B):** Understand and Plan first. This question isn't really about p. It's about the expression $\frac{x^{a+b}}{x^b}$, which can be simplified by subtracting the exponent in the denominator from the exponent in the numerator:

$$\frac{x^{a+b}}{x^b} = x^{a+b-(b)} = x^a$$

So this question may be rephrased as a potential combo: What is x^a ?

You may need to know x and a individually in order for a statement to be sufficient. In certain cases, though, you would not need to know x and a individually. (As just one example, if x is 1, then a is not needed, because 1 to any power will always be 1.)

(1) INSUFFICIENT: Knowing that x is 5 is not sufficient without knowing a.

(2) SUFFICIENT: Anything to the 0 power is 1. The only exception to the rule is 0, because 0^0 is undefined. However, the problem states that p is a positive integer, so x cannot equal 0.

The correct answer is **(B):** Statement (2) is sufficient, but statement (1) is not.

6. **(D) $4(3^{47})$:** Use the rules of exponents to simplify each expression:

(A) $(3^4)^{12} = 3^{48}$

(B) $\left[\left(3^{30}\right)^{12}\right]^{\frac{1}{10}} = 3^{\left(30 \times 12 \times \frac{1}{10}\right)} = 3^{3 \times 12} = 3^{36}$

(C) $3^{30} + 3^{30} + 3^{30} = 3(3^{30}) = 3^{31}$ (Since both values have the same base, combine to get 3^{31}.)

(D) $4(3^{47})$ Cannot be simplified further.

(E) $\left(3^{90}\right)^{\frac{1}{2}} = 3^{\frac{90}{2}} = 3^{45}$

Answer choices (A) and (D) are larger than (B), (C), and (E). Compare (A) and (D):

(A) 3^{48}

(D) $4(3^{47})$

The difficult part to compare is the exponent. Is there any way to get the same exponent?

Factor one 3 out of answer (A): $3(3^{47})$. This is less than $4(3^{47})$, so answer **(D)** is greater.

7. **(B) 12^{y+1}:** Glance at the answers. There are no terms added together, so there must be some way to combine the individual terms in this problem. Factor out common terms from each expression. Use the terms-are-identical shortcut discussed in this chapter:

$$\left(4^y + 4^y + 4^y + 4^y\right)\left(3^y + 3^y + 3^y\right)$$

$$\left(4^y\right)(4)\left(3^y\right)(3)$$

$$\left(4^{y+1}\right)\left(3^{y+1}\right)$$

$$(4 \times 3)^{y+1}$$

$$12^{y+1}$$

8. **(B):** The question asks for the combo $x + y$ and specifies that x and y are integers.

    (1) INSUFFICIENT: $3^x = 81$

    You could solve for the value of x, but the statement does not provide any information about the value of y, so this statement is not sufficient. Don't solve for x now; check statement (2) first.

    (2) SUFFICIENT:

$$5^x = \frac{25}{5^y}$$

$$\left(5^x\right)\left(5^y\right) = 25$$

$$5^{x+y} = 5^2$$

$$x + y = 2$$

    Note that, if you do not do the math (or you do it incorrectly), you may think that this statement is not enough to answer the question. In that case, you may have fallen into a C-Trap: The two statements together are definitely enough, but the answer cannot be (C) because one of the statements works by itself.

    The correct answer is **(B):** Statement (2) is sufficient, but statement (1) is not.

9. **9:** With exponential equations such as this one, the key is to recognize that as long as the exponents are all integers, each side of the equation must have the same number of each type of prime factor. Break down each base into prime factors and set the exponents equal to each other:

$$\left(2^{18}\right)\left(5^m\right) = \left(20^n\right)$$

$$2^{18} \times 5^m = (2 \times 2 \times 5)^n$$

$2^{18} \times 5^m = 2^{2n} \times 5^n$ Because m and n have to be integers, there must be the **same**

$18 = 2n;\ m = n$ **number of 2's** on either side of the equation and there must be

$n = 9;\ m = n = 9$ the **same number of 5's** on either side of the equation. Thus, $18 = 2n$ and $m = n$.

10. **(A)** ***AB:*** This is a "must be" PS problem! You can test cases. A is positive, so call it $A = 2$. B^3A is negative. If A is positive, then the B^3 term must be negative. Call it $B = -1$.

Double-check that you chose numbers that follow the facts in the problem. A is positive and $B^3A = (-1)^3(2) = -2$. This is negative, which is what the problem states. Good, check the answers. Leave in anything that's negative. Cross off anything that's non-negative.

(A) $AB = (2)(-1) = -2$. Leave this in.

(B) $B^2A = (-1)^2(2) = 2$. Eliminate.

(C) $B^4 = (-1)^4 = 1$. Eliminate.

(D) $\dfrac{A}{B^2} = \dfrac{2}{(-1)^2} = 2$. Eliminate.

(E) $-\dfrac{B}{A} = -\dfrac{-1}{2} = \dfrac{1}{2}$. Eliminate.

Alternatively, you can think it through theoretically, if you feel comfortable with this math. Since A is positive, B^3 must be negative. Therefore, B must be negative. That specific answer isn't among the choices, so keep thinking. If A is positive and B is negative, the product AB must be negative.

Roots

In This Chapter

- Roots and Fractional Exponents

- Simplifying a Root

- Imperfect vs. Perfect Squares

- Memorize: Squares and Square Roots

- Memorize: Cubes and Cube Roots

In this chapter, you will learn how exponents and roots are related, as well as how to manipulate and simplify both square and cube roots. You'll also learn about perfect squares and you'll memorize commonly used squares, cubes, square roots, and cube roots.

CHAPTER 12 Roots

Roots are the reverse of exponents. You can square something (multiply a number by itself) or you can take the square root of a number (find what number, multiplied by itself, would give you the starting number). For example, $4^2 = 16$ and $\sqrt{16} = 4$…but there's a little intricacy to the GMAT on that second part.

Compare the following two equations:

$$x^2 = 16 \qquad x = \sqrt{16}$$

Although they may seem very similar, there is an important difference. There are two solutions to the equation on the left: $x = 4$ or $x = -4$. There is only *one* solution to the equation on the right: $x = 4$.

If the GMAT itself gives you a square root symbol (e.g., $\sqrt{16}$), *only* use the positive root.

If, on the other hand, the equation contains a squared variable (e.g., x^2), and *you* take the square root, use both the positive and the negative solutions:

$$\text{Given: } x^2 = 16 \qquad x = \sqrt{16}$$
$$\text{Solve: } x = \pm 4 \qquad x = 4$$

This rule applies for any even root (square root, 4th root, 6th root, etc.). For example:

$$\sqrt[4]{81} = 3$$

Odd roots (cube root, 5th root, 7th root, etc.) also have only one solution.

Odd roots, like odd exponents, keep the sign of the base. For example:

$$\text{If } \sqrt[3]{-27} = x, \text{ what is } x?$$

The correct answer is -3, because $(-3)(-3)(-3) = -27$.

By the way, the root symbol is also called a **radical sign**.

Roots and Fractional Exponents

Fractional exponents are the link between roots and exponents. For example:

$$\sqrt{x} = \sqrt[2]{x^1} = x^{\frac{1}{2}}$$

Any number that isn't raised to a power has an implied power of 1, so x can be written x^1. And any root can be written with that little number in the "v" of the radical sign, telling you which root to take (if no number is written there, a square root—or root of 2—is assumed).

Take those two numbers, the 1 and the 2, and write them as a fraction. The exponent of the base x is always the numerator of the fraction. The radical number is always the denominator of the fraction.

Try this problem:

What is $64^{\frac{1}{3}}$?

The numerator of the fraction is 1, so raise the base to the power of 1: 64^1. The denominator is 3, so take the cube root: $\sqrt[3]{64^1}$. In order to determine that root, break 64 down:

$$64 = 4 \times 4 \times 4 = 4^3$$

The value 64 is equal to 4^3, so $64^{\frac{1}{3}} = \sqrt[3]{64} = \sqrt[3]{4^3} = 4^{\left(\frac{3}{3}\right)} = 4^1 = 4$.

As a shortcut, if a number is raised to a certain power and also rooted to that same value, you can cancel out the power and the root. In this case, 4 is raised to the power of 3 but also cube-rooted, so cancel the two operations out to get 4.

Try another one:

What is $\left(\frac{1}{8}\right)^{-\frac{4}{3}}$?

Because the exponent is negative, first take the reciprocal of the base, $\left(\frac{1}{8}\right)$, and change the exponent to its positive equivalent. Next, deal with the root and the power. You can do them in whichever order is easier for you:

$$\left(\frac{1}{8}\right)^{-\frac{4}{3}} = 8^{\frac{4}{3}} = \sqrt[3]{8^4} = \left(\sqrt[3]{8}\right)^4 = (2)^4 = 16$$

Above, it's easier to take the cube first, so move that exponent of 4 to the outside. Take the cube root of 8 (which is 2) and then raise the result to the power of 4.

Try one more:

Express $\sqrt[4]{\sqrt{x}}$ as a fractional exponent.

Transform the individual roots into exponents. The square root is equivalent to an exponent of $\frac{1}{2}$, and the fourth root is equivalent to an exponent of $\frac{1}{4}$:

$$\sqrt[4]{\sqrt{x}} = \sqrt[4]{x^{\frac{1}{2}}} = \left(x^{\frac{1}{2}}\right)^{\frac{1}{4}} = x^{\frac{1}{8}}$$

The value $x^{\frac{1}{8}}$ can also be written as $\sqrt[8]{x}$.

Simplifying a Root

Sometimes there are two numbers inside the radical sign that you'd like to combine, if possible. Other times, you may have two different radical signs to simplify. There are certain rules to follow regarding when you can and cannot simplify.

When Can You Simplify Roots?

You can only simplify roots in the ways described below when the roots are connected via multiplication or division. If two roots are added or subtracted, you cannot use this method.

How Can You Simplify Roots?

When multiplying roots, you can split up a larger product into its separate factors, saving you from having to compute large numbers. For example:

$$\sqrt{25 \times 16} = \sqrt{25} \times \sqrt{16} = 5 \times 4 = 20$$

There are two numbers under the same radical sign and each one is a perfect square. Because they are multiplied together, you can take the square root of each first and then multiply them. Here's another example:

$$\sqrt{50} \times \sqrt{18} = \sqrt{50 \times 18} = \sqrt{2 \times 25 \times 2 \times 9} = \sqrt{4 \times 25 \times 9} = 2 \times 5 \times 3 = 30$$

First, the two numbers are not under the same radical, but because they are multiplied, you can combine them under one radical. Next, 50 and 18 are not perfect squares. In this case, break down the numbers into factors and recombine in order to find any perfect squares, then take the square root.

Division of roots works the same way. You can split a larger quotient into two parts. You can also combine two roots that are being divided into a single root. For example:

$$\sqrt{\frac{144}{16}} = \frac{\sqrt{144}}{\sqrt{16}} = \frac{12}{4} = 3$$

$$\frac{\sqrt{72}}{\sqrt{8}} = \sqrt{\frac{72}{8}} = \sqrt{9} = 3$$

However, if the two numbers are added or subtracted, you *cannot* split them apart or put them together. You have to leave them as they are. For example:

$$\sqrt{16 + 9} \rightarrow \sqrt{16} + \sqrt{9}$$
$$\sqrt{25} \qquad\qquad 4 + 3 \qquad \text{This move is illegal.}$$
$$5 \qquad \neq \qquad 7$$

$$\sqrt{16} + \sqrt{9} \quad \rightarrow \quad \sqrt{16 + 9}$$
$$7 \qquad \neq \qquad 5 \qquad \text{So is the reverse.}$$

You may only separate or combine the *product* ($\times$) or *quotient* ($\div$) of two roots. You cannot separate or combine the *sum* or *difference* of two roots.

In this case, first add the numbers together, then take the square root:

$$\sqrt{16 + 9} = \sqrt{25} = 5$$

In this case, first take the square root, then add:

$$\sqrt{16} + \sqrt{9} = 4 + 3 = 7$$

You *can* add two terms together if they have the same value under square root signs. Add only the numbers in front of the roots:

$$2\sqrt{3} + 4\sqrt{3} = 6\sqrt{3}$$

Treat the stuff under the root similar to a variable: $2x + 3x = 5x$. In other words, two x terms plus three x terms gives you five x terms. In the same way, above, two $\sqrt{3}$ terms plus four $\sqrt{3}$ terms gives you six $\sqrt{3}$ terms.

Imperfect vs. Perfect Squares

Not all square roots yield an integer. For example, $\sqrt{52}$ is the root of an imperfect square. It will not yield an integer answer because no integer multiplied by itself will yield 52.

Simplifying Roots of Imperfect Squares

Some imperfect squares can be simplified into multiples of smaller square roots. For an imperfect square such as $\sqrt{52}$, you can rewrite $\sqrt{52}$ as a product of primes under the radical:

$$\sqrt{52} = \sqrt{2 \times 2 \times 13}$$

Since this is a *square* root, look for *pairs* of numbers under the radical. In this case, there is a pair of 2's. Since $\sqrt{2 \times 2} = \sqrt{4} = 2$, you can rewrite $\sqrt{52}$ as follows:

$$\sqrt{52} = \sqrt{4 \times 13} = 2 \times \sqrt{13} = 2\sqrt{13}$$

Basically, identify a pair. Then, pull one of the pair out in front of the radical and eliminate the other number in the pair. Leave any unpaired numbers (13, in this case) under the radical.

Look at another example:

Simplify $\sqrt{72}$.

You can rewrite $\sqrt{72}$ as a product of primes:

$$\sqrt{72} = \sqrt{2 \times 2 \times 2 \times 3 \times 3}$$

Since there are a pair of 2's and a pair of 3's inside the radical, you can pull out one of each:

$$\sqrt{72} = 2 \times 3 \times \sqrt{2} = 6\sqrt{2}$$

Memorize: Squares and Square Roots

Memorize the following squares and square roots, as they often appear on the GMAT. If rote memorization is not a strength for you, take the time to learn the squares that are most likely to pop up on the GMAT: 1 through 12, as well as 15 and 20.

$1^2 = 1$	$\sqrt{1} = 1$
$1.4^2 \approx 2$	$\sqrt{2} \approx 1.4$
$1.7^2 \approx 3$	$\sqrt{3} \approx 1.7$
$2^2 = 4$	$\sqrt{4} = 2$
$3^2 = 9$	$\sqrt{9} = 3$
$4^2 = 16$	$\sqrt{16} = 4$
$5^2 = 25$	$\sqrt{25} = 5$
$6^2 = 36$	$\sqrt{36} = 6$
$7^2 = 49$	$\sqrt{49} = 7$
$8^2 = 64$	$\sqrt{64} = 8$
$9^2 = 81$	$\sqrt{81} = 9$
$10^2 = 100$	$\sqrt{100} = 10$
$11^2 = 121$	$\sqrt{121} = 11$
$12^2 = 144$	$\sqrt{144} = 12$
$13^2 = 169$	$\sqrt{169} = 13$
$14^2 = 196$	$\sqrt{196} = 14$
$15^2 = 225$	$\sqrt{225} = 15$
$16^2 = 256$	$\sqrt{256} = 16$
$20^2 = 400$	$\sqrt{400} = 20$
$25^2 = 625$	$\sqrt{625} = 25$
$30^2 = 900$	$\sqrt{900} = 30$

Memorize: Cubes and Cube Roots

Memorize the following cubes and cube roots, as they often appear on the GMAT:

$1^3 = 1$	$\sqrt[3]{1} = 1$
$2^3 = 8$	$\sqrt[3]{8} = 2$
$3^3 = 27$	$\sqrt[3]{27} = 3$
$4^3 = 64$	$\sqrt[3]{64} = 4$
$5^3 = 125$	$\sqrt[3]{125} = 5$
$10^3 = 1,000$	$\sqrt[3]{1,000} = 10$

Problem Set

Now that you've finished the chapter, try the following problems.

1. For each of these statements, indicate whether the statement is TRUE or FALSE:

    (a) If $x^2 = 11$, then $x = \sqrt{11}$.

    (b) If $x^3 = 11$, then $x = \sqrt[3]{11}$.

    (c) If $x^4 = 16$, then $x = 2$.

    (d) If $x^5 = 32$, then $x = 2$.

2. $\sqrt{18} \div \sqrt{2}$

3. $\left(\dfrac{1}{125}\right)^{-\frac{1}{3}}$

4. $\sqrt{63} + \sqrt{28}$

5. $\sqrt[3]{100 - 36}$

6. Estimate: $\sqrt{60}$

    (A) 6.5

    (B) 7.7

    (C) 8.2

7. $\sqrt{150} - \sqrt{96}$

8. $10\sqrt{12} \div 2\sqrt{3}$

    (A) 4

    (B) 10

    (C) $10\sqrt{2}$

    (D) $10\sqrt{3}$

9. $\dfrac{\sqrt[4]{64}}{\sqrt[4]{4}}$

10. If $xy \neq 0$ and $\sqrt{\dfrac{xy}{3}} = x$, what is y?

    (1) $\dfrac{x}{y} = \dfrac{1}{3}$

    (2) $x = 3$

Solutions

1. (a) **FALSE:** The problem gave you x^2, so you may have two roots, positive and negative. The exponent of 2 is even, so indeed there are both positive and negative roots. If $x^2 = 11$, then $|x| = \sqrt{11}$. Thus, x could be either $\sqrt{11}$ or $-\sqrt{11}$.

    (b) **TRUE:** Odd exponents preserve the sign of the original expression. Therefore, if x^3 is positive, then x must itself be positive. If $x^3 = 11$, then x must be $\sqrt[3]{11}$.

    (c) **FALSE:** Even exponents hide the sign of the original number, so both positive and negative answers are possible. If $x^4 = 16$, then x could be either 2 or -2.

    (d) **TRUE:** Odd exponents preserve the sign of the original expression. Therefore, if x^5 is positive, then x must itself be positive. If $x^5 = 32$, then x must be 2.

2. **3:**
    $$\sqrt{18} \div \sqrt{2} = \sqrt{18 \div 2} = \sqrt{9} = 3$$

3. **5:**
    $$\left(\frac{1}{125}\right)^{-\frac{1}{3}} = 125^{\frac{1}{3}} = \sqrt[3]{125} = \sqrt[3]{5 \times 5 \times 5} = 5$$

4. **$5\sqrt{7}$:** These two roots are added together, so you cannot combine them under one root to start. Simplify separately. At the end, you can combine them because the values under the roots are the same:
    $$\sqrt{63} + \sqrt{28} = \left(\sqrt{9 \times 7}\right) + \left(\sqrt{4 \times 7}\right) = 3\sqrt{7} + 2\sqrt{7} = 5\sqrt{7}$$

5. **4:**
    $$\sqrt[3]{100 - 36} = \sqrt[3]{64} = 4$$

6. **(B) 7.7:** The number 60 is in between two perfect squares—49, which is 7^2, and 64, which is 8^2. The answer, then, must be between 7 and 8 and only answer **(B)** qualifies.

    If you did have to estimate the answer more carefully, here's how: The difference between 64 and 49 is 15, so 60 is a little more than $\frac{2}{3}$ of the way toward 64 from 49. A reasonable estimate for $\sqrt{60}$, then, would be about 7.7, which is a little more than $\frac{2}{3}$ toward 8 from 7.

7. **$\sqrt{6}$:**
    $$\sqrt{150} - \sqrt{96} = \left(\sqrt{25 \times 6}\right) - \left(\sqrt{16 \times 6}\right) = 5\sqrt{6} - 4\sqrt{6} = \sqrt{6}$$

8.   **(B) 10:** You can solve algebraically or estimate. Here's the algebraic solution:

$$10\sqrt{12} \div 2\sqrt{3} = \frac{10\sqrt{4 \times 3}}{2\sqrt{3}} = \frac{20\sqrt{3}}{2\sqrt{3}} = 10$$

Alternatively, you could approximate the values of the square roots. Since 12 is about halfway between 3^2 and 4^2, use 3.5 as an estimate. Also, the square root of 3 is on the memorization list. It equals about 1.7:

$$\frac{10\sqrt{12}}{2\sqrt{3}} \approx \frac{10 \times 3.5}{2 \times 1.7} \approx \frac{35}{3.4} \approx 10$$

Answer **(B)** is the same as the estimate.

9.   **2:**

$$\frac{\sqrt[4]{64}}{\sqrt[4]{4}} = \sqrt[4]{\frac{64}{4}} = \sqrt[4]{16} = 2$$

Note: Since the problem started you with a square root sign, solve for only the positive value.

10. **(B):** The question asks for the value of y, so isolate y in the given equation:

$$\sqrt{\frac{xy}{3}} = x$$

$$\frac{xy}{3} = x^2$$

$$xy = 3x^2 \quad \text{It's okay to divide by } x \text{ since you know that } x \text{ is not 0.}$$

$$y = 3x$$

In other words, if you can find the value of x, then you can also find the value of y. Rephrase the question: What is y or what is x?

(1) INSUFFICIENT: Statement (1) provides the value of $\frac{x}{y}$, but does not provide the value of x and y individually. For example, x could be 1 and y could be 3, or x could be 2 and y could be 6. There are at least two different values for y (or for x), so this statement is not sufficient.

(2) SUFFICIENT: Given x, you can find y.

This problem is a reminder that sometimes what might appear to be a combo question might just involve "school" algebra of solving for a single variable.

The correct answer is **(B):** Statement (2) is sufficient, but statement (1) is not.

Strategy: Arithmetic vs. Algebra 2

In This Chapter

- Good Numbers for Test Cases

- Good Numbers for Smart Numbers

- Problem Solving: Pop Quiz

- Avoid 0 or 1 When Choosing Smart Numbers

In this chapter, you will learn how to select good numbers when using the Test Cases or Smart Numbers strategies.

CHAPTER 13 Strategy: Arithmetic vs. Algebra 2

In an earlier strategy chapter, you learned three ways to turn an algebra problem into an arithmetic (real numbers) problem: Test Cases (TC), Smart Numbers (SN), and Work Backwards (WB). Two of these three types, TC and SN, require you to choose your own numbers and that's the focus of this chapter. (For the third, WB, you'll use the values given in the answer choices.)

One important note: At first, you may find yourself avoiding these test-taking approaches and instead using the textbook approaches that worked for you in school. You've practiced algebra for years, after all, and you've only been using these test-taking techniques for a short period of time. Keep practicing; you'll get better! Every high scorer on the Quant section will tell you that using these strategies where appropriate is invaluable to getting through Quant on time and with a sufficiently consistent performance to reach a top score.

Let's start with a summary of each of the three strategies.

Test Cases

- Data Sufficiency: Use when the problem allows multiple possible values for the unknowns. Try at least two different cases to see whether you can get a different answer (Yes *and* No; two *different* values).

- Problem Solving: Use when the problem asks a *must be* or *could be* question. Test cases until only one answer choice remains.

Choose Smart Numbers

- Problem Solving only

- When you see variable expressions or relative values (such as percents, fractions, ratios) in the answers, check the problem to see whether you can use smart numbers.

- If the problem never gives you a real number for that variable or relative value, you can use smart numbers.

Work Backwards

- Problem Solving only

- When the answer choices are relatively "nice" real numbers, check the problem to see whether you can work backwards.

- If the problem asks you to solve for what would be a single variable (if you were to set things up algebraically), you can work backwards.
- Start from answer (B) or (D).

Working backwards allows you to use the numbers given in the answer choices, but for the first two methods, you'll need to decide what numbers to use—and the guidelines can vary based on the strategy and on what that problem is testing. Knowing how to pick good numbers will save you time and mental effort on the GMAT.

Good Numbers for Test Cases

When using the Test Cases (TC) strategy, your goal is to find two valid cases that result in different answers so that you can prove a statement insufficient (on DS) or prove an answer incorrect (on PS).

When testing cases, people usually start with a small positive integer; that's often a good idea. But it can also be useful to test numbers that have "weird" properties: 0, 1, negatives, primes, fractions between 0 and 1, and so on.

Weird numbers are good ones to try because weird properties often give you a different answer to the question—for example, a Yes and a No answer (on a Yes/No problem) or two different values (on a Value problem). On DS, as soon as you can find two different answers, you've proven that the statement is insufficient.

Consider this problem:

> Is $c = d$?
>
> (1) $cd = 1$
>
> (2) $|c| = d$

Step 1: Understand. At a glance, it's DS. The question asks whether c and d have the same value; jot that down. Glance at the statements. There's an absolute value symbol in one, so negative vs. positive is probably going to come into play.

This is a "theory" problem; it uses variables to ask or say something about certain relationships, but there are no individual numbers that you're locked into using for c and d. Choose your own numbers to test out what would happen in various scenarios (or cases). In short, you can test cases!

Step 2: Plan. Given that absolute value symbol in statement (2), try a negative number. It's also a good idea to pause and ask yourself: What kind of case will give a Yes answer and what kind of case will give a No answer?

In this problem, if c and d are the same number, the answer is Yes. If c and d are different numbers, the answer is No. Your goal when testing cases on this problem: Find one case where they are equal and one case where they're not equal.

Step 3: Solve. Now that you have a plan, do the necessary work to solve. Follow a few guidelines to set up your first case. First, you're only allowed to try numbers that make the *facts* in the problem true. (The statements are always facts. Any givens in the question stem—*not* including the question itself—are facts.)

Second, try numbers that make your job easier. Third, try anything you like for your first case, but for your second case, pause and think about what kinds of other or weird numbers might give you a *different* answer.

Y/N $\boxed{?}$ Is $c = d$? AD / BCE

(1) $cd = 1$

	c	d	V	c=d?
#1	1	1	✓	Y
#2	2	0.5	✓	N

In the first case, start with the simplest weird numbers you can think of. For example, try $c = 1$ and $d = 1$. After you've chosen your numbers, pause for a moment to check that you chose Valid (V) numbers. Do your numbers fit all of the facts given in the question stem and in this statement? (Don't include the second statement.)

The only fact so far is that $cd = 1$. The chosen numbers, $c = d = 1$, correlate with this fact, so your numbers are valid. Continue solving. In this first case, the answer is Yes: $c = d$.

Time to try a second case. Pause for a second. You just got a Yes answer. What would need to happen in order to get a No answer instead?

You would need to find a case in which c does not equal d. Can you think of a case for which $c \neq d$ and they multiply to 1? The product of reciprocals equals 1: $c = 2$ and $d = 0.5$. Pause to make sure this is a valid case; it is. This case gives a No answer. There are two different answers, so statement (1) overall returns a Sometimes Yes/Sometimes No answer; statement (1) is not sufficient to answer the question.

It doesn't matter in which order you try cases, as long as you're trying valid numbers. Try the first valid case you think of and see what answer you get. Then pause to think about what kinds of numbers might give you a different result and try that case next.

Now, test the second statement:

$$Y/N \qquad \boxed{?} \quad \text{Is } c=d? \qquad \cancel{AD} \\ BCE$$

(1) cd = 1	(2) |c| = d

	c	d	V	c=d?
#1	1	1	✓	Y
#2	2	0.5	✓	N

(NS)

	c	d	V	c=d?
#1	1	1	✓	Y
#2	-1	1	✓	N

Since this statement contains an absolute value symbol, try negatives where you can—though it's fine to begin with the "simpler" $c = d = 1$ case, which is a valid case and yields a Yes answer for the second statement. What could give a No answer?

Try a negative! If $c = -1$ and $d = 1$, the answer is No ($c \neq d$), so statement (2) is not sufficient to answer the question. Cross off answer (B).

Put both statements together. First, scan the cases you've already tried. Did you try the same set of numbers for each statement? Yes, $c = d = 1$ worked for each statement individually, so this case will also work for the two statements together. There's your Yes case. Can you find a No?

$$(1 + 2)$$

$$\#1: \ c = 1, d = 1 \ \rightarrow \ Y$$

$$\#2:$$

$$|c| = d$$

$$-1 \text{ or } 1 \ \rightarrow \ 1$$

$$-2 \text{ or } 2 \ \rightarrow \ 2$$

$$\cdots$$

You can try some numbers to see—but first think about how the math works in order to figure out what numbers to try. Start with statement (2) because it has the weirder constraint. What kinds of numbers are allowed? The "plain" value (ignoring the positive/negative sign) must be the same for c and d—the only difference is that c could have a negative sign (but it might not).

What does that mean for statement (1)? This one says that they have to multiply to *positive* 1. In this case, both numbers have to have the same sign—either both positive or both negative:

$$(1 + 2)$$

$$\#1: \ c = 1, \ d = 1 \ \rightarrow \ Y$$

$$\#2:$$

$$cd = 1 \qquad\qquad |c| = d$$

$$\downarrow \qquad\qquad\qquad \cancel{-1} \text{ or } 1 \rightarrow 1$$

$$\text{same sign} \qquad\qquad \cancel{-2} \text{ or } 2 \rightarrow 2$$

$$\cdots$$

$$\text{both pos, same value}$$
$$1 = 1$$
$$c = d \ !$$

So the only possibility left from statement (2) is that the two numbers are the same. The case where c is negative and d is positive doesn't pass the test for statement (1)—that is, a negative c and a positive d would be an invalid case. And since the two values have to multiply to 1, c and d must each equal 1. Therefore, c must in fact equal d, always, using the two statements together.

The correct answer is (C).

Let's recap. When testing cases, your goal is to try to find two conflicting cases (e.g., a Yes and a No) in order to prove a statement insufficient (on DS) or an answer choice incorrect (on PS). As such, you want to try numbers that have certain weird characteristics that might serve to give you these different answers. What kinds of numbers? That will depend on clues you find in the specific problem you're trying to solve.

For example, the problem you just did had an absolute value symbol, so that was a clue to try negatives and positives.

In the Exponents chapter, you learned that squaring most numbers will make them larger—but that squaring a fraction between 0 and 1 will make that fraction smaller. In addition, squaring 0 or 1 will result in no change. So if you need to test cases on a problem that includes exponents, think about trying 0, 1, or fractions between 0 and 1 (as long as you're allowed to—you can only try numbers that are valid for the given facts in the problem).

Start keeping a list or make flash cards to help you remember the clues that will point you toward certain numbers to test.

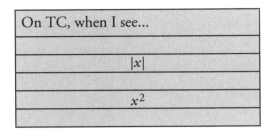
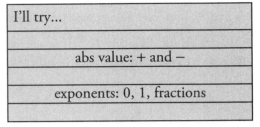

On TC, when I see...		I'll try...
$|x|$		abs value: $+$ and $-$
x^2		exponents: 0, 1, fractions

Good Numbers for Smart Numbers

The considerations for "good" numbers are different when you **choose smart numbers**. Here, you usually *don't* want to go for the weird numbers, because your goal is to pick numbers that will lead directly to the correct answer—so you don't want those numbers doing weird things in the middle of the problem.

When choosing numbers for SN, avoid 0 and 1. Also avoid numbers that already appear in the problem. (When you become very practiced, you may decide to break this rule and use one of these numbers for some very good reason—but for right now, follow these guidelines.)

If you have to pick values for two or more variables, choose different values for each variable. If appropriate, pick numbers that have different characteristics—for example, if the problem has some clue that causes you to think that even/odd concepts are being tested, then choose one even and one odd.

Finally, think about what's going on in the problem and try to choose numbers that will make your task easier.

Try this problem:

> A store sold a packet of 10 identical pens for a total of x dollars. The store originally purchased the packet of pens for 80% of the amount for which it sold the packet. In terms of x, how much profit did the store make on a single pen?
>
> (A) $\dfrac{x}{5}$
>
> (B) $\dfrac{x}{10}$
>
> (C) $\dfrac{4x}{5}$
>
> (D) $\dfrac{x}{50}$
>
> (E) $\dfrac{4x}{50}$

Step 1: Understand. At a glance, this is PS. The answers contain variables. Can you use smart numbers? Yes, the problem talks about a price for the pens but never mentions a real number for price anywhere along the way. The question asks how much *profit* was made on *one* pen. Finally, note that Profit = Revenue − Cost (the GMAT expects you to know this formula).

Step 2: Plan. Make your life easy and choose a number that will work nicely in the problem. You bought 10 pens for x dollars. The problem asks for the profit in terms of just 1 pen, not all 10, so you're going to need to divide by 10 at some point. Choose something that is a multiple of 10. Make this small but not 10 itself (in general, avoid choosing numbers that already appear in the problem). Try $x = \$20$.

Step 3: Solve. The store sold the 10 pens for a total of $20, or $2 per pen. The store earned a revenue of $2 per pen.

Its *cost* for the pens was 80% of the sales price, so its *profit* is 20% of the sales price. Use benchmarks to find 20% of $2:

$$100\% = \$2$$
$$10\% = \$0.20$$
$$20\% = \$0.40$$

The profit for one pen was $0.40.

None of the answers say $0.40 though. Plug $x = 20$ into the answers and look for the one that matches $0.40. At any point that you can tell that a particular answer will *not* equal $0.40, stop and cross off that answer:

(A) $\dfrac{x}{5} = \dfrac{20}{5} =$ not 0.4

(B) $\dfrac{x}{10} = \dfrac{20}{10} =$ not 0.4

(C) $\dfrac{4x}{5} = \dfrac{4(20)}{5} =$ too big

(D) $\dfrac{x}{50} = \dfrac{20}{50} = 0.4 =$ a match!

(E) $\dfrac{4x}{50} = \dfrac{4(20)}{50} = \dfrac{80}{50} =$ too big

The correct answer is (D).

Here's the algebraic solution:

The store sold 10 pens for a total of x dollars, or $\dfrac{x}{10}$ dollars per pen. The store bought the pens for 80% of that sale price. Profit equals revenue minus cost:

$$(\text{Profit per pen}) = (\text{Revenue per pen}) - (\text{Cost per pen})$$
$$P = \frac{x}{10} - \frac{4}{5}\left(\frac{x}{10}\right)$$
$$P = \frac{x}{10} - \frac{4x}{50}$$
$$P = \frac{5x}{50} - \frac{4x}{50}$$
$$P = \frac{x}{50}$$

The correct answer is (D). That may seem like fewer steps, but it's harder to set up. And take a look at some of the wrong answers:

(A) $\frac{x}{5}$ Mistake: Assume x is cost per pen, instead of $\frac{x}{10}$.

(C) $\frac{4x}{5}$ Mistake: Assume x is cost per pen, instead of $\frac{x}{10}$, *and* solve for cost rather than profit.

(E) $\frac{4x}{50}$ Mistake: Solve for cost rather than profit.

It's very easy, when doing algebra, to make either of those mistakes—or both. And the most common algebraic mistakes are always built into the answers on PS. You have a much better chance of avoiding those mistakes when you are working with real numbers (because everybody is better at arithmetic than algebra).

As a general rule, if you find the algebra very easy, go ahead and solve that way. When the algebra becomes harder for you, though, then switch to smart numbers. If you realize you made a careless mistake with the algebra, that may be a signal to try smart numbers instead.

You can, of course, make careless mistakes whether using algebra or real numbers. Whichever approach you choose to use, do make sure to write down what your variables stand for (in the above, x = total $) and double-check what you're solving for (profit for *one* pen).

Problem Solving: Pop Quiz

On Data Sufficiency, you can use only Test Cases. But on Problem Solving, you can use all three strategies, so part of your task will be to quickly identify which strategy is appropriate for any given question.

Pop Quiz! Take about 30 seconds to decide for both questions which strategy you could use. Then go ahead and try the two problems:

1. The price of a certain computer is increased by 10%, and then the new price is increased by an additional 5%. The new price is what percent of the original price?

    (A) 120%
    (B) 119.5%
    (C) 117%
    (D) 115.5%
    (E) 115%

2. If $ab > 0$, which of the following must be negative?

    (A) $a + b$
    (B) $|a| + b$
    (C) $b - a$
    (D) $\frac{a}{b}$
    (E) $-\frac{a}{b}$

Ready? What did you think?

Use...	When you see...
Test Cases	Data Sufficiency "theory" problem OR
	Problem Solving with a *must be* or *could be* question
Smart Numbers	Problem Solving with variables or relative values (percents, fractions, ratios) in the answers and *no* real numbers given for the variables or for items mentioned in the problem (e.g., number of cats, cups of sugar, dollars)
Work Backwards	Problem Solving with real values in the answers. The answer choices represent a single variable in the problem.

The first problem is a Smart Numbers problem and the second one is a Test Cases problem.

> The price of a certain computer is increased by 10%, and then the new price is increased by an additional 1%. The new price is what percent of the original price?
>
> (A) 120%
> (B) 119.5%
> (C) 117%
> (D) 115.5%
> (E) 115%

Step 1: Understand. PS with percentages in the answers. Check the problem: no real values given for the price. You can use smart numbers or solve algebraically.

Step 2: Plan. Think through what's going on. First, the price goes up 10%, and then the new price goes up another 5%. This is successive percent increase, so the increase is *not* just 10% + 5% = 15%. Further, it has to be *more* than 15% because the second (5%) increase is based on a larger starting number. Cross off answer (E).

Working algebraically on this problem is likely to be pretty annoying. Try choosing a smart number instead. Since this is a percent problem, use 100. (On percent problems in general, unless the number 100 shows up in the problem, it's a good idea to use 100 as your smart number.)

Step 3: Solve. Starting price is $100.

First increase: $100 + 10% = $100 + $10 = $110

Second increase: $110 + 5% = $110 + $5.50 = $115.50

Don't forget to use benchmarks when calculating percents! To get 5% of a number, take 10% and divide that by 2:

$$\text{Percentage:} \ \frac{\text{new}}{\text{orig}} \times 100 = \frac{115.5}{100} \times 100 = 115.5\%$$

Notice, at the end, how you both divide and multiply by 100, so they cancel out? This is why choosing 100 on a percent problem is a good idea.

The correct answer is (D).

The second problem was the Test Cases problem.

If $ab > 0$, which of the following must be negative?

(A) $a + b$

(B) $|a| + b$

(C) $b - a$

(D) $\dfrac{a}{b}$

(E) $-\dfrac{a}{b}$

Step 1: Understand. PS. Asks a *must be* "theory" question, so test cases. Jot down $ab > 0$.

Step 2: Plan. Think about the kinds of numbers that you could try: 0 and 1, fractions, negatives, etc. What would be good to try here?

Since the question asks what must be negative, you'd want to include negatives in the mix. Also, what does the inequality $ab > 0$ signify? Two things multiply together to be positive. First, that means neither variable can be 0, so don't try 0. It also means that the two numbers have to have the same sign, either both positive or both negative.

Step 3: Solve. Go straight for a negative-negative case:

$$a = -1$$
$$b = -2$$

(A) $a + b$	neg
(B) $|a| + b$	neg
(C) $b - a$	neg
(D) $\dfrac{a}{b}$	~~pos~~
(E) $-\dfrac{a}{b}$	neg

The question wants to know what must be negative, so cross off anything that's positive. When you're done, review any answers still in the mix to see what you might want to change in your next case in order to get a positive answer next time.

For example, choice (A) is negative for the first set of numbers, but you're allowed to choose positive numbers, too. And if you do, choice (A) will drop out. So will choice (B). You may even notice some of these things as you work through your first case; if so, jot down a reminder for what to use for your second case.

$$a = -1 \qquad a = 2$$
$$b = -2 \qquad b = 1$$

		$a=-1, b=-2$	$a=2, b=1$
(A)	$a+b$	~~neg~~	~~pos~~
(B)	$|a|+b$	~~neg~~	~~pos~~
(C)	$b-a$	neg	neg
(D)	$\dfrac{a}{b}$	~~pos~~	
(E)	$-\dfrac{a}{b}$	neg	neg

Choices (C) and (E) both stayed negative. If you're going to use positive values, then you need variable *b* to be larger than variable *a* in order to get choice (C) to drop out. Prove it to yourself with a concrete case:

$$a = -1 \qquad a = 2 \qquad a = 1$$
$$b = -2 \qquad b = 1 \qquad b = 2$$

		$a=-1, b=-2$	$a=2, b=1$	$a=1, b=2$
(A)	$a+b$	~~neg~~	~~pos~~	
(B)	$|a|+b$	~~neg~~	~~pos~~	
(C)	$b-a$	~~neg~~	~~neg~~	~~pos~~
(D)	$\dfrac{a}{b}$	~~pos~~		
(E)	$-\dfrac{a}{b}$	neg	neg	neg ✓

Finally! The correct answer is (E). No matter what you try, this one stays negative.

As you worked through the problem, you might have begun to "see" the theory. For instance, on that last step, you might have felt comfortable that answer (C) would drop out as soon as you made variable *b* larger than variable *a*. Any time you feel confident in your reasoning, it's okay not to plug in actual values to test. You're still testing the case—you're just using number characteristics rather than specific numbers.

Note one more thing. If you know that you're prone to careless mistakes on any specific kinds of math (e.g., absolute values or fractions), then write out the math itself, not just the "pos" and "neg" designations.

Everyone makes careless errors with some kinds of seemingly simple math. Know your own patterns to help you minimize mistakes!

Avoid 0 or 1 When Choosing Smart Numbers

For the Smart Numbers strategy, you've learned to avoid using 0, 1, or a number that appears elsewhere in the problem. Here's why. Try this example:

> A truck can carry *x* shipping containers and each container can hold *y* gallons of milk. If one truck is filled to capacity and a second truck is half full, how many gallons of milk are they carrying, in terms of *x* and *y* ?
>
> (A) $x + 0.5y$
>
> (B) $x + y$
>
> (C) $0.5xy$
>
> (D) $1.5xy$
>
> (E) $2xy$

13

Step 1: Understand. PS. Variables in the answers. No real numbers in the problem. You can use smart numbers, if you like.

What's the actual story? One truck holds some number of shipping containers and each shipping container holds some number of gallons of milk. And there are two trucks. Sketch something out. It doesn't need to be pretty! Just use the sketch to help understand the story.

There are two trucks. One's full and the other is half full. Each one has the same number of shipping containers (how about 1?) and each container can carry…how about 3 gallons of milk?

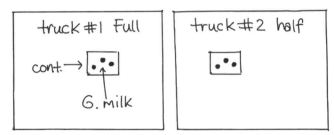

Don't worry at this stage about whether those are the right numbers to pick (it turns out that what's sketched above doesn't quite fit all the facts in the story—so you will have to adjust). Just focus on understanding the story first.

Step 2: Plan. Once you understand, you can decide what to do. The drawing shows $x = 1$ and $y = 3$. At this stage, you'd normally tell yourself, "Whoops, I'm not supposed to use 1 on smart numbers," but keep going so that you can see what could happen when you do.

Step 3: Solve. Okay, $x = 1$ and $y = 3$. Each truck has one shipping container. The first truck is filled to capacity, so it carries a total of 3 gallons of milk. The second is half full, so it carries 1.5 gallons…ugh, decimals are annoying.

That's okay! Just go back and tweak your drawing/numbers to give you integer values instead. What if $x = 1$ and $y = 2$, instead? Now, here's the scenario: The first truck is filled to capacity, so it has 2 gallons of milk. The second is half full, so it carries 1 gallon; together, the two trucks carry 3 gallons of milk.

Plug $x = 1$ and $y = 2$ into the answers to find the one that equals 3:

(A) $x + 0.5y = 1 + (0.5)(2) = 2$

(B) $x + y = 1 + 2 = 3$ Match!

(C) $0.5xy = (0.5)(1)(2) = 1$

(D) $1.5xy = (1.5)(1)(2) = 3$ Wait a second—this one matches, too!

(E) $2xy = 2(1)(2) = 4$

In rare circumstances, when using the Smart Numbers strategy, the number you choose could work for more than one answer choice. The odds are greatly increased if you choose 0, 1, or a number that already appears in the problem—so that's why you want to avoid those numbers when using the Smart Numbers strategy. (Incidentally, this is the same reason why you *do* want to use 0 or 1 when testing cases on PS. Because that can make multiple answers drop out at once!)

If you do get two answers that work, now what? If you think you've spent too much time already, guess between (B) and (D), the two answers that worked; you still have a 50/50 chance. Or, if you have time, try a different set of numbers in the problem—but you only need to check answers (B) and (D) when you get to the end.

Try $x = 2$ containers and $y = 3$ gallons of milk per container instead.

The first truck is now carrying $(2)(3) = 6$ gallons of milk. The second carries half that, or 3 gallons. Together, they carry 9 gallons of milk.

Try (B) and (D):

(B) $x + y = 2 + 3 = 5$ Not a match

(D) $1.5xy = (1.5)(2)(3) = 9$ Match!

The correct answer is (D).

If you follow the guidelines for choosing numbers, then the "two answers work!" situation is much less likely to occur:

- Avoid 0 and 1.
- Avoid numbers that appear elsewhere in the problem.
- If you have to choose multiple numbers, choose different numbers.

If you do accidentally find yourself in this situation and you have the time, then go back, change one of the numbers in your problem, and do the math again. If you don't have time, just choose one of the two answers that did work and move on.

Finally, this is important enough to repeat: At first, you may find yourself always choosing the textbook or algebraic approach. You've practiced algebra for years, after all, and you've only been using these test-taking techniques for a short period of time. Keep practicing; you'll get better!

Problem Set

Practice your test-taking strategies: Smart Numbers, Test Cases, Work Backwards. Try the algebraic/ textbook way as well to compare methods. When you're done, ask yourself which way you prefer to solve *this* problem and why.

On the real test, you won't have time to try both methods; you'll have to make a decision and go with it. Learn *how* to make that decision while studying; then, the next time a new problem pops up in front of you, you'll be able to make a quick (and good!) decision about what to do.

1. Seamus has 3 times as many marbles as Ronit, and Taj has 7 times as many marbles as Ronit. If Seamus has s marbles, then, in terms of s, how many marbles do Seamus, Ronit, and Taj have together?

   (A) $\frac{3}{7}s$

   (B) $\frac{7}{3}s$

   (C) $\frac{11}{3}s$

   (D) $7s$

   (E) $11s$

2. Machine X produces cartons at a uniform rate of 90 every 3 minutes, and Machine Y produces cartons at a uniform rate of 100 every 2 minutes. Working simultaneously, the two machines would produce a total of 560 cartons in how many minutes?

   (A) 7

   (B) 6

   (C) 5

   (D) 4

   (E) 3

3. If $x = a + b$ and $y = a + 2b$, then what is $a - b$, in terms of x and y ?

   (A) $2y - 3x$

   (B) $3y - 2x$

   (C) $2x - 3y$

   (D) $2x + 3y$

   (E) $3x - 2y$

4. If $x < y$, which of the following must be true?

   (A) $x < y^2$

   (B) $x^2 < y$

   (C) $x^2 < y^2$

   (D) $(x - y)^2 > 0$

   (E) $x^3 > y$

Save the next problems for review after you finish this entire guide.

5. A train travels at a constant rate. If the train takes 13 minutes to travel m kilometers, how long will the train take to travel n kilometers?

    (A) $\dfrac{13m}{n}$

    (B) $\dfrac{13n}{m}$

    (C) $13mn$

    (D) $\dfrac{n}{13}$

    (E) $\dfrac{m}{13}$

6. A manager split a bonus award among four employees. The first employee received $\frac{1}{3}$ of the total, the second received $\frac{1}{4}$ of the total, the third received $\frac{1}{5}$ of the total, and the fourth received the remaining \$195. What was the total bonus amount awarded to the four employees?

    (A) \$500

    (B) \$600

    (C) \$750

    (D) \$900

    (E) \$1,000

13

Solutions

1. **(C)** $\frac{11}{3}s$**:** The problem will be easier to solve if you can choose smart numbers that will give you all integers as you solve. Both Seamus and Taj have a multiple of the number of marbles that Ronit has, so begin by picking for Ronit, not for Seamus. If Ronit has 2 marbles, then Seamus has $(3)(2) = 6$ marbles and Taj has $(7)(2) = 14$ marbles. Together, the three have 22 marbles.

    Plug $s = 6$ into the answers (remember that the problem asks about Seamus's starting number, not Ronit's!), and look for a match of 22:

    (A) $\frac{3}{7}s =$ not an integer

    (B) $\frac{7}{3}s = \frac{7}{3}(6) = 14$. Not a match.

    (C) $\frac{11}{3}s = \frac{11}{3}(6) = 22$. Match!

    (D) $7s = 42$. Not a match.

    (E) $11s =$ too large

    Alternatively, you can use an algebraic approach. Begin by translating the first sentence into equations:

    $$s = 3r$$
    $$t = 7r$$

    The question asks for the sum of the three:

    $$s + r + t = ?$$

    The answers use only s, so figure out how to substitute to leave only s in the equation:

    $$r = \frac{s}{3}$$
    $$t = 7r = 7\left(\frac{s}{3}\right)$$

    Substitute those into the question:

    $$s + r + t$$
    $$s + \frac{s}{3} + 7\left(\frac{s}{3}\right)$$
    $$\frac{3s}{3} + \frac{s}{3} + \frac{7s}{3}$$
    $$\frac{11s}{3}$$

2. **(A) 7:** The answer choices are real numbers and they represent a single variable in the problem (how long it would take the two machines together to produce 560 cartons). Work backwards from the answers. Start with answer (B) or (D).

Minutes	X 90 cart in 3 min	Y 100 cart in 2 min	Total cartons produced	= 560 ?
(B) 6	180	300	480	No

Answer (B) is incorrect; in 6 minutes, the two machines will have produced only 480 cartons, not 560. Further, the number of minutes must be greater than 6 (in order for more cartons to be produced).

Only answer (A) is greater than 6, so it must be correct.

If you're not sure about that reasoning, try answer (D) next. In 4 minutes, the two machines produce 320 cartons, even fewer! This confirms the trend that a lower number of minutes will produce fewer cartons, so the answer must be **(A)**.

3. **(E) $3x - 2y$:** With so many variables, choosing smart numbers will probably be more efficient. Because x and y can be found by certain sums of a and b, pick for a and b, then calculate x and y.

If $a = 5$ and $b = 2$, then $x = 5 + 2 = 7$ and $y = 5 + 2(2) = 9$. The difference is $a - b = 5 - 2 = 3$.

Plug $x = 7$ and $y = 9$ into the answers and look for a match of 3:

(A) $2y - 3x = 2(9) - 3(7) = 18 - 21 =$ negative

(B) $3y - 2x = 3(9) - 2(7) = 27 - 14 =$ not 3

(C) $2x - 3y = 2(7) - 3(9) = 14 - 27 =$ negative

(D) $2x + 3y = 2(7) + 3(9) =$ too big

(E) $3x - 2y = 3(7) - 2(9) = 21 - 18 = 3.$ Match!

You can also use an algebraic approach.

Given: $x = a + b$
Given: $y = a + 2b$
What is $a - b$?

The answers use only x and y, so figure out how to rewrite the given equations to plug into the question, using only x and y.

If you subtract the two equations, you'll get x and y in terms of b alone:

$$y = a + 2b$$
$$\underline{- (x = a + b)}$$
$$y - x = b$$

Multiply the $x = a + b$ equation by 2 and perform the same operation to get x and y in terms of a alone:

$$2x = 2a + 2b$$
$$\underline{- (y = a + 2b)}$$
$$2x - y = a$$

Then, find $a - b$:

$$(2x - y) - (y - x)$$
$$2x - y - y + x$$
$$3x - 2y$$

4.   **(D)** $(x - y)^2 > 0$: The *must be* language signals that you can (and probably want to) test cases on this problem. The only constraint given is that x is less than y. The answers contain exponents and one contains > 0, so test negatives and fractions between 0 and 1, as well as 0 and 1 themselves.

Answer	$x = 0$ $y = 1$	$x = -1$ $y = 0$	$x = \frac{1}{4}$ $y = \frac{1}{2}$
(A) $x < y^2$	$0 < 1$ True	$-1 < 0$ True	(A) $\frac{1}{4} < \frac{1}{4}$ False
(B) $x^2 < y$	$0 < 1$ True	$1 < 0$ False	already eliminated
(C) $x^2 < y^2$	$0 < 1$ True	$1 < 0$ False	already eliminated
(D) $(x - y)^2 > 0$	$1 > 0$ True	$1 > 0$ True	(D) $\left(-\frac{1}{4}\right)^2 = \frac{1}{16} > 0$ True!
(E) $x^3 > y$	$0 > 1$ False	already eliminated	

Try the easiest combo first, something involving 0 and 1. That only knocks out one answer, but it helps you to think about what's going on with the math. Sometimes x is squared, sometimes y is squared, so put a negative number into the mix next. (Note: You no longer have to try answer (E); it drops out after the first case.)

When x is -1 and y is 0, two more answers drop out, but two are still left. Fractions between 0 and 1 do interesting things when squared, so try those next. In this final case, answer (A) is false. Answer **(D)** is true throughout all of the tests, so it's the correct answer.

5.   **(B)** $\frac{13n}{m}$: The problem never provides a real number for the distance that the train travels, just the variables m and n, so you can choose your own smart number. A small number like 2 is often a good one to choose—but that turns out not to be a great number in this case. Why?

The train takes 13 minutes to travel 2 kilometers, so the train's rate is 2 kilometers per 13 minutes. That's not a nice number. Choose something that will result in an integer, such as $m = 26$ kilometers. Now, the train is going $\frac{26 \text{ km}}{13 \text{ min}} = 2 \frac{\text{km}}{\text{min}}$.

Next, how long will the train take to go n kilometers? If $n = 10$, then the train will take 5 minutes to go 10 kilometers.

Find a match in the answers. Plug $m = 26$ and $n = 10$ into the answers. Your goal is to find an answer choice that equals 5. If you can tell that a certain answer will *not* equal 5, cross it off without calculating exactly what it does equal:

(A) $\frac{13m}{n} = \frac{13(26)}{10} =$ too big

(B) $\frac{13n}{m} = \frac{13(10)}{26} =$ maybe. Simplify to confirm: $\frac{1(10)}{2} = 5$ Match!

(C) $13mn = 13(10)(26) =$ too big

(D) $\frac{n}{13} = \frac{10}{13} =$ fraction

(E) $\frac{m}{13} = \frac{26}{13} = 2$. Not a match.

6. **(D) $900:** You can solve this problem algebraically or you can work backwards. You'd have to find a common denominator across three fractions to solve algebraically, so it may be faster to work backwards, since the fractions are relatively easy ones and the numbers in the answers are pretty nice. Start with answer (B).

	#1 $\left(\frac{1}{3}\right)$	#2 $\left(\frac{1}{4}\right)$	#3 $\left(\frac{1}{5}\right)$	#4 ($195)	Sum to the choice?
(B) 600	200	150	120	195	NO

To find a third, divide by 3. To find a fourth, divide by 2 twice. To find a fifth, or 20%, take 10% and double it.

The total won't be $600 because three of the numbers end in a 0 and the fourth ends in a 5, so answer (B) isn't correct. Is this answer too big or too small? Examine the first three figures—the ones that can actually change from answer choice to answer choice.

The first three figures add up to 470. If the total is 600, then the fourth person would get a bonus of 130. But the fourth person's bonus is actually 195, so this answer choice falls short. You need a larger number. Cross off answers (A) and (B) and try (D) next.

	#1 $\left(\frac{1}{3}\right)$	#2 $\left(\frac{1}{4}\right)$	#3 $\left(\frac{1}{5}\right)$	#4 ($195)	Sum to the choice?
(B) 600	200	150	120	195	NO
(D) 900	300	225	180	195	Yes!

This could be right, since two of the answers end in 5 now. Add them up, but make your job easier; 195 is an annoying value, so take 5 from the 225 and add it to the 195.

Don't do: $300 + 225 + 180 + 195$

Instead, do: $300 + 220 + 180 + 200 = 300 + 400 + 200 = 900$

The total matches the starting point, so this choice is the correct answer.

Quadratic Equations

In This Chapter

In this chapter, you will learn how to factor and expand quadratic equations, and you'll memorize three special quadratics (known as the special products) that will save you time and mental energy on the GMAT. You'll also learn some common ways that the GMAT likes to disguise quadratic equations—and how to recognize and strip away those disguises.

CHAPTER 14 Quadratic Equations

One special type of equation is called the **quadratic equation**. Here are some examples of quadratic equations:

$$x^2 + 3x + 8 = 12 \qquad w^2 - 16w + 1 = 0 \qquad 2y^2 - y + 5 = 8$$

The standard form of a quadratic equation is $ax^2 + bx + c = 0$, where a, b, and c are constants and a does not equal 0.

Here are other ways of writing quadratics (in nonstandard form):

$$x^2 = 3x + 4 \qquad a = 5a^2 \qquad 6 - b = 7b^2$$

Like other even-exponent equations, quadratic equations generally have two solutions. That is, there are usually two possible values of x (or whatever the variable is) that make the equation *true*.

Factoring Quadratic Equations

The following example illustrates the process for solving quadratic equations:

If $x^2 + 3x + 8 = 12$, what is x?

To start, move everything to the left side of the equals sign so that the equation is equal to 0. Put the left side in the form $ax^2 + bx + c$ (where a, b, and c are typically integers on the GMAT):

$$x^2 + 3x + 8 = 12 \qquad \text{Subtract 12 from both sides to set the right side to 0.}$$
$$x^2 + 3x - 4 = 0$$

Next, factor the equation. In order to factor, you generally need to think about two terms in the equation. Assuming that $a = 1$ (which is often the case on GMAT quadratic equation problems), focus on the two terms b and c. (If a is not equal to 1, divide everything in the equation by a to make a equal to 1.)

$$x^2 + 3x - 4 = 0$$

Rewrite the equation in the form $(x + \quad)(x + \quad)$, where the blanks represent two spaces you're leaving for numbers that you're about to calculate.

In order to factor this equation, find two integers whose product is equal to c (-4 in this equation) and whose sum is equal to b (3 in this equation).

In the original equation, $a = 1$, $b = 3$, and $c = -4$. To fill in the blanks, find the pair of numbers that will *multiply* to -4 and *add* to $+3$. The GMAT will typically make these integers, so think in those terms. In order for c to be negative, the numbers in the blanks will have to have the opposite signs. Now think of the specific values that are possible:

$$x^2 + 3x - 4 = 0$$
$$(x + \quad)(x - \quad) = 0$$

For example, 2 and -2 multiply to -4, but they do not add to 3, so this is not the right pairing. The other integer possibility is some combination of 4 and 1. Which one should get the negative sign in order to add to positive 3 ?

Make the 4 positive and the 1 negative: 4 and -1 multiply to -4 and add to 3. Place these in the spaces in the parentheses:

$$x^2 + 3x - 4 = 0$$
$$(x + 4)(x - 1) = 0$$

The two terms on the left-hand side multiply to 0, so one or both of the terms must be equal to 0. As another example, if you know that $M \times N = 0$, then you know that either $M = 0$ or $N = 0$ (or both M and N are 0).

In this problem, set each factor in parentheses independently to 0 and solve for x:

$$x + 4 = 0 \quad \text{OR} \quad x - 1 = 0$$
$$x = -4 \qquad\qquad x = 1$$

Therefore, the two solutions of the quadratic equation $x^2 + 3x + 8 = 12$ are -4 and 1. The solutions of a quadratic equation are also sometimes called its *roots*. If you see the word *root* in conjunction with a quadratic equation, this word is a synonym for *solution*.

Disguised Quadratics

The GMAT will often attempt to disguise quadratic equations by putting them in forms that do not quite look like the traditional form of $ax^2 + bx + c = 0$.

Here is a very common "disguised" form for a quadratic:

$$3w^2 = 6w$$

This is a quadratic equation because it contains both a w^2 term and a plain w term. The classic misake is to try to solve this equation without thinking of it as a quadratic:

$$3w^2 = 6w \qquad \text{Divide both sides by } w.$$
$$3w = 6 \qquad \text{Divide both sides by 3.}$$
$$w = 2$$

The value 2 is one possible solution to this equation—but there's another! If you solve this equation without factoring it like a quadratic, you will miss one of the solutions. Here is how it should be solved:

$$3w^2 = 6w$$
$$3w^2 - 6w = 0$$
$$w(3w - 6) = 0$$

Setting both factors equal to 0 yields the following solutions:

$$w = 0 \quad \text{OR} \quad 3w - 6 = 0$$
$$3w = 6$$
$$w = 2$$

If you recognize that $3w^2 = 6w$ is a disguised quadratic, you will find both solutions instead of accidentally missing one (in this case, the solution $w = 0$).

Here is another example of a disguised quadratic:

Solve for b, given that $\frac{36}{b} = b - 5$.

At first glance, this does not look like a quadratic equation at all. But it's annoying to have a variable on the bottom of a fraction, so try to get rid of that. Watch what happens:

$$\frac{36}{b} = b - 5 \qquad \text{Multiply both sides of the equation by } b.$$
$$36 = b^2 - 5b$$

Now this looks like a quadratic! Solve it by factoring:

$$36 = b^2 - 5b \qquad \text{Subtract 36 from both sides to set the equation equal to 0.}$$
$$b^2 - 5b - 36 = 0$$
$$(b - 9)(b + 4) = 0 \qquad \text{Thus, } b = 9 \text{ or } b = -4.$$

Some quadratics are hidden within more difficult equations, such as higher order equations (in which a variable is raised to the power of 3 or more). On the GMAT, these equations can almost always be factored to find the hidden quadratic expression. For example:

Solve for x, given that $x^3 + 2x^2 - 3x = 0$.

$$x^3 + 2x^2 - 3x = 0 \qquad \text{Factor out an } x \text{ from each term.}$$
$$x\left(x^2 + 2x - 3\right) = 0$$

Now, factor the quadratic:

$$x\left(x^2 + 2x - 3\right) = 0$$
$$x(x + 3)(x - 1) = 0$$
$$x = 0 \quad \text{OR} \quad x + 3 = 0 \quad \text{OR} \quad x - 1 = 0$$

This equation has *three* solutions: 0, −3, and 1.

This example illustrates a general rule:

> If you have a quadratic expression equal to 0, *and* you can factor an x out of the expression, then $x = 0$ is a solution of the equation.

Do not just divide both sides by x. If you do so, you will eliminate the solution $x = 0$. You are only allowed to divide by a variable if you are absolutely sure that the variable does not equal 0.

Taking the Square Root

So far you have seen how to solve quadratic equations by setting one side of the equation equal to 0 and factoring. However, some quadratic problems can be solved without setting one side equal to 0. If the other side of the equation is a perfect square, the problem can be solved by taking the square root of both sides of the equation. For example:

If $(z + 3)^2 = 25$, what is z ?

Take the square root of both sides of the equation to solve for z. You just have to consider both the positive and the negative square root:

$$\sqrt{(z + 3)^2} = \sqrt{25}$$
$$z + 3 = \pm 5$$
$$z = -3 \pm 5$$
$$z = \{2, -8\}$$

Going in Reverse: Use FOIL

Instead of starting with a quadratic equation and factoring it, you may need to start with factors and rewrite them as a quadratic equation (this is known as *expanding* the quadratic). To do this, use a multiplication process called FOIL: First, Outer, Inner, Last.

To change the expression $(x + 7)(x - 3)$ into a quadratic equation, use FOIL as follows:

First: Multiply the *first term* of each factor together: $(x)(x) = x^2$.

Outer: Multiply the *outer terms* of the expression together: $(x)(-3) = -3x$.

Inner: Multiply the *inner terms* of the expression together: $(7)(x) = 7x$.

Last: Multiply the *last term* of each factor together: $(7)(-3) = -21$.

Now, there are four terms: $x^2 - 3x + 7x - 21$. Combine the two middle terms for the fully simplified quadratic expression: $x^2 + 4x - 21$.

If you encounter a quadratic equation or expression, try factoring it. On the other hand, if you encounter the product of factors such as $(x + 7)(x - 3)$, you may need to use FOIL. Note that if the product of factors equals 0, you should be ready to *interpret* the meaning. For instance, if you are given $(x + k)(x - m) = 0$, then you know that $x = -k$ or $x = m$.

One-Solution Quadratics

Not all quadratic equations have two solutions. Some have only one solution. One-solution quadratics are also called perfect square quadratics, because both roots are the same. Consider the following examples:

$$x^2 + 8x + 16 = 0$$
$$(x + 4)(x + 4) = 0 \qquad \text{Here, the only solution for } x \text{ is } -4.$$
$$(x + 4)^2 = 0$$

$$x^2 - 6x + 9 = 0$$
$$(x - 3)(x - 3) = 0 \qquad \text{Here, the only solution for } x \text{ is } 3.$$
$$(x - 3)^2 = 0$$

When you see a quadratic equation, look for two solutions, but be aware that some circumstances will lead to just one solution. As long as you understand how the math works, you'll know when you should have two solutions and when you should have just one.

Zero in the Denominator: Undefined

When 0 appears in the denominator of an expression, then that expression is called *undefined*. The GMAT (thankfully!) doesn't go into this territory. Consider the following:

What are the solutions to the equation $\dfrac{x^2 + x - 12}{x - 2} = 0$?

For such a question, the GMAT would always first tell you that $x \neq 2$. If x did equal 2, then the bottom of that equation would be 0—and the GMAT won't allow that.

The numerator contains a quadratic equation. Since it is a good idea to start solving quadratic equations by factoring, factor this numerator as follows:

$$\frac{x^2 + x - 12}{x - 2} = 0 \rightarrow \frac{(x - 3)(x + 4)}{x - 2} = 0$$

If either of the factors in the numerator is 0, then the entire expression equals 0. Thus, the solutions (roots) to this equation are $x = 3$ or $x = -4$. (And, for the purposes of finding the roots, you can ignore the denominator, since the test will tell you that it does not equal 0.)

14

The Three Special Products

Three quadratic expressions called **Special Products** come up so frequently on the GMAT that it pays to memorize them. They are GMAT favorites! Make flash cards and drill them until you immediately recognize these three expressions and know how to factor (or distribute) each one automatically. This will usually put you on the path toward the solution to the problem.

		Memorize these!
Special Product 1:	$x^2 - y^2 = (x + y)(x - y)$	
Special Product 2:	$x^2 + 2xy + y^2 = (x + y)(x + y) = (x + y)^2$	
Special Product 3:	$x^2 - 2xy + y^2 = (x - y)(x - y) = (x - y)^2$	

You may also need to identify these products when they are presented in other forms. For example, $a^2 - 1$ can be factored as $(a + 1)(a - 1)$. Similarly, $(a + b)^2$ can be distributed as $a^2 + 2ab + b^2$.

Within an equation, you may need to recognize these special products in pieces. For instance, if you see $a^2 + b^2 = 9 + 2ab$, move the $2ab$ term to the left, yielding $a^2 - 2ab + b^2 = 9$. This quadratic can then be factored to $(a - b)^2 = 9$, or $a - b = \pm 3$. For example:

Simplify $\dfrac{x^2 + 4x + 4}{x^2 - 4}$, given that x does not equal 2 or −2.

Both the numerator and denominator of this fraction can be factored:

$$\frac{(x + 2)(x + 2)}{(x + 2)(x - 2)}$$

The expression $x + 2$ can be canceled out from the numerator and denominator:

$$\frac{x^2 + 4x + 4}{x^2 - 4} = \frac{x + 2}{x - 2}$$

Problem Set

Now that you've finished the chapter, try the following problems.

1. $(3 - \sqrt{7})(3 + \sqrt{7}) =$

2. If -4 is a root for x in the equation $x^2 + kx + 8 = 0$, what is k?

3. If 8 and -4 are the solutions for x, which of the following could be the equation?

   (A) $x^2 - 4x - 32 = 0$

   (B) $x^2 - 4x + 32 = 0$

   (C) $x^2 + 4x - 12 = 0$

   (D) $x^2 + 4x + 32 = 0$

   (E) $x^2 + 4x + 12 = 0$

4. If $x^2 + k = G$ and x is an integer, which of the following could be the value of $G - k$?

   (A) 7

   (B) 8

   (C) 9

   (D) 10

   (E) 11

5. What is y?

   (1) $x = 4y - 4$

   (2) $xy = 8$

6. If $\dfrac{d}{4} + \dfrac{8}{d} + 3 = 0$, what is d?

7. If $x \neq -3$ and $\dfrac{x^2 + 6x + 9}{x + 3} = 7$, what is x?

8. If $z^2 - 10z + 25 = 9$, what are the possible values for z?

9. If $a \neq 2$ and $ab \neq 0$, which of the following is equal to $\dfrac{b(a^2 - 4)}{ab - 2b}$?

   (A) ab

   (B) a

   (C) $a + 2$

   (D) a^2

   (E) $2b$

Solutions

1. **2:** You can use the special product or FOIL to simplify. The special product is faster—but you have to have it memorized.

    The original expression is in the form $(x - y)(x + y)$, which is one of the three special products. Since $(x - y)(x + y) = x^2 - y^2$, the expression in this problem simplifies to this:

    $$3^2 - \left(\sqrt{7}\right)^2 = 9 - 7 = 2$$

    Alternatively, FOIL to solve:

    $$
    \begin{aligned}
    &\text{F: } 3 \times 3 = 9 \\
    &\text{O: } 3 \times \sqrt{7} = 3\sqrt{7} \\
    &\text{I: } -\sqrt{7} \times 3 = -3\sqrt{7} \\
    &\underline{\text{L: } -\sqrt{7} \times \sqrt{7} = -7} \\
    &\text{FOIL: } 9 + 3\sqrt{7} - 3\sqrt{7} - 7 = 2
    \end{aligned}
    $$

2. **6:** The word *root* is a synonym for *solution*. If -4 is a solution, then $(x + 4)$ must be one of the factors of the quadratic equation. The other factor is $(x + ?)$.

    $$x^2 + kx + 8 = 0$$
    $$(x + 4)(x + ?) = 0$$

    The product of 4 and ? must be equal to 8; thus, the other factor is $(x + 2)$. Next, the sum of 4 and 2 must be equal to k. Therefore, $k = 6$.

    Alternatively, if -4 is a solution, then it is a possible value for x. Plug it into the equation for x and solve for k:

    $$x^2 + kx + 8 = 0$$
    $$16 - 4k + 8 = 0$$
    $$24 = 4k$$
    $$k = 6$$

3. **(A)** $x^2 - 4x - 32 = 0$: If the solutions to the equation are 8 and -4, the factored form of the equation is $(x - 8)\,(x + 4) = 0$.

    Scan the answers. Most of them have a different c term (-32, 32, -12, or 12), so check just that last part first. That's the L in FOIL: $(-8)(4) = -32$. Only answer (A) has 32 as the c term, so it must be the answer. (If more than one had that same number, then you would have to do the full FOIL.)

4. **(C) 9:** The problem states that x is an integer. It also asks for the combo $G - k$. Rearrange the expression to isolate the combo on one side:

    $$x^2 + k = G$$
    $$x^2 = G - k$$

14

Because you know that x is an integer, x^2 is a perfect square (the square of an integer). Therefore, $G - k$ is also a perfect square. The only perfect square among the answer choices is the number 9.

5. **(E):** The question asks for the value of y. You must be able to find one definitive value in order to say that a statement is sufficient.

    (1) INSUFFICIENT: This statement contains x and y, so it is not sufficient to find y alone.

    (2) INSUFFICIENT: This statement contains x and y, so it is not sufficient to find y alone.

    (1) AND (2) INSUFFICIENT: The two equations are $x = 4y - 4$ and $xy = 8$. The second equation is nonlinear (it multiplies the variables rather than adding or subtracting them), so when you combine them, you're likely to get a quadratic—which typically leads to more than one solution.

    Solve until you can tell whether you're going to get one solution or more than one. First, because the problem asked for y, isolate x in one of the equations. Luckily, this is already done in the first equation. Substitute into the second:

    $$x = 4y - 4 \rightarrow (4y - 4)y = 8$$
    $$4y^2 - 4y = 8$$
    $$y^2 - y = 2$$
    $$y^2 - y - 2 = 0$$
    $$(y + 1)(y - 2) = 0$$

    If you are able to tell before that last line that you will get two different answers, you can stop at that point.

    The correct answer is **(E)**: Nothing given is sufficient to answer the question.

6. $\{-8, -4\}$: Multiply the entire equation by $4d$ (to eliminate the fractions) and factor:

    $$d^2 + 32 + 12d = 0$$
    $$d^2 + 12d + 32 = 0$$
    $$(d + 8)(d + 4) = 0$$

    $$d + 8 = 0 \quad \text{OR} \quad d + 4 = 0$$
    $$d = -8 \qquad\qquad d = -4$$

7. **4:** The problem states that x is not -3, so you can divide out the term on the bottom of the fraction:

    $$\frac{x^2 + 6x + 9}{x + 3} = 7$$
    $$\frac{(x + 3)(x + 3)}{x + 3} = 7$$
    $$\frac{(x + 3)\,\cancel{(x + 3)}}{\cancel{x + 3}} = 7$$
    $$x + 3 = 7$$
    $$x = 4$$

8. **{2, 8}:** The right-hand side is a perfect square (9), so check whether the left-hand side is as well. And it is!

$$z^2 - 10z + 25 = 9$$
$$(z - 5)^2 = 9$$
$$\sqrt{(z - 5)^2} = \sqrt{9}$$
$$z - 5 = \pm 3$$
$$z = 5 \pm 3$$

9. **(C)** $a + 2$: There are variables in the answers and no real values given in the problem, so choose smart numbers. The number 2 is not allowed for a and the number 4 appears in the expression, so try $a = 3$ and $b = 5$, and remember to simplify before you multiply:

$$\frac{b(a^2 - 4)}{ab - 2b} =$$
$$\frac{(5)((3)^2 - 4)}{(3)(5) - 2(5)} =$$
$$\frac{5(9 - 4)}{15 - 10} =$$
$$\frac{5(5)}{5} = 5$$

Now, plug $a = 3$ and $b = 5$ into the answer choices and look for a matching answer of 5:

(A) $ab = (3)(5) = 15$

(B) $a = (3) = 3$

(C) $a + 2 = (3) + 2 = 5$ Match!

(D) $a^2 = (3)^2 = 9$

(E) $2b = 2(5) = 10$

Alternatively, you can solve algebraically. Begin by factoring the given expression, then simplify:

$$\frac{b(a + 2)(a - 2)}{b(a - 2)} = a + 2$$

Everything divides out except for the $a + 2$ term. If you spot that quickly, then the algebraic solution is faster. If not, then the algebra can get messy and the smart numbers solution may be better.

Formulas

In This Chapter

- Plug-In Formulas

- Functions

- Variable Substitution in Functions

- Sequence Formulas

- Recursive Sequences

- Linear Sequence Problems: Alternative Method

In this chapter, you will learn how to simplify and solve standard "plug-in" formulas, functions, and sequences (including both regular and recursive sequences).

CHAPTER 15 **Formulas**

Formulas are another means by which the GMAT tests your ability to work with unknowns. Formulas are specific equations that can involve multiple variables and these problems may be pure math or real-life/story problems. There are four major types of formula problems on the GMAT:

1. Plug-in formulas

2. Functions

3. Sequence formulas

4. Strange symbol formulas

The first three types are covered in this chapter. The final category is fairly rare; if you want to learn about strange symbol formulas, see the supplemental study material for this guide, found online.

Plug-In Formulas

The most basic GMAT formula problems provide you with a formula and ask you to solve for one of the variables in the formula by plugging in given values for the other variables. For example:

> The formula for determining an individual's comedic aptitude, C, on a given day is defined as $\frac{QL}{J}$, where J represents the number of jokes told, Q represents the overall joke quality on a scale of 1 to 10, and L represents the number of individual laughs generated. If Niko told 12 jokes, generated 18 laughs, and earned a comedic aptitude of 10.5, what was the overall quality of Niko's jokes?

The first sentence is providing a formula, though it may not look like it. When a variable is *defined as* a combination of some other variables, write a formula:

$$C = \frac{QL}{J}$$

Next, plug the given values into the formula in order to solve for the unknown variable Q:

$$C = \frac{QL}{J}$$
$$10.5 = \frac{18Q}{12}$$
$$Q = \frac{10.5(12)}{18}$$
$$Q = \frac{10.5(2)}{3}$$
$$Q = \frac{21}{3} = 7$$

The quality of Niko's jokes was rated a 7.

Notice that you will typically have to do some rearrangement after plugging in the numbers in order to isolate the desired unknown. The actual computations are typically not very complex (though do remember to simplify before you multiply!). Formula problems are tricky because the given formula is unfamiliar. Do not be intimidated. Figure out how to write down the equation, plug in the numbers carefully, and solve for the required unknown.

Functions

Functions are very much like the "magic boxes" you may have learned about in elementary school. For example:

> You put a 2 into the magic box, and a 7 comes out. You put a 3 into the magic box, and a 9 comes out. You put a 4 into the magic box, and an 11 comes out.

There are many possible ways to describe what the magic box is doing to your number. One possibility is that the magic box is doubling your number and adding 3:

$$2(2) + 3 = 7 \qquad 2(3) + 3 = 9 \qquad 2(4) + 3 = 11$$

Assuming that this is the case, this description would yield the following rule for this magic box: $2x + 3$. This rule can be written in function form as:

$$f(x) = 2x + 3$$

The function f represents the rule that the magic box is using to transform your number. The test might give you the function and say something like "What is $f(3)$?" The direction is telling you to put 3 into the function wherever you see an x, so 3 is the *input*:

$$f(3) = 2x + 3 \rightarrow 2(3) + 3 = 6 + 3 = 9$$

The answer is 9, so 9 is the *output*. By the way, that $f(x)$ form is read "f of x," not fx. It does *not* mean "f times x!" The letter f does not stand for a variable; rather, it stands for the rule that dictates how the input x changes into the output (answer).

Here are some other examples of functions. What do they have in common?

$$f(x) = 4x^2 - 11$$

$$g(t) = t^3 + \sqrt{t} - \frac{2t}{5}$$

They always start with that *letter*(*letter*) format. Most of the time, the first letter will be an f, g, or h. Whenever you see $f(x)$, it's saying "for the function f, follow this rule for any value of x."

The *domain* of a function indicates the possible inputs. The *range* of a function indicates the possible outputs. For instance, the function $f(x) = x^2$ can take any input (x can be anything) but never produces a negative number (because you can't square something and have the result be negative). So the domain is $x =$ all numbers, but the range is $f(x) \geq 0$.

The most basic type of function problem asks you to input the numerical value (say, 5) in place of the independent variable (x) in order to determine the value of the function. For example:

> If $f(x) = x^2 - 2$, what is the value of $f(5)$?

Apply the given rule:

$$f(5) = (5)^2 - 2 = 25 - 2 = 23$$

Variable Substitution in Functions

This type of function problem is slightly more complicated. Instead of finding the output value for a numerical input, you must find the output when the input is an algebraic expression. For example:

If $f(z) = z^2 - \frac{z}{3}$, what is the value of $f(w + 6)$?

Input the variable expression $(w + 6)$ in place of the independent variable (z) to determine the value of the function:

$$f(w + 6) = (w + 6)^2 - \frac{w + 6}{3}$$

Compare this equation to the equation for $f(z)$. The expression $(w + 6)$ has taken the place of every z in the original equation. In a sense, you are treating the expression $(w + 6)$ as one thing, as if it were a single letter or variable.

If you needed to simplify the right side, you would do so using standard algebraic simplification.

You could also be told the output and asked to find the input. For example:

If $f(x) = 3x + 2$ and $f(x) = 5$, what is x?

The first equation is the function ("given an input x, put it in the form $3x + 2$"). The second equation, though, represents an output: For some particular value of x, the output is 5. What is that value of x? To solve, set the function equal to the output:

$$3x + 2 = 5$$
$$3x = 3$$
$$x = 1$$

When $x = 1$, the output of the function is 5.

Sequence Formulas

A **sequence** is a collection of numbers in a set order. For example, $\{1, 4, 9, 16, 25\}$ is a sequence, as is $\{1, 1, 2, 3, 5, 8\}$. Sequences do not necessarily go in increasing order and it's possible to have repeated numbers.

Every sequence is defined by a rule, which you can use to find the values of terms:

$$A_n = 9n + 3$$

Find the first term (A_1) by plugging $n = 1$ into the equation: $A_1 = 12$.

Find the second term (A_2) by plugging $n = 2$ into the equation: $A_2 = 21$.

Find the nth term (A_n) by plugging n into the equation.

15

Here's another example:

If $S_n = 15n - 7$, what is the value of $S_5 - S_3$?

This question is asking for the difference between the fifth term and the third term of the sequence, or $S_5 - S_3$:

$$S_5 - S_3 = 15(5) - 7 - \left[15(3) - 7\right]$$
$$= 75 - 7 - 45 + 7$$
$$= 75 - 45$$
$$= 30$$

Recursive Sequences

Occasionally, a sequence will be defined *recursively*. A **recursive sequence** defines each term relative to other terms in that same sequence, something like "each term is equal to the previous term plus 2."

Take a look at this example:

If $a_n = 2a_{n-1} - 4$ and $a_6 = -4$, what is the value of a_4?

You can recognize that this is recursive because it doesn't have just an a_n term. It also has an a_{n-1} term. That second term refers to a different term in the same sequence; if you see this, you have a recursive sequence.

Solve the problem. If a_n represents the nth term, then a_{n-1} is the term right before a_n. You are given the value of the sixth term, and need to figure out the value of the fourth term. Keep track of this on your scrap paper:

$$\underline{\hspace{3cm}} \quad \underline{\hspace{3cm}} \quad \underline{\hspace{1cm}-4\hspace{1cm}}$$
$$a_4 \qquad\qquad a_5 \qquad\qquad a_6$$

Use the value of the sixth term (a_6) to find the value of the fifth term (a_5):

$$a_6 = 2a_5 - 4$$
$$(-4) = 2a_5 - 4$$
$$0 = 2a_5$$
$$0 = a_5$$

The value of the fifth term is 0:

$$\underline{\hspace{3cm}} \quad \underline{\hspace{1cm}0\hspace{1cm}} \quad \underline{\hspace{1cm}-4\hspace{1cm}}$$
$$a_4 \qquad\qquad a_5 \qquad\qquad a_6$$

Now use the fifth term to find the fourth term:

$$a_5 = 2a_4 - 4$$
$$(0) = 2a_4 - 4$$
$$4 = 2a_4$$
$$2 = a_4$$

The value of the fourth term is 2.

When a sequence is defined recursively, the question will have to give you the value of at least one of the terms. Use that value to find the value of the desired term.

Linear Sequence Problems: Alternative Method

For **linear sequences**, in which the same number is added to any term to yield the next term, you can use the following alternative method:

> If each number in a sequence is 3 more than the previous number, and the 6th number is 32, what is the 50th number in the sequence?

Instead of finding the rule for this sequence, consider the following reasoning: From the 6th to the 50th term, there are 44 "jumps" of 3 each. Since $44 \times 3 = 132$, there is an increase of 132 from the 6th term to the 50th term:

$$32 + 132 = 164$$

15

Problem Set

Now that you've finished the chapter, try the following problems.

1. If $A_n = 3 - 8n$, what is A_1?

2. If $A_n = 3 - 8n$, what is $A_{11} - A_9$?

3. If $f(x) = 2x^2 - 12$, what is the value of $f\left(2\sqrt{3}\right)$?

4. If $a_n = \dfrac{a_{n-1} \times a_{n-2}}{2}$, $a_5 = -6$, and $a_6 = -18$, what is the value of a_3?

5. Hugo lies on top of a building, throwing pennies straight down to the street below. The formula for the height, H, that a penny falls is $H = Vt + 5t^2$, where V is the original velocity of the penny (how fast Hugo throws it when it leaves his hand) and t is equal to the time it takes to hit the ground, in seconds. Hugo throws the penny from a height of 60 meters at an initial speed of 20 meters per second. How long does it take, in seconds, for the penny to hit the ground?

    (A) 2
    (B) 20
    (C) 200

6. Life expectancy is defined by the formula $L = \dfrac{6SB}{G}$, where S = shoe size, B = average monthly electric bill in dollars, and G = GMAT score. If Melvin's GMAT score is twice his monthly electric bill, and his life expectancy is 75, what is his shoe size?

7. The "competitive edge" of a baseball team is defined by the formula $\sqrt{\dfrac{W}{L}}$, where W represents the number of the team's wins and L represents the number of the team's losses. This year, the GMAT All-Stars had 3 times as many wins and one-half as many losses as they had last year. By what factor did their "competitive edge" increase?

8. If $t(x) = 4x^3a$ and $t(3) = 27$, what is $t(2)$?

9. The first term in an arithmetic sequence is -5 and the second term is -3. What is the 50th term? (In an arithmetic sequence, the difference between successive terms is constant.)

10. Challenge problem: If $f(x) = 2x^2 - 4$ and $g(x) = 2x$, for what values of x will $f(x) = g(x)$?

15

15

Answers and explanations follow on the next page. ▶ ▶ ▶

Solutions

1. **−5:** Substitute 1 in for n and solve:

    $$A_n = 3 - 8_n$$
    $$A_1 = 3 - 8(1)$$
    $$= 3 - 8$$
    $$= -5$$

2. **−16:** Substitute 11 and 9 in for n and solve:

    $$A_{11} - A_9 = 3 - 8(11) - \left[3 - 8(9)\right]$$
    $$= 3 - 88 - 3 + 72$$
    $$= 0 - 88 + 72$$
    $$= -16$$

3. **12:** Plug in the given value for x and solve:

    $$f(x) = 2\left(2\sqrt{3}\right)^2 - 12$$
    $$= 2(2)^2 \left(\sqrt{3}\right)^2 - 12$$
    $$= (2 \times 4 \times 3) - 12$$
    $$= 24 - 12$$
    $$= 12$$

4. **−2:** According to the formula, $a_3 = \dfrac{a_2 \times a_1}{2}$. But you aren't given a_1 or a_2. Instead, you're given a_5 and a_6. You have to work backwards from the fifth and sixth terms of the sequence to find the third term. Notice what happens if you plug $n = 6$ into the formula:

    $$a_6 = \frac{a_5 \times a_4}{2}$$

    Plug in the values of a_5 and a_6 to solve for the value of a_4:

    $$-18 = \frac{-6 \times a_4}{2}$$
    $$-36 = -6 \times a_4$$
    $$6 = a_4$$

    Now, use the fourth and fifth terms of the sequence to solve for a_3:

    $$a_5 = \frac{a_4 \times a_3}{2}$$
    $$-6 = \frac{6 \times a_3}{2}$$
    $$-12 = 6 \times a_3$$
    $$-2 = a_3$$

15

5. **(A) 2 seconds:** If you feel comfortable thinking through the scenario, you can estimate. The penny drops from 60 meters at a speed of 20 meters per second, so it should take no more than 3 seconds to drop. (It will take less than 3 seconds, in fact, since gravity will cause the speed to increase.) Only answer **(A)** is close. Here's how to do the algebra:

$$H = Vt + 5t^2$$
$$60 = 20t + 5t^2$$
$$5t^2 + 20t - 60 = 0$$
$$5\left(t^2 + 4t - 12\right) = 0$$
$$5\left(t+6\right)\left(t-2\right) = 0$$

$$t + 6 = 0 \qquad \text{OR} \qquad t - 2 = 0$$
$$t = -6 \qquad\qquad t = 2$$

Since a time must be positive, discard the negative value for t.

6. **Size 25:** The problem states that $G = 2B$, so substitute $2B$ for G in the formula, then simplify:

$$\frac{6SB}{2B} = 75$$
$$3S = 75$$
$$S = 25$$

You could also pick smart numbers for G and B as long as they fit the relationship described in the problem: G is twice B. Try $G = 4$ and $B = 2$. Then, substitute in your smart numbers and solve for S:

$$\frac{6S(2)}{4} = 75$$
$$3S = 75$$
$$S = 25$$

7. $\sqrt{6}$: The question says the competitive edge (call that c) *is defined by* a certain expression, so write a formula:

$$c = \sqrt{\frac{W}{L}}$$

Pick numbers to see what happens to the competitive edge when W is tripled and L is halved. If the original value of W is 4 and the original value of L is 2, the original value of c is $\sqrt{\frac{4}{2}} = \sqrt{2}$.

If W triples to 12 and L is halved to 1, the new value of c is $\sqrt{\frac{12}{1}} = \sqrt{12}$. The competitive edge has increased from $\sqrt{2}$ to $\sqrt{12}$. Therefore:

$$\frac{\sqrt{12}}{\sqrt{2}} = \frac{\sqrt{12}}{\sqrt{2}} = \sqrt{6}$$

The competitive edge has increased by a factor of $\sqrt{6}$. (You can also ask yourself: What do I need to multiply $\sqrt{2}$ by to get to $\sqrt{12}$?)

8. **8:** The problem contains a function, t, into which you plug values for x. The function also contains a separate variable, a. First, use the given information $t(3) = 27$ to find the value for a:

$$t(x) = 4x^3 a$$

$$t(3) \rightarrow 4(3)^3 a = 27$$

$$4(27)a = 27$$

$$4a = 1$$

$$a = \frac{1}{4}$$

Next, plug that back into the function to find the value of $t(2)$:

$$t(x) = 4x^3 a$$

$$t(2) = 4(2)^3 \left(\frac{1}{4}\right)$$

$$t(2) = 4(8)\left(\frac{1}{4}\right)$$

$$t(2) = 8$$

9. **93:** The first term is -5 and the second term is -3, so you are adding $+2$ to each successive term. How many times do you have to add 2? There are $50 - 1 = 49$ additional "steps" after the first term, so you have to add $+2$ a total of 49 times, beginning with your starting point of -5: $-5 + 2(49) = 93$.

10. **$\{-1, 2\}$:** To find the values for which $f(x) = g(x)$, set the functions equal to each other:

$$2x^2 - 4 = 2x$$

$$2x^2 - 2x - 4 = 0$$

$$2\left(x^2 - x - 2\right) = 0$$

$$2(x - 2)(x + 1) = 0$$

$$x - 2 = 0 \quad \text{OR} \quad x + 1 = 0$$

$$x = 2 \qquad \qquad x = -1$$

15

Inequalities and Max/Min

In This Chapter

- Flip the Sign
- Combining Inequalities: Line 'Em Up!
- Manipulating Compound Inequalities
- Combining Inequalities: Add 'Em Up!
- Maximizing and Minimizing
- Square-Rooting Inequalities

In this chapter, you will learn how to simplify and solve inequalities (almost the same as equations, but not quite!). You'll also learn about a common question feature that shows up on the GMAT: the max/min variation, in which you're asked to find the maximum or minimum possible value of something.

CHAPTER 16 Inequalities and Max/Min

Unlike equations, which relate two equivalent quantities, **inequalities** compare quantities that have different values. Inequalities are used to express four kinds of relationships, illustrated by the following examples:

1. x is less than 4.

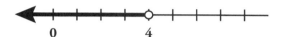
$x < 4$

2. x is less than or equal to 4.

$x \leq 4$

3. x is greater than 4.

$x > 4$

4. x is greater than or equal to 4.

$x \geq 4$

Number lines, such as those shown above, are an excellent way to visualize exactly what a given inequality means.

When you see inequalities with 0 on one side of the inequality (> 0 or < 0), the problem is likely testing positive and negative characteristics. You'll learn more about this later.

Here are some common inequality statements on the GMAT, as well as what they imply:

Statement	Implication
$xy > 0$	x and y are *both positive* OR *both negative*.
$xy < 0$	x and y have *different signs* (one positive, one negative).
$x^2 - x < 0$ $x^2 < x$	These are two different versions of the same inequality. Both mean that $0 < x < 1$.

Why is that last one true? The inequality to the left is saying that, when you square a number, it gets smaller. Only a very narrow set of circumstances makes this true; most of the time, when you square a number it gets larger.

If you square any negative number, it becomes positive (and, therefore, larger). If you square any positive number greater than 1, it gets larger.

If you square 0, it stays 0. If you square 1, it stays 1. These are the only two numbers that stay the same when you square them.

Finally, if you square a value between 0 and 1, this is the one cirumstance in which the value gets smaller.

Flip the Sign

Most operations that can be performed on equations can be performed on inequalities. For example, in order to simplify an inequality (e.g., $2 + x < 5$), you can add or subtract a constant on both sides:

$$
\begin{array}{ll}
2 + x < 5 & x - 5 < 9 \\
\underline{-2 \qquad -2} & \underline{\quad +5 + 5} \\
x < 3 & x \quad < 14
\end{array}
$$

You can also add or subtract a variable expression on both sides:

$$
\begin{array}{ll}
y + x < 5 & x - ab < 9 \\
\underline{-y \qquad\quad -y} & \underline{\quad + ab \qquad + ab} \\
x < 5 - y & x \qquad < 9 + ab
\end{array}
$$

You can multiply or divide by a *positive* number on both sides:

$$
\begin{array}{ll}
2x < 6 & 0.2x < 1 \\
\underline{\div 2 \ \div 2} & \underline{\times 5 \quad \times 5} \\
x < 3 & x < 5
\end{array}
$$

One procedure, however, is very different for inequalities: When you multiply or divide an inequality by a negative number, the inequality sign flips! For example:

If $4 - 3x < 10$, what is the range of possible values for x ?

$$
\begin{array}{lll}
4 \quad - \quad 3x \quad < \quad 10 & \\
\underline{-4 \qquad\qquad\qquad\quad -4} & \text{First, subtract 4 from both sides.} \\
-3x \quad < \quad 6 & \\
\underline{\div -3 \quad \div -3} & \text{Next, divide by } -3. \\
x \quad > \quad -2 & \text{Because you're dividing by a negative, flip the inequality sign.}
\end{array}
$$

Do not multiply or divide an inequality by a variable unless you know the sign of the number that the variable stands for. If you don't know whether that number is positive or negative, then you don't know whether to flip the inequality sign.

Combining Inequalities: Line 'Em Up!

Many GMAT inequality problems involve more than one inequality. To solve such problems, you may need to convert several inequalities to a compound inequality, which is a series of inequalities strung together, such as $2 < 3 < 4$. To convert multiple inequalities to a compound inequality, first line up the variables, then combine. For example:

> If $x > 8$, $x < 17$, and $x + 5 < 19$, what is the range of possible values for x ?

First, solve any inequalities that need to be solved. In this example, only the last inequality needs to be solved:

$$x + 5 < 19$$
$$x < 14$$

Second, rearrange the inequalities so that all the inequality symbols point in the same direction, and then line up the common variables in the inequalities:

$$8 < x$$
$$x < 17$$
$$x < 14$$

Finally, put the information together. Notice that $x < 14$ is more limiting than $x < 17$ (in other words, whenever $x < 14$, x will always be less than 17, but not vice versa). The range, then, is $8 < x < 14$ rather than $8 < x < 17$. Discard the less limiting inequality, $x < 17$. Try another example:

> If $u < t$ and $b > r$ and $f < t$ and $r > t$, is $b > u$?

Combine the four given inequalities by simplifying and lining up the common variables.

First, align all inequalities in the same direction: $u < t$, $r < b$, $f < t$, and $t < r$.

Then, line up any like variables . . .   . . . and combine.

$$u < t$$
$$\phantom{u <} r < b$$
$$f < t$$
$$\phantom{f <} t < r$$

$$u < t < r < b$$
$$f < t < r < b$$

In this problem, it is not possible to combine all the information into a single compound inequality. Both u and f are less than t, but you do not know the relationship between u and f.

The answer to the question is yes, b is greater than u.

Manipulating Compound Inequalities

Sometimes a problem with compound inequalities will require you to manipulate the inequalities in order to solve the problem. You can perform operations on a compound inequality as long as you remember to perform those operations on every term in the inequality, not just the outside terms. For example:

$x + 3 < y < x + 5 \not\to x < y < x + 2$ **INCORRECT**: You must subtract 3 from *every* term in the inequality.

$x + 3 < y < x + 5 \to x < y - 3 < x + 2$ CORRECT

$\frac{c}{2} \leq b - 3 \leq \frac{d}{2} \to c \leq b - 3 \leq d$ **INCORRECT**: You must multiply by 2 in *every* term in the inequality.

$\frac{c}{2} \leq b - 3 \leq \frac{d}{2} \to c \leq 2b - 6 \leq d$ CORRECT

Combining Inequalities: Add 'Em Up!

You can also combine inequalities by adding the inequalities together. In order to add inequalities, the inequality signs must face in the same direction. (Don't subtract inequalities, though—ever.) For example:

Is $a + 2b < c + 2d$?

(1) $a < c$

(2) $d > b$

Assume that you've already tried the two statements individually and neither was sufficient by itself. In order to test the statements together, add the inequalities together to see whether they match the question. First, line up the inequalities so that they are all facing the same direction:

$a < c$
$b < d$

Then, take the sum of the two inequalities to try to prove the result. Add them up once, then take a look. It's not quite the same. What's missing? You need another b and d, so add the second inequality *again*:

$$
\begin{array}{r}
a \quad\ \ < c \\
+ \quad b < \quad d \\
\hline
a + b < c + d \\
+ \quad b < \quad d \\
\hline
a + 2b < c + 2d
\end{array}
$$

If you use both statements, you can answer the question. Therefore, the answer is **(C)**.

You also could have multiplied the second inequality by 2 before summing so that the result matched the original question:

$$
\begin{array}{r}
a \quad\ \ < c \\
+ \quad 2b < \quad 2d \\
\hline
a + 2b < c + 2d
\end{array}
$$

You might not notice that at first, though. Adding one of each inequality the first time is a good way to understand what's going on with the math; that can help you to notice that you need to double one of the inequalities (i.e., use it twice).

You can also multiply inequalities together as long as all possible values of the inequalities are positive, though this doesn't show up a lot on the GMAT.

But remember this: *Never subtract or divide inequalities.*

Maximizing and Minimizing

Some problems ask you to find the maximum or minimum of multiple possible solutions; these are called max/min problems for short.

As you work through the problem, look for the spots where you have flexibility to try multiple possible values. Then, think about what the problem asked you to do. For instance, if the problem asked you to find the maximum value for something, where else in the problem do you need to maximize or minimize values in order to accomplish your overall goal? Try an example:

If $2y + 3 \leq 11$ and $1 \leq x \leq 5$, what is the maximum possible value for xy?

Which combinations of extreme values will maximize the value of the product xy? First, simplify whatever you can. The x inequality is already simplified, but the y inequality can be simplified further:

$$2y + 3 \leq 11$$
$$2y \leq 8$$
$$y \leq 4$$

Next, examine the extreme ends of each range. If a range includes 0, it's also a good idea to note that, since 0 can have an unusual effect in problems:

Extreme Values for x	**Extreme Values for y**
The lowest value for x is 1.	There is no lower limit to y.
The highest value for x is 5.	The highest value for y is 4.
	y could be 0.

Now, consider the different scenarios for x and y that could lead to the maximum possible value for xy. The value of y could be positive or negative, but x must be positive. A positive times a negative has to be negative, and that won't be the maximum value, so ignore all negative values for y.

The value of 0 for y also won't help to maximize the value of xy. If you're restricted to positives, then you want to maximize the value of each individual number in order to get the maximum possible product.

In this case, xy is maximized when $x = 5$ and $y = 4$, with a result that $xy = 20$.

How does the situation change if this is the problem:

If $-20 \leq 2y \leq 8$ and $-3 \leq x \leq 5$, what is the maximum possible value for xy?

The first inequality simplifies to $-10 \leq y \leq 4$. Also, this time, both x and y could be negative—and a negative times a negative is positive—so you have to consider the negative scenario this time:

Extreme Values for x   **Extreme Values for y**

The lowest value for x is -3.   The lowest value for y is -10.

The highest value for x is 5.   The highest value for y is 4.

x could be 0. y could be 0.

Max scenario 1: Positive × Positive. Use the largest possible values for each:

$x = 5$ and $y = 4$, so $xy = 20$

Max scenario 2: Negative × Negative. Use the smallest possible values for each:

$x = -3$ and $y = -10$, so $xy = 30$

In this problem, the maximum value for xy is obtained when using the smallest possible values for x and y. The maximum value is 30.

When you see max/min language in a problem, first jot down whether the problem is asking you to maximize or to minimize. Next, identify the parts of the problem where you have the flexibility to maximize or minimize some values. Finally, consider the different possible scenarios—you may need to test two or three options in order to figure out the correct answer.

Square-Rooting Inequalities

Just like equations involving even exponents, inequality problems involving even exponents require you to consider *two* scenarios. Consider this example:

If $x^2 < 4$, what are the possible values for x?

To solve this problem, recall that when given x^2 and solving for x, you'll have two solutions: the positive version and the negative version. For example, if $x^2 = 4$, then $x = \pm 2$.

Something similar happens when you solve an inequality, with one important difference:

$x^2 < 4$

$x < 2$ and $x > -2$

If x is positive, then $x < 2$. So far, this is how you would normally solve.

But, if x is negative, then taking the square root is the equivalent of dividing by a negative, so you have to flip the inequality sign: $x > -2$.

Here is another example:

If $10 + x^2 \geq 19$, what is the range of possible values for x?

$$10 + x^2 \geq 19$$
$$x^2 \geq 9$$
$$x \geq 3 \quad \text{AND} \quad x \leq -3$$

If x is positive, then $x \geq 3$, but if x is negative, then $x \leq -3$.

Advanced material for the Algebra unit (primarily covering additional strategies for equations, formulas, and inequalities) can be found in Atlas, Manhattan Prep's online learning platform. Use the online material only if you feel that you have mastered everything in the Algebra unit of this strategy guide and only if you are aiming for a Quant section score of 48 or higher.

16

Problem Set

Now that you've finished the chapter, try the following problems.

1. Which of the following is equivalent to $-3x + 7 \leq 2x + 32$?

   (A) $x \geq -5$

   (B) $x \geq 5$

   (C) $x \leq 5$

   (D) $x \leq -5$

2. If $G^2 < G$, which of the following could be G ?

   (A) $\quad 1$

   (B) $\dfrac{23}{7}$

   (C) $\dfrac{7}{23}$

   (D) -4

   (E) -2

3. If $5B > 4B + 1$, is $B^2 > 1$?

4. If $|A| > 19$, which of the following could NOT be equal to A ?

   (A) $\quad 26$

   (B) $\quad 22$

   (C) $\quad 18$

   (D) -20

   (E) -24

5. If $-10 \leq a \leq 5$ and $7 \leq b \leq 10$, what is the least possible value of $|a - b|$?

   (A) -2

   (B) $\quad 0$

   (C) $\quad 2$

   (D) $\quad 3$

   (E) $\quad 5$

Save the following problems for review after you finish this entire guide.

6. If a > 7, a + 4 > 13, and 2a < 30, which of the following must be true?

    (A) 9 < a < 15

    (B) 11 < a < 15

    (C) 15 < a < 20

    (D) 13 < a < 15

7. If $d > a$ and $L < a$, which of the following cannot be true?

    (A) $d + L = 14$

    (B) $d - L = 7$

    (C) $d - L = 1$

    (D) $a - d = 9$

    (E) $a + d = 9$

8. A retailer sells only radios and clocks. If there are currently exactly 42 total items in inventory, how many of them are radios?

    (1) The retailer has more than 26 radios in inventory.

    (2) The retailer has less than twice as many radios as clocks in inventory.

9. If $4x - 12 \geq x + 9$, which of the following must be true?

    (A) $x > 6$

    (B) $x < 7$

    (C) $x > 7$

    (D) $x > 8$

    (E) $x < 8$

10. If $0 < ab < ac$, is a negative?

    (1) $c < 0$

    (2) $b > c$

16

Solutions

1. **(A)** $x \geq -5$:

$$-3x + 7 \leq 2x + 32$$
$$-5x \leq 25$$
$$x \geq -5$$

2. **(C)** $\dfrac{7}{23}$: If G^2 is less than G, then G must be positive (since G^2 itself has to be 0 or positive). In addition, only values between 0 and 1 get smaller when you square them. Thus, $0 < G < 1$. Only the value in answer **(C)** is between 0 and 1.

3. **Yes:**

$$5B > 4B + 1$$
$$B > 1$$

   For any number greater than 1, the square of the number is also greater than 1, so $B^2 > 1$.

4. **(C) 18:** If $|A| > 19$, then $A > 19$ OR $A < -19$. The only answer choice that does not satisfy either of these inequalities is **(C)**, 18.

5. **(C) 2:** The question asks for the least possible value, so this is a max/min problem. Take some time during the Understand and Plan phases to think about what it means to minimize the value of $|a - b|$.

   How low can an absolute value go? It can never be negative. Glance at the answers—choice (A) can't be correct.

   An absolute value can be 0 or positive. Glance at the answers again—0 is in the running. Since the question asks for the least possible value, start there. What would need to happen in order for $|a - b| = 0$ to be true?

   The values for a and b would have to be identical. But this isn't possible, since a is between -10 and 5, inclusive, and b is between 7 and 10 inclusive. Eliminate choice (B) and move on to the next smallest value, 2.

   In order for the absolute value to be 2, the actual difference would have to be either 2 or -2. In other words, a and b would have to be 2 apart (though it doesn't matter which one is larger than the other). Is that a possible outcome? Yes, when $a = 5$ and $b = 7$.

   Alternatively, try each of the four extreme cases:

   Case 1: $|-10 - 7| = 17$

   Case 2: $|-10 - 10| = 20$

   Case 3: $|5 - 7| = 2$

   Case 4: $|5 - 10| = 5$

   The least possible value is 2. Note that answer (A) is a trap. The value of $5 - 7$ is -2, but the value of $|5 - 7|$ is 2, and the question asks about the absolute value.

6. **(A) $9 < a < 15$:** First, solve the second and third inequalities. The second one, $a + 4 > 13$, becomes $a > 9$. The third one, $2a < 30$, becomes $a < 15$.

    Next, make all of the inequality symbols point in the same direction. Then, line up the inequalities based on the variable a to combine:

    $$9 < a$$
    $$a < 15 \rightarrow 9 < a < 15$$
    $$7 < a$$

    If 7 and 9 are both less than a, the limiting factor is the larger value, 9. (If a is greater than both 7 and 9, then overall a is greater than 9.) Therefore, a is between 9 and 15.

    Notice that, in all of the incorrect answers, the low end is too high. For example, answer (B) indicates that a cannot be 11, but a could in fact be 11. The correct answer will both keep out all the impossible values of a *and* include all the possible values of a.

7. **(D) $a - d = 9$:** The *cannot be true* language signals an opportunity to test cases. The wording of the question indicates that the four wrong answers all could be true—so start with answer (A) and see which cases you can create. If you get hung up on a particular answer, maybe that's the one that can't be true. Leave that one aside and keep going with the others.

    The question stem indicates that d is greater than a but L is less than a. In other words: $L < a < d$. Test cases, making sure to try only numbers that follow this constraint:

    $$L < a$$
    $$a < d \rightarrow L < a < d$$

Answers to test	Given $L < a < d$ Test	Does it work?
(A) $d + L = 14$	$d = 10, L = 4$	Yes
(B) $d - L = 7$	$d = 10, L = 3$	Yes
(C) $d - L = 1$	$d = 10, L = 9$	Yes
(D) $a - d = 9$	$a = 10, d = $ bigger…?	…?
(E) $a + d = 9$	$a = 4, d = 5$	Yes

    For four of the answers, it's possible to choose values that follow the constraint that $L < a < d$. For answer **(D)**, though, this is impossible. The value for a has to be *less* than the value for d, so whatever you try to choose will end up with a negative answer, not positive 9.

8. **(C):** First, assign variables ($r =$ number of radios and $c =$ number of clocks) so that you can jot down the information in the question stem:

    $$r + c = 42$$

    The question asks for r. Note that, if you can find c, then you can find r, so the rephrased question is this: What is r OR What is c ?

    (1) INSUFFICIENT: This indicates that $r \geq 27$, so r could equal 27, 28, 29, etc.

(2) INSUFFICIENT: This statement is tricky to translate. First, pretend that it says that there are twice as many radios as clocks. That translates to $r = 2c$. Then, add in the inequality: There are *less than twice as many radios*: $r < 2c$.

Combine this information with the original equation $r + c = 42$:

$$r < 2c$$
$$r + c = 42$$

Isolate c in the second equation, then substitute into the inequality:

$$c = 42 - r$$
$$r < 2c$$
$$r < 2(42 - r)$$
$$r < 84 - 2r$$
$$3r < 84$$
$$r < 28$$

This information on its own is insufficient; r could be 27, 26, and so on.

(1) AND (2) SUFFICIENT: Statement (1) tells you $r \geq 27$, and statement (2) tells you $r < 28$. Therefore, r must equal 27.

The correct answer is **(C)**: Both statements together are sufficient, but neither one alone is sufficient.

9. **(A) $x > 6$:** What must be true? You might want to test some cases. First, though, simplify that annoying inequality:

$$
\begin{aligned}
4x - 12 &\geq x + 9 \\
3x &\geq 21 \\
x &\geq 7
\end{aligned}
$$

Careful. None of the answers match exactly. So test a couple of cases first before you choose something—make sure you understand what's going on. If $x \geq 7$, then x could be 7 itself.

Answers to test	Test #1: If $x = 7$ Answer true?	Test #2: If $x = 8$ Answer true?
(A) $x > 6$	Yes. Keep.	Yes. Keep.
(B) $x < 7$	No. Eliminate.	(ignore)
(C) $x > 7$	No. Eliminate.	(ignore)
(D) $x > 8$	No. Eliminate.	(ignore)
(E) $x < 8$	Yes. Keep.	No. Eliminate. Done!

The only answer that works every time is answer **(A)**.

10. **(D):** If $0 < ab < ac$, then $0 < ac$. Since ab is positive, a and b must have the same sign. Since ac is also positive, the same applies to a and c. Therefore, a, b, and c must all have the same sign.

The question stem also indicates that $ab < ac$. You can't divide out the a, though, since if a were negative, you would need to flip the inequality. Leave it for now.

(1) SUFFICIENT: Statement (1) indicates that c is negative. Therefore, since a and c share the same sign, a is negative.

(2) SUFFICIENT: Statement (2) is trickier. The statement indicates that $b > c$, but the question stem indicates that $ab < ac$. When you multiply both sides of $b > c$ by a, the inequality sign gets flipped. The only time an inequality sign flips is when you multiple or divide by a negative, so a must be negative.

Another option for statement (2) is to test cases. Pick values for b and c that adhere to the statement $b > c$, and then evaluate what values of a can make the inequality given in the question true. You also know that both ab and bc are greater than 0, so you only need to test cases where all the variables have the same sign.

Case	b	c	a	$0 < ab < ac$
1	3	2	1	$0 < 3 < 2$ ✗
2	−2	−3	−1	$0 < 2 < 3$ ✓

Only case 2, in which all the variables are negative, is valid. Thus, a must be negative; statement (2) is sufficient.

The correct answer is **(D)**: Each statement alone is sufficient.

UNIT THREE

Word Problems

In this unit, you'll learn how to translate, organize, and solve all kinds of story problems, including how to logic your way to an answer on many types of these problems; topics include rates, work, overlapping sets, statistics, and consecutive integers. You'll also learn advanced methods for the Choose Smart Numbers and Work Backwards strategies.

In This Unit

Translations

In This Chapter

- Pay Attention to Units

- Common Relationships

In this chapter, you will learn how to translate stories into math. You'll also learn certain common formulas that the GMAT expects you to know (e.g., Profit = Revenue − Cost), as well as how to convert among different types of units (e.g., meters to kilometers).

CHAPTER 17 **Translations**

Story problems are prevalent on the GMAT and can come in any form: Word Problems, Fractions, Percents, Algebra, and so on. Tackle story problems using your standard 3-step approach to solving: Understand, Plan, Solve.

Step 1: Understand: What's the Story?

Glance at the problem: The first thing you'll notice is a lot of text. Also note whether it is Problem Solving or Data Sufficiency. Do the answers or statements give you any quick clues about possible approaches? (Example: "Nice" real numbers in the answers on PS might lead you to work backwards. An annoying or complicated equation anywhere in the problem or statements signals a chance to rephrase or simplify.)

Often, on story problems, it's best to read the entire problem before you begin to jot down the information. In fact, you might move this task to your Plan phase.

Step 2: Plan: Choose an Approach

Your task is two-fold: Turn the story into math and then decide how you want to approach it. You can use either the Algebraic method or one of the test-taking strategies (Work Backwards, Choose Smart Numbers, Test Cases, and so on). One more thing: Choose variables that tell you what they are (more on this below).

Step 3: Solve: Go for It!

Now that you understand and have a plan, go ahead and solve. (If you don't understand or have a plan, don't try to solve. Guess and move on.)

Try this problem:

> A candy company sells premium chocolate candies at $5 per pound and regular chocolate candies at $4 per pound in increments of whole pounds only. If Bronte buys a 7-pound box of chocolate candies that costs $31, how many pounds of premium chocolate candies are in the box?
>
> (A) 1
> (B) 2
> (C) 3
> (D) 4
> (E) 5

Ready?

Step 1: **Understand.** The first glance indicates that this is a PS story problem. The answers are small whole numbers, so this might be a candidate for working backwards. Jot down WB on your scrap paper to remind yourself later.

Now, read the story and get oriented. There are two different kinds of candies. You have to buy in whole-pound increments. Bronte (abbreviate this to B from now on, even in your head) buys a 7-pound box that cost $31. It asks how many pounds were premium candies. That's a lot of information. Push the *jot* task to the Plan step.

Step 2: **Plan.** B probably bought both kinds of candies. How can you know? Glance at the answers. The choices are 1 through 5, so B had to buy *some* premium candies but couldn't have bought all 7 pounds. So, yes, B bought both kinds of candies. Call premium candies *P* and regular candies *R*. (Don't just use *x* and *y* every time. Choose variables that tell you what they are. You don't want to accidentally solve for the wrong thing!)

The question asks specifically for the number of pounds of premium candies. This represents a single variable in the problem (*P*), so working backwards would be a good strategy here.

Here's one way to organize this story on paper:

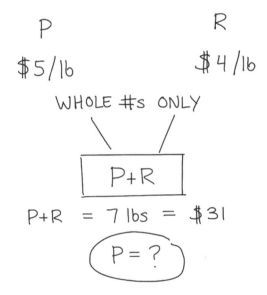

Step 3: **Solve.** Start with either answer (B) or answer (D), your choice:

	P=	R=	$P\\ 5P	$R\\ 4R	= $31?
(A)					
(B)	2	5	5(2)=10	4(5)=20	No.\ Too small.
(C)					
(D)					
(E)					

Answer (B) is incorrect. The number only added up to $30 and it needs to add up to $31. Which direction do you need to go to find the correct answer?

You need to add a dollar, so you need more of the more expensive chocolate. Which one is more expensive? The premium brand is, so you need more of that type. Cross off answer (A) as well, since that would mean fewer pounds of the premium brand.

Next, if you feel comfortable with this, you can actually think your way through the rest of the math. Answer (B) came to $30, but B spent $31, so you need to add just one more dollar. The difference in price between P and R is also just one dollar. So if you add one pound of P and take away one pound of R, you'll pay one more dollar. The answer must be (C), 3 pounds.

If you're not comfortable thinking that through, that's fine—just go back to the standard process and try answer (D) next. Use the scratch paper setup you already have, and run the new answer choice through the same process.

If P is 4, then R is 3. The cost is $(5)(4) + (4)(3) = 20 + 12 = \$32$. This is too much, so answer (D) is incorrect. Then examine the pattern. Answer (B) was too small at $30 and answer (D) was too large at $32, so answer (C) must be correct.

Either way, the correct answer is (C).

You can also solve algebraically, but fair warning: On this problem, since the answer choice values are such nice numbers, the algebra is probably more annoying than working backwards. It's still a good idea to know how this works, though, because you may need to use algebra on a different one. For example:

$p =$ pounds of premium chocolate candies

$r =$ pounds of regular chocolate candies

You would also want to write down something similar to this:

$p =$ _____?

What else can you write down? Bronte bought a 7-pound box of the candies. Both premium and regular make up that 7 pounds, so you can write an equation:

$p + r = 7$

The other given concerns the total cost of the box, $31. The total cost is equal to the cost of the premium chocolates plus the cost of the regular chocolates.

This is a relationship the GMAT expects you to know: *Total Cost = Unit Price × Quantity*. You can express total cost using information you already have:

Total Cost of Box $= \$31$

Cost of Premiums $= (5 \text{ \$/pound}) \times (p \text{ pounds}) = 5p$

Cost of Regulars $= (4 \text{ \$/pound}) \times (r \text{ pounds}) = 4r$

Note that you can translate "dollars per pound" to "$/pound." In general, the word *per* is translated as "divided by."

17

Put that all together to get the second equation:

$$31 = 5p + 4r$$

Here's your current scratch paper; how can you solve?

$p = \text{\# prem}$
$r = \text{\# reg}$
$p + r = 7$
$31 = 5p + 4r$
$p = \underline{\qquad}?$

When you have two equations with two variables, the most efficient way to find the desired value is to eliminate the unwanted variable in order to solve for the desired variable.

You're looking for p. To eliminate r, first isolate it in one of the equations. It is easier to isolate r in the first equation:

$$r + p = 7 \longrightarrow r = 7 - p$$

Now, replace r with $(7 - p)$ in the second equation and solve for p:

$$31 = 5p + 4(7 - p)$$
$$31 = 5p + 28 - 4p$$
$$3 = p$$

The correct answer is (C).

Story problems typically toss a lot of information at you, which is why it is so important to have a good process. Understand the story first—and possibly hold off on jotting down the math until you start to figure out your Plan. When you Understand and have a Plan, then you can go ahead and Solve.

One last thing: A lot of stories have what's called a *hidden integer constraint*. If the story is talking about people or cars or marbles, there's an assumption that you have only whole numbers of people or cars or marbles. You'll never have 1.2 people or half of a car.

Pay Attention to Units

Unlike problems that test pure algebra, Word Problems have a context or story. The values, both unknown and known, have a meaning. Practically, this means that every value in a Word Problem has units.

Every equation that correctly represents a relationship has units that make sense. Most relationships are either additive or multiplicative.

17

Additive Relationships

In the chocolates problem, there were two additive relationships:

$$\text{pounds } p + \text{pounds } r = 7 \text{ pounds}$$

$$\$31 = \text{cost of } p + \text{cost of } r$$

For each equation, the units of every term are the same; for example, pounds plus pounds equals pounds.

Multiplicative Relationships

Remember this relationship?

$$\text{Total Cost} = \text{Unit Price} \times \text{Quantity}$$

In the problem, the cost of p is $5 per pound and the cost of r is $4 per pound. If you're solving algebraically, it works out this way:

$$5 \left(\frac{\text{dollars}}{\text{pound}} \right) \times p \text{ (pounds)} = 5p \text{ (dollars)}$$

$$4 \left(\frac{\text{dollars}}{\text{pound}} \right) \times r \text{ (pounds)} = 4r \text{ (dollars)}$$

For multiplicative relationships, treat units like numerators and denominators. Units that are multiplied together *do* change.

In the equations above, pounds in the denominator of the first term cancel out pounds in the numerator of the second term, leaving dollars as the final units:

$$5 \left(\frac{\text{dollars}}{\cancel{\text{pounds}}} \right) \times p \left(\cancel{\text{pounds}} \right) = 5p \text{ (dollars)}$$

Look at the formula for area to see what happens to the same units when they appear on the same side of the fraction (l = length and w = width):

$$l \text{ (feet)} \times w \text{ (feet)} = lw \left(\text{feet}^2 \right)$$

Keep track of the units to stay on track in the calculation.

Common Relationships

The GMAT will assume that you have mastered the following relationships. Notice that for all of these relationships, the units follow the rules laid out in the previous section:

- Total Cost (\$) = Unit Price (\$/unit) × Quantity Purchased (units)
- Profit (\$) = Revenue (\$) − Cost (\$)
- Total Earnings (\$) = Wage Rate (\$/hour) × Hours Worked (hours)
- Miles = Miles per Hour × Hours
- Miles = Miles per Gallon × Gallons

Units Conversion

When values with units are multiplied or divided, the units change. This property is the basis of using **conversion factors** to convert units. A conversion factor is a fraction whose numerator and denominator have different units but the same value.

For instance, how many seconds are in 7 minutes? There are 60 seconds in a minute. In this case, $\frac{60 \text{ seconds}}{1 \text{ minute}}$ is a conversion factor. Because the numerator and denominator are the same, multiplying by a conversion factor is just a sneaky way of multiplying by 1. The multiplication looks like this:

$$7 \text{ minutes} \times \frac{60 \text{ seconds}}{1 \text{ minute}} = 420 \text{ seconds}$$

Because you are multiplying, you can cancel minutes, leaving the desired units (seconds).

Questions will occasionally center around your ability to convert units. Try the following example:

> A certain medicine requires 4 doses per day. If each dose is 150 milligrams, how many milligrams of medicine will a person have taken after the end of the third day, if the medicine is used as directed?

For any question that involves unit conversion, there will have to be some concrete value given. In this case, you were told that the time period is three days, that there are 4 doses/day, and that 1 dose equals 150 milligrams.

Now, you need to know what the question wants. It's asking for the number of milligrams of medicine that will be taken in that time. How can you combine all of those givens so that the only units that remain are milligrams?

Combine the calculations into one big expression:

$$3 \text{ days} \times \frac{4 \text{ doses}}{1 \text{ day}} \times \frac{150 \text{ milligrams}}{1 \text{ dose}} = 1,800 \text{ milligrams}$$

During the GMAT, you may not actually write out the units for each piece of multiplication. If you don't, however, make sure that your conversion factors are set up properly to cancel out the units you don't want and to leave the units you do want.

Finally, keep an eye out for more of these relationships! For instance, rate and work problems are also built on a common relationship that you're expected to know for the test; you'll learn about that relationship later.

Advanced material for the Word Problems unit (primarily covering additional strategies for overlapping sets and consecutive integers) can be found in Atlas, Manhattan Prep's online learning platform. Use the online material only if you feel that you have mastered everything in the Word Problems unit of this strategy guide and only if you are aiming for a Quant section score of 48 or higher.

17

Problem Set

Now that you've finished the chapter, try the following problems.

1. United Telephone charges a base rate of $10.00 for service, plus an additional charge of $0.25 per minute. Atlantic Call charges a base rate of $12.00 for service, plus an additional charge of $0.20 per minute. For what number of minutes would the bills for each telephone company be the same?

2. Caleb spends $72.50 on 50 hamburgers for the marching band. If single burgers cost $1.00 each and double burgers cost $1.50 each, how many double burgers did he buy?

3. Carina has 100 ounces of coffee divided into packages of 5 or 10 ounces. If she has 2 more 5-ounce packages than 10-ounce packages, how many 10-ounce packages does she have?

   (A)   2
   (B)   4
   (C)   6
   (D)   8
   (E)   10

4. A circus earned $150,000 in ticket revenue by selling 1,800 VIP and Standard tickets. They sold 25% more Standard tickets than VIP tickets. If the revenue from Standard tickets represents one-third of the total ticket revenue, what is the price of a VIP ticket?

Solutions

1. **40 minutes:** Let x = the number of minutes.

    A call made by United Telephone costs $10.00 plus $0.25 per minute: $10 + 0.25x$.

    A call made by Atlantic Call costs $12.00 plus $0.20 per minute: $12 + 0.20x$.

    Set the expressions equal to each other and solve for x:

    $$10 + 0.25x = 12 + 0.20x$$
    $$0.05x = 2$$
    $$x = 40$$

    For that last math step, you can multiply both sides by 100 to get rid of the decimal ($5x = 200$), then solve. You could also recognize that 0.05 is the same as 5% and use percent benchmarks to solve. If 5% of a number equals 2, then 10% of the number equals 4, and 100% of the number equals 40.

2. **45 double burgers:** Let s = the number of single burgers purchased and d = the number of double burgers purchased:

    Caleb bought 50 burgers: Caleb spent $72.50 in all:

    $$s + d = 50$$ $$s + 1.5d = 72.5$$

    Combine the two equations by subtracting equation 1 from equation 2:

    $$s + 1.5d = 72.50$$
    $$-\,(s + d = 50)$$
    $$\overline{0.5d = 22.5}$$
    $$d = 45$$

3. **(C) 6:** The answers are small integers and represent a single variable in the problem, so work backwards to solve. Set up a table to keep your work organized as you test the answer choices. Start with answer (B) or (D).

    Let T equal the number of 10-ounce packages and F equal the number of 5-ounce packages. *Last* refers to the value in the previous column.

$T =$	Amt in 10 oz $(T \times 10)$	Amt in 5 oz $(100 - \text{last})$	$F = (\text{last}/5)$	$F - T = 2$?
(B) 4	40 oz	60 oz	12	$12 - 4 = 8$ No
(D) 8	80 oz	20 oz	4	$4 - 8 = -4$ No

    Answer (B) is too large and answer (D) is too small; the correct answer must be in between the two.

17

Alternatively, solve via algebra. Let F equal the number of 5-ounce packages and T equal the number of 10-ounce packages:

Carina has 100 ounces of coffee:

$$5F + 10T = 100$$

She has 2 more 5-ounce packages than 10-ounce packages:

$$F = T + 2$$

Combine the equations by substituting the value of F from equation 2 into equation 1:

$$5(T + 2) + 10T = 100$$
$$5T + 10 + 10T = 100$$
$$15T + 10 = 100$$
$$15T = 90$$
$$T = 6$$

4. **$125:** To answer this question correctly, make sure to differentiate between the *price* of tickets and the *quantity* of tickets sold. Let V equal the number of VIP tickets sold and S equal the number of Standard tickets sold.

The question indicates that the circus sold a total of 1,800 tickets, and that the circus sold 25% more Standard tickets than VIP tickets. Create two equations:

$$V + S = 1,800 \qquad 1.25V = S$$

Use these equations to figure out how many VIP tickets were sold:

$$V + S = 1,800$$
$$V + (1.25V) = 1,800$$
$$2.25V = 1,800$$
$$\frac{9}{4}V = 1,800$$
$$V = 1,800 \left(\frac{4}{9}\right)$$
$$V = 800$$

Now, find the cost per VIP ticket. The circus earned $150,000 in ticket revenue, and Standard tickets represented one-third of that revenue. Therefore, Standard tickets accounted for $\frac{1}{3} \times \$150,000 = \$50,000$. VIP tickets then accounted for the other $100,000 in revenue.

Thus, $\dfrac{100,000}{800} = \dfrac{1,000}{8} = \$125$ per VIP ticket.

Strategy: Logic It Out

In This Chapter

- Draw It Out

- Maximizing and Minimizing

- Write Out the Scenarios

- When in Doubt, Logic It Out

In this chapter, you will learn how to logic your way to answers on all kinds of story problems, including drawing out a story, listing out and testing scenarios, maximizing and minimizing, and more.

CHAPTER 18 Strategy: Logic It Out

Numerous times throughout this guide, you've learned how to use real numbers or to sketch out a story—basically, to use a more "real-world" approach to perform the necessary math.

This chapter contains more ways to **logic it out** on the GMAT.

Try this problem:

> Five identical pieces of wire are soldered together end-to-end to form one longer wire, with the pieces overlapping by 4 centimeters at each joint. If the wire thus made is exactly 1 meter long, how long, in centimeters, is each of the identical pieces? (1 meter = 100 centimeters)
>
> (A) 21.2
> (B) 22
> (C) 23.2
> (D) 24
> (E) 25.4

The setup of this problem is unusual, so draw out the scenario in order to understand what the problem is describing:

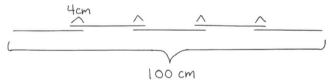

How many overlapping areas are there? Many people make the mistake of thinking that, because there are five pieces of wire, there are also five spots where the wires join. It turns out that there are only four joints! Sketch out weird scenarios to catch these kinds of details.

The total length is 100 centimeters plus those extra amounts where the wires overlap. What happens when you solder the wire together? Consider just the first two segments. Imagine that each one is 10 centimeters long (they aren't—this is just to understand what's going on and to help you figure out your plan).

If two 10-centimeter wires were laid end-to-end with no overlap, the length would be 20 centimeters. But since the two are overlapped, you'll lose a portion of that length. How much?

$$10 \text{\textemdash\textemdash\textemdash} \text{\textemdash\textemdash\textemdash} 10$$

$$\underline{10}$$
$$\underline{} \quad 4 \qquad 6$$

$$\underline{10}$$
$$\underline{}$$
$$\qquad\qquad 6$$

When they're soldered (melted) together, you don't lose *both* of the overlapping segments—if you did, then there would be a gap in the wire. The two pieces wouldn't actually be connected. Rather, think of it as though the top 4-centimeter segment stays, but the bottom one "disappears" (because it gets melted into the top one). So the length is $10 + 6 = 16$ centimeters. You've lost the length of *one* of the overlapping segments, or 4 centimeters.

Back to the given problem. There are four overlapping segments. You lose 4 centimeters at each connection, so you'll lose a total of 16 centimeters. The full length *before* the wires are soldered together—shown in the first picture—is $100 + 16 = 116$ centimeters.

Because there are five wires, the length of each one is $\dfrac{116}{5} = \ldots$ wait! That's a little annoying without a calculator. Break it into pieces that are more easily divisible by 5:

$$\frac{100 + 15 + 1}{5}$$

$$\frac{100}{5} = 20 \qquad \frac{15}{5} = 3 \qquad \frac{1}{5} = 0.2$$

The length is 23.2. Keep an eye on the answer choices as you do this math. Once you realize that the answer is 23-point-*something*, you can stop.

The correct answer is (C).

This problem can also be done algebraically; the relevant equation is $5x - 4(4) = 100$, where x is the length of each wire. Those who don't draw it out, though, are more likely to think that there are five joints and mistakenly write the equation as $5x - 5(4) = 100$, which leads to trap answer (D) 24.

Draw It Out

There are multiple ways that you can avoid "textbook" math to get to the answer more quickly and easily on the GMAT. Whenever you find a problem that could actually be happening to someone in the real world, ask yourself: If I were in this situation right now, how would I try to figure out the answer?

You almost certainly wouldn't start writing equations. Instead, you'd sketch out the situation using a combination of logic, math, and just trying out numbers or scenarios.

How could you sketch out this problem?

> A train travels at a constant rate of 90 kilometers/hour. How many hours does it take the train to travel 450,000 meters? (1 kilometer = 1,000 meters)

First, 450,000 meters is a really annoying number—but the problem gives you a conversion metric. And the rate is in kilometers per hour, so definitely convert the ugly meters figure to kilometers. Divide by 1,000 to convert this distance to 450 kilometers.

Logic it out: You're driving the train and you're going a steady 90 kilometers/hour. How long is it going to take you to go 450 kilometers? After an hour, you've gone 90 kilometers. After two hours, you've gone 180. What's the pattern?

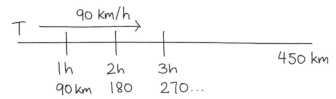

It's all in multiples of 90. It's going to take you five multiples, or 5 hours, to get to 450. (By the way, if you like, you can make the numbers easier to look at by chopping a 0 off of each one. You're driving 9 kilometers every hour and want to go 45 kilometers total. That will take 5 hours.)

A problem could also ask something like this:

> A train leaves a station at 1 p.m. and travels at a constant rate of 90 kilometers/hour. At what time does the train reach the next station, a distance of 450,000 meters? (1 kilometer = 1,000 meters)

It still takes the train 5 hours to travel that distance, but the answer is now 1 p.m. + 5 hours = 6 p.m. As on any problem, take note of what the question wants you to find; a good (and very annoying!) trap answer on this problem would be 5 p.m.

Most of the time, the GMAT will ask for the stopwatch time; occasionally, it will ask you to solve in terms of clock times.

There are usually multiple ways to draw out the problem to get to the answer, so you aren't stuck trying to figure out the main textbook math method. Put yourself in the situation and ask yourself how you would go about this in the real world. You'd almost never start writing a bunch of equations; rather, you'd use logic and estimation to get to a close-enough answer.

Rate and work problems, in particular, often lend themselves well to using logic to solve. You'll see more of these in the next chapter.

18

Maximizing and Minimizing

As you learned a little earlier in this guide, a story problem might ask you to find the minimum or maximum possible value of something.

For example:

> There are enough available spaces on a school team to select at most $\frac{1}{3}$ of the 50 students trying out for the team. What is the greatest number of students that could be rejected while still filling all available spaces for the team?
>
> (A) 16
> (B) 17
> (C) 33
> (D) 34
> (E) 35

You're asked to maximize the number of *rejected* students. Think about what else you may need to minimize (or maximize) in the problem in order to maximize this number.

First, fill all available spaces on the team. If at most $\frac{1}{3}$ of the students can be selected, then at most $\frac{50}{3}$, or $16\frac{2}{3}$, students can be selected. It's impossible to select $\frac{2}{3}$ of a person, though! Is the maximum possible 16 or 17?

If the *maximum* is 16 and a bit, then you can't go up to 17. Round down to 16. (Note that both of these values are in the answers; they're traps!)

The maximum number of rejected students, then, is $50 - 16 = 34$. The correct answer is (D).

This problem has a hidden *integer constraint*. Notice also that you have to be careful to round in the right direction—not up, but down. If the maximum number of available spaces is $16\frac{2}{3}$, then 17 students is more than that max, so round down to 16.

Try another. How would you logic this problem out?

> Orange Computers is breaking up its conference attendees into groups. Each group must have exactly 1 person from Division A, 2 people from Division B, and 3 people from Division C. There are 20 people from Division A, 30 people from Division B, and 40 people from Division C at the conference. What is the smallest number of people who will NOT be able to be assigned to a group?
>
> (A) 12
> (B) 5
> (C) 2
> (D) 1
> (E) 0

18

You're in charge of the conference and you have to figure this out. First, you need to **understand** what the parameters are. Jot down the given information on your scrap paper:

Div.	Total People	Per Group
A	20	1
B	30	2
C	40	3

Plan. The goal is to place as many people as possible in groups. Consider Division A. There are 20 of these people and you need 1 per group, so that's 20 groups…

Oh, wait. For 20 groups, you'd need 40 people from B and there are only 30, so that won't work. There have to be fewer than 20 groups. (And, incidentally, this proves that at least 1 person will be without a group, so the answer can't be 0.) Hmm. If starting with Division B, you'd have 15 groups, but that would require 45 people from Division C and there are only 40.

The most constrained or limited group is Division C because you need 3 in each group and you only have 40 people overall, for a maximum of 13 groups. So start there.

Solve. Division C can make 13 groups of 3, using a total of 39 people. One person is left without a group. Glance at the answers. Answer (E) can't be correct, since at least 1 person is already without a group (if you didn't already notice this earlier).

Next, Division B will use $13 \times 2 = 26$ people. There are 4 Division B people left without a group. So there are at least 5 total without a group now; eliminate answers (C) and (D).

You'll also need 13 people from Division A, leaving 7 more without a group. Look at the answers. Don't even bother to add up the numbers—the answer must be more than 5, so answer (A) must be correct.

Some max/min problems will be more like the first one, where the path of the math is fairly straightforward, but you have to make decisions along the way about maximizing or minimizing other pieces in order to get to your desired answer.

In others, the starting point won't be so obvious. As with the second problem, you'll try a couple of scenarios until you find the limiting factor, and then you'll follow the math from there.

In both cases, make sure to pay attention to any constraints, especially those not explicitly stated. People and saxophones and rabbits cannot be split into fractional parts.

Write Out the Scenarios

Here's another variation on how to use logic:

> During a week-long sale at a car dealership, the greatest number of cars sold on any one day was 12. If at least 2 cars were sold each day, was the average (arithmetic mean) daily number of cars sold during that week greater than 6 ?
>
> (1)   During that week, the second fewest number of cars sold on any one day was 4.
>
> (2)   During that week, the median number of cars sold was 10.

Note: The average is found by taking the sum of a set of numbers and dividing by the number of terms. The median is the middle number in a set of numbers arranged in increasing order. You'll learn more about statistics a bit later in this guide—but you can solve this problem even though you haven't relearned much of anything about stats yet!

Pretend you're the manager of the car dealership and the owner has asked you to figure this out. Your manager knows you're not a mathematician. . .and you don't need to be to do this.

You know that the highest day was 12, but you don't know which day of the week that was. And at least 2 cars were sold each day, but more cars could have been sold. The problem allows multiple possible scenarios, so how could you draw something that shows what you know but allows for flexibility?

Glance at the statements. They provide information about the fewest number of sales and the median number of sales.

Since it's asking about median, try organizing the number of sales from smallest to largest.

Draw out seven slots (one for each day) and add the information given in the question stem:

$$\underline{\geq2} \quad \underline{} \quad \underline{} \quad \underline{} \quad \underline{} \quad \underline{} \quad \underline{12}$$

The problem indicates that at least 2 cars were sold on each day, so the smallest number has to be at least 2 (though it could be greater). The greatest number sold on any one day was 12. The other days have to be somewhere in this range from 2 to 12, *inclusive*. You are allowed to have two days on which the same number of cars were sold.

The question asks whether the average number of daily sales for the week is more than 6. Because this is a Yes/No DS question, test each statement to see whether it can give you both a "Yes, the average is more than 6" answer and a "No, the average is not more than 6" answer. If so, then you'll know the statement is insufficient.

(1)   During that week, the second smallest number of cars sold on any one day was 4.

Draw out a version of the scenario that includes statement (1):

$$\underline{\geq2} \quad \underline{4} \quad \underline{} \quad \underline{} \quad \underline{} \quad \underline{} \quad \underline{12}$$

Can you find a way to make the average less than 6? Keep the first day at 2 and make the other days as small as possible. You can use the same number more than once:

$$\underline{\geq2} \quad \underline{4} \quad \underline{4} \quad \underline{4} \quad \underline{4} \quad \underline{4} \quad \underline{12}$$

If the first day is 2, the sum of the numbers is 34. The average is $\frac{34}{7}$, which is a little less than 5.

Can you also make the average greater than 6? Try making the numbers as big as you can:

$$\underline{4} \quad \underline{4} \quad \underline{12} \quad \underline{12} \quad \underline{12} \quad \underline{12} \quad \underline{12}$$

You may be able to eyeball that and tell it will be greater than 6. If not, calculate: The sum is $8 + 5(12) = 68$, so the average is $\frac{68}{7}$, which is a bit less than 10.

Statement (1) is not sufficient because the average might be greater than or less than 6.

Cross off answers (A) and (D) and move to statement (2):

> (2)   During that week, the median number of cars sold was 10.

Again, draw out the scenario (using *only* the second statement this time!). The median is the middle number or slot in the list:

$$\underline{\geq 2} \quad \underline{} \quad \underline{} \quad \underline{10} \quad \underline{} \quad \underline{} \quad \underline{12}$$

Can you make the average less than 6 ? The three lowest days could each be 2. Then, the next three days could each be 10.

$$\underline{2} \quad \underline{2} \quad \underline{2} \quad \underline{10} \quad \underline{10} \quad \underline{10} \quad \underline{12}$$

The sum is $6 + 30 + 12 = 48$. The average is $\frac{48}{7}$, or just less than 7, but greater than 6. The numbers cannot be made any smaller. First, you have to have a minimum of 2 a day. Once you hit the median of 10 in the middle slot, you have to have something greater than or equal to the median for the remaining slots to the right.

The smallest possible average is greater than 6, so this statement is sufficient to answer the question. The correct answer is (B).

If a problem talks about a set of numbers but doesn't give you the value of all of those numbers, try drawing out slots to represent each number in the set and stepping through the allowed scenarios. If it's a max/min problem, you'll probably want to test the extreme scenarios (make everything as small as possible or as large as possible) to see the range of possible outcomes.

If a problem includes information about the median, you will probably want to order the numbers from least to greatest.

When in Doubt, Logic It Out

Sketching out a problem and using logic is a fantastic way to get through some especially annoying story problems—and not just when you're in doubt. As you get better at working in this way, you'll find that these methods are very effective even when you do know how to do the "textbook" version of the math.

First, put yourself in the problem; pretend that you have to figure this out in the real world. Then, ask yourself what you would do in order to find the answer—even if just to estimate and narrow down the answers.

As you work, keep your eye on the answer choices. Often, on GMAT stories, you'll be able to stop working before you reach the "true" end of the math, because the other four answers will already have been eliminated.

18

Problem Set

Now that you've finished the chapter, try the following problems. You'll get additional chances to practice these techniques later in this guide.

1. A bookshelf holds both paperback and hardcover books. The ratio of paperback books to hardcover books is 22 to 3. How many paperback books are on the shelf?

    (1) The number of books on the shelf is between 202 and 247, inclusive.

    (2) If 18 paperback books were removed from the shelf and replaced with 18 hardcover books, the resulting ratio of paperback books to hardcover books on the shelf would be 4 to 1.

2. a, b, and c are integers in the set $\{a, 72, b, 51, c, 85\}$. Is the median of the set greater than 70 ?

    (1) $b > c > 69$

    (2) $a < c < 71$

3. Velma has exactly one week to learn all 71 Japanese hiragana characters. If she can learn at most a dozen of them on any one day and will only have time to learn four of them on Friday, what is the least number of hiragana that Velma will have to learn on Saturday?

4. A casino uses chips in $5 and $7 denominations only. Which of the following amounts CANNOT be paid out using these chips?

    (A) $31

    (B) $29

    (C) $26

    (D) $23

    (E) $21

18

Answers and explanations follow on the next page. ▶ ▶ ▶

Solutions

1. **(D):** The question stem states that the ratio of paperback books to hardcover books is 22 to 3 and asks for the number of paperback books. Set up a ratio table:

	P	*H*	Total
R	22	3	25
M			
A	⬭		

The actual number of paperbacks must be a multiple of 22, the number of hardcovers must be a multiple of 3, and the total number of books must be a multiple of 25. Use this knowledge to evaluate the statements.

(1) SUFFICIENT: There is only one multiple of 25 between 202 and 247, so the total number of books must be 225. You can find the unknown multiplier, so you can also find the number of *P*'s.

(2) SUFFICIENT: Hmm. The starting ratio can be written as an equation: $\frac{P}{H} = \frac{22}{3}$.

Then, a new ratio is given. Use this information to write a second equation: $\left(\frac{P-18}{H+18}\right) = \frac{4}{1}$. You now have two equations and two variables; can you solve?

Check to make sure that both equations are linear and that you do have two *different* equations. Cross-multiply: $3P = 22H$ and $(P-18) = 4(H+18)$. You might want to do one more step with the second one (but don't do more work than you have to do): $P = 4H + (18)(4) - 18$.

Yes, the equations are both linear (no squares or similar) and they are not the same equation. You can solve for the individual values of *P* and *H*.

The correct answer is **(D):** Each statement works alone.

2. **(A):** The set is not in increasing order already, so you're going to need to do that yourself. Draw out six spaces and imagine they contain values ordered from low to high. What would the median be? Since there are an even number of numbers, the median of a set of six integers is the average of the two middle terms (the third and fourth) when the terms are placed in order from low to high.

Glance at the statements. Together with the question stem, many scenarios are possible, so test cases on this problem.

(1) SUFFICIENT: Since the statement establishes the smallest possible values for *b* and *c*, start with the minimum case. If *c* is an integer greater than 69, the smallest *c* can be is 70. By similar logic, the smallest *b* could be is 71. In this case, the set contains the values $\{a, 51, 70, 71, 72, 85\}$. The only unknown is the value of *a*.

Try the smallest possibility for a. If $a \leq 51$, the median is halfway between 70 and 71, which is greater than 70.

$$\frac{a \leq 51}{\text{low}} \qquad \underline{51} \qquad \underbrace{\underline{c = 70} \qquad \underline{b = 71}}_{\text{median}} \qquad \underline{72} \qquad \frac{85}{\text{high}}$$

Next, place a in the middle. If $a = 70$ or 71, then the median is either between 70 and 71 or between 71 and 71—both of which are greater than 70. Here's the 71 and 71 case:

$$\frac{51}{\text{low}} \qquad \underline{c = 70} \qquad \underbrace{\underline{a = 71} \qquad \underline{b = 71}}_{\text{median}} \qquad \underline{72} \qquad \frac{85}{\text{high}}$$

If $a > 71$, the ordered set is $\{51, 70, 71, 72, a, 85\}$, so the median is between 71 and 72, or again greater than 71:

$$\frac{51}{\text{low}} \qquad \underline{c = 70} \qquad \underbrace{\underline{b = 71} \qquad \underline{72}}_{\text{median}} \qquad \underline{a = 72} \qquad \frac{85}{\text{high}}$$

In all cases, the median is greater than 70 using the *smallest* possible values for all three variables, so the answer is a definite Yes.

(2) INSUFFICIENT: Since the statement establishes the greatest possible values for a and c, start with the maximum case. If c is an integer less than 71, the greatest c can be is 70. By similar logic, the greatest a could be is 69. In this case, the set is $\{b, 51, 69, 70, 72, 85\}$. The only unknown is the value of b.

If $b \leq 51$, the ordered set is $\{b, 51, 69, 70, 72, 85\}$ and the median is halfway between 69 and 70, which is less than 70. The answer is No, the median is not greater than 70 as shown below:

$$\frac{b \leq 51}{\text{low}} \qquad \underline{51} \qquad \underbrace{\underline{a = 69} \qquad \underline{c = 70}}_{\text{median}} \qquad \underline{72} \qquad \frac{85}{\text{high}}$$

Try to get a Yes answer next. Jump much higher for b.

If $b = 90$, the ordered set is $\{51, 69, 70, 72, 85, 90\}$, the median is between 70 and 72, which is greater than 70.

Because there are both Yes and No cases, this statement is not sufficient.

The correct answer is **(A)**: Statement (1) works alone, but statement (2) does not.

3. **7**: Draw it out! Draw seven slots and label them for the days of the week. The problem states that Velma will learn 4 hiragana on Friday and at most 12 on any other day. Finally, it asked for the least possible number that she will need to learn on Saturday:

$$\frac{\leq 12}{\text{Sun}} \qquad \frac{\leq 12}{\text{M}} \qquad \frac{\leq 12}{\text{Tu}} \qquad \frac{\leq 12}{\text{W}} \qquad \frac{\leq 12}{\text{Th}} \qquad \frac{4}{\text{F}} \qquad \frac{\text{least?}}{\text{Sat}}$$

Since she'll learn 4 on Friday, she has 67 more to learn. To minimize the number of hiragana that she will have to learn on Saturday, *maximize* the number that she learns on the other days. If Velma learns the maximum of 12 hiragana from Sunday to Thursday, then she will have $67 - 5(12) = 7$ left for Saturday:

$$\frac{12}{\text{Sun}} \quad \frac{12}{\text{M}} \quad \frac{12}{\text{Tu}} \quad \frac{12}{\text{W}} \quad \frac{12}{\text{Th}} \quad \frac{4}{\text{F}} \quad \frac{7}{\text{Sat}}$$

4. **(D) $23:** The payouts will have to be in the sum of some integer number of $5 chips and some integer number of $7 chips. Which of the answer choices *cannot* be the sum? First, check the answers for any multiples of 7 and/or 5; this eliminates answer (E). Glance at the answers. The numbers are not that large, so you could try to re-create them. Write out some multiples of 5 and 7 and try to combine them to create the remaining four answers:

$$
\begin{array}{cc}
5 & 7 \\
10 & 14 \\
15 & 21 \\
20 &
\end{array}
$$

You don't need to go higher than 20 for the multiples of 5. If that went up to 25 and you added 7 more, you'd be above the greatest number in the answers. Ditto, if you went up to 28 for the multiples of 7, then added 5 more, you'd be beyond the range of answers.

Now, pair up the numbers systematically and see which answer choices you can match.
$5 + 7, 5 + 14, 5 + 21$? Bingo, that last one equals 26. Eliminate answer (C).

Next, $10 + 7, 10 + 14, 10 + 21$? Bingo again, the last one equals 31. Eliminate answer (A).

Keep going; $15 + 14 = 29$, so eliminate answer (B). The only remaining value is 23; by process of elimination, it must be the sum that cannot be paid out in these chips, so **(D)** is the correct answer.

18

Rates and Work

In This Chapter

In this chapter, you will learn how to set up and solve a variety of rate and work problems, both algebraically and by using logic. (The latter approach is often the easier one!) You'll also learn what to do with more complicated scenarios such as relative rates, average rates, and working together.

CHAPTER 19 **Rates and Work**

Rate problems come in a variety of forms on the GMAT, but all are marked by three primary components: *rate*, *time*, and either *distance* or *work*.

These three elements are related by the following equations:

Rate × Time = Distance

Rate × Time = Work

These equations can be abbreviated as $RT = D$ or as $RT = W$.

This chapter will discuss the ways in which the GMAT makes rate situations more complicated. Often, $RT = D$ problems, also known as RTD problems, will involve more than one person or vehicle traveling. Similarly, many $RT = W$ problems will involve more than one worker.

Let's get started with a review of some fundamental properties of rate problems.

Basic Motion: The RTD Chart

All basic motion problems involve three elements: rate, time, and distance.

Rate is expressed as a ratio of distance and time, with two corresponding units. Some examples of rates include 30 miles per hour, 10 meters/second, and 15 kilometers/day.

Time is expressed using a unit of time. Some examples of times include 6 hours, 23 seconds, and 5 months.

Distance is expressed using a unit of distance. Some examples of distances include 18 miles, 20 meters, and 100 kilometers.

You can make an RTD chart to organize the information for a basic motion problem. Read the problem and fill in two of the variables. Then, use the $RT = D$ formula to find the missing variable. For example:

> If a car is traveling at 30 miles per hour, how long does it take to travel 75 miles?

Fill in your RTD chart with the given information. Then, solve for the time:

	Rate (miles/hour)	×	Time (hours)	=	Distance (miles)
Car	30	×		=	75

$30t = 75$, or $t = 2.5$ hours

Up next is a much more complicated problem. Pretend you're Annika, actually hiking right now, and see what you can do with the Logic It Out approach from the prior chapter.

Annika hikes at a constant rate of 12 minutes per kilometer. She has hiked 2.75 kilometers east from the start of a hiking trail when she realizes that she has to be back at the start of the trail in 45 minutes. If Annika continues east, then turns around and retraces her path to reach the start of the trail in exactly 45 minutes, for how many kilometers total did she hike east?

(A) 2.25
(B) 2.75
(C) 3.25
(D) 3.75
(E) 4.25

This is a pretty nasty problem. You could use an RTD chart to solve algebraically. But to set that up correctly, you've got to understand the weird scenario, so start by sketching it out. (And then, it turns out, you can just keep going and solve fully that way!)

Here's Annika partway down her hiking trail, suddenly realizing that she's got 45 minutes till she needs to get back:

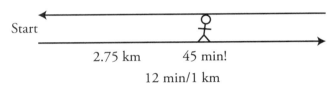

Pretend that isn't Annika at all—now, it's you. Are you going to whip out paper and pencil to start doing some algebra to figure out when to turn around? No way. You're going to use real-world logic to figure out what to do.

What do you want to figure out? The question asks how far you will have traveled east. The first part of the distance is 2.75 kilometers, but you don't know how much *farther* east you can go before turning around. Glance at the answers. Hey, the answer can't be (A) because you've already gone more than 2.25 kilometers. And the answer can only be (B) if you have to turn around right now. Do you?

First, if you didn't go a step farther, how long would it take to get back?

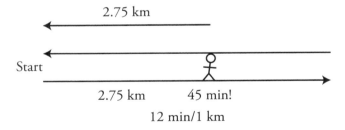

You're going to need 2.75 kilometers to get back. How long is that going to take if you're going 1 kilometer every 12 minutes? Let's see, you can go 3 kilometers in (count it out) 12, 24, 36 minutes. So if you turn around right now (at 2.75 kilometers), you'll be back in less than 36 minutes. But you still have 45 minutes to go, so answer (B) isn't correct.

The next possible answer is 3.25 kilometers. If you go that far east in total, you'd have to go another half a kilometer right now, then turn around and hike 3.25 kilometers back. How long does it take you to go 0.5 kilometer? If it takes 12 minutes to go 1 kilometer, then you'll need 6 minutes to go 0.5 kilometer.

19

So, first, you'd continue east for another 6 minutes. Then you'd turn around and hike back 3.25 kilometers. You can go 3 kilometers in 36 minutes, and you'd need another 3 minutes to go that last 0.25 kilometer, for a total of 39 minutes hiking west.

Therefore, 6 minutes east + 39 minutes west = 45 minutes total and you're back at your car. The correct answer is (C).

Here's another way to draw it out:

Go back to the beginning.

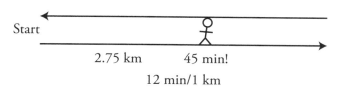

Start
2.75 km   45 min!
12 min/1 km

Step back from the problem for a second—forget that you want 2.75 kilometers plus some unknown distance. Look at your diagram. You're asking yourself how far you can travel east before you turn around and go back; that is, you want to know how far *half* of the trip is. If you can calculate the total distance, you can find the halfway mark.

To start, you travel 2.75 kilometers. Then, you travel another 45 minutes at 12 minutes per kilometer. You can count it out again or do the straight math—12 × 4 = 48—so it takes 48 minutes to go 4 kilometers. How can you find the distance for 45 minutes?

If you hike 1 kilometer in 12 minutes, then you hike 0.25 kilometer in 3 minutes. Subtract: You hike 4 − 0.25 = 3.75 kilometers in 48 − 3 = 45 minutes.

Therefore, you travel 2.75 + 3.75 = 6.5 kilometers total. Half of that, 3.25 kilometers, is spent hiking east. The correct answer is (C).

There are usually multiple ways to logic out the problem to get to the answer; you can do whatever feels easiest to you. Put yourself in the situation and ask yourself how you would go about this in the real world. You'd almost never start writing a bunch of equations; rather, you'd start just sketching out scenarios, using real-world logic and estimation to get to the answer (or close enough!).

Whenever you run across a rate or work problem, try sketching out the problem to gain practice. At first, you'll likely feel slow, but you'll gain efficiency and accuracy with practice!

Matching Units in the RTD Chart

All the units in your RTD chart must match up with one another. The two units in the rate should match up with the unit of time and the unit of distance. For example:

> An elevator operates at a constant rate of 4 seconds to rise one floor. How many floors will the elevator rise in 2 minutes?

The elevator moves 1 floor every 4 seconds: $\frac{1 \text{ floor}}{4 \text{ seconds}} = \frac{1}{4}$ floor/second.

There are two common potential mistakes people make. First, always express the rate as per *one* unit of time: one second, one minute, one hour. In the case above, the rate is the fraction $\frac{1}{4}$ of a floor per one second, not 1 floor per 4 seconds.

19

Second, the rate is *not* $\dfrac{4 \text{ seconds}}{1 \text{ floor}}$. Always express rates as *distance over time*, not as *time over distance*.

Given the rate of $\dfrac{1}{4}$ floor per second, how many floors will the elevator rise in 2 minutes?

Watch out! There is a problem with the RTD chart below. The rate is expressed in floors per second, but the time is expressed in minutes. This will yield an incorrect answer.

	R (floors/second)	$\times$	*T* (minutes)	$=$	*D* (floors)
Elevator	0.25	$\times$	2	$=$	?

To correct this table, change the time into seconds. To convert minutes to seconds, multiply 2 minutes by 60 seconds per minute, yielding 120 seconds, as shown in the chart below:

	R (floors/second)	$\times$	*T* (seconds)	$=$	*D* (floors)
Elevator	0.25	$\times$	120	$=$	?

Once the time has been converted from 2 minutes to 120 seconds, the time unit will match the rate unit, and you can solve for the distance using the $RT = D$ equation:

$$0.25(120) = d$$
$$d = 30 \text{ floors}$$

Thus, the elevator will go up 30 floors in 2 minutes.

You can also try to logic it out. Sketch out the answer as though it's happening in the real world.

You're on the elevator. Every 4 seconds, you're going to go up one floor, and you'll be on the elevator for 2 minutes. After 8 seconds, you're at floor 2. After 12 seconds, you're at floor 3. It's annoying to keep going up by increments of 4; what would be easier?

After 40 seconds, you're at floor 10. After 80 seconds, you're at floor 20. And after 120 seconds (or 2 minutes), you're at floor 30.

The RTD chart or the sketch-it-out approach may seem like overkill for problems in which you need to set up just one equation ($RT = D$ or $RT = W$) and then substitute. However, these two methods will help you to address more complicated scenarios, as you'll see in the next section.

Multiple Rates

Some rate problems on the GMAT will involve *more than one trip or traveler*. To deal with this, you will need to deal with multiple $RT = D$ relationships. Try this example:

> Amal runs a 30-mile course at a constant rate of 6 miles per hour. If Cahaya runs the same course at a constant rate and completes the course in 60 fewer minutes, how fast did Cahaya run?

Draw the scenario. This is a good idea whether you plan to continue with a logic-it-out approach or whether you plan to use an RTD chart; sketching the scenario will help you to keep the moving parts straight:

C: ?? mph, but 60 min <u>faster</u>

A: 4 mph ──────────────────────────────────▶

30 mi

Start thinking logically. What's the connection between A and C? The time: C was 60 minutes faster than A. What can you figure out around this connection? You can figure out how fast A went. If A ran 6 miles every hour and had to cover 30 miles, then A took 5 hours to go the whole 30 miles.

Therefore, C took $5 - 1 = 4$ hours to run the 30 miles. If C covered 30 miles in 4 hours, then C ran $\frac{30}{4} = 7.5$ miles in 1 hour, or 7.5 miles per hour.

Alternatively, create an RTD chart. A chart for this question has two rows, one for Amal and one for Cahaya, as shown below:

	R (miles/hour)	×	T (hours)	=	D (miles)
Amal					
Cahaya					

Pay attention to the relationships between these two equations. Try to use the minimum necessary number of variables.

For example, Cahaya ran for 60 fewer minutes, so use t and $t - 60$ minutes for the two times. To make units match, convert 60 minutes to 1 hour. If Amal ran t hours, then Cahaya ran $(t - 1)$ hours. The distance they both ran was 30 miles. Fill in this information on your chart:

	R (miles/hour)	×	T (hours)	=	D (miles)
A	6		t		30
C	?		$t - 1$		30

Now, solve for t:

$$6t = 30$$
$$t = 5$$

If $t = 5$, then Cahaya ran for $5 - 1 = 4$ hours. Now, solve for Cahaya's rate:

$$r \times 4 = 30$$
$$r = 7.5$$

For questions that involve multiple rates, start by sketching the situation. From there, decide whether you would rather logic it out or whether you would rather set up the $RT = D$ equations. Either way, look for connections, or relationships, between the different parts of the problem. These relationships will help you to be able to solve efficiently.

Relative Rates

Relative rate problems are a subset of multiple rate problems. The defining aspect of relative rate problems is that two bodies are traveling *at the same time*. There are three possible scenarios:

1. The bodies move *toward* each other.

2. The bodies move *away* from each other.

3. The bodies move in the *same direction* on the same path.

These questions can be dangerous because they can take a long time to solve using the conventional multiple rates strategy (discussed in the last section). You can save valuable time and energy by considering the *combined* rate at which the distance between the bodies changes:

Toward each other:	Away from each other:	Same direction:
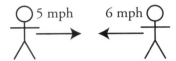		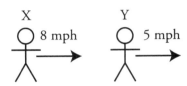
Two people decrease the distance between themselves at a rate of $5 + 6 = 11$ mph.	Two cars increase the distance between themselves at a rate of $30 + 45 = 75$ mph.	Persons X and Y decrease the distance between themselves at a rate of $8 - 5 = 3$ mph.

Try an example:

> Two people are 14 miles apart and begin walking toward each other. Person A walks 3 miles per hour, and Person B walks 4 miles per hour. How long will it take them to reach each other?

What is the combined rate of the two people? Since they are walking toward each other, they are both contributing to getting closer together at a rate of $3 + 4 = 7$ miles per hour. For every hour that they both walk, they get 7 miles closer together.

How long will it take to cover the 14 mile distance between them? Walking 7 miles an hour for 2 hours will bring them together, so the answer is 2 hours. You can literally sketch out all of the movement:

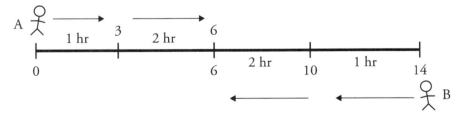

Some people might prefer an RTD chart (though the logical approach used above works on a surprising number of GMAT problems, even harder ones). Create an $RT = D$ equation for the combined rate: $3 + 4 = 7$ miles per hour.

19

	R (miles/hour)	×	T (hours)	=	D (miles)
A + B	7		t		14

$$7t = 14$$
$$t = 2$$

Note that the draw-it-out technique will still work even when the answer isn't an integer. Let's say that Person B is walking at a rate of 5 miles per hour:

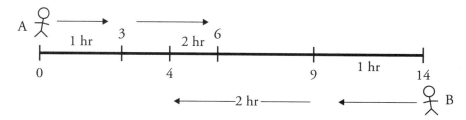

They haven't passed at 1 hour, but they have at 2 hours. You would typically be able to eliminate two or three multiple-choice answers at this stage. Next, try 1.5 hours:

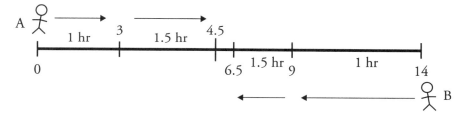

They haven't passed yet. This is usually enough for you to narrow the choices down to a single answer, though it depends on the exact mix of answer choices.

Average Rate: Find the Total Time

Consider the following problem:

> If Lior walks to work at a rate of 4 miles per hour and walks home by the same route at a rate of 6 miles per hour, what is Lior's average walking rate for the round trip?

It is very tempting to find an average rate as you would find any other average: add and divide. Thus, you might say that Lior's average rate is 5 miles per hour ($4 + 6 = 10$ and $10 \div 2 = 5$). However, this is incorrect!

If an object moves over the same distance twice, but at different rates each time, then *the average rate will NEVER be the "straight" average of the two rates given for the two legs of the journey*. Instead, because the object spends more time traveling at the slower rate, *the average rate will ALWAYS be closer to the slower of the two rates than to the faster*. Basically, the slower trip is weighted more heavily in the calculations (this is called a weighted average and you'll learn more about this in a few chapters). On DS problems, that knowledge may be enough to answer the question.

19

In order to find the average rate, first find the *total* combined distance for the trips and the *total* combined time for the trips. Use this formula:

$$\text{Average Speed} = \frac{\text{Total Distance}}{\text{Total Time}}$$

The problem above never establishes a specific distance. Because Lior walks the *same* route to work and back home, the average does not depend upon the specific distance. Whether the person or vehicle in the question goes 1 mile or 15, the *average* will be the same, so pick your own smart number for the distance.

Since 12 is a multiple of the two rates in the problem, 4 and 6, 12 is a good number to use.

Set up an RTD chart or draw out the scenario, your choice. Both approaches are shown here:

$$\frac{4 \text{ mph}}{\text{Go}} \longrightarrow \qquad \longleftarrow \frac{6 \text{ mph}}{\text{Return}}$$

12 mi

Takes 3h   *Takes 2h*

$$\frac{\text{Dist}}{\text{Time}} = \frac{24}{5} = 4.8$$

The calculations are shown in the chart, but you would typically perform these outside of the chart and then enter the information into your chart:

	Rate (miles/hour)	×	Time (hours)	=	Distance (miles)
Going	4	×	$\frac{12}{4} = 3$	=	12
Return	6	×	$\frac{12}{6} = 2$	=	12
Total	$\frac{24}{5} = 4.8$	×	$3 + 2 = 5$	=	$12 + 12 = 24$

If you like, test different numbers for the distance (try 24 or 36) to prove that you will get the same answer, regardless of the number you choose for the distance.

Basic Work Problems

Work problems are just another type of rate problem. These questions are concerned with the amount of work of some type performed rather than the distance traveled.

Work: Work takes the place of distance. Instead of $RT = D$, use the equation $RT = W$. The amount of work done is often a number of jobs completed or a number of items produced.

Time: This is the time spent working.

Rate: In work problems, the rate expresses the amount of work done in a given amount of time.

$$R = \frac{W}{T}$$

As with rate problems, always express a rate as work per unit time $\left(\frac{W}{T}\right)$. For example, if a machine produces pencils at a constant rate of 120 pencils every 30 seconds, the rate at which the machine works is $\frac{120 \text{ pencils}}{30 \text{ seconds}} = 4$ pencils/second.

Many work problems will require you to calculate a rate. Try the following problem:

> Malak can paint $\frac{2}{9}$ of a room in 40 minutes. At this rate, how long will it take Malak to paint the entire room?
>
> (A) 2 hours
>
> (B) 3 hours
>
> (C) 4 hours

You can use an RTW chart or logic it out, your choice. Both approaches are shown here.

The question asks how long it takes Malak to paint the whole room. In terms of the fraction given in the question stem, the whole job is $\frac{9}{9}$.

If Malak takes 40 minutes to paint $\frac{2}{9}$ of a room, how long would is take to paint $\frac{1}{9}$ of the room? Since $\frac{1}{9}$ is half as much as $\frac{2}{9}$, it would take half as long, or 20 minutes.

If it takes 20 minutes to paint $\frac{1}{9}$ of the room, then it takes 9 times as long to paint the whole room: $(20)(9) = 180$ minutes, or 3 hours. The correct answer is (B).

Alternatively, set up an RTW chart with your known information to find Malak's rate; note that the given information is in minutes but the question asks for hours, so at some point you'll need to convert from minutes to hours:

	R (rooms/hour)	×	T (hours)	=	W (rooms)
Malak	r		$\frac{2}{3}$		$\frac{2}{9}$

Now, solve for the rate:

$$r \times \frac{2}{3} = \frac{2}{9}$$
$$r = \frac{2}{9} \times \frac{3}{2} = \frac{1}{3}$$

Malak paints $\frac{1}{3}$ of the room every hour. Painting the whole room is the same as doing $\frac{3}{3}$ of the job, so it will take a total of 3 hours to complete. The correct answer is (B).

One interesting item. Malak's rate is $\frac{1}{3}$ and the time to complete the whole job is 3. These two numbers, $\frac{1}{3}$ and 3, are reciprocals. It will always be the case that the rate and the time it takes to do 100% of the job are reciprocals—that knowledge may save you some calculation time on some problems.

19

Working Together: Add the Rates

More often than not, work problems will involve more than one worker. When two or more workers are performing the same task, their rates can be added together. For instance, if Machine A can make 5 boxes in an hour, and Machine B can make 12 boxes in an hour, then working together the two machines can make $5 + 12 = 17$ boxes per hour.

Likewise, if Ren can complete $\frac{1}{3}$ of a task in an hour and Serena can complete $\frac{1}{2}$ of that task in an hour, then working together they can complete $\frac{1}{3} + \frac{1}{2} = \frac{5}{6}$ of the task every hour.

If, on the other hand, one worker is undoing the work of the other, subtract the rates. For example, if one hose is filling a pool at a rate of 3 gallons per minute, but another hose is draining the pool at a rate of 1 gallon per minute, the pool is being filled at a rate of $3 - 1 = 2$ gallons per minute.

Try the following problem:

> Machine A fills soda bottles at a constant rate of 60 bottles every 12 minutes, and Machine B fills soda bottles at a constant rate of 120 bottles every 8 minutes. How many bottles can both machines working together at their respective rates fill in 25 minutes?

First, check the given rate information against the question. It's asking about a 25-minute time frame. It would be easy to take the given information and "scale it up" for a 24-minute time frame (Machine A fills 120 bottles every 24 minutes, and Machine B fills 360 bottles every 24 minutes). If this problem had multiple-choice answers, you would want to glance at them at this point to see whether you can get away with rounding from here.

That's not the case on this problem, though. Instead, begin by putting the rates in proper form (per 1 unit of time):

$$\text{Rate}_{\text{Machine A}} = \frac{60 \text{ bottles}}{12 \text{ minutes}} = 5 \text{ bottles/minute}$$

$$\text{Rate}_{\text{Machine B}} = \frac{120 \text{ bottles}}{8 \text{ minutes}} = 15 \text{ bottles/minute}$$

Working together, they fill $5 + 15 = 20$ bottles every minute. In 25 minutes, then, they would fill $(20)(25) = 500$ bottles.

If you're not sure about that final calculation, you can fill out an RTW chart. Let b be the number of bottles filled:

	R (bottles/minute)	×	T (minutes)	=	W (bottles)
A + B	20		25		b

$b = 20 \times 25 = 500$ bottles

Even as work problems become more complex, there are still only a few relevant relationships:

- $RT = W$
- When two machines (or similar) are both contributing to the same job, add the rates.
- If one machine is undermining or taking away from a job, subtract the rate of that machine.

Try another example:

> Alejandro, working alone, can build a doghouse in 4 hours. Betty can build the same doghouse in 3 hours. If Betty and Carey, working together, can build the doghouse twice as fast as Alejandro can alone, how long would it take Carey, working alone, to build the doghouse?

Begin by solving for the rate that each person works. Let c represent the number of hours it takes Carey to build the doghouse.

Alejandro can build $\frac{1}{4}$ of the doghouse every hour, Betty can build $\frac{1}{3}$ of the doghouse every hour, and Carey can build $\frac{1}{c}$ of the doghouse every hour.

The problem states that Betty and Carey, working together, can build the doghouse twice as fast as Alejandro. In other words, their rate is twice Alejandro's rate:

$$\text{Rate}_B + \text{Rate}_C = 2\left(\text{Rate}_A\right)$$
$$\frac{1}{3} + \frac{1}{c} = 2\left(\frac{1}{4}\right)$$
$$\frac{1}{c} = \frac{1}{2} - \frac{1}{3} = \frac{1}{6}$$
$$c = 6$$

It takes Carey 6 hours to build the doghouse alone.

You can also logic it out. Alejandro takes 4 hours to build the doghouse, and Betty takes 3 hours.

Betty and Carey together can build the doghouse twice as fast as Alejandro. It takes Alejandro 4 hours, so Betty and Carey together take 2 hours.

What portion of the doghouse will Betty do in that 2 hours? Since she can do the whole thing in 3 hours, she'll have $\frac{2}{3}$ of it done in 2 hours. Therefore, Carey will have to do the other $\frac{1}{3}$ of the doghouse in 2 hours.

That's Carey's rate; use it to figure out how long Carey will take to do the whole job alone:

$$2 \text{ hours} \rightarrow \frac{1}{3} \text{ of job}$$
$$6 \text{ hours} \rightarrow \frac{3}{3} \text{ of job}$$

19

When dealing with multiple rates, be sure to express rates per unit time. When the work involves completing a task, treat completing the task as doing 100% of the work. Once you know the rates of every worker, add the rates of workers who work together to complete the same task.

Problem Set

Now that you've finished the chapter, try the following problems.

1. An empty bucket is filled with paint at a constant rate, and after 6 minutes the bucket is filled to $\frac{3}{10}$ of its capacity. How much more time will it take to fill the bucket to full capacity?

2. Two hoses are pouring water into an empty pool. Hose 1 alone would fill up the pool in 6 hours. Hose 2 alone would fill up the pool in 4 hours. How long would it take for both hoses to fill up two-thirds of the pool?

    (A) 1 hour 36 minutes

    (B) 2 hours 24 minutes

    (C) 5 hours

3. Did it take a certain ship less than 3 hours to travel 9 kilometers? (1 kilometer = 1,000 meters)

    (1) The ship's average speed over the 9 kilometers was greater than 55 meters per minute.

    (B) The ship's average speed over the 9 kilometers was less than 60 meters per minute.

4. Twelve identical machines, running continuously at the same constant rate, take 8 days to complete a shipment. How many additional machines, each running at the same constant rate, would be needed to reduce the time required to complete a shipment by 2 days?

    (A) 2

    (B) 3

    (C) 4

    (D) 6

    (E) 9

5. Al and Barb shared the driving on a certain trip. What fraction of the total distance did Al drive?

    (1) Al drove for $\frac{3}{4}$ as much time as Barb did.

    (2) Al's average driving speed for the entire trip was $\frac{4}{5}$ of Barb's average driving speed for the trip.

6. Nicky and Chadi begin running a race at the same time, though Nicky starts the race 36 meters ahead of Chadi. If Chadi runs at a pace of 5 meters per second and Nicky runs at a pace of only 3 meters per second, how many seconds will Nicky have run by the time Chadi passes him?

    (A) 15 seconds

    (B) 18 seconds

    (C) 25 seconds

    (D) 30 seconds

    (E) 45 seconds.

19

7. Mary, working at a steady rate, can perform a task in m hours. Nadir, working at a steady rate, can perform the same task in n hours. Is $m < n$?

    (1) The time it would take Mary and Nadir to perform the task together, each working at their respective constant rates, is greater than $\frac{m}{2}$.

    (2) The time it would take Mary and Nadir to perform the task together, each working at their respective constant rates, is less than $\frac{n}{2}$.

Solutions

1. **14 minutes:** The question asks how much more time it will take to finish filling the bucket. You would need another $\frac{7}{10}$ to fill the bucket. One way to go from $\frac{3}{10}$ to $\frac{7}{10}$ is this:

    $\frac{3}{10}$ capacity $\rightarrow$ 6 minutes

    $\frac{1}{10}$ capacity $\rightarrow$ 2 minutes

    To get to $\frac{7}{10}$ capacity, multiply by 7: It will take (2 minutes)(7) = 14 minutes.

    Alternatively, assign a smart number for the capacity of the bucket. The logic is the same, but this approach allows you to work with more whole numbers and fewer fractions. The bucket is initially filled to $\frac{3}{10}$ of its capacity, so pick a multiple of 10.

    If the capacity is 20 (call it gallons), then the bucket is currently $\frac{3}{10} \times 20 = 6$ gallons full. It took 6 minutes for the bucket to get this full, so the bucket is filling at a rate of 1 gallon per minute.

    There are $20 - 6 = 14$ more gallons to go until the bucket is full, so it will take another 14 minutes to fill.

2. **(A) 1 hour 36 minutes:** The question is a bit unusual. It doesn't ask how long it will take to fill the pool to capacity but how long it will take to fill the pool to *two-thirds* of capacity. Ideally, try to solve directly for this value.

    To start, glance at the answers. First, they're fairly far apart, so you may be able to estimate. Second, if the second hose alone can fill the pool completely in 4 hours, then it can't take more time than that for the two hoses together to fill the pool to two-thirds of capacity. Eliminate answer (C). There are only two answers left; take the math as far as you need to in order to tell whether it will take more or less than 2 hours.

    If Hose 1 can fill the pool in 6 hours, its rate is $\frac{1}{6}$ "pool per hour," or the fraction of the job it can do in 1 hour. Likewise, if Hose 2 can fill the pool in 4 hours, its rate is $\frac{1}{4}$ pool per hour. Therefore, the combined rate is $\frac{5}{12}$ pool per hour $\left(\frac{1}{4} + \frac{1}{6} = \frac{5}{12}\right)$.

    Convert $\frac{2}{3}$ of capacity to have the same denominator: $\frac{2}{3} \rightarrow \frac{8}{12}$.

    After 1 hour, the pool is $\frac{5}{12}$ full. After 2 hours, the pool is $\frac{10}{12}$ full. This is too much! It takes less than 2 hours to get to $\frac{8}{12}$ full. The only possible answer is **(A)**.

19

3. **(A):** The statements provide rates in meters per minute but the question asks how many hours it takes to go a certain number of kilometers. A good first step here is to figure out how fast the ship would have to travel to cover 9 kilometers in 3 hours. Create an RTD chart, and convert kilometers to meters and hours to minutes:

	R (meters/minute)	×	T (minutes)	=	D (meters)
	r		180		9,000

$$180r = 9,000$$
$$r = 50$$

The question asks whether the ship traveled 9 kilometers in *less than* 3 hours. If it took less time, the ship would have to have traveled *faster* than 50 meters/minute. Therefore, the question is really asking, was $r > 50$ meters/minute?

(1) SUFFICIENT: If the average speed of the ship was greater than 55 meters per minute, then $r > 55$. Thus, r is definitely greater than 50.

(2) INSUFFICIENT: If the average speed of the ship was less than 60 meters per minute, then $r < 60$. The value of r could be greater or less than 50.

The correct answer is **(A)**: Statement (1) alone is sufficient, but statement (2) is not.

4. **(C) 4:** This is a complicated story. Lay it out carefully before you figure out how to solve. All the machines run at the same rate, so you can ignore that potential aspect of things. There are 12 machines to start and they take 8 days to do the job. The problem states that the time required will be reduced *by* 2 days—so that's a total of 6 days. (Note the trap: The problem writer is hoping you'll think the time was reduced *to* 2 days.)

If you feel really comfortable with work problems, there's a neat shortcut you can use. Twelve machines complete the job in 8 days, or $(12r)(8) = 1$ job. An unknown number of machines (call it n) completes the job in 6 days, or $(nr)(6) = 1$ job. The left sides of those two equations equal the same thing, so you can set them equal to each other and solve:

$$(12r)(8) = (nr)(6)$$
$$\frac{(12)(8)}{6} = \frac{nr}{r}$$
$$(2)(8) = n$$
$$n = 16$$

The *new* number of machines is 16. The *added* number of machines is $16 - 12 = 4$.

If that doesn't work for you, use the standard RTW approach. Let the work rate of 1 machine be r. Then the work rate of 12 machines is $12r$, and you can set up an RTW chart:

	R	×	T	=	W
Original	$12r$		8		$96r$

19

The shipment work is then 96*r*. To figure out how many machines are needed to complete this work in $8 - 2 = 6$ days, set up another row and solve for the unknown rate:

	R	×	*T*	=	*W*
Original	12*r*		8		96*r*
New	⬭		6		96*r*

Therefore, there are $\dfrac{96r}{6} = 16r$ machines in total, or $16 - 12 = 4$ additional machines.

5. **(C):** The problem asks for a relative value, not the actual value. Rephrase the question as follows: What is the ratio of Al's driving distance to the entire distance driven? Alternatively, since the entire distance is the sum of only Al's distance and Barb's distance, you can find the ratio of Al's distance to Barb's distance:

    (1) INSUFFICIENT: Knowing only the relative amount of time each drove indicates nothing about distance driven.

    (2) INSUFFICIENT: Knowing only the relative rates at which each drove indicates nothing about distance driven.

    (1) AND (2) SUFFICIENT: Set up an RTD chart to combine the information:

	R	×	*T*	=	*D*
Al	$\left(\dfrac{4}{5}\right)r$		$\left(\dfrac{3}{4}\right)t$		$\left(\dfrac{3}{5}\right)rt$
Barb	*r*		*t*		*rt*
Total					$\left(\dfrac{8}{5}\right)rt$

Call the distance measurement *miles*. The total trip distance was $\dfrac{8}{5}$ miles or 1.6 miles (ignore the *rt*, since that's identical for all three entries for distance). Bob drove 0.6 miles of the total distance, so he drove $\dfrac{0.6}{1.6}$ of the distance.

The correct answer is **(C):** The two statements work together, but neither one works alone.

6. **(B) 18 seconds:** Save time on this problem by considering the rate at which Chadi closes the gap with Nicky. If Nicky runs at a rate of 3 meters per second and Chadi runs at a rate of 5 meters per second, then Chadi catches up at a rate of $5 - 3 = 2$ meters per second. Since Nicky starts off 36 meters ahead of Chadi, Chadi needs to make up 36 meters to catch up to Nicky. If Chadi closes the gap by 2 meters per second, then it will take Chadi $\dfrac{36}{2} = 18$ seconds to catch up to Nicky.

19

Alternatively, use a single $RT = D$ equation. The rate at which Chadi catches up to Nicky is 2 meters per second, and the distance is 36 meters (because that's how far apart Nicky and Chadi are):

	R (meters/second)	×	T (seconds)	=	D (meters)
	2		t		36

$$2t = 36$$
$$t = 18$$

A third way to solve this problem is to draw it out. Draw Nicky and Chadi's starting points:

Next, map out how their positions will change over time. It will take a while for Chadi to catch up to Nicky; Chadi runs 5 meters per second and needs to make up 36 meters. Map out their progress in increments of 10 seconds rather than 1 second (looking at the answer choices is another way to get this hint; the smallest answer is 15):

Seconds	Nicky's Position = 36 + 3 meters/second	Chadi's position = 5 meters/second
0	36	0
10	36 + 3(10) = 66	5(10) = 50
20	36 + 3(20) = 96	5(20) = 100

After 20 seconds, Chadi has just passed Nicky, so Chadi overtook Nicky at some time between 10 and 20 seconds. Only answers (A) and (B) are in this range. You could test answer (A) at this point or logic it out. The two runners are much closer together after 20 seconds ($100 - 96 = 4$ meters) than they are after 10 seconds ($66 - 50 = 16$ meters). Thus, the exact time Chadi passed Nicki must be closer to 20 seconds than 10 seconds.

7. **(D):** The question asks whether $m < n$, or whether Mary is faster than Nadir. There are three possibilities: They work at the same rate, Mary is faster, or Nadir is faster. If the two people work at exactly the same rate, then together they would complete the job in half the time it would take to work alone.

(1) SUFFICIENT: What does $\frac{m}{2}$ represent? Since m is the time it takes Mary to do the job alone, $\frac{m}{2}$ is half of that—or the time it would take two identical Mary clones to do the job. This statement indicates that, when Mary and Nadir do the job, they will spend *more* time than two Mary clones would take—so Nadir must be slowing down the job. In other words, Yes, $m < n$.

Put some concrete numbers on this to help understand. For example, say that Mary can do the job in 5 hours, or $m = 5$. Two Mary clones would do the job in 2.5 hours, or $\frac{m}{2} = 2.5$. But this statement says that Mary and Nadir take *longer* than $\frac{m}{2}$, so Nadir must be slowing down the job. In other words, Yes, $m < n$.

19

(2) SUFFICIENT: Use similar logic. Since n is the time it takes Nadir to do the job alone, $\frac{n}{2}$ is half of that—or the time it would take two identical Nadir clones to do the job. This statement indicates that, when Mary and Nadir do the job, they will spend *less* time than two Nadir clones would take—so Mary must be speeding up the job. In other words, Yes, $m < n$.

Use some concrete numbers again to check the logic: If Nadir can do the job in 6 hours, or $n = 6$, then two Nadir clones would do the job in 3 hours, or $\frac{n}{2} = 3$. But this statement says that Mary and Nadir take *less* than $\frac{n}{2}$, so Mary must be speeding up the job. In other words, Yes, $m < n$.

The correct answer is **(D)**: Each statement alone is sufficient.

Overlapping Sets

In This Chapter

- The Double-Set Matrix
- Overlapping Sets and Percents
- Overlapping Sets and Algebraic Representation

In this chapter, you will learn how to organize and solve overlapping set stories in both percent and algebraic form.

CHAPTER 20 Overlapping Sets

Stories that involve two (or more) given sets of data that partially intersect with each other are termed **overlapping sets**. For example:

> Of 30 integers, 15 are in set A, 22 are in set B, and 8 are in both sets A and B. How many of the integers are in NEITHER set A nor set B ?

This problem involves two sets, A and B. The two sets overlap because some of the numbers are in both sets. Thus, these two sets can actually be divided into four categories:

1. Numbers in set A

2. Numbers in set B

3. Numbers in both A and B

4. Numbers in neither A nor B

Solving double-set GMAT problems, such as in the example above, involves finding values for one of these four categories.

The Double-Set Matrix

For GMAT problems involving only *two* sets of data, the most efficient tool is the **double-set matrix**. Here's how to set one up, using the previous example:

> Of 30 integers, 15 are in set A, 22 are in set B, and 8 are in both set A and B. How many of the integers are in NEITHER set A nor set B ?

First, set up a table:

	A	Not A	Total
B			
Not B			
Total			

For two data sets, you'll always have four columns and four rows. The final column and the final row will always be labeled Total. Next, ask yourself what the two data sets are. In this case, the sets are A and B. A particular value can be either in set A or not in set A. These are called *mutually exclusive*, a term you'll hear in graduate school. Label the columns so that the mutually exclusive options A and not A are side by side. Likewise, a particular value can be either in set B or not in set B.

This box shows the overlap.

	A	Not *A*	Total
B	8		22
Not *B*			
Total	15		30

This box shows the total members in set *B*.

This box in the lower right corner is the key. This tells you how many distinct members exist in the overall group.

This box shows the total members in set *A*.

This box shows the members in NEITHER set.

Once the information given in the problem has been filled in, as in the chart below, complete the rest of the chart. Each row and each column sum to a total value as shown here:

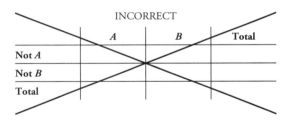

	A	Not *A*	Total
B	8	14	22
Not *B*	7	1	8
Total	15	15	30

The question asks for the number of integers that are in *neither* set. Look at the chart to find the number of integers that are Not *A* and Not *B*; the answer is 1.

There are two important points to remember. First, you likely will not need to fill in the entire chart; you only have to fill in enough to get the particular value that the question asked you to find. To that end, before you start solving, put a circle in the box that you want to find.

Second, when you construct a double-set matrix, the rows must correspond to the *mutually exclusive options* for one decision: You have *A* or you don't have *A*. Likewise, the columns should correspond to the mutually exclusive options for the other decision: You have *B* or you don't have *B*. Do *not* draw the table this way:

INCORRECT

	A	*B*	Total
Not *A*			
Not *B*			
Total			

Once you've set up the matrix, take a moment to check the logic of a couple of the boxes. In the incorrect example, the first open box shows the intersection of *A* and Not *A*. How many items can be both in *A* and not in *A* at the same time? Zero. The same is true of *B* and Not *B*. It's also the case that you could have some items in both *A* and *B*, but the matrix doesn't contain any box that allows that combination. Logically, then, this cannot be the correct set-up for the matrix.

One final note: Venn diagrams (overlapping circles) can also be used for these problems, but the double-set matrix is strongly recommended for problems with only two sets of data points. The double-set matrix conveniently displays *all* possible combinations of options, including the totals, whereas the Venn diagram displays only a subset of the combinations.

20

Overlapping Sets and Percents

Many overlapping sets problems involve *percents* or *fractions*. The double-set matrix is still effective on these problems, especially if you choose a smart number for the grand total. For problems involving percents, choose a total of 100. For problems involving fractions, choose a common denominator for the total. For example, choose 15 if the problem mentions categories that are $\frac{1}{3}$ and $\frac{2}{5}$ of the total. For example:

> The books on a bookshelf are either hardcover or paperback. Sixty percent of the books are paperback and half of the hardcover books are fiction. If 40% of the paperback books are fiction, what percent of the books are nonfiction?
>
> (A) 30
>
> (B) 40
>
> (C) 44
>
> (D) 56
>
> (E) 60

First, set up your chart. The two groups are fiction/nonfiction and hardcover/paperback. Because the problem uses only percentages, no real numbers, choose 100 for the total number of books. The problem asks for the percentage that are nonfiction; put a circle in that box.

Then, begin to fill in the other information given in the problem. The second sentence indicates that 60% of the books are paperback. That allows you to figure out the portion that are hardcover, since the two have to add up to 100. You also know that half of the hardcover books are fiction; therefore, half of the hardcover books are nonfiction. Fill in the table:

	F	NF	Total
HC	50% Tot HC = 20	50% Tot HC = 20	100 − 60 = 40
PB	40% Tot PB = 24		60
Total		⬯	100

Next, add the information from the third sentence and solve for the desired box. Of the paperbacks, 40% are fiction; there are 60 paperbacks, so 40% is 24. (Take 10%, then multiply by 4: $(6)(4) = 24$.) Now, you have a choice. You can solve to the right or solve down in order to get to the circle. Here's how to solve down:

	F	NF	Total
HC	50% Tot HC = 20	50% Tot HC = 20	$x = 40$
PB	40% Tot PB = 24		60
Total	20 + 24 = 44	100 − 44 = 56	100

You don't need to complete the entire chart, since you have already answered the question asked in the problem. If you want to check your work—and you have the time!—you can complete the matrix. The last box you fill in must work both vertically and horizontally.

20

The correct answer is (D), 56. There are some traps built into the answer choices. The last number before the answer, 44, is in the answer choices; this number represents an adjacent category, fiction, rather than the desired category, nonfiction. Someone choosing (C) solved for the wrong box.

Note one important thing about this pair of answers, 44 and 56: They add up to 100%! Trap answer (C) has a name: It's an evil twin. One of the most common careless mistakes people make is to solve for the wrong thing. In this case, you would do everything correctly, right up to the end, and then just choose the wrong answer.

Evil twins pop up on all kinds of story problems, not just ones that involve percents. When you see that a story problem contains two adjacent things you could have solved for (nonfiction *or* fiction, in this case, or the number of cats vs. the number of dogs), and the answers contain real numbers, glance at those answers first to see whether evil twins are present. In this case, there are *two* pairs of evil twins adding up to 100: the pair 44/56 and the pair 40/60. Answer choice (A), 30, is the odd one out, so if you have to guess, don't guess that one.

The other pairing, 40/60, is the result of a calculation error along the way. The problem states that 40% of the paperbacks are fiction. If someone mistakenly reads that as 40% of *all* of the books are fiction, then she would put 40 in the fiction total box and calculate the final answer as 60. Alternatively, if someone did place the 40% properly in the paperback fiction box but mistakenly took 40% of 100 rather than 40% of 60, then she would put 60 in the fiction total box and calculate the final answer as 40.

As with any problem, only use smart numbers if the problem contains only relative values (such as fractions and/or percents), but no actual *numbers* of items or people. In that case, go ahead and pick a total of 100 (for percent problems) or a common denominator (for fraction problems). If actual quantities appear anywhere in the problem, though, then all the totals are already determined. In that case, you cannot assign numbers, but must solve for them instead.

Overlapping Sets and Algebraic Representation

When solving overlapping sets problems, pay close attention to the wording of the problem. For example, consider this problem:

> A researcher estimates that 10% of the children in the world are between the ages of 8 and 18 and dislike soccer, and that 50% of the children who like soccer are between the ages of 8 and 18. If 40% of the children in the world are between the ages of 8 and 18, what percentage of children in the world are under age 8 and dislike the game of soccer? (Assume all children are between the ages of 0 and 18.)

It is tempting to fill in the number 50 to represent the percent of children aged 8 to 18 who like soccer. However, this approach is incorrect:

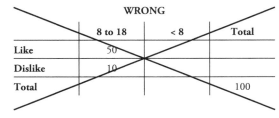

You'll need some of your Sentence Correction skills here. The sentence says that 50% of the children *who like soccer* are between the ages of 8 and 18. This is different from saying that 50% of the children *in the world* are between the ages of 8 and 18. The children *who like soccer* are a subset—a smaller number—of *all* of the children in the world.

You do not yet know how many children like soccer, so you can't actually find the 50% figure (yet!). Instead, represent the unknown total number of children who like soccer with the variable x. Then, represent the number of children aged 8 to 18 who like soccer with the expression $0.5x$:

	8 to 18	< 8	Total
Like	$0.5x$		x
Dislike	10		
Total	40		100

The "8 to 18 + Like" box must equal $40 - 10 = 30$; set up an equation to solve for x:

$$0.5x = 30$$
$$x = 60$$

Fill in whatever you need to get to the desired cell. Here's one possible path:

	8 to 18	< 8	Total
Like	$0.5x = 30$		$x = 60$
Dislike	10	30	40
Total	40		100

Therefore, 30% of the children are under age 8 and dislike soccer.

Problem Set

Now that you've finished the chapter, try the following problems.

1. Set *A* contains 16 even integers, and set *B* contains 22 integers that are all multiples of 3. If 7 of the integers fall into both sets *A* and *B*, how many integers are in exactly one of the two sets?

2. Of the 28 people in a park, 12 are children and the rest are adults. Eight people have to leave the park at 3 p.m.; the rest will stay. If, after 3 p.m., there are 6 children still in the park, how many adults are still in the park?

    (A) 2
    (B) 8
    (C) 11
    (D) 14
    (E) 20

Save the following problems for review after you finish this entire guide.

3. Of the students at a certain high school, 40% take physics. Of those students who don't take physics, 20% do take calculus. What percentage of students take neither physics nor calculus?

4. Of 30 snakes at the reptile house, 10 have stripes, 21 are poisonous, and 5 have no stripes and are not poisonous. How many of the snakes both have stripes and are poisonous?

5. At a car dealership, 10% of all cars are red and have heated seats, and 75% of cars without heated seats are red. If 40% of all of the cars are red, what percent of the cars have heated seats?

    (A) 25%
    (B) 40%
    (C) 60%
    (D) 75%
    (E) 85%

Answers and explanations follow on the next page. ▶ ▶ ▶

Solutions

1. **24 integers:** Use a double-set matrix to solve this problem. First, fill in the numbers given in the problem: 16 integers total in set A and 22 integers total in set B. There are 7 integers in the overlap of sets A and B. Next, use subtraction to solve for the number of integers in set A but not in set B (9) and the number of integers in set B but not in set A (15). Finally, add those two numbers: $9 + 15 = 24$.

	A	**Not A**	**Total**
B	7	**15**	22
Not B	9		
Total	16		

2. **(D) 14:** Use a double-set matrix to solve this problem. First, fill in the numbers given in the problem: There are 28 people total; 12 are children, and the rest ($28 - 12 = 16$) are adults; 8 leave at 3 p.m. and the rest ($28 - 8 = 20$) stay. Next, 6 children stay in the park after 3 p.m. Since there are a total of 20 people in the park after 3 p.m., the remaining 14 people who stay must be adults. Here is the table:

	C	**A**	**Total**
Leave			8
Stay	6	**14**	**20**
Total	12	**16**	28

    Notice that there are two pairs of evil twins in the answers choices. Answers (A) and (D) sum to 16, the total number of adults. If you thought the question asked how many adults left the park, rather than stayed, you would come up with answer (A).

    Answers (B) and (E) sum to 28, the total number of people in the park. If you thought the question asked for the total number of people who stayed in the park, rather than just the adults who stayed, you might choose answer (E).

3. **48%:** Since all the numbers in this problem are given in percentages, assign a grand total of 100 students. The problem indicates that 40% of all high school students take physics, so fill in 40 for this total. The number who don't take physics must be $100 - 40 = 60$.

    Next, 20% of those students who do not take physics do take calculus. (It does not say that 20% of *all* students take calculus!) According to the table, 60 students do not take physics, so 20% of those, or 12, do take calculus. Therefore, fill in 12 for the students who take calculus but not physics. Finally, subtract: $60 - 12 = 48$ students take neither physics nor calculus.

	P	**No P**	**Total**
C		12	
No C		48	
Total	40	**60**	100

4. **6:** Use a double-set matrix to solve this problem. First, fill in the numbers given in the problem: 30 snakes total, 10 with stripes (and therefore 20 without), 21 that are poisonous (and therefore 9 that are not), and 5 that are neither striped nor poisonous. Use subtraction to fill in enough of the chart to answer the question (one way is shown below). A total of 6 snakes have stripes and are poisonous.

	S	Not S	Total
P	6		21
Not P	4	5	9
Total	10	20	30

5. **(C) 60%:** Use a double-set matrix to solve this problem. Since all the numbers in this problem are given in percentages, assign a grand total of 100 cars. The problem indicates that 10% of all cars are red and have heated seats, so enter 10 in the R + HS cell. It also indicates that 75% *of cars without heated seats* are red. At this point, you don't know how many cars don't have heated seats, so assign the variable x to represent the Total Not HS. Of these cars, 75% are red, so enter $0.75x$ in the R + Not HS cell.

    Next, 40% of all cars are red, so enter 40 in the Total R cell. Column R has to add up $(10 + 0.75x = 40)$, so the R + Not HS cell $(0.75x)$ must equal 30. Solve the equation to find that $x = 40$. If 40 cars do not have heated seats, then 60 have heated seats. Therefore, 60% of all of the cars have heated seats as shown in the table below:

	R	Not R	Total
HS	10		60
Not HS	$0.75x = 30$		$x = 40$
Total	40		100

Did you notice the two pairs of evil twins that add to 100 in this problem? Answers (A) and (D) are one pair, and answers (B) and (C) are the other. You might get answer (B) if you solved for the cars without, rather than with, heated seats. You could get answers (A) or (D) if you focused on red cars as opposed to all cars.

Statistics

In This Chapter

In this chapter, you will learn how to calculate averages in a variety of situations, as well as how to lay out median problems and how to logic your way through standard deviation problems.

CHAPTER 21 **Statistics**

Averages

The **average** (or the **arithmetic mean**) of a set is given by the following formula:

$$\textbf{Average} = \frac{\textbf{Sum}}{\textbf{\# of terms}}, \text{ which is abbreviated as } A = \frac{S}{n}.$$

The sum, S, refers to the sum of all the terms in the set.
The number, n, refers to the number of terms that are in the set.
The average, A, refers to the average value (arithmetic mean) of the terms in the set.

The language in an average problem will often refer to an arithmetic mean. However, occasionally, the concept is implied. "The cost per employee, if equally shared, is $20" means that the *average* cost per employee is $20. Likewise, the "per capita income" is the average income per person in an area.

Here's a commonly used variation of the average formula:

$$\text{Average} \times \text{Number of terms} = \text{Sum, or } A \times n = S$$

Using the Average Formula

Every GMAT problem dealing with averages can be solved using some form of the average formula. In general, if the average is unknown, the first formula, $A = \frac{S}{n}$, will solve the problem more directly. If the average is known, the second formula, $A \times n = S$, is better.

When you see any GMAT average problem, write down the average formula. Then, fill in any of the three variables (S, n, and A) that are given in the problem. Try an example:

> The sum of 6 numbers is 90. What is the average term?

$A = \dfrac{S}{n}$ The sum, S, is given as 90. The number of terms, n, is given as 6.

By plugging in, you can solve for the average: $\dfrac{90}{6} = 15$.

Notice that you do *not* need to know each term in the set to find the average!

Sometimes, using the average formula will be more involved. For example:

> If the average of the set {2, 5, 5, 7, 8, 9, x} is 6.1, what is the value of x ?

Plug the given information into the average formula, and solve for x:

$A \times n = S$ $(6.1)(7 \text{ terms}) = 2 + 5 + 5 + 7 + 8 + 9 + x$

$$42.7 = 36 + x$$
$$6.7 = x$$

More complex average problems involve setting up two average formulas. For example:

> Sam earned a $2,000 commission on a big sale, raising his average commission by $100.
> If Sam's new average commission is $900, how many sales has he made?

To keep track of two average formulas in the same problem, you can set up a table. Sam's new average commission is $900, and this is $100 higher than his old average, so his old average was $800.

Note that the Number and Sum columns add up to give the new cumulative values, but the values in the Average column do *not* add up:

	Average	$\times$	**Number**	$=$	**Sum**
Old total	800	$\times$	n	$=$	$800n$
This sale	2,000	$\times$	1	$=$	2,000
New total	900	$\times$	$n + 1$	$=$	$900(n + 1)$
	DON'T add vertically		add vertically		add vertically

The right-hand (Sum) column gives the equation you need:

$$800n + 2,000 = 900(n + 1)$$
$$800n + 2,000 = 900n + 900$$
$$1,100 = 100n$$
$$11 = n$$

Since you are looking for the new number of sales, which is $n + 1$, Sam has made a total of 12 sales.

Median: The Middle Number

Some GMAT problems feature another stats concept: The **median**, or middle value in a list of values placed in increasing order. The median is calculated in one of two ways, depending on the number of data points in the set:

1. For sets containing an *odd* number of values, the median is the *unique middle value* when the data are arranged in increasing (or decreasing) order. For example, the median of the set {5, 17, 24, 25, 28} is the unique middle number, 24.

2. For sets containing an *even* number of values, the median is the *average (arithmetic mean) of the two middle values* when the data are arranged in increasing (or decreasing) order. For example, the median of the set {3, 4, 9, 9} is the mean of the two middle values (4 and 9), or 6.5.

Notice that the median of a set containing an *odd* number of values must be an actual value in the set. However, the median of a set containing an *even* number of values does not have to be in the set—and indeed will not be, unless the two middle values are equal.

Medians of Sets Containing Unknown Values

Unlike the arithmetic mean, the median of a set depends only on the one or two values in the middle of the ordered set. Therefore, you may be able to determine a specific value for the median of a set *even if one or more unknowns are present.*

For example, consider the unordered set {x, 2, 5, 11, 11, 12, 33}. No matter whether x is less than 11, equal to 11, or greater than 11, the median of the resulting set will be 11. (Try substituting different values of x to see why the median does not change.)

By contrast, the median of the unordered set {x, 2, 5, 11, 12, 12, 33} depends on x. If x is 11 or less, the median is 11. If x is between 11 and 12, the median is x. Finally, if x is 12 or more, the median is 12.

Standard Deviation

The mean and median both give *average* or *representative* values for a set, but they do not tell the whole story. It is possible for two sets to have the same average but to differ widely in how spread out their values are. For example, both of these sets have an average and median of 5: {2, 4, 6, 8} and {0, 0, 10, 10}.

To describe the spread, or variation, of the data in a set, use a different measure: the **Standard Deviation** (SD).

Standard deviation indicates how far from the average (mean) the data points typically fall. Therefore:

- A small SD indicates that a set is clustered closely around the average (arithmetic mean) value. In the two sets given earlier, the set {2, 4, 6, 8} has the smaller SD.

- A large SD indicates that the set is spread out widely, with some points appearing far from the mean. In the two sets given earlier, the set {0, 0, 10, 10} has the larger SD.

What about the set {5, 5, 5, 5}? When a set contains all the same value, the numbers are not spread out at all, so the SD is 0.

For most sets, even if you know both the average and the SD of a set, you cannot tell what the numbers are in that set. Multiple possible combinations of numbers can result in the same average and the same SD. The exception is any set with an SD of 0. For example, if the SD is 0 and the average is 13, then all of the members of that set must equal 13. (You still don't know, though, how many instances of 13 are in the set; There might be 1 or 1,000.)

	Set 1	Set 2	Set 3
Mean = 5 Median = 5	{5, 5, 5, 5}	{2, 4, 6, 8}	{0, 0, 10, 10}
Difference from the mean of 5 (in absolute terms)	{0, 0, 0, 0} SD = 0 An SD of 0 means that all the numbers in the set are equal.	{3, 1, 1, 3} moderately spread out SD = moderate (technically, SD = $\sqrt{5} \approx 2.24$ but you won't have to calculate this!)	{5, 5, 5, 5} more spread out (technically, SD = 5) If every absolute difference from the mean is equal, then the SD equals that difference.

21

You might be asking how to calculate the $\sqrt{5}$ shown as the SD for the second set. The good news is that you do not need to know—the GMAT will not ask you to calculate a specific SD unless a shortcut exists, such as knowing that the SD is 0 if all of the numbers in the set are identical. If you just pay attention to what the *average spread* is doing, you'll be able to answer all GMAT standard deviation problems, which involve either 1) *changes* in the SD when a set is transformed or 2) *comparisons* of the SDs of two or more sets. Just remember that the more spread out the numbers, the larger the SD.

If you see a problem focusing on changes in the SD, ask yourself whether the changes move the data closer to the mean, farther from the mean, or neither. If you see a problem requiring comparisons, ask yourself which set is more spread out from its mean.

Following are some sample problems to help illustrate SD properties:

1. Which set has the greater standard deviation: {1, 2, 3, 4, 6} or {441, 442, 443, 444, 445}?

2. If each data point in a set is increased by 7, does the set's standard deviation increase, decrease, or remain constant?

3. If each data point in a set is increased by a factor of 7, does the set's standard deviation increase, decrease, or remain constant? (Assume that the set consists of different numbers.)

Answers and explanations follow on the next page. ▶ ▶ ▶

Answer Key

1. **The first set has the greater SD.** One way to understand this is to observe that the gaps between its numbers are, on average, slightly bigger than the gaps in the second set (because the last two numbers are 2 units apart). Another way to resolve the issue is to observe that the set {441, 442, 443, 444, 445} would have the same standard deviation as {1, 2, 3, 4, 5}. Replacing 5 with 6, which is farther from the mean, will increase the SD of that set.

2. **The SD will not change.** "Increased by 7" means that the number 7 is *added* to each data point in the set. This transformation will not affect any of the gaps between the data points, and thus it will not affect how far the data points are from the mean. If the set were plotted on a number line, this transformation would merely slide the points 7 units to the right, taking all the gaps and the mean along with them.

3. **The SD will increase.** "Increased by a *factor* of 7" means that each data point is multiplied by 7. This transformation will make all the gaps between points 7 times as big as they originally were. Thus, each point will fall 7 times as far from the mean. The SD will increase by a factor of 7. Why did the problem specify that the set consists of different numbers? If each data point in the set was the same, then the SD would be 0. Multiplying each data point by 7 would still result in a set of identical numbers and an identical SD of 0.
    •

Problem Set

Now that you've finished the chapter, try the following problems.

1. The average (arithmetic mean) of 11 numbers is 10. When one number is eliminated, the average of the remaining numbers is 9.3. What is the eliminated number?

2. Given the set of numbers {4, 5, 5, 6, 7, 8, 21}, how much higher is the mean than the median?

3. For an entire class of students, the mean score on a test was 60, and the standard deviation was 15. If Eike's score was within 2 standard deviations of the mean, what is the lowest score Eike could have received?

4. Matt earned a $1,000 commission on a big sale, raising his average commission by $150. If Matt's new average commission is $400, how many sales has he made?

Save the following problems for review after you finish this entire guide.

5. If the average of x and y is 50, and the average of y and z is 80, what is the value of $z - x$?

    (A) 20
    (B) 30
    (C) 50
    (D) 60
    (E) 80

6. The median price of all houses sold in the Seaside Hills neighborhood last year was $450,000. Was the average (arithmetic mean) price of the houses sold last year greater than $400,000 ?

    (1) The most expensive house sold in Seaside Hills last year was sold for $800,000.
    (2) Exactly three houses were sold in Seaside Hills last year.

Solutions

1. **17:** If the average of 11 numbers is 10, their sum is $11 \times 10 = 110$. After one number is eliminated, the average is 9.3, so the sum of the 10 remaining numbers is $10 \times 9.3 = 93$. The number eliminated is the difference between these sums: $110 - 93 = 17$.

2. **2:** The mean of the set is the sum of the numbers divided by the number of terms. First, group numbers to make it easier to add them up. For example, $4 + 6 = 10$, $5 + 5 = 10$ and $7 + 8 = 15$. The mean is $56 \div 7 = 8$. The median is the middle number in the set, which is 6. The difference between the two numbers is 2.

3. **30:** Eike's score was within 2 standard deviations of the mean. Since 1 standard deviation is 15, her score is no more than $15 \times 2 = 30$ points from the mean. The lowest possible score she could have received, then, is $60 - 30$, which is equal to 30.

4. **5:** For this kind of problem, you can do your calculations just in terms of the "extra" money that Matt made, over his prior average.

    Before the big sale, Matt's average commission was $250. For the big sale, he got a commission of $1,000. Count the first $250 toward his original average and the other $750 as his "extra" money. If he hadn't made any extra money, then his average would have stayed at $250. But he did make $750 extra, so how does that impact the average?

    Imagine that, prior to the big sale, Matt had made exactly one other sale. Then, the big sale with an extra $750 would increase his average across two sales by $\frac{750}{2} = 375$. His average actually increased by only $150, so he must have made more than two sales. If he had had two prior sales with an average of $250, then adding the extra $750 from the third sale would increase the average by $\frac{750}{3} = 250$. In short, you can calculate the increase in the average using this shortcut:

    $$\frac{\text{Extra Amount}}{\text{\# of Sales}} = \text{Increase in Average}$$

    In this problem, $\frac{750}{\text{\# of sales}} = 150$, so Matt had 5 total sales.

    Alternatively, you can solve algebraically. Before the big sale, Matt's average commission was $250, so the sum of the previous sales was $S = 250n$. After the sale, three things happened: The sum of Matt's commissions increased by $1,000, the number of sales he made increased by 1, and his average commission was $400. Express this algebraically with the following equation:

    $$S + 1,000 = 400(n + 1)$$
    $$250n + 1,000 = 400(n + 1)$$
    $$250n + 1,000 = 400n + 400$$
    $$150n = 600$$
    $$n = 4$$

    Before the big commission, Matt had made 4 sales. Including the big commission, Matt made 5 sales.

5. **(D) 60:** This is an interesting hybrid problem. At first glance, it may seem like a candidate for working backwards, since the answers are real numbers. However, it asks for a relative value: the difference betweeen z and x. In this case, you can choose smart numbers for the values of the individual variables, as long as those numbers make the given facts true.

Let $x = 40$ and $y = 60$ (the average must be equal to 50). Next, the average of y and z must be 80. If $y = 60$, then z has to be 100. Therefore, $z - x = 100 - 40 = 60$.

You can also solve algebraically, though that is more cumbersome on this problem. First, translate the given information:

$$\frac{x + y}{2} = 50 \qquad \frac{y + z}{2} = 80$$

The first equation can be rearranged to give $x = 100 - y$. The second equation can be rearranged to give $z = 160 - y$. Plug the information into $z - x$ and solve:

$$\begin{aligned} z - x &= (160 - y) - (100 - y) \\ &= 160 - y - 100 + y \\ &= 160 - 100 \\ &= 60 \end{aligned}$$

6. **(C):** The question stem provides information about a median for a data set and asks whether the average of the same data set was greater than $400,000, which can be abbreviated $400K. When you're given a median, it's often a good idea to draw out dashes for each item in the set (e.g., for a three-item set: __ __ __), but this question stem doesn't indicate how many items are in the set. And that's your first clue as to how to think about this information.

If the set contains exactly one item, then that item is $450K and the average is also $450K. If the set contains two items, then the two items must again average to $450K, since the median of a two-item set is found by averaging the two items. So if you know that the set has one or two items, then the average matches the median ($450K).

If the set contains exactly three items, then the middle item is $450K, but the least expensive item could be anything between 0 and $450K and the most-expensive item could be anything from $450K to infinity. That flexibility would allow an average below or above $400K. The same will be true for a four-item set, a five-item set, and so on. If the set has three or more items, then you'd have to be given more information in order to be able to find the average.

Glance at the statements. Begin with statement (2) on this one.

(2) INSUFFICIENT: Three houses were sold, but no additional information is given. It's not possible, therefore, to calculate anything about the average price for all three houses.

(1) INSUFFICIENT: The most expensive house was $800K, but how many houses were sold? It could have been two, in which case the average equals the median, $450K. In this case, the answer to the question is Yes, the average is greater than $400K.

21

But there could also have been more houses sold. Imagine that five houses were sold for the following prices: \$1, \$1, \$450K, \$450K, and \$800K. The average would be approximately $\frac{\$1,700K}{5}$. That value is less than \$400K, so the answer is No. (For the average to be \$400K, the numerator would have to be \$2,000K.)

(1) AND (2) SUFFICIENT: If three houses (an odd number) were sold, then the median must be the price of one of the houses, so two of the three houses were sold for \$450K and \$800K, respectively. If the third house sold for \$1 (almost the minimum, which is actually \$0), the average would be $\frac{\$1 + \$450K + \$800K}{3}$. Is that value going to be greater than \$400K or less than \$400K? The sum of the prices is greater than \$1,200K, so the average of the three prices is greater than \$400K. This is the minimum average possible, so the answer is Always Yes.

The correct answer is **(C)**: The two statements are sufficient when used together, but neither one works alone.

Weighted Averages

In This Chapter

- The Algebraic Method
- The Teeter-Totter Method
- Mixtures, Percents, and Ratios

In this chapter, you will learn how to recognize weighted average and mixture problems and how to use both logical and algebraic approaches to solve.

CHAPTER 22 Weighted Averages

The concept of **weighted averages** will come up all the time in graduate school—and in the general business world. It's worth spending some extra time digging in to understand this topic. If you can get to the point that you can think logically about weighted averages, as this chapter shows, you'll be in a strong position to talk about similar quant topics in grad school and beyond.

The regular formula for averages, $A = \dfrac{S}{n}$, applies only to sets of data consisting of individual values that are equally weighted—that is, all of the values "count" equally toward the average. For example, if you earn 100 on one exam and 80 on another exam, an equally weighted average of your scores is 90.

Some averages, however, are weighted more heavily toward certain data points. For example, imagine that your teacher tells you that your midterm exam will count for 40% of your grade and your final exam will count for 60% of your grade. If you can score a perfect 100 on only one of those components, which one would you want it to be?

Your final exam, of course! It counts more heavily toward your final grade. Next, imagine that you score 100 on your final exam but only 80 on your midterm exam. What is the weighted average of those two scores?

Any average has to be between the two starting points, in this case 100 and 80. The *regular* average would be 90. Is the weighted average higher or lower than the regular average of 90?

The final exam counts for more than 50% of your final score, so the weighted average must be closer to the final exam score of 100 than to 80. The weighted average must be between 90 and 100.

That knowledge is usually enough to get you to the right answer on a Data Sufficiency problem and it can often be enough to get to the right answer even on a Problem Solving problem. If you do need to calculate further, there are two ways to calculate the exact value: *algebraically* or via the *Teeter-Totter*.

The Algebraic Method

The **algebraic method** can be time-consuming without a calculator. It's usually only worth using if you have two data points and relatively easy numbers. It is worth *understanding*, though, because this will allow you to understand and remember the faster method introduced in the next section.

First, think about how a regular (nonweighted) average works. In a regular average, each item has exactly equal weight. For example, if there are two items, both are weighted $\frac{1}{2}$. If your teacher weighted your two exams equally, then this would be the calculation:

$$100\left(\frac{1}{2}\right) + 80\left(\frac{1}{2}\right) = 50 + 40 = 90$$

That is, the average is 90, exactly halfway between 80 and 100. The initial equation could be rearranged in this way:

$$100\left(\frac{1}{2}\right) + 80\left(\frac{1}{2}\right) = \frac{1}{2}(100 + 80) = \frac{100 + 80}{2}$$

Is that starting to look familiar? That's the average formula: Find the sum of the two numbers and divide by 2. Technically, regular averages all have these equal weightings, so you can always write the equation in the simplified form: $\dfrac{\text{Sum}}{\text{\# of Terms}}$

Weighted averages are solved using the same initial formula, but the weightings are not $\frac{1}{2}$ for each of the two terms.

You scored 100 on your final exam and it has a 60%, or $\frac{3}{5}$, weighting. You scored 80 on your midterm and it has a 40%, or $\frac{2}{5}$, weighting. Here's what that looks like:

$$100\left(\frac{3}{5}\right) + 80\left(\frac{2}{5}\right) = ?$$
$$60 + 32 = 92$$

The weighted average is 92.

If you're going to solve algebraically for a weighted average, you always have to use the "long" form of the average equation. You'll always have a component multiplied by its weighting, and then the next component multiplied by its weighting, and so on:

$$\text{Weighted Average} = (\text{Component 1})(\text{Weighting 1}) + (\text{Component 2})(\text{Weighting 2})$$

You can have more than two components. The GMAT typically sticks to two or three.

The Teeter-Totter Method

The **Teeter-Totter method** is very efficient as long as you understand what a weighted average is and how the concept works in general. If you struggle with the concept, then you may want to stick with the algebraic method—and just guess if you get a complicated one that's too annoying to solve algebraically.

The problem is the same: You scored 100 on your final exam and it has a $\frac{3}{5}$ weighting. You scored 80 on your midterm and it has a $\frac{2}{5}$ weighting. What is your final grade?

As with the algebraic method, begin by thinking about what would happen if you had two evenly weighted scores:

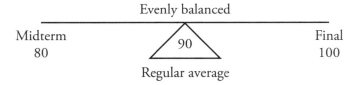

If you had a "regular" average, then the teeter-totter would be perfectly balanced and you would have an average of 90, halfway between 80 and 100.

In this case, though, you have a weighted average. Which way does the teeter-totter tilt?

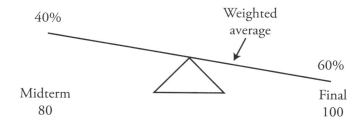

The final exam is weighted more heavily. The weighted average "slips" down toward the heavier end of the teeter-totter, so you know that the weighted average must be between 90 and 100. On DS problems, this is usually enough to determine whether a statement is sufficient!

On a PS problem, you might have a mix of answers such as the following: 82, 90, 92, 98, 105. You can knock out 82, 90, and 105 immediately, since they aren't between 90 and 100.

The two remaining answers, 92 and 98, are at opposite ends of the possible spectrum. Look at the weightings you were given: Are they pretty close to the regular weighting of $\frac{1}{2}$ or 50/50? If so, then the answer should be closer to the regular average (90 in this case).

Or are the given weightings really far from the 50/50 regular average calculation? If so, then the answer should be farther away from the regular average.

In this problem, the weightings are $\frac{3}{5}$ and $\frac{2}{5}$, or 60/40. This is pretty close to the 50/50 case, so the answer should be closer to 90—and, indeed, 92 is the correct answer.

If you do have to calculate the exact weighted average, here's what you do: The two ends of the teeter-totter are 80 and 100, and the difference between them is 20. Write that down. The final exam has a weighting of 60%, so it is responsible for 60% of that length of 20. Find 60% of 20: It is equal to 12. The average will weigh down the 100 end of the teeter totter more:

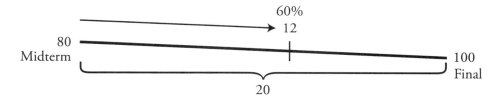

Therefore, the average is 80 + 12, which sums to 92 (and this makes logical sense; the value is between 90 and 100).

You don't need to draw out a full teeter-totter, but do draw at least the sloped line. Use logic to know which side is heavier. Calculate the "length" of the line (the difference between the two ends) and use it to calculate the value of the heavier weighting (in this case, 12); then, add that weight to the lighter side to see how far it tilts the teeter-totter down to the heavier side.

Imagine the situation were reversed: The score of 80 had the 60% weighting and the score of 100 had only a 40% weighting. In this case, you would start from the lighter end of the teeter-totter (the 100 end) and subtract instead:

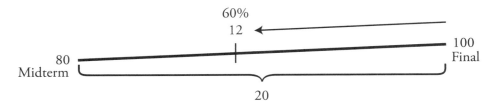

In this case, the average needs to be closer to the midterm end, so start from the higher (lighter) end, 100. Subtract from that end: $100 - 12 = 88$. Again, this makes logical sense: This time, the answer should be between 80 and 90.

In both cases, draw the sloped line and place the final number in roughly the appropriate position. That step will tell you which end is the lighter end and whether you'll need to add from the smaller end $(80 + 12)$ or subtract from the larger end $(100 - 12)$.

What if the problem changed the given information? Try this:

> You score 80 on your midterm exam and 100 on your final exam. Only these two exams make up your final grade of 92. How heavily did your teacher weight the final exam?

First, draw your teeter-totter:

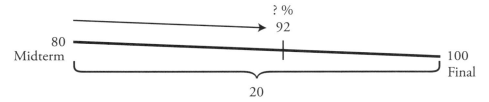

In this case, you still know the two end points (and the length), but now you're given the final average of 92 and you have to figure out the weighting that results in that average.

Because the weighted average is closer to 100 than to 80, you know that 100 is the heavier weight, so your final exam should be weighted more than 50%. But it shouldn't be a lot more, because 92 is not that much higher than the regular/unweighted average of 90. Depending on the answer choices, this might be enough to find the correct answer.

If you do need to calculate more precisely, find the longer of the two distances. In this case, that's between 80 and 92:

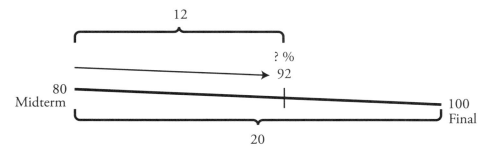

The weighting of the heavier (final exam) side is the fractional part 12 over the total length 20: $\frac{12}{20} = \frac{3}{5}$, which is equal to 60%.

If the problem had asked you to calculate the weighting of the *less*-heavily weighted value, the midterm exam, then you would find the *shorter* of the two distances, 8, and divide by the total distance, 20: $\frac{8}{20} = \frac{2}{5}$, which is equal to 40%.

Try this DS problem:

> The average number of students per class at School X is 25 and the average number of students per class at School Y is 33. Is the average number of students per class for both schools combined less than 29 ?
>
> (1) There are 12 classes in School X.
>
> (2) There are more classes in School X than in School Y.

Because this is a DS problem, there's a very good chance that you will not have to complete the calculations. In this case, try the teeter-totter method.

First, the question stem provides this information:

X (weight?) 25 ——————— △ ? ——————— (weight?) 33 Y

You don't know how to tilt the teeter-totter, because you don't know enough information yet. The question itself, though, implies something very intriguing.

If the two schools are equally weighted, then the regular average would be 29. What would have to be true to make the average *less* than 29?

The teeter-totter would have to be tilted down toward School X; this school would be weighted more heavily. Keep this in mind as you examine the statements:

> (1) There are 12 classes in School X.

This statement doesn't provide any information about School Y, so it's impossible to tell whether one school is weighted more heavily. Statement (1) is not sufficient. Eliminate answers (A) and (D).

> (2) There are more classes in School X than in School Y.

If there are more classes over at School X, then the weighted average has to tilt down toward this school:

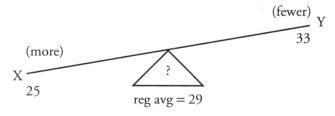

As a result, the weighted average has to be less than the regular average of 29.

Statement (2) is sufficient; the correct answer is (B).

On weighted average problems, you can choose whether to use the algebraic method or the teeter-totter method. The teeter-totter method is generally faster—*if* you really understand how weighted averages work. Try both methods out on some *Official Guide* problems and decide which one is better for you.

Mixtures, Percents, and Ratios

Percents and ratios can also show up in weighted average problems, particularly in the form of mixtures.

First, try this regular mixtures problem (you don't need to calculate a weighted average for this one):

> A 400 milliliter solution is 20% alcohol by volume. If 100 milliliters of water is added, what is the new concentration of alcohol, as a percent of volume?
>
> (A)   5%
> (B)   10%
> (C)   12%
> (D)   12.5%
> (E)   16%

To start, you have two liquid solutions: a 400 milliliter solution that is 20% alcohol and 80% something else and a 100 milliliter solution that is 100% water (and therefore 0% alcohol).

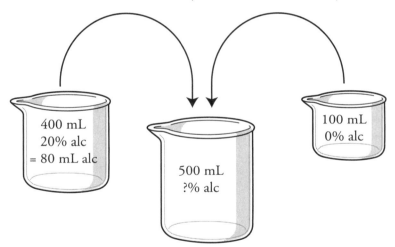

You can actually calculate the milliliters of alcohol in the 400 milliliter beaker: 20% of 400 is 80 milliliters. The 100 milliliter beaker doesn't contribute any alcohol at all, so the 500 milliliter beaker contains a total of 80 milliliters of alcohol. The big beaker, then, is $\frac{80}{500} = \frac{8}{50} = \frac{16}{100} = 16\%$ alcohol. The correct answer is (E).

In this case, only one of the two beakers contributed alcohol to the mixture. What happens when both parts of the problem contribute to the desired mixture?

Try this example:

> Kris-P cereal is 10% sugar by weight, whereas healthier but less delicious Bran-O cereal is 2% sugar by weight. To make a delicious and healthy mixture that is 4% sugar, what should be the ratio of Kris-P cereal to Bran-O cereal, by weight?
>
> (A) 1 : 2
>
> (B) 1 : 3
>
> (C) 1 : 4
>
> (D) 3 : 1
>
> (E) 4 : 1

You can use the algebraic method or the teeter-totter—your choice. Both solutions are shown below.

The question asks for a ratio. Note that you don't necessarily need to know the real values of something in order to find a ratio. Call the weight of Kris-P cereal K and the weight of Bran-O cereal B.

To solve algebraically, set up an equation:

$$0.1K + 0.02B = 0.04(K + B)$$

Kris-P is weighted 10% and Bran-O is weighted 2%. The final mixture (the sum of the two components K and B) is weighted 4%.

Because the question asks for the ratio of K to B, manipulate the equation to solve for $\frac{K}{B}$. First, multiply the whole equation by 100 to get rid of the decimals. Then, simplify from there:

$$10K + 2B = 4(K + B)$$
$$10K + 2B = 4K + 4B$$
$$6K = 2B$$
$$\frac{K}{B} = \frac{2}{6} = \frac{1}{3}$$

The ratio of Kris-P to Bran-O is 1 : 3. The correct answer is (B).

To use your teeter-totter, start drawing:

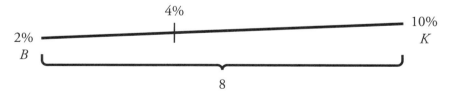

Because 4% is closer to 2%, the Bran-O side is heavier. Calculate the distance between the two ends: $10 - 2 = 8$. Finally, find the distances of the two subparts of the line:

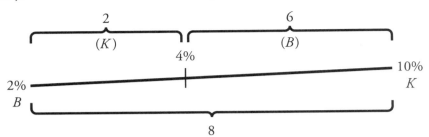

The smaller number, 2, is associated with the less-heavily weighted end (Kris-P, 10%). Note that the 10% K figure is on the other end of the teeter-totter; it will always be the case that the subpart is associated with the opposite end of the teeter-totter.

The larger number, 6, is associated with the more heavily weighted end (Bran-O, 2%). Again, it will always be the case that the subpart is associated with the opposite end of the teeter-totter.

Therefore, the ratio of Kris-P to Bran-O is 2 : 6, or 1 : 3, which is answer (B).

You can choose whether to use algebra or the teeter-totter; try out both to see which works best for you in various circumstances.

Problem Set

Now that you've finished the chapter, try these problems.

1. Imani has won 40% of the first 25 poker games she played this week. If she wins 80% of the remaining games she plays this week, how many additional games must Imani play in order to win 60% of all games for the week?

2. Hot dog vendors sold an average of 66 hot dogs per stand. Trainee vendors averaged 70 hot dogs sold. The ratio of non-trainee vendors to trainee vendors was 1 : 2. What was the average number of hot dogs sold by the non-trainee vendors?

Save these problems for review after you finish this entire guide.

3. Tickets to a play cost $10 for children and $25 for adults. If 100 tickets were sold, were more adult tickets sold than children's tickets?

    (1)   The average revenue per ticket was $18.25.

    (2)   The revenue from ticket sales exceeded $1,800.

4. A feed store sells two varieties of birdseed: Brand A, which is 40% millet and 60% sunflower, and Brand B, which is 65% millet and 35% safflower. If a customer purchases a mix of the two types of birdseed that is 50% millet, what percent of the mix is Brand A?

    (A)   15%

    (B)   40%

    (C)   50%

    (D)   60%

    (E)   85%

5. On a particular exam, the seniors in a history class averaged 86 points and the juniors in the class averaged 80 points. If the overall class average was 82 points, what was the ratio of seniors to juniors in the class?

6. A mixture of lean ground beef (10% fat) and super-lean ground beef (3% fat) has a total fat content of 8%. What is the ratio of lean ground beef to super-lean ground beef?

Solutions

1. **25 additional games:** This is a weighted averages problem. You can calculate this algebraically, but sketch it out first to understand the moving parts:

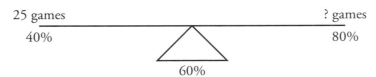

Which way should the teeter-totter tilt, to the right or to the left?

Actually, it doesn't tilt at all. Since 60% is exactly halfway between 40% and 80%, this isn't a weighted average at all; it's a regular average, where the two sides are equally weighted.

Since that's the case, the number of games at each end should match. Since Imani played 25 games for the 40%-win-rate group, she must also have played 25 games for the 80%-win-rate group. No algebra needed!

2. **58 hot dogs:** You can save yourself some calculation time by using smart numbers for part of this problem. The overall average of hot dogs sold is 66; trainees sold an average of 70. The ratio of non-trainees to trainees is 1 : 2, so just assume there was one actual non-trainee and two actual trainees (these are your smart numbers):

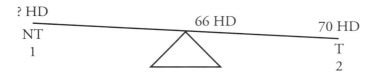

The teeter-totter is tilted toward the trainees. If those two trainees sold 70 hot dogs each, then those two people sold 140 hot dogs together. The overall average is 66 hot dogs and there were three people selling hot dogs, so there was an overall total of $(66)(3) = 198$ hot dogs sold. The one non-trainee, then, must have sold $198 - 140 = 58$ hot dogs.

But this can be solved in an even more streamlined way. The overall sum of $(66)(3)$ hot dogs sold must stay constant. If the two trainees sold 70 hot dogs each, then each one sold 4 hot dogs above the average, for a total of 8 extra hot dogs above the average of 66. In order for the overall average to be 66, those 8 extra hot dogs have to be taken away from the other group—in this case, the one non-trainee. The non-trainee, therefore, must have sold $66 - 8 = 58$ hot dogs.

3. **(D):** First things first: How would you recognize that this question is about weighted averages? The two different prices for tickets are like two different data points, and the number of tickets sold will act as the weight. If more adult tickets were sold, then the average ticket price will be closer to $25. If more children's tickets were sold, then the average ticket price will be closer to $10.

(1) SUFFICIENT: $18.25 is closer to $25 than to $10, so there must have been more adult tickets sold than children's tickets. Statement (1) is sufficient.

(2) SUFFICIENT: The total revenue from ticket sales exceeded $1,800. How are ticket sales calculated?

To figure that out, look at the information in the question stem again. One hundred tickets were sold. Consider two extreme scenarios:

$$100 \text{ children's tickets sold} = 100 \times \$10 = \$1{,}000 \text{ revenue}$$
$$100 \text{ adult tickets sold} = 100 \times \$25 = \$2{,}500 \text{ revenue}$$

If there were an equal number of adult and children's tickets sold, the revenue would be an average of $1,000 and $2,500, or $1,750. That's the connection to weighted averages. If the revenue is greater than $1,800, it is closer to $2,500 than to $1,000, which means more adult tickets must have been sold. Statement (2) is also sufficient.

The correct answer is (D): Each statement works alone.

4.   (D) 60%: The mixtures contain various things, but the question is only about the percent of millet, so ignore the other ingredients. Brand A is 40% millet and Brand B is 65% millet. The mixture is 50% millet, so this is a weighted averages problem. Sketch it out:

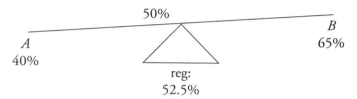

The regular average of 40% and 65% is halfway between, or 52.5%. If there were 50% of each brand in the mix, then the percentage of millet would be 52.5%.

The actual weighted average is 50%; this is closer to 40%, so there's more of Brand A in the mix. The correct answer has to be more than 50%, so eliminate answers (A), (B), and (C).

Compare the diagram to the two remaining answers. Is the given average of 50% closer to the regular average in the middle or closer to the extreme end of 40%? Since it's closer to the regular average (which represents a 50/50 mixture), the correct answer must be 60%, not 85%.

5.   **1 : 2:** The seniors in the class scored 4 points higher on average than the entire class. Similarly, the juniors scored 2 points lower on average than the class. Draw a teeter-totter to solve:

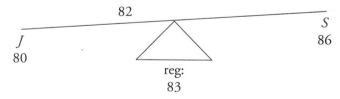

There are more juniors because the weighted average is closer to the 80 side of the teeter-totter. What's the ratio of the two parts?

The total distance of the line is 6, broken down into two portions of 2 and 4. Which is which?

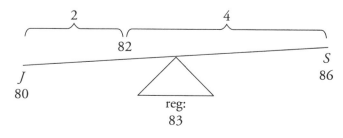

Think logically: There are fewer seniors than juniors, so the ratio of seniors to juniors must be 2 : 4, or 1 : 2. (You might also remember that these parts are always associated with the opposite end of the teeter-totter, so the 2 portion is associated with seniors and the 4 portion is associated with juniors.)

6. **5 : 2:** The question asks for the ratio of the two types of beef, so you don't need to worry about the actual amount of beef.

To set up this problem algebraically, first set up an equation, letting L be lean beef and S be super-lean beef:

$$1L + 0.03S = 0.08(L + S)$$

The question asks for the ratio of L to S, or $\dfrac{L}{S}$. First, multiply the equation by 100 to get rid of the decimals, then solve:

$$10L + 3S = 8(L + S)$$
$$10L + 3S = 8L + 8S$$
$$2L = 5S$$
$$\frac{L}{S} = \frac{5}{2}$$

Alternatively, draw a teeter-totter:

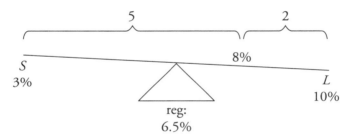

There's more lean ground beef, because 8% is closer to 10%. What's the ratio?

The "length" of the line is $10 - 3 = 7$. The lean (L) side is associated with the larger number, 5, and the super-lean (S) side is associated with the smaller number, 2. The ratio of $L : S = 5 : 2$.

Strategy: Arithmetic vs. Algebra 3

In This Chapter

- Choosing Numbers for Smart Numbers
- Pick for Any Unknown on Smart Numbers
- Smart Numbers Disguised as Working Backwards
- Logic It Out and Work Backwards

In this chapter, you will learn more advanced approaches for the Choose Smart Numbers, Work Backwards, and Logic It Out strategies, including when to choose certain kinds of numbers, how to work more flexibly with smart numbers, and how to both work backwards and logic it out on the same problem.

CHAPTER 23 Strategy: Arithmetic vs. Algebra 3

This chapter focuses on more advanced techniques for handling harder Smart Numbers, Work Backwards, and Logic It Out problems. (The Arithmetic vs. Algebra 4 chapter will cover advanced techniques for the Test Cases strategy.)

Try this problem:

> Cost is expressed by the formula tb^4. If b is doubled and t remains the same, the new cost is how many times greater than the original cost?
>
> (A)   1.2
> (B)   2
> (C)   6
> (D)   8
> (E)   16

You can use an algebraic approach on this problem—and the algebraic approach is really streamlined *if* you know how to set it up. Here's how:

$$\text{Original} = tb^4$$

$$\text{New} = t(2b)^4 = 16tb^4$$

$$\frac{\text{New}}{\text{Old}} = \frac{16tb^4}{tb^4} = 16$$

The correct answer is (E). If you feel comfortable with this algebraic approach, go for it. More people, though, will be unsure about that approach or setup. Instead, use one of the approaches built for standardized tests.

At first glance, the problem might seem like a candidate for working backwards—there are real numbers in the answer choices. In fact, though, those numbers are *relative* values, not actual ones: They represent the multiplier to go from the original cost to the new cost. If the multiplier were 5, then it wouldn't matter whether your original cost was $10 or $10 million—you'd still multiply the original cost by 5 to get the new one.

Further, there are never any real values given for the cost. This is actually a Smart Numbers problem!

The original cost is defined as tb^4. Choose something for b that isn't very large, since you're going to have to raise it to a power of 4. Try $b = 2$ and $t = 3$:

$$\text{Original cost} = tb^4 = 3\left(2^4\right)$$

The numbers are a little annoying, so don't keep multiplying that out. Just leave it for now; later, you may be able to simplify before you multiply. (This applies in general to the whole test. Don't do math that you might not have to do! Defer the work.) Keep in mind that you're looking for opportunities to divide out either the 3 or the 2^4 or both!

Next, figure out the new cost. The value of b doubles, but t stays the same:

$$\text{New cost} = t(2b)^4$$
$$= 3(2 \times 2)^4$$
$$= (3)(2^4)(2^4)$$

Since you're looking for opportunities to divide out a 3 or a 2^4, don't combine the bases 2 and 2 to make a 4^4. Instead, distribute the exponent to each 2 and keep them separate.

The question asks how many times greater the new cost is than the old one, or New $= y$(Old). In other words, divide the new by the old to find the multiplier:

$$\frac{\text{New}}{\text{Old}} = \frac{(\cancel{3})(\cancel{2^4})(2^4)}{(\cancel{3})(\cancel{2^4})} = 2^4 = 16$$

The math with real numbers is the same math as the algebra—in both cases, everything cancels out except for the 16. Using real numbers can just help you to see how the math works and to set it up correctly.

Choosing Numbers for Smart Numbers

Earlier in this guide, you learned how to choose good numbers for certain strategies. This section summarizes the earlier guidelines for the Smart Numbers strategy and adds some new ones.

First, you always have to follow any constraints given in a problem. For example, if the problem says that x is a positive integer, then you can only try positive integers for x.

When using the Smart Numbers strategy on Problem Solving problems, the general guidelines are to avoid 0, 1, and numbers that appear in the problem. If you have to choose for more than one variable, choose different numbers for each variable.

In addition to the above, try to choose numbers that will work well in the problem. Here are some of the most common ways in which you'll choose numbers on the exam.

Choosing Smart Numbers	
When I see. . .	*I'll choose. . .*
Percents	100 or 50
Fractions (part to whole)	A common denominator for all of the fractions
Ratios (even if in fraction form)	The parts of the ratio
	e.g. The number of dogs is $\frac{3}{4}$ the number of cats.
	e.g. The ratio of dogs to cats is 3 : 4.
	Use 3 dogs to 4 cats.

Choosing Smart Numbers	
That I'll need to divide	A multiple of the divisor
	e.g. Someone bought 8 pens for *x* dollars.
	Use a multiple of 8; if $x = 16$, then the pens were $2 each.
Variation of dividing:	Values that will give integers when calculating a rate
Rate or work problems	Rate = Distance (or Work) divided by Time
A lot of multiplication or exponents	Smaller numbers (e.g. 2)
A variable under a square root sign	A perfect square, such as 4
A variable under a cube root sign	A perfect cube, such as 8
2 or more variables; choosing for one will determine the value of the other(s)	*Don't* default to choosing for the first variable mentioned. Think about it.
	What's the easiest starting point?
	e.g. If $x + y = a$ and $x - y = b$, it's easier to choose *x* and *y* than *a* and *b*.
	e.g. If Pool A's capacity is twice Pool B's capacity, choose for the smaller capacity first, then multiply by 2 to get the larger capacity.

On more advanced problems, you may see two such clues and have to decide which one to use first. This is what your Plan phase is for—to figure out which characteristic you should prioritize.

As you study, continue adding to the list above as you come across more examples of smart numbers and find your own ways to decide how to choose specific numbers.

Pick for Any Unknown on Smart Numbers

On a Smart Numbers problem, it's often easiest to pick for the actual variables in the problem. Sometimes, though, it's easier to pick for a different unknown, *not* the variable that shows up in the problem and answer choices.

Here's an example:

A truck is filled to $\frac{1}{4}$ of its maximum weight capacity. An additional *y* pounds are added such that the truck is now filled to $\frac{7}{8}$ of its capacity. In terms of *y*, what is the maximum weight capacity of the truck, in pounds?

(A) $\frac{5}{8}y$

(B) $\frac{5}{4}y$

(C) $\frac{8}{5}y$

Understand. This is a PS problem with variable expressions in the answers and no real value ever given for the weight. You can choose smart numbers. The question asks for the maximum capacity. The variable *y* represents the additional weight added to the truck to go from $\frac{1}{4}$ to $\frac{7}{8}$ of capacity.

Plan. What kind of value for y would be a "good" number, given that y covers the gap between $\frac{1}{4}$ and $\frac{7}{8}$ of the truck's capacity? That's an annoying question. This problem would be a lot easier if it *gave* the maximum capacity and *asked* you to find y.

Guess what? You're actually allowed to choose for whatever unknown you would like. If you think it's easier to choose for the answer/ending value and then work from the end of the problem to the beginning to solve for the starting variable, go right ahead!

The two fractions have denominators of 4 and 8, so choose a value for the total capacity that works nicely with both: 8.

Solve. If the total capacity of the truck is 8 pounds (it's a *really* small truck!), then at first it contains 2 pounds of material. Later, it contains 7 pounds, so $y = 5$ pounds were added. Plug this value into the answers and look for the answer that equals the total capacity of 8:

(A) $\frac{5}{8}y = \frac{5}{8}(5) \neq 8$ Eliminate

(B) $\frac{5}{4}y = \frac{5}{4}(5) \neq 8$ Eliminate

(C) $\frac{8}{5}y = \frac{8}{5}(5) = 8$ Match!

The correct answer is (C).

When using smart numbers, you can always choose where to start. Most of the time, it will be easier to choose for the given variable, but if you ever find yourself thinking that the math would be easier if they had given the end value, go ahead and reverse the process. Choose your own value for that ending point and work your way to the variable.

By the way, one of the answer choices doesn't make logical sense—though most people don't stop to consider the problem in this way. The variable y represents a subset of the truck's capacity, since it's the amount of capacity that allows the truck to go from $\frac{1}{4}$ to $\frac{7}{8}$ full. The answer choices represent the total capacity of the truck. Logically, the total capacity must be greater than a subset of the capacity, so the correct answer must be y times a number greater than 1. Answer (A) is illogical because the value of the fraction is less than 1.

You don't absolutely have to learn to spot those kinds of traps—but if you do, that can help you to narrow down answers when you need to guess. It can also help you to avoid careless mistakes—if you know logically that the fraction should be greater than 1, but you end up getting answer (A), you'll know to check your work.

Smart Numbers Disguised as Working Backwards

Some problems do have real numbers in the answer choices, but can still be solved via smart numbers.

Try this problem:

> A company pays the same hourly rate to all of its employees. Four people work for 8 hours each and earn a total of y dollars collectively. How many people need to work for 20 hours each in order to earn a total of $1.25y$ dollars collectively?
>
> (A) 1
> (B) 2
> (C) 3

Understand. This problem fits all of the hallmarks of a working backwards problem—"nice" real numbers in the answers, and those answers represent a single variable in the problem—but there's a hitch. What do you do with that variable y in the story?

The y represents the dollars earned for a certain number of hours worked. Later, the problem uses $1.25y$ to represent the dollars earned for a different number of hours worked. The problem also states that the hourly pay rate is the same for everyone, but it *never* gives a real number for rate of pay or for dollars anywhere in the problem.

That's a characteristic of smart numbers! If the problem keeps talking about something but never gives you a real number for that something, you're allowed to choose your own number—so go for it!

Plan. Choose your own pay rate and work through the problem accordingly. How about $10/hour? (You may be tempted to go with something like $15. Don't think real world. Make your task as easy as you can.)

Solve. The pay rate is $10 per hour. In the first scenario, four people work for 8 hours each, or a total of 32 hours. Collectively, they are paid $(32)(10) = \$320$. This is y.

The problem asks about a second scenario in which the workers earn $1.25y$. This is 25% greater than y itself, so take 25%, or $\frac{1}{4}$, of y and add to y: $320 + 80 = \$400$.

Aside: To find 25%, you can benchmark: $25\% = 10\% + 10\% + 5\% = 32 + 32 + 16 = 80$. Alternatively, to find $\frac{1}{4}$, divide by 2 twice: $\frac{320}{2} = \frac{160}{2} = 80$.

In order to earn a total of $400 at a pay rate of $10 per hour, the workers must have collectively worked a total of 40 hours. For the second scenario, the problem states that the workers worked 20 hours each, so there must have been 2 workers to work a total of 40 hours.

The correct answer is (B).

Note: You can also solve this problem by choosing a value for the variable y and then calculating the pay rate. You'd need to divide y by both 4 (people) and 8 (hours each) to find the hourly rate, so $y = 32$ might be a good fit. (This would work out to a pay rate of $1/hour.) As on any Smart Numbers problem, start with whatever seems easiest or most natural to you.

Whenever a problem talks about some variable and never gives you a real value for that variable, you can choose your own number for that thing—even if the problem gives you real numbers for other items in the problem, including the answer choices.

Logic It Out and Work Backwards

Try this problem:

> Train X is traveling at a constant speed of 30 miles per hour, and Train Y is traveling at a constant speed of 40 miles per hour. If the two trains are traveling in the same direction along the same route but Train X is 25 miles ahead of Train Y, how many hours will pass before Train Y is 10 miles ahead of Train X?
>
> (A) 1.5
> (B) 2.0
> (C) 2.5
> (D) 3.0
> (E) 3.5

Understand. Glance at the answers before reading the problem. They're all small numbers—so when you read the problem, check whether you can work backwards. The problem itself involves two trains moving in certain ways, so sketch out the story. The question does ask for a single variable in the problem (the number of hours it will take for a certain scenario to happen), so you can work backwards. Sketch the story out to make sure you know all of the moving parts:

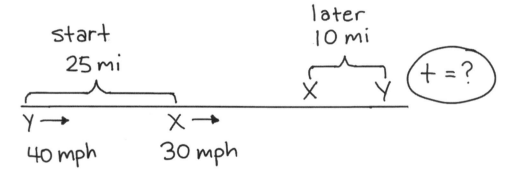

Plan. Think about how to use the sketch to make it easier to work backwards. The answer choices represent the amount of time that both trains move. You know the rates of both trains, so for each answer choice that you try, you could sketch another line below and map out how the trains move each hour (or half hour) of the trip.

Solve. Try answer (B) first:

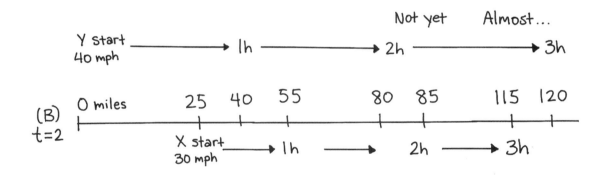

Train Y hasn't passed Train X yet by the 2-hour mark, so answer (B) is incorrect and answer (A) must be wrong, too. Cross off both.

Glance at the answers. Answer (D) is 3 hours, so just extend the line a little farther to find where the trains are after 1 more hour:

Close! But not quite. Train Y has passed Train X, but it is not yet 10 miles ahead of Train X. So (D) isn't long enough.

Only answer (E) represents a longer time, so it must be the correct answer.

You can also solve algebraically. The most efficient algebraic method is shown below.

Because the problem focuses on the difference in movement between the two trains, find the difference in distance and the difference in rate, then plug into the Rate-Time-Distance (RTD) formula.

The two trains are currently 25 miles apart, with X ahead of Y. The problem asks you to solve for the time at which Y has moved 10 miles ahead of X. Therefore, Y has to catch up to X to erase that initial 25-mile deficit and then move an additional 10 miles beyond X. In other words, Y has to travel an additional $25 + 10 = 35$ miles farther than X travels. Use 35 as the distance in the RTD formula.

For every hour that the two trains travel, Y goes 10 miles per hour faster (since it travels 40 miles per hour to X's 30 miles per hour). Use 10 miles per hour as the rate in the RTD formula:

$$\frac{35 \text{ miles}}{10 \text{ miles per hour}} = 3.5 \text{ hours}$$

When the algebra for a particular problem feels easier for you, that solution can be quite efficient—but on a problem that you find complex, it's easy to mess up the equation. As you study, think about when you would want to use an algebraic approach (usually when the problem feels straightforward to you) and when you would want to draw it out and work backwards (usually when the problem feels more complex). If you study how to make the best choice for you, then you can react quickly on test day.

23

Problem Set

Pop quiz! The problems in this set may cover any strategies from the entire guide up to this point.

1. In a college class, each student's overall grade is calculated by averaging the student's grades on t different exams. Up until the last exam, Wei had earned an average exam grade of $0.75g$. After earning a grade of g on the last exam, Wei's overall grade in the class was $0.8g$. What is the value of t ?

    (A) 2
    (B) 3
    (C) 4
    (D) 5
    (E) 6

2. If $a = 2.4d7$, and d represents a digit from 0 to 9, is d greater than 4 ?

    (1) If a were rounded to the nearest hundredth, the new number would be greater than a.
    (2) If a were rounded to the nearest tenth, the new number would be greater than a.

3. The Crandall's hot tub has a capacity of x liters and is half full. Their swimming pool, which has a capacity of y liters, is filled to four-fifths of its capacity. If enough water is drained from the swimming pool to fill the hot tub to capacity, the pool is now how many liters short of full capacity, in terms of x and y ?

    (A) $0.8y - 0.5x$
    (B) $0.8y + 0.5x$
    (C) $0.2y + 0.5x$
    (D) $0.3(y - x)$
    (E) $0.3(y + x)$

4. Four brothers split a sum of money between them. The first brother received 50% of the total, the second received 25% of the total, the third received 20% of the total, and the fourth received the remaining $4. The first brother received how much more money than the third brother received?

    (A) $4
    (B) $16
    (C) $20
    (D) $24
    (E) $36

5. A rental car agency owns a total of $5x$ cars and $2x$ trucks, where x is a positive integer. If the agency purchases c new cars, will the new ratio of cars to trucks be at least 3 to 1 ?

    (1) $c = x + 5$
    (2) $x = 11$

Save the following problems for review after you finish this entire guide.

6. Teachers and students at a school are solving problems. There are twice as many students as teachers, and each student solves 3 more problems than each teacher. If teachers solve 24 of the 90 total problems solved, how many problems does each teacher solve?

    (A) 3
    (B) 4
    (C) 5
    (D) 6
    (E) 8

7. If b is an integer, is 1.3 multiplied by b an integer?

    (1) b is a multiple of 3.
    (2) 0.7 multiplied by b is an integer.

8. Vimbai spends $\frac{3}{8}$ of her monthly paycheck on rent and $\frac{1}{4}$ on food. Her roommate, Carrie, who earns twice as much as Vimbai, spends $\frac{1}{4}$ of her monthly paycheck on rent and $\frac{1}{2}$ on food. If the two roommates decide to donate the remainder of their money to charity each month, what fraction of their combined monthly income will they donate?

    (A) $\frac{5}{24}$
    (B) $\frac{7}{24}$
    (C) $\frac{11}{24}$
    (D) $\frac{17}{24}$
    (E) $\frac{19}{24}$

Solutions

1. **(D) 5:** The answer choices contain real numbers, represented by t in the problem, but the problem also contains an unspecified value, g. No real value is ever given for g, so choose your own. You'll need to take both 0.75 and 0.8 of g, so chose a value that will work well in both calculations.

    Let $g = 100$. Wei's average for all but the last exam (or $t - 1$ exams) was 75. The last exam grade was 100. The sum of all of the grades is $75(t - 1) + 100$. The total number of tests is t. Plug these values and variables into the average formula and solve for t:

    $$\text{Average} = \frac{\text{Sum}}{\text{\# of Terms}}$$
    $$80 = \frac{75(t - 1) + 100}{t}$$
    $$80t = 75(t - 1) + 100$$
    $$80t = 75t - 75 + 100$$
    $$5t = 25$$
    $$t = 5$$

    Wei took a total of 5 exams.

2. **(B):** The variable d represents a single digit, so it could be any digit from 0 to 9. The question doesn't ask for the value of d; rather, it asks whether d is greater than 4. This is a Yes/No question. What would be sufficient and what would not? If you can tell that $d > 4$, the information is sufficient. If you can tell that $d \leq 4$, the information is sufficient. If d could cross over the "barrier" of 4 (that is, it could be 4 or 5), the information is not sufficient—so you may want to test the numbers 4 and 5 specifically.

    (1) INSUFFICIENT: In the representation $a = 2.4d7$, the hundredths digit is the variable d. Test some cases to see what happens to a when you round to d.

    This statement is complex, so think about what you're allowed to try. If $d = 5$, then $a = 2.457$. Rounding to the nearest hundredth produces 2.46, which is indeed greater than 2.457. It's valid, then, to choose $d = 5$. In this case, is d greater than 4 ? Yes.

    Can you think of another case that would give a No answer?

    Try $d = 4$. In this case, $a = 2.447$. Rounding to the nearest hundredth produces 2.45, which is indeed greater than 2.447. It's valid to choose $d = 4$. In this case, is d greater than 4 ? No.

    Because the answer is Sometimes Yes/Sometimes No, this statement is not sufficient.

    (2) SUFFICIENT: The tenths digit of $a = 2.4d7$ is 4. Two outcomes are possible when rounding to the tenths digit: 2.4 or 2.5. The value 2.4 would be smaller than the starting number; only the value 2.5 would be greater. In order to make the rounded value 2.5, the value of the next digit to the right, d, has to be 5 or greater. According to this statement, Yes, d is always greater than 4.

    The correct answer is **(B)**: Statement (2) is sufficient, but statement (1) is not.

3. **(C) $0.2y + 0.5x$:** The answers contain the variables x and y; the question stem never offers real values for these variables, so you can choose your own smart numbers. The problem contains two fractions: The hot tub is *half* full and the pool is filled to *four-fifths* of its capacity. The two capacities are not related (that is, once you pick for one variable, the other variable is not automatically determined), so you'll have to pick two numbers. Pick something divisible by 2 for x and divisible by 5 for y. Try $x = 4$ and $y = 10$:

$$x = \text{H cap} = 4 \qquad\qquad \text{Half full} = 2$$
$$y = \text{P cap} = 10 \qquad\qquad \tfrac{4}{5} \text{ full} = 8$$

The hot tub, with a capacity of 4, is half full, so there are 2 liters of water in the hot tub. The pool, with a capacity of 10, is four-fifths full, so there are 8 liters in the pool.

Next, the problem says that water is siphoned off from the pool and put into the hot tub. How much? The hot tub needs 2 more liters to be full, so subtract 2 from the pool. The pool now has only 6 liters, so it is 4 liters short of its capacity of 10.

Plug $x = 4$ and $y = 10$ into the answer choices and look for an answer that matches: 4 liters short.

(A) $0.8y - 0.5x = (0.8)(10) - (0.5)(4) = 8 - 2 = 6$

(B) $0.8y + 0.5x = (0.8)(10) + (0.5)(4) =$ too big, since (A) was too big.

(C) $0.2y + 0.5x = (0.2)(10) + (0.5)(4) = 2 + 2 = 4$ Match!

(D) $0.3(y - x) = 0.3(10 - 4) = 0.3(6) =$ not an integer

(E) $0.3(y + x) = 0.3(10 + 4) = 0.3(14) =$ not an integer

4. **(D) \$24:** The answer choices are "nice" integers; check the question stem to see whether you can work backwards.

The question asks for the difference between Brother 1 and Brother 3. If you started with answer (B), 16, what values would you choose for each brother? They can be anything, as long as the difference is 16.

Don't work backwards on this problem. (This is why the strategy specifies that the question should ask for a single variable in the problem.) Do the actual math to solve.

The first three brothers got $50\% + 25\% + 20\% = 95\%$ of the money. The fourth brother, then, got the remaining 5%, and that 5% is equal to \$4.

If $5\% = \$4$, then $10\% = \$8$, and $100\% = \$80$. The total amount of money is \$80. The first brother got 50%, or \$40, and the third brother got 20%, or \$16. The difference is $\$40 - \$16 = \$24$.

5. **(A):** This is a Yes/No question and it asks an *at least* question, so expect to use an inequality to translate into math. The story problem discusses ratios using the variables c and x. Glance at the statements. The second statement provides a value for the unknown x. The first statement would allow you to find c if you know x. So is the answer (C)?

That's probably too good to be true. Be suspicious—this might be a C-Trap. Jot down the information from the question stem. The current number of cars to trucks is $5x$ to $2x$, or a ratio of $5 : 2$. If there are c more cars, then there are a total of $5x + c$ cars. The question asks whether this new situation has a car-to-truck ratio of *at least* $3 : 1$. Use this information to set up a proportion for the question: Is the ratio of the new number of cars to the number of trucks at least 3 to 1 ?

$$\text{Is } \frac{\text{Cars}}{\text{Trucks}} = \frac{5x + c}{2x} \geq \frac{3}{1}?$$

The left-hand side shows the real-number representation for cars and trucks after c cars are added. The right-hand side shows the ratio for the same scenario. The question asks whether that ratio is *at least* 3 : 1, so use the greater-than-or-equal-to symbol.

Fractions are annoying; can you cross-multiply to simplify the equation? Yes, the problem indicates that x is positive, so don't switch the direction of the inequality sign when you cross-multiply:

Is $5x + c \geq 6x$?
Is $c \geq x$?

This is the rephrased question. Statement (2) is easier, so start there.

(2) INSUFFICIENT: This statement provides no information about c, so it's not possible to tell whether c $\geq$ x.

(1) SUFFICIENT: The question stem states that x is a positive integer. Take any positive integer and add 5; what happens? The number gets larger, so c does have to be greater than x. (In fact, this would work with any number, positive or negative, integer or fraction.) This information is sufficient to answer the question Always Yes.

The correct answer is **(A)**: Statement (1) is sufficient alone, but statement (2) is not.

6. **(E) 8:** The answers contain easy integers, so check whether you can work backwards. The question does ask for a single variable, so you can. (Note: The problem might seem pretty straightforward at first glance, but there are three variables: number of teachers, number of students, and number of problems solved. This will make for a very messy algebraic solution. Even if you really like algebra, consider working backwards on this problem.)

The problem gives enough information to solve for the total number of problems solved by students. If teachers solve 24 out of the 90 problems, then the students must solve $90 - 24 = 66$ problems.

The answers represent the number of problems solved by each teacher. Each student solves 3 more than each teacher, so start by adding 3 to each answer choice:

	Prob per T:	$\rightarrow$	Prob per S:
(A)	3	$\rightarrow$	6
(B)	4	$\rightarrow$	7
(C)	5	$\rightarrow$	8
(D)	6	$\rightarrow$	9
(E)	8	$\rightarrow$	11

(# of students)(# problems solved per student) = 66

The students solve a total of 66 problems, and there must be an integer-number of students (no partial people!), so the number of problems solved per student must be a factor of 66. Only answers (A) and (E) qualify; eliminate the other three.

Try either remaining answer. If the one you try is incorrect, then the correct answer has to be the other one.

Prob per T	Prob per S (Prob per T + 3)	# S (66 ÷ prior)	# S = twice # T
(A) 3	6	$\frac{66}{6} = 11$	5.5 teachers...

There are supposed to be twice as many students as teachers, so that would be 5.5 teachers ... no good! The only remaining answer is **(E)**. (If you try it: problems per teacher = 8, problems per student = 11, # of students = 6, # of teachers = 3. The teachers solve $(8)(3) = 24$ problems, which is what the problem said, so this answer is correct.)

7. **(B):** This is a Yes/No question. The question stem establishes that b is an integer and asks whether 1.3 multiplied by b is an integer. Before jumping to the statements, think about what kinds of values for b would allow $1.3b$ to be an integer.

For example, if $b = 10$, then $1.3b$ would be 13. Any multiple of 10 would also return a Yes answer. The value 5 would not return an integer, but 10 (a multiple of 5) would. The value 3 would not return an integer, but 30 (a multiple of 3) would ...

(1) INSUFFICIENT: If b is a multiple of 3, then b could be 3 itself, so $1.3b$ would not be an integer, and the answer is No. (You don't necessarily need to find the value in order to tell that it won't be an integer, but $(3)(1.3) = 3.9$.)

Alternatively, b could be 30, and then $1.3b$ would be $(1.3)(10)(3)$. This is an integer, so the answer is Yes. The answer is Sometimes Yes/Sometimes No, so this statement is not sufficient.

(2) SUFFICIENT: If 0.7 multiplied by b is an integer, then b could be 10. In this case, $1.3b$ is also an integer, and the answer is Yes.

Try to find a No answer. If $b = 1$, then $0.7b$ is not an integer, so this is an invalid case. Discard it. If $b = 2$, then $0.7b$ is also not an integer, so this is another invalid case. Discard it. In fact, none of the integers 1 through 9 will make $0.7b$ an integer. Why not?

When multiplying a decimal by an integer, you'll always need to insert the same number of decimal places into the product: for example, $(0.7)(2) = 1.4$ and $(0.7)(3) = 2.1$. When you get up to $(0.7)(10)$, the answer is technically 7.0—but that digit after the decimal place is a 0, so now you have an integer. In other words, in order for $0.7b$ to be an integer, b has to contain a multiple of 10. And since b contains a multiple of 10, the value of $1.3b$ has to be an integer as well. Using statement (2), the answer to the question *Is 1.3b an integer?* is Always Yes.

The correct answer is **(B):** Statement (2) alone is sufficient, but statement (1) alone is not.

8. **(B)** $\frac{17}{24}$: The answer choices represent a relative amount, so use smart numbers to solve. The question asks what fraction of their total income Vimbai and Carrie will donate, or $\frac{\text{combined donation}}{\text{combined total}}$.

Since the denominators in the problem are 8, 4, and 2, assign Vimbai a monthly paycheck of $8. Assign Carrie, who earns twice as much, a monthly paycheck of $16. Total income is $8 + $16 = $24. The roommates' monthly expenses break down as follows:

	Rent	Food	Left over/to donate
V	$\frac{3}{8}$ of 8 = 3	$\frac{1}{4}$ of 8 = 2	8 − (3 + 2) = 3
C	$\frac{1}{4}$ of 16 = 4	$\frac{1}{2}$ of 16 = 8	16 − (4 + 8) = 4

Vimbai and Carrie will donate a total of $3 + $4 = $7 out of their combined monthly income of $24.

Notice the two pairs of evil twins: Answers (A) and (E) sum to 1, as do answers (B) and (D). Answer (D) represents the fraction of total income that Vimbai and Carrie *spend*, rather than donate, a classic GMAT trap on this kind of question. Answer (A) results from using the same income for Vimbai and Carrie (but doing everything else correctly). And answer (E) makes both of those mistakes. Avoid guessing (C) on this problem, since it does not have an evil twin at all.

Consecutive Integers

In This Chapter

- Evenly Spaced Sets
- Counting Integers: Add 1 before You Are Done
- Properties of Evenly Spaced Sets
- The Sum of Consecutive Integers

In this chapter,you will learn how to recognize and solve problems involving consecutive integers and other evenly spaced sets, as well as how to determine the number of integers in a large set and the sum of the integers in a set.

CHAPTER 24 Consecutive Integers

Consecutive integers are integers that follow one after another from a given starting point, without skipping any integers. For example, 4, 5, 6, and 7 are consecutive integers, but 4, 6, 7, and 9 are not. There are many other types of consecutive patterns. For example:

Consecutive even integers: 8, 10, 12, 14

(8, 10, 14, and 16 is incorrect, as it skips 12)

Consecutive primes: 11, 13, 17, 19

(11, 13, 15, and 17 is incorrect, as 15 is not prime)

Evenly Spaced Sets

In **evenly spaced sets**, the values of the numbers in the set go up or down by the same amount (or **increment**) from one item in the sequence to the next. For example, the set {4, 7, 10, 13, 16} is evenly spaced because each value increases by 3 over the previous value. Think of this as the broadest grouping—the biggest circle in the diagram shown below:

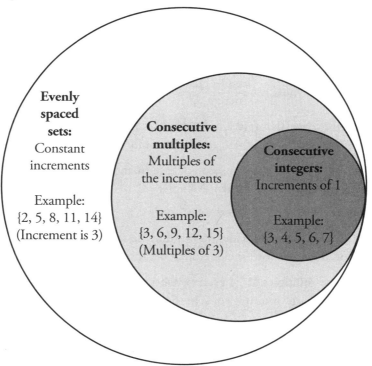

Within that circle is the subset **consecutive multiples**. These are special cases of evenly spaced sets in which all of the values in the set are multiples of the increment. For example, in the set {12, 16, 20, 24}, the values increase from one to the next by 4, and each element is a multiple of 4. Sets of consecutive multiples must be composed of integers.

The inner circle, **consecutive integers**, holds special cases of consecutive multiples: All of the values in the set increase by 1, and all integers are multiples of 1. For example, {12, 13, 14, 15, 16} is a set of consecutive integers.

Counting Integers: Add 1 before You Are Done

How many integers are there from 6 to 10, inclusive? Four, right? No! There are actually *five* integers from 6 to 10. Count them: 6, 7, 8, 9, 10.

How did that happen? When you subtract $(10 - 6 = 4)$, you are actually subtracting out the lower extreme, 6; that number is not included in the count. If you *do* want to include it in the count, then add 1 before you're done. For example:

> How many integers are there from 14 to 765, inclusive?

The word *inclusive* indicates that you need to include both numbers at the ends of the range in your count. The formula is (**Last − First + 1**): $765 - 14 + 1 = 752$.

This is straightforward when you are dealing with consecutive integers. Sometimes, however, the question will ask about consecutive multiples.

In this case, if you subtract the greatest number from the least and add 1, you will be overcounting. For example, "All of the even integers between 12 and 24, inclusive" yields seven integers: 12, 14, 16, 18, 20, 22, and 24. However, (Last − First + 1) would yield $(24 - 12 + 1) = 13$, which is too big. How do you amend this? Since the items in the list are going up by increments of 2 (you are counting only the even numbers), divide (Last − First) by 2. Then, add the 1 before you're done:

$$\frac{(\text{Last} - \text{First})}{\text{Increment}} + 1 = \frac{(24 - 12)}{2} + 1 = 6 + 1 = 7$$

For consecutive multiples, the formula is $\dfrac{(\text{Last} - \text{First})}{\text{Increment}} + 1$.

The bigger the increment, the lower that fraction will go. This makes logical sense, since a bigger increment between numbers in the range means that there are fewer numbers to be counted in that range.

Sometimes, it is easier to list the terms of a consecutive pattern and count them, especially if the list is short or if one or both of the extremes are omitted. For example:

> How many multiples of 7 are there between 10 and 40 ?

First, note that the question says *between* 10 and 40 but does not include the word *inclusive*. So don't include 10 or 40 in this count. (Also, don't include them because neither one is a multiple of 7!)

Second, there aren't that many multiples of 7 in such a short range, so it may be fastest to just write them down: 14, 21, 28, 35. There are four multiples of 7 in the given range. Try another example:

> How many multiples of 7 are there between 10 and 80 ?

This time, it would be more annoying to write out the possibilities. Instead, find the least multiple of 7 and the greatest multiple of 7 in that range and use those as your First and Last numbers. The least one is 14 and the greatest is 77. Now use the formula:

$$\frac{(\text{Last} - \text{First})}{\text{Increment}} + 1 = \frac{(77 - 14)}{7} + 1 = \frac{63}{7} + 1 = 9 + 1 = 10$$

Properties of Evenly Spaced Sets

The following properties apply to all **evenly spaced sets**:

1. The average (arithmetic mean) and median are equal to each other. For example:

    > What is the arithmetic mean of 4, 8, 12, 16, and 20 ?

    In this example, the median is 12. Since this is an evenly spaced set, the arithmetic mean (average) is also 12. Now, try another example:

    > What is the arithmetic mean of 4, 8, 12, 16, 20, and 24 ?

    In this example, the median is the average (arithmetic mean) of the two middle numbers, or the average of 12 and 16. Thus, the median is 14. Since this is an evenly spaced set, the average of the set is also 14.

    In a set with an odd number of evenly spaced integers, such as the first example above, the median/average will always be a member of the set (and, therefore, an integer).

    In a set with an even number of evenly spaced integers, such as the second example above, the median/average will *not* be a member of the set, since you'll always have to average the two middle numbers of the set in order to find the median.

2. The mean and median of the set are equal to the average of the First and Last terms. For example:

    > What is the arithmetic mean of 4, 8, 12, 16, and 20 ?

    In this example, the arithmetic mean and median are both equal to $\dfrac{(4+20)}{2} = 12$. Now, try another example:

    > What is the arithmetic mean of 4, 8, 12, 16, 20, and 24 ?

    In this example, the arithmetic mean and median are both equal to $\dfrac{(4+24)}{2} = 14$.

    For all evenly spaced sets, the average equals $\dfrac{\textbf{First} + \textbf{Last}}{\textbf{2}}$.

The Sum of Consecutive Integers

Consider this problem:

> What is the sum of all the integers from 20 to 50, inclusive?
>
> (A) 990
>
> (B) 1,085
>
> (C) 1,167

Adding all those integers would take much more time than you have for a GMAT problem. Since the set is evenly spaced, though, there's a way to calculate the sum:

Sum of Evenly Spaced Set = Average $\times$ Number of Terms

First, use the first and last terms of the set to find the average:

$$\frac{20 + 50}{2} = 35$$

Find the number of terms: 50 − 20 + 1 = 31. Then, plug these values into the formula to find the sum:

Sum = (35)(31)

Glance at the answer choices to see how far you have to go with the calculation. The answers are fairly close together, so standard estimation doesn't seem like a great bet.

But the math you have to do is multiplication, so check the units digits of the answers. All three are different, so you can find just the units digits of (35)(31) and you're done. In multiplication, the units digit of the answer depends only on the units digits of the starting numbers. In this case, (5)(1) = 5, so choose the answer with a units digit of 5.

The correct answer is (B).

Advanced material for the Word Problems unit (primarily covering additional strategies for overlapping sets and consecutive integers) can be found in Atlas, Manhattan Prep's online learning platform. Use the online material only if you feel that you have mastered everything in the Word Problems unit of this strategy guide and only if you are aiming for a Quant section score of 48 or higher.

24

Problem Set

Now that you've finished the chapter, try these problems.

1. How many terms are there in the set of consecutive integers from −18 to 33, inclusive?

2. What is the sum of all the positive integers up to 100, inclusive?

Save the following problems for review after you finish this entire guide.

3. In a sequence of eight consecutive integers, how much greater is the sum of the last four integers than the sum of the first four integers?

4. If the sum of the last three integers in a set of six consecutive integers is 624, what is the sum of the first three integers of the set?

5. The operation $x \Rightarrow y$ is defined as the sum of all integers from x to y, inclusive. For example, $3 \Rightarrow 7 = 3 + 4 + 5 + 6 + 7$. What is the value of $(100 \Rightarrow 150) - (125 \Rightarrow 150)$?

24

Solutions

1. **52:** Number of terms = First − Last + 1:

$$33 - (-18) + 1 = 52$$

2. **5,050:** Sum = (Average)(Number of Terms). To find the average, take the average of the first and last terms in the set: $\frac{1 + 100}{2} = 50.5$. To find the sum, find the difference between the last and the first and then add 1 before you're done: $(100 - 1) + 1$. Finally, multiply 100 by 50.5 to find the sum of all the integers in the set: $100 \times 50.5 = 5,050$.

3. **16:** The problem never specifies a set of numbers, so it must be the case that you get the same outcome no matter what numbers you use. In that case, choose your own set of numbers!

   For example, try 1, 2, 3, 4, 5, 6, 7, and 8. The sum of the first four integers is 10. The sum of the last four integers is 26. The difference is $26 - 10 = 16$.

   If you want to get extra fancy, line up those eight numbers in two rows as follows:

$$\begin{array}{cccc} 1 & 2 & 3 & 4 \\ 5 & 6 & 7 & 8 \end{array}$$

   What is the problem asking you? Find the difference between the sum of the top row and the sum of the bottom row. Make this easier by first finding the *differences*, not the sums. For instance, the difference between 1 and 5 is +4. Likewise, the difference between 2 and 6 is +4. The same is true for all numbers in the set (since they're all consecutive!), so the total difference is $4 + 4 + 4 + 4 = (4)(4) = 16$.

   Here's how to solve algebraically. The numbers can be represented as follows: n, $(n + 1)$, $(n + 2)$, $(n + 3)$, $(n + 4)$, $(n + 5)$, $(n + 6)$, and $(n + 7)$.

   First, find the sum of the first four integers:

$$n + (n + 1) + (n + 2) + (n + 3) = 4n + 6$$

   Then, find the sum of the next four integers:

$$(n + 4) + (n + 5) + (n + 6) + (n + 7) = 4n + 22$$

   The difference between these two partial sums is:

$$(4n + 22) - (4n + 6) = 22 - 6 = 16$$

4. **615:** Think of the set of integers as n, $(n + 1)$, $(n + 2)$, $(n + 3)$, $(n + 4)$, and $(n + 5)$. Thus, $(n + 3) + (n + 4) + (n + 5) = 3n + 12 = 624$. Don't solve that quite yet, though—it's a little annoying. What does the problem want you to find?

   It asks for $n + (n + 1) + (n + 2) = 3n + 3$. Look back at the other equation.

   If $3n + 12 = 624$, then $3n + 3$ is 9 less than 624, or $624 - 9 = 615$.

24

Alternatively, another way you could solve this algebraically is to line up the algebraic expressions for each number so that you can subtract one from the other directly:

Sum of the last three integers

$$(n + 3) \;+\; (n + 4) \;+\; (n + 5)$$

Less the sum of the first three integers

$$- \quad \big[n \;+\; (n + 1) \;+\; (n + 2)\big]$$

$$3 \;+\; 3 \;+\; 3 \;=\; 9$$

Thus, the sum of the last three numbers is 9 greater than the sum of the first three numbers, so the sum of the first three numbers is $624 - 9 = 615$.

5. **2,800:** Definitely take your time to understand what's going on. This problem contains two components: the sum of all the numbers from 100 to 150 and the sum of all the numbers from 125 to 150. Since the problem asks for the *difference* between these components, you are essentially finding just the sum of all the numbers from 100 to 124 (because you will subtract out the value of the numbers from 125 to 150). You can think of this logically by visualizing a simpler problem: Find the difference $(1 \Rightarrow 5) - (3 \Rightarrow 5)$. Set up an equation:

$$1 + 2 + 3 + 4 + 5$$
$$- \quad 3 + 4 + 5$$
$$1 + 2$$

Back to the given problem. Find the sum of the integers from 100 to 124. Use the Sum = Average × Number of Terms formula.

There are 25 numbers from 100 to 124 $(124 - 100 + 1)$. To find the sum of these numbers, multiply by the average term:

$$\text{Average: } \frac{100 + 124}{2} = 112$$
$$\text{Sum: } 25 \times 112 = 25 \times 100 + 25 \times 12 = 2{,}500 + 300 = 2{,}800$$

UNIT FOUR

Number Properties

In this unit, you'll learn all about number properties, including how to handle divisibility, primes, odds and evens, positives and negatives, combinatorics, and probability. You'll also learn advanced strategies for testing cases on number properties problems.

In This Unit

- Chapter 25: Divisibility and Primes

- Chapter 26: Odds, Evens, Positives, and Negatives

- Chapter 27: Strategy: Arithmetic vs. Algebra 4

- Chapter 28: Combinatorics

- Chapter 29: Probability

Divisibility and Primes

In This Chapter

In this chapter, you will learn number property rules specific to positive integers, including a special subset of positive integers called primes. You'll learn how to find multiples, factor pairs, and prime factors of integers and how to address divisibility topics. Finally, you'll learn different ways that the GMAT will present this information and how the test might disguise the information—as well as how to strip away the disguise!

CHAPTER 25 Divisibility and Primes

The special properties of integers form the basis of most number properties problems on the GMAT. **Integers** are whole numbers, such as 0, 1, 2, and 3, that have no fractional part. Integers include positive numbers (1, 2, 3 …), negative numbers (−1, −2, −3 …), and the number 0.

Arithmetic Rules

Most arithmetic operations on integers will result in an integer. For example:

$4 + 5 = 9$	$(-2) + 1 = -1$	The sum of two integers is always an integer.
$4 - 5 = -1$	$(-2) - (-3) = 1$	The difference of two integers is always an integer.
$4 \times 5 = 20$	$(-2) \times 3 = -6$	The product of two integers is always an integer.

Division, however, is different. Sometimes the result is an integer, and sometimes it is not:

$8 \div 2 = 4$	This result is an integer …
$2 \div 8 = \frac{1}{4}$	… but this one isn't. (By the way, the result of division is called the **quotient**.)

An integer is said to be **divisible** by another number if the result, or quotient, is an integer.

For example, 21 is divisible by 3 because 21 divided by 3 results in an integer $(21 \div 3 = 7)$. However, 21 is not divisible by 4 because 21 divided by 4 results in a non-integer $(21 \div 4 = 5.25)$.

You can also talk about divisibility in terms of remainders. One number is divisible by another if the result has a remainder of 0. For example, 21 is divisible by 3 because 21 divided by 3 yields 7 with a remainder of 0. On the other hand, 21 is not divisible by 4 because 21 divided by 4 yields 5 with a remainder of 1.

Here are some more examples:

$8 \div 2 = 4$	Therefore, 8 is divisible by 2.
	You can also say that 2 is a **divisor** or **factor** of 8.
$2 \div 8 = 0.25$	Therefore, 2 is *not* divisible by 8.
$(-6) \div 2 = -3$	Therefore, −6 is divisible by 2.
$(-6) \div (-4) = 1.5$	Therefore, −6 is *not* divisible by −4.

Rules of Divisibility by Certain Integers

The **divisibility rules** are very useful shortcuts to determine whether an integer is divisible by 2, 3, 4, 5, 6, 8, 9, and 10.

An integer is divisible by

2 if the integer is even.
For example, 12 is divisible by 2, but 13 is not. Integers that are divisible by 2 are called **even**, and integers that are not divisible by 2 are called **odd**. You can tell whether a number is even by checking to see whether the units (ones) digit is 0, 2, 4, 6, or 8. For example, 1,234,567 is odd, because 7 is odd, whereas 2,345,678 is even, because 8 is even.

3 if the sum of the integer's digits is divisible by 3.
For example, 72 is divisible by 3 because the sum of its digits is $7 + 2 = 9$, which is divisible by 3. By contrast, 83 is not divisible by 3, because the sum of its digits is 11, which is not divisible by 3.

4 if the integer is divisible by 2 *twice* or if the last two digits are divisible by 4.
For example, 28 is divisible by 4 because you can divide it by 2 twice and get an integer result ($28 \div 2 = 14$ and $14 \div 2 = 7$). For larger numbers, check only the last two digits. For example, 23,456 is divisible by 4 because 56 is divisible by 4, but 25,678 is not divisible by 4 because 78 is not divisible by 4.

5 if the integer ends in 0 or 5.
For example, 75 and 80 are divisible by 5, but 77 and 83 are not.

6 if the integer is divisible by *both* 2 and 3.
For example, 48 is divisible by 6 since it is divisible by 2 (it ends with an 8, which is even) AND by 3 ($4 + 8 = 12$, which is divisible by 3).

8 if the integer is divisible by 2 three times or if the last three digits are divisible by 8.
For example, 32 is divisible by 8 since you can divide it by 2 three times and get an integer result ($32 \div 2 = 16$, $16 \div 2 = 8$, and $8 \div 2 = 4$). For larger numbers, check only the last three digits. For example, 23,456 is divisible by 8 because 456 is divisible by 8, whereas 23,556 is not divisible by 8 because 556 is not divisible by 8.

9 if the sum of the integer's digits is divisible by 9.
Since the sum of the digits of 4,185 is $4 + 1 + 8 + 5 = 18$, it is divisible by 9. By contrast, 3,459 is not divisible by 9, because the sum of its digits is 21, which is not divisible by 9.

10 if the integer ends in 0.
Because it ends in a zero, 670 is divisible by 10, but 675 is not.

The GMAT can also test these divisibility rules in reverse. For example, if you are told that a number has a ones digit equal to 0, you can infer that that number is divisible by 2, by 5, and by 10. Similarly, if you are told that the sum of the digits of x is equal to 21, you can infer that x is divisible by 3 but *not* by 9.

There is no rule listed for divisibility by 7 because there isn't a relatively easy rule for this. The simplest way to check for divisibility by 7, or by any other number not found in this list, is to perform long division—that is, if you have to divide at all. First, check whether you can estimate or otherwise avoid annoying math!

Factors and Multiples

Factors and multiples are essentially opposite terms.

A **factor** is a positive integer that divides evenly into an integer. For example, what are the factors of 8? The factors (or divisors) are 1, 2, 4, and 8. A factor of an integer is smaller than or equal to that integer.

A **multiple** of an integer is formed by multiplying that integer by any integer. What are the multiples of 8? The multiples include 8, 16, 24, and 32 (and keep going forever). On the GMAT, multiples of an integer are equal to or larger than that integer.

Note that an integer is always both a factor and a multiple of itself; for example, 8 is both a factor of and a multiple of 8. In addition, 1 is a factor of *every* integer.

An easy way to find all the factors of *small* integers is to use **factor pairs**. Factor pairs for any integer are the pairs of factors that, when multiplied together, yield that integer. For example, the factor pairs of 8 are (1, 8) and (2, 4).

To find the factor pairs of a number such as 72, start with the most basic factors: 1 and 72. Then, "walk upwards" from 1, testing to see whether different numbers are factors of 72. Once you find a number that is a factor of 72, find its partner by dividing 72 by the factor. Keep walking upwards until all factors are exhausted.

Here's how to find factor pairs, step-by-step:

1. Make a table with two columns labeled *Small* and *Large*.

2. Start with 1 in the Small column and 72 in the Large column.

3. Test the next possible factor of 72 (which is 2); 2 is a factor of 72, so write 2 underneath the 1 in your table. Divide 72 by 2 to find the factor pair: 36. Write 36 in the Large column.

4. Repeat this process until the numbers in the Small and the Large columns run into each other. In this case, once you have tested 8 and found that 9 is its paired factor, you can stop.

Small	Large
1	72
2	36
3	24
4	18
6	12
8	9

Fewer Factors, More Multiples

It can be easy to confuse factors and multiples. Use the mnemonic **Fewer Factors, More Multiples** to help remember the difference. Every positive integer has a limited number of factors. Factors divide into the integer and are therefore less than or equal to the integer. For example, there are only four factors of 8: 1, 2, 4, and 8.

By contrast, every positive integer has infinite multiples. These multiply out from the integer and are therefore greater than or equal to the integer. For example, the first five multiples of 8 are 8, 16, 24, 32, and 40, but you could go on listing multiples of 8 forever.

Factors, multiples, and divisibility are very closely related concepts. For example, 3 is a factor (or a divisor) of 12. This is the same as saying that 12 is a multiple of 3 or that 12 is divisible by 3.

On the GMAT, this terminology is often used interchangeably in order to make the problem seem harder than it actually is. Be aware of the different ways that the GMAT can phrase information about divisibility. Moreover, try to convert all such statements to the same terminology. For example, all of the following statements *say exactly the same thing*:

- 12 is divisible by 3.
- 12 is a multiple of 3.
- $\frac{12}{3}$ is an integer.
- 12 is equal to $3n$, where n is an integer.
- 12 items can be shared among 3 people so that each person has the same number of items.
- 3 is a divisor of 12, or 3 is a factor of 12.
- 3 divides 12.
- $\frac{12}{3}$ yields a remainder of 0.
- 3 goes into 12 evenly.

When you see language similar to the above, you can translate it and write it down in whatever form works best for your brain. Practice recognizing that all of these forms are really telling you the same piece of information.

Divisibility and Addition/Subtraction

If you add two multiples of 7, you get another multiple of 7. Try it: $35 + 21 = 56$. This is always mathematically valid because this is the math that's happening: $(5 \times 7) + (3 \times 7) = (5 + 3) \times 7 = 8 \times 7$.

Likewise, if you subtract two multiples of 7, you get another multiple of 7. Try it: $35 - 21 = 14$. Again, this is what's happening with the math: $(5 \times 7) - (3 \times 7) = (5 - 3) \times 7 = 2 \times 7$.

This pattern holds true for the multiples of any integer N. If you add or subtract multiples of N, the result is a multiple of N. You can restate this principle using any of the disguises noted earlier: For example, if N is a divisor of x and of y, then N is a divisor of $x + y$.

Primes

Prime numbers are a very important topic on the GMAT. A prime number is any positive integer with *exactly two* different factors: 1 and itself. In other words, a prime number has *no* factors *other* than 1 and itself. For example, 7 is prime because the only factors of 7 are 1 and 7. However, 8 is not prime because it has more than two factors: 1, 2, 4, and 8.

The number 1 is a special case. It has exactly one factor (itself), so it does not qualify as prime (which needs exactly two factors). The number 1 is unique in that 1 has just one factor, while all the other non-prime positive integers (officially known as *composite* numbers) have three or more factors.

1	Primes (2, 3, 5, 7, ...)	Composites (4, 6, 8, 9, ...)
Exactly one factor: 1	Exactly two factors: 1 Itself	Three or more factors: 1 Itself Other(s) between 1 and itself

The first prime number is 2, which is also the only even prime. The first ten prime numbers are 2, 3, 5, 7, 11, 13, 17, 19, 23, and 29. Memorizing these primes will save you time on the test.

Prime Factorization

Earlier, you learned how to find the factor pairs of a number. You can also find the **prime factors** of a number. Every number has its own unique mix of prime factors, so breaking a number down to its prime factors can be very useful on the GMAT.

Create a prime factor tree, as shown below with the number 72. Test different numbers to find one that goes into 72 without leaving a remainder. Once you find such a number, split 72 into factors, as shown here:

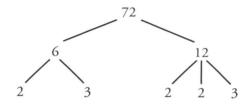

For example, 72 is divisible by 6, so it can be split into 6 and $72 \div 6 = 12$. Then, repeat this process on 6 and 12 until every branch on the tree ends at a prime number. Once you have only primes, stop, because you cannot split prime numbers into two smaller factors. In this example, 72 splits into 5 total prime factors (including repeats): $2 \times 2 \times 2 \times 3 \times 3$. In general, write prime factors for a number in increasing order, as shown.

Prime factorization is an extremely important tool to use on the GMAT. Once you know the prime factors of a number, you can determine *all* the factors of that number, even for large numbers. The factors can be found by building all the possible products of the prime factors; the next section shows how.

Factor Foundation Rule

The GMAT expects you to know the factor foundation rule: **If *a* is a factor of *b*, and *b* is a factor of *c*, then *a* is a factor of *c*.** In other words, any integer is divisible by all of its factors—and it is also divisible by all of the factors of its factors.

For example, if 72 is divisible by 12, then 72 is also divisible by all the factors of 12 (1, 2, 3, 4, 6, and 12). Written another way, if 12 is a factor of 72, then all the factors of 12 are also factors of 72. The factor foundation rule allows you to conceive of factors as building blocks in a foundation; for example, 12 and 6 are factors, or building blocks, of 72 (because 12×6 builds 72).

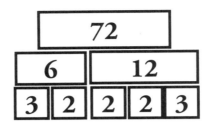

The number 12, in turn, is built from its own factors; for example, 4×3 builds 12. Thus, if 12 is part of the foundation of 72 and 12 in turn rests on the foundation built by its prime factors (2, 2, and 3), then 72 is also built on the foundation of 2, 2, and 3.

You can use the bottom level—the prime building blocks—to find (almost) any factor of 72. First, write them in increasing order: $2 \times 2 \times 2 \times 3 \times 3$. (The one factor you won't find here is the factor of 1. Just remember that all numbers always have 1 as a factor.)

Back to the building blocks. First, 2 and 3 are factors of 72. Next, you can multiply any combination of the building blocks to find larger factors. For example, $2 \times 2 = 4$ is a factor of 72. So is $2 \times 3 = 6$.

You can combine any of the prime factors you like to find any factors of 72. For example, if the test asks you whether 24 is a factor of 72, you could divide to find out—but that would get annoying as the numbers get larger. Instead, find the prime factors of 24 (which are 2, 2, 2, and 3), and check whether they're on the list for 72. They are, so 24 is also a factor of 72.

The Prime Box

You can organize this information with a tool called a prime box. A **prime box** is exactly what its name implies: a box that holds all the prime factors of a number (in other words, the lowest-level building blocks). Here are prime boxes for 72, 12, and 125:

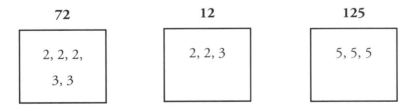

Do repeat copies of the prime factors if the number has multiple copies of that prime factor. What goes in the box should actually multiply up to the main number.

You can use the prime box to test whether or not a specific number is a factor of another number. For example:

Is 27 a factor of 72 ?

72

| 2, 2, 2, |
| 3, 3 |

$27 = 3 \times 3 \times 3$, but 72 only has *two* 3's in its prime box. It's not possible to make 27 from the prime factors of 72, so 27 is not a factor of 72.

Now, try another example:

If the integer *n* is divisible by 8 and 15, is *n* divisible by 12 ?

n

| 2, 2, 2, 3, 5, . . . ? |

First, factor both numbers: $8 = 2 \times 2 \times 2$ and $15 = 3 \times 5$. Although you don't know what *n* is, *n* has to be divisible by any number made up of those primes.

$12 = 2 \times 2 \times 3$. All of those factors appear in *n*'s box, so yes, *n* is also divisible by 12.

What if integer *k* is divisible by 8 and by 10? First, factor: $8 = 2 \times 2 \times 2$ and $10 = 2 \times 5$. Next, combine...actually, wait. Don't combine yet. If the two numbers have any *overlapping* factors, then you first have to strip out any overlap. The number 10 has one factor of 2 and the number 8 has three factors of 2, so they overlap on one factor of 2. Strip out that one factor. The prime box for *k* is $2 \times 2 \times 2 \times 5$.

Notice the ellipses and question mark ("... ?") in the prime box of *n*. This indicates that you have created a **partial prime box** of *n*. Whereas the *complete* set of prime factors of 72 can be calculated and put into its prime box, you only have a *partial* list of prime factors of *n*, because *n* is an unknown number. You know that *n* is divisible by 8 and 15, but you do *not* know what additional primes, if any, *n* has in its prime box.

Most of the time, when building a prime box for a *variable*, you will use a partial prime box, but when building a prime box for a *number*, you will use a complete prime box.

Remainders

Most of this chapter has focused on numbers that are divisible by other numbers (factors)—that is, numbers that have an integer result. This section, however, discusses what happens when a number, such as 8, is divided by a *non*-factor, such as 5.

Every division has four parts:

1. The **dividend** is the number being divided. In $8 \div 5$, the dividend is 8.

2. The **divisor** is the number that is dividing. In $8 \div 5$, the divisor is 5.

3. The **quotient** is the number of times that the divisor goes into the dividend *completely*. The quotient is always an integer. In $8 \div 5$, the quotient is 1 because 5 goes into 8 one (1) time completely.

4. The **remainder** is what is left over. In $8 \div 5$, the remainder is 3 because 3 is left over after 5 goes into 8 once.

Putting it all together, you have $8 \div 5 = 1$, with a remainder of 3.

On the GMAT, it's not unusual to see the word *remainder*. The other terms (*dividend*, *divisor*, and *quotient*) are much less common; they could appear but most people won't see them. Factor that knowledge into your decision as to whether to memorize these terms.

As another example, the number 17 is not divisible by 5. When you divide 17 by 5 using long division, you get 3 with a remainder of 2:

$$\begin{array}{r} 3 \\ 5\overline{)17} \\ -15 \\ \hline 2 \end{array}$$

The quotient is 3 because 15 is the largest multiple of 5 smaller than 17, and 15 ÷ 5 = 3. The remainder is 2 because 17 is 2 more than a multiple of 5 (15).

You can also express this relationship as a general formula:

Dividend = Quotient × Divisor + Remainder
(or, Dividend = Multiple of Divisor + Remainder)

Finally, it is possible to have a remainder of 0. A remainder of 0 occurs when one number actually is divisible by another. For example, 20 ÷ 5 = 4 remainder 0. Most of the time, you won't need to notice that something has a remainder of 0, but the GMAT might use this to disguise information. If the test tells you that n divided by 5 has a remainder of 0, it's really telling you that n is divisible by 5. (You could also say it's telling you that n is a multiple of 5.)

Advanced material for the Number Properties unit (primarily covering additional strategies for divisibility and primes, combinatorics, and probability) can be found in Atlas, Manhattan Prep's online learning platform. Use the online material only if you feel that you have mastered everything in the Number Properties unit of this strategy guide and only if you are aiming for a Quant section score of 48 or higher.

Problem Set

For questions 1–6, answer each question with one of three responses: Always Yes, Always No, or Sometimes Yes/Sometimes No. If your answer is Sometimes, use two numerical examples to show how to get a Yes and a No.

All variables in problems 1–6 are integers.

1. If a is divided by 7 or by 18, an integer results. Is $\frac{a}{42}$ an integer?

2. If 80 is a factor of r, is 15 a factor of r ?

3. If 7 is a factor of n and 7 is a factor of p, is $n + p$ divisible by 7 ?

4. If j is divisible by 12 and 10, is j divisible by 24 ?

5. If 6 is a divisor of r and r is a factor of s, is 6 a factor of s ?

6. If s is a multiple of 12 and t is a multiple of 12, is $7s + 5t$ a multiple of 12 ?

Save the following problem set for review after you finish this entire guide.

7. A skeet shooting competition awards points for each round as follows: The first-place finisher receives 11 points, the second-place finisher receives 7 points, the third-place finisher receives 5 points, and the fourth-place finisher receives 2 points. No other points are awarded. Jordan competes in several rounds of the skeet shooting competition and receives points in each round. If the product of all of the points Jordan receives equals 84,700, in how many rounds does Jordan participate?

   (A) 2
   (B) 3
   (C) 7
   (D) 9
   (E) 11

8. If x, y, and z are integers, is x even?

   (1) $10^x = (4^y)(5^z)$
   (2) $3^{x + 5} = 27^{y + 1}$

25

Solutions

1. **Always Yes:**

    a

    | 2, 3, 3, |
    | 7, . . .? |

    If *a* is divisible by 7 and by 18, its prime factors include all of the factors of those two numbers: 2, 3, 3, and 7, as shown in the prime box. Therefore, any integer that can be constructed as a product of any of these prime factors is also a factor of *a*. $42 = 2 \times 3 \times 7$, all of which are in the prime box, so 42 is also a factor of *a*.

2. **Sometimes Yes/Sometimes No:**

    r

    | 2, 2, 2, |
    | 2, 5, . . .? |

    If *r* is divisible by 80, its prime factors include 2, 2, 2, 2, and 5, as shown in the prime box. Therefore, any integer that can be constructed as a product of any of these prime factors is also a factor of *r*. $15 = 3 \times 5$. The factor 5 is in the prime box, but the 3 may or may not be. For example, if $r = 80$, then No, 15 is *not* a factor of *r*, but if $r = 240$ (which is 80×3), then Yes, 15 *is* a factor of *r*.

3. **Always Yes:** If two numbers are both multiples of the same number, then their *sum* is also a multiple of that same number. Since *n* and *p* share the common factor 7, the sum of *n* and *p* must also be divisible by 7.

4. **Sometimes Yes/Sometimes No:**

j	*j*	*j*
2, 2, 3, . . .?	2, 5, . . .?	2, 2, 3, 5, . . .?

    Careful! The number 12 contains 2, 2, and 4. The number 10 contains 2 and 5. But you can't (necessarily) put all of those numbers in the combined prime box for *j*. First, check for overlap. The two boxes overlap on one factor of 2, so strip out one 2, leaving you with $2 \times 2 \times 3 \times 5$ for *j*'s prime box.

    Next, the question asks whether *j* is divisible by 24, which equals $2 \times 2 \times 2 \times 3$. The prime box of *j* contains at least two 2's and *could* contain more but it doesn't have to. The number 24 requires three 2's. Therefore, you may or may not be able to create 24 from *j*'s prime box; 24 is not necessarily a factor of *j*.

    Prove it with numbers. The smallest possible value of *j* is $2 \times 2 \times 3 \times 5 = 60$. This number is *not* divisible by 24, so if $j = 60$, the answer is No. Alternatively, *j* could equal 120 (which is 60×2), in which case *j* is divisible by 24 and the answer is Yes.

5. **Always Yes:** By the factor foundation rule, if 6 is a factor of *r* and *r* is a factor of *s*, then 6 is a factor of *s*.

6. **Always Yes:** If *s* is a multiple of 12, then so is 7*s*. If *t* is a multiple of 12, then so is 5*t*. Since 7*s* and 5*t* are both multiples of 12, then their sum $(7s + 5t)$ is also a multiple of 12.

7. **(C) 7:** The values for scoring first, second, third, and fourth place in the competition are all prime numbers—when this happens, it is never a coincidence. Notice also that the problem mentions a *product* involving those prime numbers. Those two pieces together signal a prime factor problem. Take that ugly number and break it down into its prime factors:

$$84,700 = 847 \times 100$$

847 is a pretty annoying number to have to break down. But the problem indicates that it must be some combination of 2, 5, 7, and 11. It doesn't contain any 2s or 5s, so it must be some combination of 7 and/or 11.

Break the number into parts that are more easily divisible by 7:

$$700 = 7 \times 100$$
$$140 = 7 \times 20$$
$$7 = 7 \times 1$$

$700 + 140 + 7$ adds up to 847. To get there, you need a total of $100 + 20 + 1 = 121 \times 7$. The 7 part of that is a prime, but the 121 can be broken down further. (And don't forget about the initial value of 100—that still needs to be broken down, too!)

$$847 = 7 \times 121 = 7 \times 11 \times 11$$

$$100 = 10 \times 10 = 2 \times 2 \times 5 \times 5$$

Thus, Jordan received first place twice (11 points each), second place once (7 points each), third place twice (5 points each), and fourth place twice (2 points each). Jordan competed in a total of 7 rounds.

8. **(A):** The question stem establishes that x, y, and z are all integers and asks whether x is even. This is a Yes/No question. An even integer will end in 0, 2, 4, 6, or 8.

    (1) SUFFICIENT: Statement (1) indicates that $10^x = (4^y)(5^z)$. The variables are all in the exponents, so break the bases down to primes so that you can get the variables out of the exponents:

$$10^x = \left(4^y\right)\left(5^z\right)$$
$$(2 \times 5)^x = \left(2^2\right)^y\left(5^z\right)$$
$$2^x 5^x = 2^{2y} 5^z$$

Next, drop the bases and set the corresponding exponents equal to each other: $x = 2y$ and $x = z$. (You're allowed to do this even with multiple variables as long as everything is broken down into primes.) If $x = 2y$, and y is an integer (as given in the question stem), x must be even, since it equals 2 times an integer. The answer is Always Yes.

(2) INSUFFICIENT: Statement (2) indicates that $3^{x+5} = 27^{y+1}$. Break the bases down to primes so that you can get the variables out of the exponents. Since y is an integer, x must be 2 smaller than a multiple of 3, but that does not tell you whether x is even. If $y = 1$, then $x = 1$ (odd), but if $y = 2$, then $x = 4$ (even). Therefore:

$$3^{x+5} = 27^{y+1}$$
$$3^{x+5} = \left(3^3\right)^{y+1}$$
$$3^{x+5} = 3^{3y+3}$$

Drop the bases and set the corresponding exponents equal to each other: $x + 5 = 3y + 3$. Simplify: $x = 3y - 2$. The variable y is an integer but it could be odd or even. If y is odd, then $3y$ is also odd, as is $3y - 2$. In this case, x would be odd. However, if y is even, then $3y$ is also even, as is $3y - 2$. In this case, x would be even.

The correct answer is **(A)**: Statement (1) alone is sufficient, but statement (2) is not.

25

Odds, Evens, Positives, and Negatives

In This Chapter

- Arithmetic Rules of Odds and Evens
- Representing Odds and Evens Algebraically
- Positives and Negatives
- Absolute Value: Absolutely Positive
- A Double Negative = A Positive
- Multiplying and Dividing Signed Numbers
- Disguised Positives and Negatives
- The Sum of Two Primes

In this chapter, you will learn how positive and negative concepts are tested on the exam for both integers and non-integers. You will also learn about odd and even rules, which apply only to integers. Finally, you'll learn how to recognize these topics when the GMAT disguises them at times.

CHAPTER 26 Odds, Evens, Positives, and Negatives

Even numbers are integers that are divisible by 2. Odd numbers are integers that are not divisible by 2. All integers are either even or odd. For example:

Evens: 0, 2, 4, 6, 8, 10, 12 . . .   Odds: 1, 3, 5, 7, 9, 11 . . .

Note that 0 is an even integer. When 0 is divided by 2, the result is an integer—so 0 is even.

Consecutive integers alternate between even and odd: 9, 10, 11, 12, 13 . . .

O, E, O, E, O . . .

Negative integers are also either even or odd:

Evens: −2, −4, −6, −8, −10, −12 . . .   Odds: −1, −3, −5, −7, −9, −11 . . .

Arithmetic Rules of Odds and Evens

The GMAT tests your knowledge of how odd and even numbers combine through addition, subtraction, multiplication, and division. Rules for adding, subtracting, multiplying, and dividing odd and even numbers can be derived by testing out simple numbers, but it pays to memorize the following rules for operating with odds and evens, as they are extremely useful for certain GMAT math questions.

Addition and subtraction:

Even ± Even = Even $8 + 6 = 14$

Odd ± Odd = Even $7 + 9 = 16$

Even ± Odd = Odd $7 + 8 = 15$

If they're the same, the sum (or difference) will be even. If they're different, the sum (or difference) will be odd.

Multiplication:

Even × Even = Even $2 \times 4 = 8$

Even × Odd = Even $4 \times 3 = 12$

Odd × Odd = Odd $3 \times 5 = 15$

If one even number is present, the product will be even. If you have only odd numbers, the product will be odd.

If you multiply together several even integers, the result will be divisible by higher and higher powers of 2 because each even number will contribute at least one 2 to the factors of the product.

For example, if there are two even integers in a set of integers being multiplied together, the result will be divisible by (at least) 4:

$$\mathbf{2} \times 5 \times \mathbf{6} = 60 \qquad \text{(divisible by 4)}$$

If there are three even integers in a set of integers being multiplied together, the result will be divisible by (at least) 8:

$$\mathbf{2} \times 5 \times \mathbf{6} \times \mathbf{10} = 600 \qquad \text{(divisible by 8)}$$

Division:

There are no guaranteed outcomes in division, because the division of two integers may not yield an integer result. In these cases, you'll have to try the actual numbers given. The divisibility tools outlined in Chapter 1 can help you determine the outcome.

Representing Odds and Evens Algebraically

Try this problem:

Is positive integer m odd?

(1) $m = 2k + 1$, where k is an integer.

(2) m is a multiple of 3.

Statement (2) is easier to attack. The variable m could be 3, which is odd, or 6, which is even. This statement is NOT sufficient to determine whether m is odd.

Statement (1) is a bit trickier. An even number is a multiple of 2, so any even number can be represented as $2n$, where n is an integer. An odd number is always one more than an even number, so the subsequent odd number could be written $2n + 1$. When you see this notation in future (even if the variable is different, as it is in the given problem), note that the problem is signaling that something is odd.

Statement (1) indicates that $m = 2k + 1$, where k is an integer, so m must be odd. Statement (1) is sufficient to answer the question: Yes, m is odd.

The answer is (A): Statement (1) is sufficient alone, but statement (2) is not.

The GMAT will sometimes use this notation to disguise information about odds and evens; add it to your list of "GMAT codes" to know for the test.

Positives and Negatives

Numbers can be either positive or negative (except the number 0, which is neither):

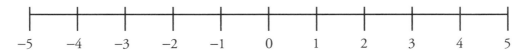

On the number line, negative numbers are all to the left of the number 0. Positive numbers are all to the right of the number 0.

Note that a variable (such as x) can have either a positive or a negative value, unless there is evidence otherwise. The variable x is not necessarily positive, nor is $-x$ necessarily negative. For example, if $x = -3$, then $-x = 3$.

Absolute Value: Absolutely Positive

Absolute value can be a component of positive/negative problems. The **absolute value** of a number answers this question: How far away is the number from 0 on the number line? For example, the number 5 is exactly 5 units away from 0, so the absolute value of 5 equals 5. Mathematically, this is written using the symbol for absolute value: $|5| = 5$. To find the absolute value of -5, look at the number line again: -5 is also exactly 5 units away from 0. Thus, the absolute value of -5 equals 5, or, in mathematical symbols, $|-5| = 5$.

Absolute value is always positive, because it disregards the direction (positive or negative) from which the number approaches 0 on the number line. When you interpret a number in an absolute value sign, just think: absolutely positive! (Except, of course, for 0, because $|0| = 0$. This is the smallest possible absolute value.)

One more thing: 5 and -5 are the same distance from 0; in other words, 0 is located halfway between them. In general, if two numbers are opposites of each other, then they have the same absolute value, and 0 is halfway between. If $x = -y$, then one of the two scenarios below is true:

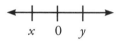 

(You cannot tell which variable is positive and which is negative without more information.)

A Double Negative = A Positive

A **double negative** occurs when a minus sign is in front of a negative number (which already has its own negative sign). For example:

What is $7 - (-3)$?

As you learned in English class, two negatives yield a positive:

$$7 - (-3) = 7 + 3 = 10$$

This is a very easy step to miss, especially when the double negative is somewhat hidden. For example:

What is $7 - (12 - x)$?

Many people will make the mistake of computing this as $7 - 12 - x$. However, notice the first minus sign has to be distributed to both terms in the parentheses, so the second term ends up with a double minus sign. This expression is simplified as $7 - 12 - (-x) = 7 - 12 + x$.

Multiplying and Dividing Signed Numbers

When you multiply or divide numbers, positive or negative, follow these rules to keep the signs straight:

Even number of negative signs = **positive**	0 negative signs: $7 \times 8 = 56$	2 negative signs: $(-7) \times (-2) = 14$
Odd number of negative signs = **negative**	1 negative sign: $-7 \times 8 = -56$	3 negative signs: $(-1) \times (-2) \times (-3) = -6$

Try this Data Sufficiency problem:

> Is the product of all of the elements in set S negative?
>
> (1) All of the elements in set S are negative.
>
> (2) There are 5 negative numbers in set S.

The problem asks whether the product of all of the elements is negative. Based on the rule above, it seems as though you just need to know whether there are an odd or even number of negative numbers in the set. There is one other number, though, to consider: 0. If you forgot about that while doing the problem, try it again right now.

Statement (1) indicates that everything in set S is negative, but you don't know whether there are an odd or even number of terms in the set, so this information is not sufficient to answer the question.

Statement (2) indicates that there are 5 negative numbers in the set. When the GMAT says something like this, you *can* conclude that there are exactly 5 negative numbers in the set (and no more). There could also be other numbers in the set (such as 0 or positive numbers). If there are 5 negative numbers and no others, then the product would be negative. If there are 5 negative numbers and other positive numbers, then the product would still be negative. But if 0 is in the mix, then the product is 0, which is not negative. So this statement is also not sufficient by itself.

Combined, set S contains 5 negative numbers *and nothing else*, so this information is sufficient to know that the product of the elements in set S must be negative. The correct answer is (C): The two statements are sufficient together, but neither one works alone.

Disguised Positives and Negatives

Some Positive/Negative questions are disguised as inequalities. This generally occurs whenever a problem tells you that a quantity is greater than or less than 0, or asks you whether a quantity is greater than or less than 0. For example:

> If $\dfrac{a-b}{c} < 0$, is $a > b$?
>
> (1) $c < 0$
>
> (2) $a + b < 0$

The fact that $\dfrac{a-b}{c} < 0$ indicates that the numerator and denominator have *different* signs. That is, either the entire numerator $(a - b)$ is positive and the denominator c is negative, or vice versa.

Statement (1) establishes that c is negative. Therefore, $a - b$ must be positive:

$$a - b > 0$$
$$a > b$$

Statement (1) is sufficient: Yes, a must be greater than b.

Statement (2) indicates that the sum of a and b is negative. Test some cases. If a is 2 and b is -5, then the sum is negative (so this is a valid case). In this case, Yes, $a > b$. If, on the other hand, a is -5 and b is 2, then the sum is negative (so this is a valid case). In this case, No, a is not greater than b. This statement is not sufficient to answer the question.

The correct answer is (A): Statement (1) is sufficient by itself, but statement (2) is not.

Generally speaking, whenever you see inequalities with the number 0 on either side of the inequality, test positive and negative cases to help solve the problem.

The Sum of Two Primes

All prime numbers are odd, except the number 2. (All even numbers greater than 2 are divisible by 2, so they cannot be prime.) Thus, the sum of any two primes will be even (odd + odd = even), *unless* one of those primes is the number 2.

If a problem tells you that the sum of two primes is odd, one of those primes must be the number 2 and the other prime must not be 2. Conversely, if you know that 2 *cannot* be one of the primes in the sum, then the sum of the two primes must be even. Try an example:

If a and b are both prime numbers greater than 10, which of the following CANNOT be true?

I. ab is an even number.

II.   The difference between a and b equals 117.

III. The sum of a and b is even.

(A) I only

(B) I and II only

(C) I and III only

(D) II and III only

(E) I, II, and III

The question asks what cannot be true; jot that down. Since a and b are both prime numbers greater than 10, they must both be odd. Therefore, ab must be an odd number, so statement I cannot be true. This statement has to be included in the correct answer, so eliminate answer (D).

Similarly, if a and b are both odd, then $a - b$ cannot equal 117 (an odd number). The difference between two odd numbers must be even. Therefore, statement II cannot be true. Eliminate answers (A) and (C).

Finally, since a and b are both odd, $a + b$ must be even, so statement III will always be true. Statements I and II cannot be true, so the correct answer is (B).

26

Problem Set

For questions 1–6, answer each question with one of three responses: Always Yes, Always No, or Sometimes Yes/Sometimes No. Try to explain each answer using the rules you learned in this section.

All variables in questions 1–6 are integers.

1. If $x \div y$ yields an odd integer, is x odd?

2. If $a + b$ is even, is ab even?

3. If c, d, and e are consecutive integers, is cde even?

4. If h is even, j is odd, and k is odd, is $k(h + j)$ odd?

5. If n, p, q, and r are consecutive integers, is their sum even?

6. If xy is even and z is even, is $x + z$ even?

7. Simplify $\dfrac{-30}{5} - \dfrac{18 - 9}{-3}$.

8. Simplify $\dfrac{20 \times (-7)}{-35 \times (-2)}$.

9. If x, y, and z are prime numbers and $x < y < z$, what is the value of x?

    (1) xy is even.

    (2) xz is even.

Save the following problem set for review after you finish this entire guide.

10. If c and d are integers, is $c - 3d$ even?

    (1) c and d are odd.

    (2) $-2d$ is odd.

11. Is the integer x odd?

    (1) $2(y + x)$ is an odd integer.

    (2) $2y$ is an odd integer.

Answers and explanations follow on the next page. ▶ ▶ ▶

Solutions

1. **Sometimes Yes/Sometimes No:** There are no guaranteed outcomes in division. For example, if $x = 6$ and $y = 2$, then $6 \div 2 = 3$ and x is even. Alternatively, if $x = 9$ and $y = 3$, then $9 \div 3 = 3$ and x is odd.

2. **Sometimes Yes/Sometimes No:** If $a + b$ is even, a and b are either both odd or both even. If they are both odd, ab is odd. If they are both even, ab is even.

3. **Always Yes:** Since all integers alternate between even and odd, at least one of the consecutive integers, c, d, or e, must be even. Therefore, the product cde must be even.

4. **Always Yes:** If h is even and j is odd, then $h + j$ must be odd, since $E + O = O$. Therefore, $k(h + j) = \text{odd(odd)}$, which is always odd.

5. **Always Yes:** If n, p, q, and r are consecutive integers, two of them must be odd and two of them must be even. Pair them up to add them: $O + O = E$ and $E + E = E$. Finally, add those two results: $E + E = E$.

6. **Sometimes Yes/Sometimes No:** If xy is even, then either x or y (or both x and y) must be even. Given that z is even, $x + z$ could be either $O + E$ or $E + E$. If $x + z = O + E = O$, the answer is No. If $x + z = E + E = E$, the answer is Yes.

7. **-3:** This is a two-step subtraction problem. First, simplify each fraction. The first fraction simplifies to $\dfrac{-30}{5} = -6$, and the second fraction simplifies to $\dfrac{9}{-3} = -3$. The final answer is $-6 - (-3) = -6 + 3 = -3$.

8. **-2:** The sign of the first product, $20 \times (-7)$, is negative. The sign of the second product, $-35 \times (-2)$, is positive. Therefore, -140 divided by 70 is -2.

9. **(D):** This is a Value question. The value of each variable is prime and x is the smallest of the three.

   (1) SUFFICIENT: If xy is even, then x is even or y is even. Only one prime number is even: the number 2. Since $x < y$, x must equal 2, since that's the smallest prime number.

   (2) SUFFICIENT: Similarly, if xz is even, then x is even or z is even. Since $x < z$, x must equal 2, because 2 is the smallest and only even prime number.

   The correct answer is **(D)**: Each statement is sufficient by itself.

10. **(A):** This is a Yes/No question. The two variables are both integers. In order for the difference $c - 3d$ to be even, the two terms (c and $3d$) either both have to be even or both have to be odd.

    (1) SUFFICIENT: If both c and d are odd, then $c - 3d$ equals $O - (3 \times O) = O - O = E$.

    (2) INSUFFICIENT: If $c - 2d$ is odd, then c must be odd, because $2d$ will always be even. However, this indicates nothing about d. If d is also odd, then the difference $c - 3d$ is even. But if d is even, then the difference $c - 3d$ is odd.

    The correct answer is **(A)**: Statement (1) is sufficient by itself, but statement (2) is not.

11. **(E):** This is a Yes/No question. The stem establishes that x is an integer and asks whether it's odd. Glance at the two statements. The second one provides no information about x, so start with this one.

(2) INSUFFICIENT: This statement indicates nothing about x. The question stem also doesn't provide any facts about the relationship between x and y, so this statement is not sufficient.

(1) INSUFFICIENT: $2(y + x)$ is an odd integer. The standard rule states that 2 multiplied by any integer is even, so how is it possible that 2 multiplied by something could yield an odd integer? The value in the parentheses must not be an integer itself. For example, the decimal 1.5 times 2 yields the odd integer 3. List some other possibilities:

$$2(y + x) = 1, 3, 5, 7, 9, \text{ etc.}$$
$$(y + x) = \frac{1}{2}, \frac{3}{2}, \frac{5}{2}, \frac{7}{2}, \frac{9}{2}, \text{ etc.}$$

The variable x is an integer, so y must be a fraction in order to get such a fractional sum.

Case 1: If $y = 0.5$ and $x = 0$, then $2(y + x) = 2(0.5) = 1$, so this is a valid case to test. In this case, No, x is not odd. (The number 0 is even.)

Case 2: If $y = 0.5$ and $x = 1$, then $2(y + x) = 2(1.5) = 3$, so this is a valid case to test. In this case, Yes, x is odd.

(1) AND (2) INSUFFICIENT: Statement (1) indicates that y must be a fraction or decimal in the pattern 0.5, 1.5, 2.5, etc. How does statement (2) add to this information?

$$2y = \text{odd}$$
$$y = \frac{\text{odd}}{2}$$

Odd integers divided by 2 will turn into fractions: $\frac{1}{2}, \frac{3}{2}, \frac{5}{2}, \ldots$

This is the same information conveyed by statement (1); the two statements are identical twins. Identical twins must be either answer (D) or (E). Answer (D) has already been knocked out, so the answer must be (E).

The correct answer is **(E)**: Using the two together is still not sufficient to answer the question.

Strategy: Arithmetic vs. Algebra 4

In This Chapter

- How to Test Cases
- Choosing Numbers for Testing Cases
- Review Your Work

In this chapter, you will learn advanced strategies for testing cases as well as methods for reviewing your work on problems and pushing your learning as far as you can. The review methods can be used on all GMAT problems—quant, verbal, and integrated reasoning.

CHAPTER 27 Strategy: Arithmetic vs. Algebra 4

Number Properties concepts lend themselves very well to testing cases, so it's common to see these on the GMAT. Most will be in the form of Data Sufficiency, though you may see one or two Problem Solving versions.

Set a timer for 8 minutes and try the following four-problem set under official exam conditions. Do the problems in order. Choose an answer before moving to the next problem (even if you have to guess).

Your main goal is to finish the set. Have an answer—any answer!—for all four problems by the time your timer goes off (i.e., by the time the test ends). Ready? Go!

1. Does positive integer b have a factor n such that $1 < n < b$?

   (1) $b = 2k$, where k is an integer greater than 1.

   (2) k is a factor of b, where k is an integer greater than 1.

2. If $xy \neq 0$, is $\dfrac{x}{y} < \dfrac{2x}{y}$?

   (1) y is positive.

   (2) xy is positive.

3. If x and y are integers and $1 < x < y$, what is the value of y ?

   (1) $xy = 15$

   (2) The product of 42 and x is 126.

4. Is integer p even?

   (1) $2p + 1$ is odd.

   (2) $\dfrac{p}{2}$ is even.

Before you read further, how do you think that went?

Do you have an answer for each question? On the real test, there's a penalty for not answering all of the questions.

How was your time management? In hindsight, do you think you should have cut off a particular problem more quickly or spent more time on a particular problem?

Full disclosure: Most people will find the first two problems harder than the last two. Did you spend too much time on either or both and then have to rush to finish? This can easily happen on the real test as well, so think about whether you should have bailed on one of the problems in order to be able to finish the set. Everyone needs to do this on the real test, so practice doing so!

Do you think you chose the best solution methods (for you)? Do you have any ideas for alternative approaches that you could have tried? Feel free to try any of the problems again using any other approaches that you would like.

Before checking the solutions to the problem set, review how to test cases and then analyze the process you used on the problem set.

How to Test Cases

This section summarizes how to test cases on Data Sufficiency problems and on Problem Solving problems.

Don't look yet, but the solutions to the problem set are a little later in this chapter. Consider how your process compared to the testing cases summary below. You may want to try the problems again before you look at the solutions.

Testing Cases on Data Sufficiency

Understand: First, **recognize** that you can test cases. The question stem and the statement will allow for multiple possible values; they don't lock you into using one set of values.

Articulate the *facts* given in the problem and separate them from the *question* that is being asked. Remind yourself of your goal when testing cases on DS: Try to find two different answers so that you can call that statement Not Sufficient and move on.

Plan: First, **think about** any **constraints** you're given. The constraints are the facts given in the problem and can be found in *two* places: (1) the question stem and (2) the two statements. You are only allowed to try numbers that fit the given facts. (As you work on one statement alone, ignore any facts given in the *other* statement.)

Next, use the given facts as clues to figure out what kinds of numbers you *do* want to try. These clues will help you to find the kinds of numbers that will give you different answers (more on this in the next section of this chapter).

Solve: Then, **test one set of numbers**. Choose your values, write them down, then check your numbers against the facts in the problem to make sure that you have chosen a valid case. If your chosen numbers "break" any of the facts—that is, make any fact in the question stem or the statement on which you're working right now false—*discard* that case. All of the given facts must be true, so any numbers you choose must go along with those facts. Cross an invalid case off on your scratch paper and start again.

If you have a valid case, solve to find an answer to the question. On a Yes/No question, you will get either a Yes or a No. On a Value question, you will get a particular value.

Then, try to find a second case that gives you a *different* answer. Remind yourself of what a "different" answer looks like for this problem. For example, if the question is "Is $b > 5$?" and your first answer is Yes, then you would want to find a No case. For this particular question, a No case would only occur when b is equal to or less than 5, so choose such a value for your second case.

If you can find two different answers, you're done! That statement has a Sometimes Yes/Sometimes No answer, so you can cross off the relevant answer(s) on your grid and move to the next step in your DS process.

If you keep getting the same answer, try to to articulate *why* this is happening. If you are trying the same kind of number each time, then you may need to try a different kind of number to find that opposite case—so trying to articulate what's happening can prompt you to try a specific kind of number that will yield a different answer.

Alternatively, articulating what's happening with the math may demonstrate that you will always get that same answer—in other words, that this statement is sufficient.

At times, you may get the same answer after a few cases but not be able to articulate what's happening. If you're not sure why but you also don't see how to get a different answer after trying a few different kinds of numbers, don't keep sitting on this problem. Go ahead and call this statement sufficient and move on.

Testing Cases on Problem Solving

There weren't any PS problems in the set, but it's still a good idea to review that process.

Understand: First, during the Understand step, **recognize** that you can test cases. The question will ask what *must* or *could be* a certain thing (true, false, or a certain characteristic).

Articulate the *facts* given in the problem and separate them from the *question* that is being asked. Remind yourself of your goal when testing cases on PS: to try to find a value that takes this answer choice out of the running. (For example, if it asks what could be *true*, try to find a value to make an answer *false*, and then you know you can cross it off forever.)

Plan: During the Plan step, first **think about** any **constraints** you're given. The constraints are the facts given in the problem. You are only allowed to try numbers that fit the given facts.

Next, use the given facts as clues to figure out what kinds of numbers you *do* want to try. These clues will help you to find the kinds of numbers that will give you the result you're looking for.

Solve: Then, **test one set of numbers**. Choose your values, write them down, then check your numbers against the facts in the problem to make sure that you have chosen a valid case. If your chosen numbers "break" any given facts, *discard* that case. Cross it off on your scratch paper and start again.

If you have a valid case, test it across all five answer choices and cross off any answers that fail the test. Then, look at the remaining answer choices and think about what kind of case to try next. What might help you to knock out one (or more) of the remaining choices? Repeat until you're down to one answer (or you get stuck; in that case, guess from the remaining answers and move on).

Choosing Numbers for Testing Cases

One more thing before diving into the solutions for the problem set: Review the guidelines for good numbers to use when testing cases. If this sparks any ideas for the problems in that set, feel free to retry any of them before looking at the solutions.

First, you always have to follow any constraints given in a problem. For example, if the problem says that *x* is positive, then you can only try positive values for *x*—but you may want to try both integers and non-integers.

When using the Test Cases strategy on either Data Sufficiency or Problem Solving problems, the general guidelines are to try numbers that are really easy to use and are likely to give you opposite, or different, answers.

The table below contains some common clues that can help you to decide what kinds of numbers to test. The first column refers to a given or fact, not the question. Only the givens or facts constrain what you're allowed to try. Also, some entries will show both mathematical symbols and words for the same concept—the test can tell you something in math or in words.

Testing Cases	
When I see (given/fact) . . .	*I'll choose . . .*
That I can test cases	0 and 1 if I can
Positive	Integers if possible/easy; fractions if needed
Non-negative	0 and positive (don't forget 0!)
(A) > 0 or greater than 0	(A) Positive
(B) < 0 or less than 0	(B) Negative
(C) $|x|$	(C) Positive and negative
Divisible by 2 or 4	Even
x and y are integers and $x = y + 1$	Odd and even
(A) x^2 (B) x^3 (C) $x^2 < x$	(A) hides sign (could be pos or neg); 0 and 1 (stay same); fractions between 0 and 1 get smaller (B) keeps sign; 0 and 1 (stay same); fractions between 0 and 1 get smaller (C) Fractions between 0 and 1
x and y are positive integers, and either $xy =$ (some number) or the product of x and y is (some number)	x and y are factors of the number (write out factor pairs)
(A) A number has exactly two factors.	(A) Prime
(B) A number has a factor between itself and 1.	(B) Not prime
(C) $1 < n < p$, where n is a factor of p.	(C) Not prime
(D) A number has more than two factors.	(D) Not prime
x and y are integers, and	
(A) $x + y > 0$	(A) At least one is positive.
(B) $x + y < 0$	(B) At least one is negative.
(C) $xy > 0$ or $x \div y > 0$	(C) Same sign: both positive or both negative
(D) $xy < 0$ or $x \div y < 0$	(D) Opposite signs: one positive, one negative
x and y are integers, and	
(A) $x + y =$ even	(A) Same parity: both even or both odd
(B) $x + y =$ odd	(B) Opposite parity: one even, one odd
(C) $xy =$ even	(C) At least one is even.
(D) $xy =$ odd	(D) Both are odd.

You have to choose numbers that fit all of the facts given in a problem. Often, this is straightforward. For example, if the problem tells you that x is a positive integer and that x is divisible by 3, it's not terribly difficult to process all of those facts at once and realize that you can choose 3, 6, 9, and so on.

Other combinations of facts will require additional thought. For example, a problem might say that x is an integer and that $x + 3$ is prime. If you begin by thinking about possible integer values for x, you might easily choose something that isn't prime when you add 3. It's probably safer to think of a prime number first (e.g., 7) and then figure out that x would have to be 4 in this case.

Try another one:

> If y is an integer and the remainder is 0 when $y + 2$ is divided by 5 . . . what could you use for y?

In order to get a remainder of 0, $y + 2$ must be divisible by 5. So $y + 2$ could be 5, in which case $y = 3$. Alternatively, $y + 2$ could be 10, in which case $y = 8$. Again, it's easier to start by choosing a value for $y + 2$, not for y by itself.

When you have multiple facts to account for, take your time during the Plan phase to figure out where to start your thinking as you choose values for your cases.

Now, are you ready? It's time to take a look at the solutions to the problem set.

Review Your Work

Use these solutions as a series of hints to help you review the problems. First, check just the correct answer; if you got it wrong, does knowing the right answer give you any ideas? If so, try those ideas before you read the solution.

Then, start reading the solution. The moment you read anything that gives you an idea about what to do, immediately *stop* reading the solution and try those next steps on your own. See what you can figure out for yourself. Whenever you get stuck, return to the solution—but when you get another idea, *stop* reading the solution again and push your thinking as far as you can on your own.

As you work, if you find any new "When I see X, I'll do Y" clues, add them to your flash cards or notes immediately.

Problem 1

> Does positive integer b have a factor n such that $1 < n < b$?
>
> (1) $b = 2k$, where k is an integer greater than 1.
> (2) k is a factor of b, where k is an integer greater than 1.

The correct answer is (A).

The question stem indicates that b is a positive integer and asks whether b has a factor smaller than b itself but larger than 1. The problem is a theoretical one—no real numbers are given, so you may want to test cases. First, though, take some time to understand that unusual question.

Can you think of a number that does have this trait? (You're not actually solving the problem or testing cases at this point. You're just trying to understand what they're talking about.)

The number 10 fits the description. It has a factor of 2. It also has a factor of 5. Both of those are less than 10 but greater than 1.

Can you think of a positive integer for which this description does *not* work? That is, a positive integer that does *not* have a factor less than itself but greater than 1?

Consider the number 7, a prime number, which by definition has exactly two factors: itself and 1. Any prime number would give a No answer to the question. Any composite number would give a Yes answer. (Composite numbers are all of the positive integers *besides* prime numbers and the number 1. The number 1 is the only positive integer that is neither prime nor composite. You don't need to know the term *composite* for the GMAT; you just need to know the concept.)

So the question is really asking whether b is a composite number. (If you don't want to use that term, you can also ask whether b is a "non-prime" number. That term isn't really proper from a math standpoint—but the GMAT isn't really a math test!)

Now that you understand what the question is asking, you can come up with a plan. The statements contain b and n, as well as a third variable, k. Testing cases is probably the best approach. Look at statement 1:

(1) $b = 2k$, where k is an integer greater than 1.

(1) SUFFICIENT: The statement introduces a third variable that wasn't in the question stem. This statement also says nothing about n. So it can't be sufficient, right?

Wait. It's pretty unusual for the statements to introduce a variable that didn't appear in the question stem. Examine this more closely. Given that k is an integer greater than 1, what are some possible values for b?

Case 1: If $k = 2$, then $b = 4$. Is b composite (or non-prime)? Yes.

Case 2: If $k = 3$, then $b = 6$. Is b composite (or non-prime)? Yes.

Can you get a No answer? Is there a value for k that would allow b to be prime?

It's not possible. First, b equals k multiplied by 2, so b will always be even. Second, k is at least 2, so b is at least 4. The only even prime number is 2, so if b is even and at least 4, it cannot be prime.

Statement (1) is sufficient to answer the question. Eliminate answers (B), (C), and (E).

(2) k is a factor of b, where k is an integer greater than 1.

(2) INSUFFICIENT: Try some cases.

Case 1: If $k = 2$, then b could be 4. In this case, is b composite (or non-prime)? Yes.

Given that same starting point, $k = 2$, b itself could also be 2, since any number has itself as a factor (in other words, 2 is a factor of 2).

Case 2: If $k = 2$, then b could be 2. In this case, is b composite (or non-prime)? No, in this case b is prime.

A Sometimes Yes/Sometimes No answer is not sufficient.

The correct answer is (A): Statement (1) works alone, but statement (2) does not.

Problem 2

If $xy \neq 0$, is $\dfrac{x}{y} < \dfrac{2x}{y}$?

(1) y is positive.

(2) xy is positive.

The correct answer is (B).

The question stem is annoying. The statements are pretty straightforward and the reference to *positive* indicates that this might be a Positive/Negative problem. Can you simplify or rephrase the question? Your initial instinct may be to cross-multiply to get rid of the fractions, but the question stem does not indicate whether *y* is positive or negative. As a result, you wouldn't know whether to flip the inequality sign when performing the multiplication, so taking this action is likely to make the rephrase more complicated, not less. Don't go there.

Instead, compare the two sides of the inequality. They're almost identical; the only difference is multiplying the numerator by 2. The statements hinted at a positive/negative approach, so test some cases with some easy positive and negative numbers. Note the constraint: Don't use 0 for either variable.

Statement (1) indicates that *y* is positive but says nothing about *x*. Statement (2) indicates that *x* and *y* are either both positive or both negative. It's your choice as to which seems like an easier starting point; this solution will start with statement (1).

(1) INSUFFICIENT: This statement indicates that *y* is positive but says nothing about *x*. Try cases in which *x* is both positive and negative.

Case 1: $x = 1$, $y = 2$. (Pause to verify that your numbers fit all of the facts given in the problem. They do? Carry on.)

$$\text{Is } \frac{1}{2} < \frac{2(1)}{2} \text{ ?}$$
$$\text{Is } \frac{1}{2} < 1 \text{ ? Yes.}$$

This is a Yes case. Try a negative value for *x* to see what answer that returns.

Case 2: $x = -1$, $y = 2$. (Pause. Does this fit all of the facts? Carry on.)

$$\text{Is } \frac{-1}{2} < \frac{2(-1)}{2} \text{ ?}$$
$$\text{Is } -\frac{1}{2} < -1 \text{ ? No.}$$

When *x* is negative and *y* is positive, the answer is No. Because the answer is Sometimes Yes/Sometimes No, this statement is not sufficient.

(2) SUFFICIENT: The statement indicates that *x* and *y* are either both positive or both negative. Try both cases.

First, examine the cases that you tried for statement (1) (but don't use that statement itself!). You can reuse any cases that also fit statement (2). The two variables have the same sign. The first case ($x = 1$ and $y = 2$) fits this scenario, so this case will also work for statement (2). That's your Yes case.

Note: If you use the same starting numbers for the case, the answer will always be the same—Yes, in this case—because the two statements never contradict. So when you see that you can reuse the numbers for the other statement, don't actually do the whole case. The answer will be the same.

The second case for statement (1), though, used a negative *x* and positive *y*, so that one can't be reused here. Instead, try the negative-negative case for statement (2).

27

Case 1: Reused from statement (1). Yes.

Case 2: $x = -1$, $y = -2$. (Pause. Did you fulfill all constraints? Carry on.)

$$\text{Is } \frac{-1}{-2} < \frac{2(-1)}{-2} \text{ ?}$$

$$\text{Is } \frac{1}{2} < 1 \text{ ? Yes.}$$

Hmm. That also returned a Yes case. Try to articulate what's happening with the math. The left side has $\frac{x}{y}$ and the right side has almost the same thing, $\frac{2x}{y}$. The right side can also be written $2\left(\frac{x}{y}\right)$. In other words, you're just multiplying the original fraction by 2.

If you start with any *positive* fraction and multiply it by 2, you're going to get a larger value. So when x and y are both positive, you'll always get a Yes answer.

What about when they're both negative? If they're both negative, those negative signs will actually cancel out, so you'll end up with a positive fraction. And any positive fraction multiplied by 2 will get larger. This statement is sufficient because the only possible answer is Yes.

The correct answer is (B): Statement (2) works alone, but statement (1) does not.

Problem 3

> If x and y are integers and $1 < x < y$, what is the value of y ?
>
> (1) $xy = 15$
> (2) The product of 42 and x is 126.

The correct answer is (A).

The question stem doesn't have a lot of complexity. Both variables are integers and both are greater than 1. Also, y is greater than x. The question asks for the value of y.

At first, the problem might not appear to contain any of the usual clues that can help you to tell what kind of problem is being tested. The statements talk about basic multiplication. There's nothing indicating the dividing line between positive and negative or odd and even.

Go back to the multiplication part. Both statements multiply two integers together to get a third integer. This is a clue! The two smaller numbers are factors of the larger number.

(1) SUFFICIENT: The factor pairs of 15 are (1, 15) and (3, 5). Both variables are greater than 1, so cross off the (1, 15) factor pair. And y is greater than x, so y must be 5 (and x must be 3). You have a definitive value for y, so this statement is sufficient.

(2) INSUFFICIENT: This statement allows you to find the value of x, but it indicates nothing about y.

The correct answer is (A): Statement (1) works alone, but statement (2) does not.

This problem is setting up a C-Trap. You can get the value of x from statement (2), and you could plug that into the equation in statement (1) to get the value of y. If the question stem hadn't provided the additional facts that it did, then (C) would have been the answer. But, given the question stem, statement (1) is enough on its own.

Problem 4

Is integer p even?

(1) $2p + 1$ is odd.

(2) $\frac{p}{2}$ is even.

The correct answer is (B).

The question stem establishes that p is an integer and asks whether p is even.

(1) INSUFFICIENT: If $2p + 1$ is odd, then $2p$ is even. Any integer multiplied by 2 is even, though, so p itself could be either even or odd. (If you're not sure, test a couple of numbers to see.)

(2) SUFFICIENT: Any odd number divided by 2 will result in a non-integer. So if $\frac{p}{2}$ is even, then p itself must be even. You can literally write an equation to show this:

$$\frac{p}{2} = \text{even}$$
$$p = 2(\text{even})$$

If p equals 2 times another even, then p itself must be even. (You can also test actual values to figure this out, if you prefer.)

The correct answer is (B): Statement (2) is sufficient by itself, but statement (1) is not.

Now that you've reviewed the four problems, what are your major takeaways?

How will you make better decisions around time management next time you do a problem set? Do you need to build any better habits around your DS process, how you write things down on your scratch paper, or how you solve?

27

Problem Set

Now that you've finished the chapter, try the following problems.

1. Is $pqr > 0$?

    (1) $pq > 0$

    (2) $\dfrac{q}{r} < 0$

2. If x is a positive integer, is $x^2 + 6x + 10$ odd?

    (1) $x^2 + 4x + 5$ is odd.

    (2) $x^2 + 3x + 4$ is even.

3. If x is a positive integer and $3x + 2$ is divisible by 5, then which of the following must be true?

    (A) x is divisible by 3.

    (B) $3x$ is divisible by 10.

    (C) $x - 1$ is divisible by 5.

    (D) x is odd.

    (E) $3x$ is even.

4. If p, q, and r are integers, is $pq + r$ even?

    (1) $p + r$ is even.

    (2) $q + r$ is odd.

Save these problems for review after you finish this entire guide.

5. If x is an integer and $0 < x < 24$, is $\dfrac{24}{x}$ an integer?

    (1) $\dfrac{28}{x}$ is an integer.

    (2) $\dfrac{x}{4}$ is an integer.

6. The length of a certain rectangle is a multiple of 18, and the width of the rectangle is a multiple of 12. Which of the following CANNOT be the perimeter of the rectangle?

    (A) 60

    (B) 72

    (C) 84

    (D) 96

    (E) 108

7. A university badminton club has both students and professors as members. Is the number of students in the club at least 45?

    (1) The number of professors in the club is a multiple of 8.

    (2) The number of students in the club is exactly 20% greater than the number of professors in the club.

Answers and explanations follow on the next page. ▶ ▶ ▶

Solutions

1.   **(E):** The question stem asks whether the product of three numbers is greater than 0, so this is a Yes/No question focusing on the concept of positive and negative. First, figure out what would need to be true in order for the product of three numbers to be positive.

    First, if any of the variables is 0, the answer is No. Next, if all three variables are positive, then the product will be positive. If exactly two are negative and one is positive, then the product will be positive. Finally, if exactly one or exactly three are negative, then the product will be negative.

    (1) INSUFFICIENT: If pq is greater than 0, then p and q have the same sign, either both positive or both negative. This statement says nothing about r, so r could be positive, negative, or 0. Test cases; try to get different answers.

	p	q	r	Valid?	Is $pqr > 0$?
Case 1	+	+	0	✓	No
Case 2	+	+	+	✓	Yes

    (2) INSUFFICIENT: If q divided by r is less than 0, then q and r have opposite signs. This statement says nothing about p, so p could be positive, negative, or 0. Test cases; try to get different answers.

	p	q	r	Valid?	Is $pqr > 0$?
Case 1	0	+	−	✓	No
Case 2	−	+	−	✓	Yes

    (1) AND (2) INSUFFICIENT: Using both statements together, p and q have the same sign (either both positive or both negative) and q and r have opposite signs. In other words, two of the variables have the same sign and the third has opposite signs.

	p	q	r	Valid?	Is $pqr > 0$?
Case 1	+	+	−	✓	No
Case 2	−	−	+	✓	Yes

    The correct answer is **(E):** Using the two statements together, there is still not enough information to answer the question.

2.   **(A):** The question can first be simplified by noting that if x is even, $x^2 + 6x + 10$ will be even (a No answer), and if x is odd, $x^2 + 6x + 10$ will be odd (a Yes answer). Thus, you can simplify this question: Is x odd?

    (A couple of shortcuts to save time in reaching that conclusion: The exponent on the first term can be ignored, since an even squared is still even and an odd squared is still odd. You know $6x$ will be even no matter what, since 6 is even, and obviously 10 is even no matter what. So an even plus two evens is even, and an odd plus two evens is odd.)

(1) SUFFICIENT: You can test odd and even cases or simply use number theory. If x is even, you get even + even + odd = odd, and if x is odd, you get odd + even + odd = even. Thus, since $x^2 + 4x + 5$ is odd, x is even. The answer to the rephrased question is Always No, so this statement is sufficient.

(2) INSUFFICIENT: $x^2 + 3x + 4$ is actually even regardless of what integer is plugged in for x. If x is even, you get even + even + even = even, and if x is odd, you get odd + odd + even = even. Thus, x could be odd or even, and the answer is Sometimes Yes/Sometimes No. Plugging in numbers will yield the same conclusion—x could be any integer.

Note that you should *not* factor any of the expressions above. If you wasted time factoring, remember: Factoring is meaningless if you don't have an equation set equal to 0! This problem was about number theory (or number testing), not factoring.

The correct answer is **(A)**: Statement (1) is sufficient by itself, but statement (2) is not.

3. **(C) $x - 1$ is divisible by 5:** The question stem is asking a *must be* question, so test cases on this problem. Use positive integers for x that make the following equation true:

    $$\frac{3x + 2}{5} = \text{integer}$$

    If $x = 1$, then $3(1) + 2 = 5$, which is divisible by 5. So this is a valid case to test. Check $x = 1$ against the answer choices. Answers (A), (B), and (E) are all false for this case, so eliminate them.

    Try another case. If $x = 2$, then $3(2) + 2 = 8$, which is not divisible by 5. This is an invalid case; discard it. What about $x = 3$? In this case, $3(3) + 2 = 11$. Still invalid. You can continue to try increasing integers or take a moment to think about what's happening with the math to help you find the next case. Rearrange that starting equation a little:

    $$\frac{3x + 2}{5} = \text{int}$$
    $$3x + 2 = (5)(\text{int})$$
    $$3x = (5)(\text{int}) - 2$$

    In other words, $3x$ must equal a multiple of 5 minus 2. Multiples of 5 are 5, 10, 15, 20, 25, and so on. Subtract 2 from these multiples of 5 to find the potential values of $3x$, which are 3, 8, 13, 18, 23, and so on.

    Because x itself must be an integer, $3x$ must be a multiple of 3. This narrows down the list of potential values of $3x$ to 3, 18, and so on, and the corresponding x values are 1, 6, and so on. The first case, $x = 1$, has already been tested, so the next one to try is $x = 6$.

    Case 2: $x = 6$. Verify that this is valid: $(3)(6) + 2 = 20$. This is divisible by 5, so proceed. Answers (A), (B), and (E) have already been eliminated, so test only answers (C) and (D). In this case, answer (D) is false so eliminate it. The only remaining answer is **(C)**.

4. **(E):** The Yes/No question asks whether $pq + r$ is even. What would need to be true in order for the answer to be Yes? Either both pq and r need to be even or both pq and r need to be odd.

    (1) INSUFFICIENT: You are told that $p + r$ is even. To stay organized, test all the cases that make the statement true. Both p and r are even, or both p and r are odd. For each of those scenarios, q could be odd or even. Set up a table to keep track of all of these possibilities:

27

Scenario	p	q	r	$pq + r$
1	Odd	Odd	Odd	$O \times O + O = E$
2	Odd	Even	Odd	$O \times E + O = O$
3	Even	Odd	Even	$E \times O + E = E$
4	Even	Even	Even	$E \times E + E = E$

Since $pq + r$ could be odd or even, statement (1) is not sufficient. Note that you can stop as soon as you have found contradictory cases (one odd and one even); above, for example, you could have stopped after scenario 2.

(2) INSUFFICIENT: As in statement (1), you can organize the information from statement (2) with a table. Either q is even and r is odd or q is odd and r is even, and p can be odd or even:

Scenario	p	q	r	$pq + r$
5	Odd	Even	Odd	$O \times E + O = O$
6	Even	Even	Odd	$E \times E + O = O$
7	Odd	Odd	Even	$O \times O + E = O$
8	Even	Odd	Even	$E \times O + E = E$

(1) AND (2) INSUFFICIENT: Notice that scenarios 2 and 5 are identical, as are scenarios 3 and 8. Therefore, both sets of scenarios meet the criteria laid forth in statements (1) and (2), but they yield opposite answers to the question:

Scenario	p	q	r	$pq + r$
2 & 5	Odd	Even	Odd	$O \times E + O = O$
3 & 8	Even	Odd	Even	$E \times O + E = E$

The correct answer is **(E)**: The statements are not sufficient alone or together.

5. **(C):** This Yes/No question indicates that x is an integer between (but *not* including) 0 and 24. It asks whether 24 divided by x is an integer, or $\frac{24}{x} = $ int?

The value of x would need to be a factor of 24 in order for the result to be an integer; there are a limited number of possibilities. The factor pairs for 24 are $(1, 24)$, $(2, 12)$, $(3, 8)$, and $(4, 6)$. Keep this in mind as you test cases.

(1) INSUFFICIENT: If 28 is divisible by x, then x is a factor of 28. The factors of 28 are $(1, 28)$, $(2, 14)$, and $(4, 7)$. Also follow the constraints given in the question stem: x is an integer between 0 and 24. So try anything on the factors-of-28 list besides the number 28.

Case 1: If $x = 4$, then $\frac{24}{4}$ is an integer. This is a Yes case.

Case 2: Can you get a different answer? Look over the list of factors for 28 (not including 28 itself!) and try to find one that will result in a non-integer when divided into 24. If $x = 7$, then $\frac{24}{7}$ is not an integer. This is a No case.

(2) INSUFFICIENT: If x is divisible by 4, then x is a multiple of 4, so it could be 4, 8, 12, 16, and so on. Try values only from that list.

Case 1: $x = 4$, in which case the answer to the question is Yes, $\frac{24}{4}$ is an integer.

Case 2: $x = 16$, in which case the answer to the question is No, $\frac{24}{16}$ is not an integer.

(1) AND (2) SUFFICIENT: Using both statements together, x must be both a factor of 28 and divisible by 4. First, review the factor pairs of 28. (You don't need to rewrite them—you can look at what you wrote down for the second statement.) Cross off all of the numbers that are not divisible by 4 and that are not between 0 and 24: $(\cancel{1}, \cancel{28})(\cancel{2}, \cancel{14})(4, \cancel{7})$. The only value left is $x = 4$, and the answer to the question is Yes, $\frac{24}{4}$ is an integer.

The correct answer is **(C)**: The two statements together are sufficient, but neither one works alone.

6. **(B) 72:** The length could be 18, 36, 54, and so on. The width could be 12, 24, 36, and so on. The question stem asks what *cannot* be the perimeter. This wording signals that there are multiple possible values that will work, so test cases on this problem. First, set up the information. The perimeter of a rectangle is $2(w + l)$. What's the smallest possible perimeter?

    Let $l = 18$ and $w = 12$. In this case, the perimeter is $2(18 + 12) = 2(30) = 60$. Cross off answer (A).

    What's the next possible case? You could double both values, the length to 36 and the width to 24, which would significantly increase the perimeter...but glance at those answers. They're not that much greater than 60, yet three of the four remaining answers must also work. That's your clue to first double only one of the dimensions, but leave the other the same.

    The next smallest case will be to double the width to become 24 but leave the length at 18. (Ignore the fact that this makes the width longer than the length; that's okay.) In this case, the perimeter is $2(24 + 18) = 2(42) = 84$. Eliminate answer (C).

    That skipped over answer (B). Is there another, smaller case you could have tried to get 72 as the perimeter? The length is a multiple of 18, so doubling that one (and leaving the width at 12) would lead to a larger perimeter than 84. There is no other case possible between 60 and 84, so 72 is not a possible length for the perimeter.

7. **(C):** Let s and p be the number of students and professors in the club, respectively. The question asks whether $s \geq 45$.

    (1) INSUFFICIENT: This statement provides information about the professors but not the students. The question stem did not provide any additional information about the relationship between p and s, so this statement is not sufficient to answer the question.

    (2) INSUFFICIENT: This statement provides a *relative* relationship between the number of professors and the number of students but no actual values. There is a hidden integer constraint here—both p and s must be integers—so this limits the values that could work for the given relationship. What integers will allow you to take 20% and get another integer?

Case 1: Try 100 first since this is a percent problem. Let $p = 100$ and $s = 120$. (To find 20%, take 10% and double it.) In this case, Yes, $s \geq 45$.

A No case would require an integer less than 45 that will still yield an integer when you take 20%. Benchmark your way to the smallest possible integer that will work: If 20% = 1, then 100% = $(1)(5) = 5$. Now put this number formally through the test to make sure the logic worked.

Case 2: Try $p = 5$. In this case, 20% of 5 is 1, so $s = 6$. In this case, s is less than 45, so the answer is No.

(1) AND (2) SUFFICIENT: According to statement (1), the value of p has to be 8, 16, 24, 32, and so on. According to statement (2), the smallest possible value of p is 5; the other possible values of p will be multiples of 5, or 5, 10, 15, 20, and so on.

Put the information together. The first value that is both a multiple of 8 and a multiple of 5 is $p = 40$. Now find s: 20% of $40 = 4 + 4 = 8$, so $s = 48$. This is the smallest possible value for s, so the answer is always Yes, $s \geq 45$.

The correct answer is **(C)**: Both statements together are sufficient, but neither one works alone.

27

Combinatorics

In This Chapter

In this chapter, you will learn how to set up and solve combination, or counting, problems. These questions are not very common on the GMAT and many people dislike them, so you may choose not to study certain material; the chapter will guide you in making this choice.

CHAPTER 28 **Combinatorics**

The Words *OR* and *AND*

Suppose you are at a restaurant that offers a free side dish of soup or salad with any main dish. How many possible side dishes can you order?

You have two options: the soup OR the salad. The most important part of the example is this: The word *or* means *add*. You will see this word show up again and again in both combinatorics and probability problems.

If the same restaurant offers three main dishes (steak, salmon, or pasta), then how many possible combinations of main dish and side dish are there?

There are two decisions that need to be made: a main dish AND a side dish. List out all the possible combinations:

Steak – Soup	Steak – Salad	Salmon – Soup
Salmon – Salad	Pasta – Soup	Pasta – Salad

There are six possible combinations. For a problem without many options, you can literally just write out the possibilities. You can also do some math if you know that the word *and* means *multiply*.

When you make two decisions, you make decision 1 AND decision 2. This is true whether the decisions are simultaneous (e.g., choosing a main dish and a side dish) or sequential (e.g., choosing among routes between successive towns on a road trip).

In this example, you have three options for main dishes AND two options for side dishes:

$$\text{(steak OR chicken OR salmon)} \quad \text{AND} \quad \text{(soup OR salad)}$$
$$(\;1\;+\;1\;+\;1\;)\;\times\;(\;1\;+\;1\;)\;=\;6$$
$$3\qquad\qquad\times\qquad 2\qquad=\;6$$

More straightforward combinatorics (also known as counting) problems can be solved using these two principles:

1. *OR* means *add*.
2. *AND* means *multiply*.

GMAT questions will get more complicated, of course. Try the following example:

> An office manager must choose a four-digit lock code for the office door. The first and last digits of the code must be odd, and no repetition of digits is allowed. How many different lock codes are possible?

When a question asks how many possible ways something can happen, you have a combinatorics or counting problem. In this case, the manager has to make four decisions to get a four-digit lock code. To keep track, make a slot for each digit:

$$\underline{\qquad}_{\text{Digit 1}} \times \underline{\qquad}_{\text{Digit 2}} \times \underline{\qquad}_{\text{Digit 3}} \times \underline{\qquad}_{\text{Digit 4}}$$
$$\text{AND} \qquad \text{AND} \qquad \text{AND}$$

Next, fill in the number of options for each slot. This is known as the **slot method**.

How many options are there for each digit? Start with the most constrained decisions first. There are restrictions on the first and last numbers so start there.

The first digit must be odd, so it can be 1 OR 3 OR 5 OR 7 OR 9. There are five options for the first digit. The problem also indicated that there can be no repeated numbers. Now that you have chosen the first digit (even though you don't know what the actual value will be), there are only four odd numbers remaining for the last digit. Fill in both slots:

$$\underline{\ 5\ }_{\text{Digit 1}} \times \underline{\qquad}_{\text{Digit 2}} \times \underline{\qquad}_{\text{Digit 3}} \times \underline{\ 4\ }_{\text{Digit 4}}$$
$$\text{AND} \qquad \text{AND} \qquad \text{AND}$$

Now, fill in the other two slots. Make sure to account for the lack of repetition. Ten digits exist in total (0 through 9), but two have already been used, so there are eight options remaining for the second digit and seven options for the third digit:

$$\underline{\ 5\ }_{\text{Digit 1}} \times \underline{\ 8\ }_{\text{Digit 2}} \times \underline{\ 7\ }_{\text{Digit 3}} \times \underline{\ 4\ }_{\text{Digit 4}}$$
$$\text{AND} \qquad \text{AND} \qquad \text{AND}$$

Finally, multiply this out. Look to multiply multiples of 5s and 2s together (because $5 \times 2 = 10$ and 10 is easier to multiply into other numbers). In this case, $5 \times 4 = 20$ and $8 \times 7 = 56$. The number 20 can be thought of as 2×10, so multiply $(56)(2)(10) = 1{,}120$.

When making decisions, there are two main cases:

1. Decision 1 OR Decision 2: ADD the possibilities.

2. Decision 1 AND Decision 2: MULTIPLY the possibilities.

Finally, the rest of this chapter deals with more complex scenarios. Many test-takers really dislike combinatorics; if you are one of them, you can decide to bail (guess immediately) on most combinatorics problems on the GMAT. It is possible to score well into the 700s while bailing on most combinatorics problems on the test.

If you see a more straightforward problem for which you can write out a small number of combinations, go ahead and logic it out. If you see a problem that has anything more complicated, choose your favorite letter and move on. (And, if you want to do that, you don't have to learn how to do anything else in this chapter.)

28

Arranging Groups

Another very common type of combinatorics problem asks how many different ways there are to arrange a group.

The number of ways of arranging n distinct objects, if there are no restrictions, is $n!$ (n factorial).

The term **n factorial** ($n!$) refers to the product of all the integers from 1 to n, inclusive. If you are going to go for it on medium to harder combinatorics questions, memorize the first six factorials, shown here:

$1! = 1$ $\qquad\qquad$ $4! = 4 \times 3 \times 2 \times 1 = 24$

$2! = 2 \times 1 = 2$ $\qquad\quad$ $5! = 5 \times 4 \times 3 \times 2 \times 1 = 120$

$3! = 3 \times 2 \times 1 = 6$ $\qquad$ $6! = 6 \times 5 \times 4 \times 3 \times 2 \times 1 = 720$

For example, how many ways are there to arrange four people in four chairs in a row? Using the **slot method**, there is one slot for each position in the row. If you place any one of four people in the first chair, then you can place any one of the remaining three people in the second chair. For the third and fourth chairs you have two choices and then one choice.

$$\underline{\quad 4 \quad} \times \underline{\quad 3 \quad} \times \underline{\quad 2 \quad} \times \underline{\quad 1 \quad} = 24 \text{ arrangements}$$

If you know how to think that through, you can just say, "The number of ways to arrange four people equals 4 factorial, which equals 24."

Arranging Groups Using the Anagram Grid

How many arrangements are there of the letters in the word EEL?

There are three letters, so according to the factorial formula, there should be $3! = 6$ arrangements, as follows (the two E's have subscripts to keep them straight):

E_1E_2L $\qquad$ E_1LE_2 $\qquad$ LE_1E_2

E_2E_1L $\qquad$ E_2LE_1 $\qquad$ LE_2E_1

The two arrangements in each column are considered identical. For example, E_1E_2L is the same thing as E_2E_1L; they're both EEL. There are really only three distinct arrangements:

EEL $\qquad$ ELE $\qquad$ LEE

Sometimes, you have to divide out a subset of the possible arrangements because they are identical to others in the set.

Here's how that would play out on a more GMAT-like problem:

> Seven people enter a race. There are 4 types of medals given as prizes for completing the race. The winner gets a platinum medal, the runner-up gets a gold medal, the next 2 racers each get a silver medal, and the last 3 racers all get bronze medals. What is the number of different ways the medals can be awarded?

In order to keep track of all the different categories, create an **anagram grid**. Anagram grids can be used whenever you are arranging members of a group.

28

The number of columns in the grid will always be equal to the number of members of the group. There are 7 runners in the race, so make 7 columns (labeled 1 through 7). Next, categorize each member of the group. There are 1 platinum medal, 1 gold medal, 2 silver medals, and 3 bronze medals. Note: Use only letters for the bottom row, never numbers (you'll see why in a minute).

1	2	3	4	5	6	7
P	G	S	S	B	B	B

Just as the two E's in EEL were indistinguishable, the 2 silver medals and the 3 bronze medals are indistinguishable, so 7! is not the answer. Use the top and bottom rows to create a fraction:

$$\frac{\text{Top row}}{\text{Bottom row}} = \frac{7!}{1!1!2!3!}$$

The numerator of the fraction is always the factorial of the largest number in the top row (in this case, 7!). The denominator is the product of the factorials of each *different* kind of letter in the bottom row. In this case, there are one P, one G, two S's, and three B's. (Use only letters in the bottom row to avoid mixing up the number of repeats with the numbers themselves.)

The bottom row of the fraction shows the 1! terms for both P and G, but in practice, you don't have to write out any 1! terms, since they don't make a difference to the calculation. As you simplify the fraction, look for ways to cancel out numbers in the denominator with numbers in the numerator:

$$\frac{7!}{2!3!} = \frac{7 \times 6 \times 5 \times \overset{2}{\cancel{4}} \times \cancel{3!}}{\underset{1}{\cancel{2}} \times 1 \times \cancel{3!}} = 7 \times 6 \times 5 \times 2 = 420$$

Try another problem:

A local card club will send 3 representatives to the national conference. If the local club has 8 members, how many different groups of representatives could the club send?

The problem talks about 8 members, so draw 8 columns for the anagram grid. There are 3 representatives chosen; represent them with Y. Use N to represent the 5 members of the group who are not chosen.

1	2	3	4	5	6	7	8
Y	Y	Y	N	N	N	N	N

Set up your fraction:

$$\frac{8!}{3!5!} = \frac{8 \times 7 \times \cancel{6} \times \cancel{5!}}{\left(\cancel{3} \times \cancel{2} \times 1\right)\cancel{5!}} = 8 \times 7 = 56$$

On the top of the fraction, only write out the numbers down to the largest factorial that also appears on the bottom of the fraction. In the fraction above, you can cancel out the two 5! terms without having to write them out.

Multiple Groups

So far, the discussion has revolved around two main themes: (1) making decisions and (2) arranging groups. More difficult combinatorics problems will actually combine the two topics. In other words, you may have to make multiple decisions, each of which will involve arranging different groups.

Try the following problem:

> The I Eta Pi fraternity must choose a delegation of 3 senior members and 2 junior members for an annual interfraternity conference. If I Eta Pi has 6 senior members and 5 junior members, how many different delegations are possible?

First, note that you are choosing senior members AND junior members. These are different decisions, so determine each separately and then multiply the possible arrangements.

You have to pick 3 seniors out of a group of 6. That means that 3 are chosen (and identical) and the remaining 3 are not chosen (and also identical):

$$\frac{6!}{3!3!} = \frac{6 \times 5 \times 4 \times 3!}{(3 \times 2 \times 1) \, 3!} = 5 \times 4 = 20$$

Similarly, pick 2 juniors out of a group of 5, where 2 members are chosen (and identical) and the remaining 3 members are not chosen (and also identical):

$$\frac{5!}{2!3!} = \frac{5 \times \overset{2}{4} \times 3!}{\left(_1 2 \times 1\right) 3!} = 5 \times 2 = 10$$

There are 20 possible senior delegations AND 10 possible junior delegations. Since *AND* means *multiply*, there are $20 \times 10 = 200$ possible delegations.

Problems will not always make it clear that you are dealing with multiple decisions. Try the following problem:

> The yearbook committee has to pick a color scheme for this year's yearbook. There are 7 colors to choose from (red, orange, yellow, green, blue, indigo, and violet). How many different color schemes are possible if the committee can select at most 2 colors?

Although this question concerns only one group (colors), it also involves multiple decisions. The question states there can be *at most* 2 colors chosen. In other words, the color scheme can contain 1 color OR 2 colors.

Figure out how many combinations are possible if 1 color is chosen, as well as how many are possible if 2 colors are chosen, and then add them together:

$$1 \text{ color chosen and 6 colors not chosen} = \frac{7!}{1!6!} = 7$$

$$2 \text{ colors chosen and 5 colors not chosen} = \frac{7!}{2!5!} = 21$$

Together, there are $7 + 21 = 28$ possible color schemes.

Problem Set

Now that you've finished the chapter, try the following problems.

1. In how many different ways can the letters in the word *LEVEL* be arranged?

2. A company makes 5 different types of truffles. If one package contains exactly 2 truffles of different types, how may different combinations are possible?

Save the following problems for review after you finish this entire guide.

3. A pod of 6 dolphins always swims single file, with 3 females at the front and 3 males in the rear. In how many different arrangements can the dolphins swim?

4. Mario's Pizza offers a choice of 2 types of crust, 2 types of cheese, and 5 different types of vegetables. If Linda's volleyball team decides to order a pizza with 4 types of vegetables, how many different choices do the teammates have at Mario's Pizza?

5. What is the sum of all the possible three-digit numbers that can be constructed using the digits 3, 4, and 5 if each digit can be used only once in each number?

Answers and explanations follow on the next page. ▶ ▶ ▶

Solutions

1. **30 ways:** There are two repeated E's and two repeated L's in the word *LEVEL*. To find the number of ways this word can be arranged, set up a fraction in which the numerator is the factorial of the number of letters and the denominator is the factorial of the number of each repeated letter:

$$\frac{5!}{2!2!} = \frac{5 \times \overset{2}{\cancel{4}} \times 3 \times \cancel{2!}}{\cancel{2} \times 1 \times \cancel{2!}} = 5 \times 2 \times 3 = 30$$

    Alternatively, you can solve this problem using the slot method, as long as you correct for over-counting (since there are some identical elements). There are five choices for the first letter, four for the second, and so on, making the product $5 \times 4 \times 3 \times 2 \times 1 = 120$. However, there are two sets of two indistinguishable elements each, so you must divide by 2! to account for each of these. Thus, the total number of combinations is as shown in the calculation above.

2. **10:** In every combination, 2 types of truffles will be in the package and 3 types of truffles will not. Therefore, this problem is a question about the number of anagrams that can be made from the "word" YYNNN:

1	2	3	4	5
Y	Y	N	N	N

    $$\frac{5!}{2!3!} = \frac{5 \times \overset{2}{\cancel{4}} \times \cancel{3!}}{\cancel{2} \times \cancel{3!}} = 5 \times 2 = 10$$

3. **36:** This is a multiple arrangements problem, in which you have two separate pools (females AND males). There are 3! ways in which the 3 females can swim. There are 3! ways in which the 3 males can swim. Therefore, there are $3! \times 3!$ ways in which the entire pod can swim:

    $$3! \times 3! = 6 \times 6 = 36$$

4. **20 choices:** Consider the vegetables first. Model them with the "word" YYYYN, in which four of the types are on the pizza and one is not. The number of anagrams for this "word" is in the table below:

1	2	3	4	5
Y	Y	Y	Y	N

    $$\frac{5!}{4!} = 5$$

    If each of these pizzas can also be offered in 2 choices of crust, there are $5 \times 2 = 10$ choices of pizza. The same logic applies for the cheese so there are $10 \times 2 = 20$ choices.

5. **2,664:** There are six ways in which to arrange these digits:

$$
\begin{array}{ccc}
3 & 4 & 5 \\
3 & 5 & 4 \\
4 & 3 & 5 \\
4 & 5 & 3 \\
5 & 3 & 4 \\
5 & 4 & 3 \\
\end{array}
$$

Notice that each digit appears twice in the hundreds column, twice in the tens column, and twice in the ones column. Use place value to find the sum. The sum of each digit in the hundreds column is $3 + 3 + 4 + 4 + 5 + 5 = 24$. Since this is the hundreds column, multiply this sum by 100 to get the sum of just the hundreds part of each number. Repeat this reasoning for the tens column and the ones column:

$$100(24) + 10(24) + 1(24) = 2,400 + 240 + 24 = 2,664$$

Probability

In This Chapter

- Calculate the Numerator and Denominator Separately

- More Than One Event: AND vs. OR

- $P(A) + P(\text{Not } A) = 1$

- The $1 - x$ Probability Trick

In this chapter, you will learn how to set up and solve probability problems for both single and multiple events. You'll also learn a very useful shortcut for tackling multi-part probabilities: calculating the probability of the outcome that you *don't* want (otherwise known as the $1 - x$ trick).

CHAPTER 29 Probability

Probability is a quantity that expresses the chance, or likelihood, of an event.

Think of probability as a fraction:

$$\text{Probability} = \frac{\text{Number of } \textit{desired} \text{ or } \textit{successful} \text{ outcomes}}{\text{Total number of } \textit{possible} \text{ outcomes}}$$

For instance, if you flip a coin (one side heads, the other tails), what is the probability that heads turns up? There are two possible outcomes (heads or tails), but only one of them is considered desirable (heads), so the probability is $\frac{1}{2}$.

Notice that the numerator of the fraction is *always* a subset of the denominator. If there are n possible outcomes, then the number of desirable outcomes must be between 0 and n (the number of outcomes cannot be negative). As a result, *any probability will be between 0 and 1.*

An impossible event has a probability of 0 when the desired outcome cannot happen. For example, if you flip a coin (one side heads, the other tails), what is the probability that a dragon turns up? There are no dragons on the coin, so $\frac{0}{2} = 0$. By contrast, a certain event has a probability of 1 when the number of desired outcomes is equal to the number of possible outcomes. If you flip a coin (heads or tails), what is the probability that either heads or tails turns up? $\frac{2}{2} = 1$. Those are the only two possible outcomes.

Additionally, probability can be expressed as a fraction, a decimal, or a percent. For example, $\frac{3}{4} = 0.75 = 75\%$. Depending on the problem, you can solve in any one of these forms; sometimes, you'll need to use the percent form in order to think about the number of desired outcomes and the number of possible outcomes.

Calculate the Numerator and Denominator Separately

Numerators and denominators of probabilities are related, but they must be calculated separately. Often, it will be easier to begin by calculating the denominator.

There are two ways to calculate a number of outcomes for either the numerator or the denominator:

1. Manually count the number of outcomes (if there aren't that many).

2. Use an appropriate combinatorics formula. These problems tend to be harder; if you dislike probability, you may decide to bail immediately on these kinds of problems (as there aren't typically that many on the test).

Try the following problem:

> Two number cubes with faces numbered 1 to 6 are rolled. What is the probability that the sum of the rolls is 8 ?

Start with the total number of possible outcomes (the denominator). For this calculation, you can use combinatorics. Notice that rolling two number cubes is like rolling cube 1 AND rolling cube 2. For each of these rolls, there are six possible outcomes (the numbers 1 to 6). Since AND equals multiply, there are $6 \times 6 = 36$ possible outcomes. This is the denominator of the fraction.

Next, figure out how many of those 36 possible rolls represent the desired outcome (a sum of 8). It would be complicated to come up with an appropriate combinatorics formula—and not worth the time it would take because only a limited number of combinations would work. Count them up! If the first cube turns up a 1, the other cube would need to roll a 7. This isn't possible, so eliminate that possibility. Keep counting; here are the rolls that work, in order (first roll and second roll):

2 and 6	3 and 5	4 and 4	5 and 3	6 and 2

You do actually need to include the final two in that list; a roll of 3 and then 5 is a different outcome than a roll of 5 and then 3 because both of those outcomes were counted separately in the 6×6 calculation.

There are 5 combinations that work, so the probability of a sum of 8 is $\frac{5}{36}$.

More Than One Event: AND vs. OR

Combinatorics and probability have another connection: the meaning of the words *AND* and *OR*. In probability, as well as in combinatorics, the word *AND* means multiply and the word *OR* means add. Try this example:

> There is a $\frac{1}{2}$ probability that a certain coin will turn up heads on any given toss. What is the probability that two tosses of the coin will yield heads both times?

To answer this question, calculate the probability that the coin lands on heads on the first flip AND heads on the second flip. The probability of heads on the first flip is $\frac{1}{2}$. The probability of heads on the second flip is also $\frac{1}{2}$. Since AND means multiply, the probability is $\frac{1}{2} \times \frac{1}{2} = \frac{1}{4}$.

Try another example:

> The weather report for today states that there is a 40% chance of sun, a 25% chance of rain, and a 35% chance of hail. Assuming only one of the three outcomes can happen, what is the probability that it rains or hails today?

The question is asking for the probability of rain OR hail. Therefore, the probability is 25% + 35% = 60%. The calculation would change if *both* rain and hail can happen, but don't worry about that for now.

P(A) + P(Not A) = 1

P(A) + P(Not A) = 1 is a fancy way of saying that the probability of something happening plus the probability of that thing *not* happening must sum to 1. For example, the probability that it either rains or does not rain is equal to 1: If there's a 25% chance of rain, then there must be a 75% chance that it will *not* rain. Try an example:

> A person has a 40% chance of winning a game every time he or she plays it. If there are no ties, what is the probability that Asha loses the first game played and wins the second game?

If the probability of winning the game is 40%, then the odds of *not* winning the game (losing) are 100% − 40% = 60%. Calculate the odds that Asha loses the game the first time AND wins the game the second time:

$$(60\%) \times (40\%) = 0.6 \times 0.4 = 0.24$$

The probability is 0.24, or 24%.

The 1 - *x* Probability Trick

Suppose that a salesperson makes 5 sales calls, and you want to find the likelihood that he or she makes *at least 1* sale. If you try to calculate this probability directly, you will have to confront 5 separate possibilities that constitute "success": exactly 1 sale, exactly 2 sales, exactly 3 sales, exactly 4 sales, or exactly 5 sales. This would almost certainly be more work than you can reasonably do in two minutes.

There is, however, another option. Instead of calculating the probability that the salesperson makes at least 1 sale, you can calculate the probability that the salesperson does *not* make at least 1 sale.

$$\text{Prob of at least 1 sale} + \text{prob of 0 sales} = 1$$
$$P(\geq 1) \quad + \quad P(0) \quad = 1$$
$$P(\geq 1) \quad\quad\quad\quad\quad = 1 - P(0)$$

These two outcomes (at least 1 sale or 0 sales) make up all of the possible outcomes. So if you know the probability of making 0 sales, you can subtract that from 1 to find the probability of making at least 1 sale. This is the **1 - *x* shortcut.**

Calculating just a single probability and subtracting from 1 is a lot faster than calculating 5 probabilities and adding them up. When a probability problem sets up an *at least* or *at most* scenario, look for this 1 - *x* shortcut.

For complicated probability problems, decide whether it is easier to calculate the probability you want or the probability you do *not* want. On the GMAT, most of the time, it will be faster to calculate the probability that the problem did not ask for. Try an example:

> A bag contains equal numbers of red, green, and yellow marbles. If Gurdeep pulls three marbles out of the bag, replacing each marble after picking it, what is the probability that at least one will be red?

Since the question asks whether at least one will be red, there are three possible cases to calculate: one red, two red, or three red. Instead, calculate the probability that *none* of the marbles are red. Each time Gurdeep picks a marble, there is a $\frac{2}{3}$ probability that the marble will *not* be red. The probability that all three marbles will not be red is $\frac{2}{3} \times \frac{2}{3} \times \frac{2}{3} = \frac{8}{27}$.

If the probability that *none* of the marbles is red is $\frac{8}{27}$, then the probability that at least one marble is red is $1 - \frac{8}{27} = \frac{19}{27}$.

If you need to calculate the probability of an event (P(A)), there are two ways to calculate the probability:

$$P(A) \quad \text{or} \quad 1 - P(\text{Not A})$$

When the question includes *at least* or *at most* language, the 1 - P(Not A) method is usually faster.

Advanced material for the Number Properties unit (primarily covering additional strategies for divisibility and primes, combinatorics, and probability) can be found in Atlas, Manhattan Prep's online learning platform. Use the online material only if you feel that you have mastered everything in the Number Properties unit of this strategy guide and only if you are aiming for a Quant section score of 48 or higher.

Problem Set

Now that you've finished the chapter, try the following problems. For problems 1 and 2, assume that each number cube has six sides with faces numbered 1 to 6.

1. Two number cubes are rolled. What is the probability that the sum of the two numbers will yield a 10 or lower?

2. What is the probability that the sum of two number cubes will yield a 7 on their first roll, and then when both are rolled again, their sum will again yield a 7 ?

Save the remaining problems for review after you finish this entire guide.

3. On the planned day of a picnic, there is a 30% chance of rain. If it rains, there is a 50% chance that the picnic will be canceled, but if it doesn't rain, the picnic will take place. What is the chance that the picnic will take place?

4. In a diving competition, each diver has a 20% chance of a perfect dive. The first perfect dive of the competition, but no subsequent dives, will receive a perfect score. What are the chances that the third diver will receive a perfect score on that dive? (Assume that each diver can perform only one dive.)

5. A magician has five animals in a magic hat: 3 doves and 2 rabbits. If the magician pulls two animals out of the hat at random, what is the chance that the two will be the same type of animal?

Answers and explanations follow on the next page. ▶ ▶ ▶

Solutions

1. $\frac{11}{12}$: There are a total of $6 \times 6 = 36$ possible outcomes. There are many possible ways to get the desired outcome of a sum of 10 or lower. Solve this problem by calculating the probability that the sum will be *higher* than 10 and subtracting that probability from 1. There are three combinations of two number cubes that yield a sum higher than 10: $5 + 6$, $6 + 5$, and $6 + 6$. Therefore, the probability that the sum will be higher than 10 is $\frac{3}{36}$, or $\frac{1}{12}$. The probability that the sum will be 10 or lower is $1 - \frac{1}{12} = \frac{11}{12}$.

2. $\frac{1}{36}$: There are 36 ways in which two number cubes can be thrown ($6 \times 6 = 36$). The combinations that yield a sum of 7 are $1 + 6$, $2 + 5$, $3 + 4$, $4 + 3$, $5 + 2$, and $6 + 1$, or six different combinations. Therefore, the probability of rolling a 7 is $\frac{6}{36}$, or $\frac{1}{6}$. To find the probability that this will happen twice in a row (an outcome of 7 AND 7), multiply: $\frac{1}{6} \times \frac{1}{6} = \frac{1}{36}$.

3. **85%:** There are two possible ways in which the picnic can take place:

    1. It doesn't rain: $P = 70\%$ OR

    2. It rains AND the picnic is held anyway:

    $$P = 30\%\left(\frac{1}{2}\right) = 15\%$$

    Add the probabilities together to find the total probability that the picnic will take place:

    $$70\% + 15\% = 85\%$$

4. $\frac{16}{125}$: In order for the third diver to receive a perfect score, neither of the previous two divers can receive one. Therefore, you are finding the probability of a chain of three events: that diver one will *not* get a perfect score AND diver two will *not* get a perfect score AND diver three *will* get a perfect score. Multiply the probabilities:

    $$\frac{4}{5} \times \frac{4}{5} \times \frac{1}{5} = \frac{16}{125}.$$

    The probability is $\frac{16}{125}$ that the third diver will receive a perfect score.

5. $\frac{4}{10}$ **or 40%:** Use an anagram model to determine the total number of different pairs the magician can pull out of the hat. Since two animals will be in the pair and the other three will not, use the "word" YYNNN.

A	B	C	D	E
Y	Y	N	N	N

    $\dfrac{5!}{2!3!} = \dfrac{5 \times 4}{2 \times 1} = 10$

    Thus, there are 10 possible pairs; this is the bottom of the probability fraction.

Then, list the pairs in which the animals will match. Represent the rabbits with the subscript letters a and b, and the doves with the letters x, y, and z.

Matched Pairs:
$$R_a\ R_b \qquad D_x\ D_y$$
$$D_x\ D_z \qquad D_y\ D_z$$

There are four pairs in which the animals will be a matched set: one way in which the rabbits can be chosen and three ways in which the doves can be chosen.

Therefore, the probability that the magician will randomly draw a matched set is $\dfrac{4}{10} = 40\%$.

UNIT FIVE

Geometry

In this unit, you will learn all of the geometry topics you need to know for the GMAT, including line and angle rules; definitions, formulas, and rules for polygons, triangles, and circles; and various rules associated with coordinate planes. You'll also find a cheat sheet at the end of this unit containing all of the major geometry rules and formulas on a single page. Feel free to tear it out of the book (or photocopy it) to have handy during your studies.

In This Unit

- Chapter 30: Geometry Strategy

- Chapter 31: Lines and Angles

- Chapter 32: Polygons

- Chapter 33: Triangles and Diagonals

- Chapter 34: Circles and Cylinders

- Chapter 35: Coordinate Plane

CHAPTER 30

Geometry Strategy

In This Chapter

- The Three Principles
- Understand–Plan–Solve
- Estimation

In this chapter, you will learn how to adapt the Understand–Plan–Solve process for geometry problems in particular and you'll learn how to estimate on geometry problems.

CHAPTER 30 Geometry Strategy

Before diving into the rules and formulas, take a few minutes to learn some important guidelines that will help you approach every geometry problem you will do on the GMAT.

The Three Principles

Use three general principles to succeed on geometry problems:

1. **If they don't tell you, don't assume.**

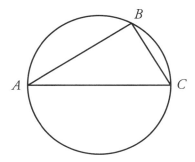

Points *A*, *B*, and *C* lie on the circle and form a triangle. Is line segment *AC* a diameter of the circle?

In the figure above, line segment *AC* does look like a diameter of the circle, but it could be just slightly off and not a diameter at all. Don't make any assumptions; just *looking* like a diameter doesn't make *AC* a diameter on the GMAT.

> **Vocab Lesson:** When a triangle lies inside a circle and the "points" (or *vertices*) of a triangle touch the circle, then the triangle is said to be *inscribed* in the circle.

2. If they give you a piece of information, use it.

Line segment *AC* passes through the center of the circle.

What can you infer from that piece of information?

If a line segment passes from one side to the other of a circle through the center, then that line segment must be a diameter of the circle. Now, you've got a connection between the triangle and the circle: The longest side of the triangle is also a diameter of the circle.

How does that help? Read on—but note that, any time you're given multiple shapes, the trick to solving the problem usually revolves around finding connections between those shapes.

3. Know your rules and formulas.

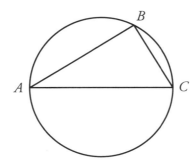

Rule:
If one of the sides of a triangle inscribed in a circle is a
diameter of the circle, then the triangle must be a right triangle.

If you inscribe a triangle in a circle (as in the figure shown above), and one side of that triangle is also a diameter of the circle, then the opposite angle (angle *B* in this diagram) has to be a right angle. It doesn't matter where you place *B* on the circle; it will still be a right angle. (Well, if you place *B* right on *A* or *C*, then *B* won't be a right angle. In that case, though, *ABC* also won't be a triangle!)

In short, it is not enough just to memorize a bunch of rules. The test writers are going to "cut up" the rules and give them to you in pieces. You need to know the rules well enough that you can put those pieces back together.

To recap:

1.   If they don't tell you, don't assume.

2.   If they give you a piece of information, use it.

3.   Know your rules and formulas.

One last thing: It turns out, thankfully, that there are a few small things you *can* take for granted on GMAT Geometry.

If the problem describes a shape as a triangle, then it really is a triangle. If the problem discusses a line, then you really do have a 180° straight line. If lines look as if they touch, they do. In other words, you can take the test at its word—it will use the word *line* in the official geometry sense—but you can't add in any extra assumptions.

If the GMAT gives you a figure or number line with points, you can assume that the points will always be in the order shown in the diagram. For instance, consider the figure below:

You can trust that both *A* and *B* are positive (because both are shown to the right of 0) and that *B* is greater than *A* (because *B* is to the right of *A*).

Figures on Problem Solving questions will be drawn to scale unless noted. Figures on Data Sufficiency questions, however, are *not* necessarily drawn to scale (and they will *not* be noted accordingly). You can still trust that lines are lines and that intersecting lines or shapes actually do intersect, including the relative positions of points, angles, and regions.

30

Understand–Plan–Solve

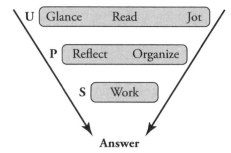

Answer

As with all other Quant problems, use the Understand–Plan–Solve approach. This will include some special steps for geometry problems.

1. Understand

If the problem mentions something for which you know a formula (e.g., the area of a circle), write down the formula. If the problem gives you a figure, redraw it on your scrap paper. If a geometry problem doesn't give you a figure, draw one anyway.

You have graph paper, so make the figure decently precise. Don't waste time or space, of course, but make the figure big enough that you can see what you're doing and accurate enough to prevent careless mistakes. For instance, if you know one side of a triangle is longer than another, draw the figure so that the longer side *looks* longer.

Finally, mark clearly what you're trying to find. Perhaps the question asks you to find the measure of angle x, which has already been labeled on the figure. Put a symbol, such as a star, next to the x to remind yourself that this is your goal. (You can use any symbol you want, as long as you use the same symbol consistently and as long as you use a symbol that will never be used by the test writers themselves.)

Perhaps the question asks you to find the perimeter of a rectangle. It would be tough to show that on the figure, so instead, write the formula for perimeter and put a star next to the P:

$$\bigstar P = 2l + 2w$$

Alternatively, write something like:

$$P = \underline{\qquad}\ ?$$

2. Plan

Are there overlapping shapes? Think about the connections between the shapes during your Plan phase.

The givens, or starting information, will allow you to infer certain other things that must be true. Are there multiple directions in which you could start to infer new information from the givens? Take a little time to think about which path looks most efficient to get you to your goal.

Not sure what to do first? That's okay. Go ahead and infer two or three things, even if you're not sure yet how that might help to get you to the answer. (If you can't find anything to infer, now might be a good time to guess and move on.)

3. Solve

As you proceed through the rest of the problem, keep adding to your drawing. Every time you infer something new, write or draw it in. (Make sure, when you first draw the figure, that you give yourself enough space to draw and write additional information on it!)

Try out the 3-step process on this problem:

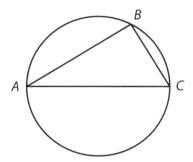

Triangle *ABC* is inscribed in the circle and line segment *AC* passes through the center of the circle. If the length of line segment *AB* is 3 and the length of line segment *AC* is 5, then what is the length of line segment *BC* ?

(A) 2

(B) 3

(C) 4

(D) 6

(E) 8

Understand. Draw the figure on your scratch paper and add the given lengths. Mark the wanted information, line segment *BC*.

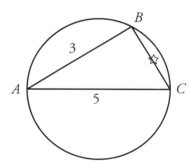

Plan. They want the length of *BC*. There are two overlapping shapes; what's the connection between the shapes? The diameter *AC* is also the hypotenuse of the triangle. What does that mean?

Solve. Given that AC is a diameter, ABC must be a right triangle and angle B must be the right angle. Great! You can use the Pythagorean theorem to solve:

$$a^2 + b^2 = c^2$$
$$3^2 + b^2 = 5^2$$
$$9 + b^2 = 25$$
$$b^2 = 16$$
$$b = 4$$

The correct answer is (C).

Don't worry if you've completely forgotten about the Pythagorean theorem or any of the other math needed to answer this question. You'll relearn how to do it all while working through this section of the guide.

Estimation

You can estimate your way to an answer on problems with certain characteristics; this technique is often helpful on geometry problems in particular.

First, it's important that the problem gives you either a figure drawn to scale or enough information to draw a figure reasonably to scale yourself. Remember that your scrap paper will be graph paper, so you can draw right angles, squares, and other dimensions reasonably accurately.

Second, the answers need to be spread far enough apart that estimating an answer will still keep you in the range of the one correct answer.

For instance, say you are given these answer choices:

(A)   25°
(B)   45°
(C)   60°
(D)   90°
(E)   110°

You might not know how to calculate the correct answer, but you might be able to tell, for example, that the desired angle is less than 90°, which will eliminate (D) and (E). Alternatively, you might be able to tell that the answer is close to 90°, allowing you to chop out (A) and (B) and possibly (C).

Try this problem, inspired by one from *The GMAT Official Guide*:

A square has a 10-centimeter diagonal. What is the area of the square, in square centimeters?

(A)   50
(B)   64
(C)   100
(D)   144
(E)   200

30

First, draw a square on your scrap paper. Remember, you'll have graph paper, so you can make a true square. Draw a diagonal and label it 10:

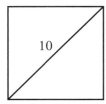

First, if the diagonal is 10, then the length of one side must be less than 10.

Next, the area of a square is s^2, where s is the length of one side. If the length of a side were 10, then the area would be 10^2, which equals 100. But the length is less than 10, so the area must also be less than 100. Eliminate answers (C), (D), and (E). There are only two answers left!

You might be thinking, That's too good to be true. . .the real test won't do that. It does; as noted, this problem and set of answer choices were inspired by a real question that was published by the makers of the GMAT.

You might also be thinking: I can just do the math, so why would I need to estimate to make a guess?

There are two reasons. First, you learn how to do harder problems by practicing your skills on easier ones, so even if you find this problem easy, learning how to estimate here will help you to do so on harder ones that you can't do the "textbook" way.

Second, you can use the rough estimation to check your work. Say that you made a calculation error and called the length of one side $10\sqrt{2}$. (There is a specific reason why someone might be susceptible to that particular mistake. If you're not sure what it is, look at this problem again after you've studied the Triangles and Diagonals chapter.)

If you accidentally call one side $10\sqrt{2}$, then you're going to calculate the area as 200, which is answer (E). If you then double-check your work via estimation, you'll realize that 200 is too big.

Advanced material for the Geometry unit can be found in Atlas, Manhattan Prep's online learning platform. Use the online material only if you feel that you have mastered everything in the Geometry unit of this strategy guide and only if you are aiming for a Quant section score of 48 or higher.

30

Problem Set

If you think you remember some (or many!) geometry rules, use this problem set as a diagnostic quiz to see where you need to review. On the other hand, if you've totally forgotten all of your geometry rules, skip this set for now and come back to the problems after working through the relevant chapters in this book.

1. If the length of an edge of cube A is one-third the length of an edge of cube B, what is the ratio of the volume of cube A to the volume of cube B ?

2.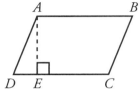

    In the figure shown above, *ABCD* is a parallelogram. The ratio of *DE* to *EC* is 1 : 3. Height *AE* has a length of 3. If quadrilateral *ABCE* has an area of 21, what is the area of *ABCD* ?

3.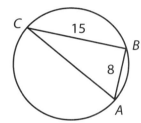

    In the figure shown above, triangle *ABC* is inscribed in a circle, such that *AC* is a diameter of the circle. If line segment *AB* has a length of 8 and line segment *BC* has a length of 15, what is the circumference of the circle?

4.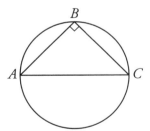

    As shown in the figure, triangle *ABC* is inscribed in a circle. Line segment *AC* is a diameter of the circle and angle *BAC* is 45°. If the area of triangle *ABC* is 72 square units, how much larger is the area of the circle than the area of triangle *ABC* ?

5.

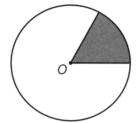

On the number line shown above, is $xy < 0$?

(1) Zero is to the left of y on the number line above.

(2) xy and yz have opposite signs.

6.

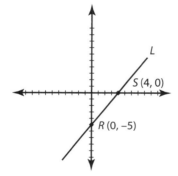

In the figure shown above, O represents the center of a circular 60-minute timer. If the minute-hand moves through the shaded region shown, does the shaded region represent more than 10 minutes on the timer?

(1) The minute-hand has a length of 10.

(2) The area of the sector is greater than 16π.

7. The side of an equilateral triangle has the same length as the diagonal of a square. What is the area of the square?

(1) The height of the equilateral triangle is equal to $6\sqrt{3}$.

(2) The area of the equilateral triangle is equal to $36\sqrt{3}$.

8.

Line L passes through points R $(0, -5)$ and S $(4, 0)$ in the figure shown. Point P with coordinates (x, y) is a point on line L and does not overlap with points R or S. Is $xy > 0$?

(1) $x > 4$

(2) $y > -5$

Solutions

1. **1 to 27:** There are no specified amounts in this question, so pick numbers. Let cube A have sides of length 1 and cube B have sides of length 3:

    $$\text{Volume of cube A} = 1 \times 1 \times 1 = 1$$
    $$\text{Volume of cube B} = 3 \times 3 \times 3 = 27$$

    Therefore, the ratio of the volume of cube A to the volume of cube B is $\frac{1}{27}$, or $1:27$.

2. **24:** First, label the lengths with the given ratio and break quadrilateral *ABCE* into two pieces: a 3 by 3*x* rectangle and a right triangle with a base of *x* and a height of 3. Add the area of each shape to get the area of quadrilateral *ABCE*:

    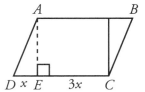

    $$(3 \times 3x) + \frac{3 \times x}{2} = 9x + 1.5x = 10.5x$$

    If *ABCE* has an area of 21, then $21 = 10.5x$, which reduces to $x = 2$. Quadrilateral *ABCD* is a parallelogram, so use the formula for area: Area = Base × Height, or $4x \times 3$. Substitute the known value of 2 for *x* and simplify:

    $$A = 4(2) \times 3 = 24$$

3. **17π:** If line segment *AC* is a diameter of the circle, then inscribed triangle *ABC* is a right triangle, with *AC* as the hypotenuse. Use the Pythagorean theorem to find the hypotenuse:

    $$8^2 + 15^2 = c^2$$
    $$64 + 225 = c^2$$
    $$289 = c^2$$
    $$c = 17$$

    The 8–15–17 right triangle is also one of the "common" right triangles; if you have it memorized, then you don't have to use the Pythagorean theorem to find diameter *AC*.

    The circumference of the circle is πd, or 17π.

4. **$72\pi - 72$:** Draw a picture. If AC is a diameter of the circle, then angle ABC is a right angle. Therefore, triangle ABC is a 45–45–90 triangle, and the base and the height are equal. Assign the variable x to represent both the base and height:

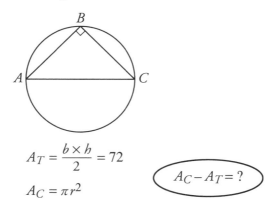

$$A_T = \frac{b \times h}{2} = 72$$

$$A_C = \pi r^2$$

$$A_C - A_T = \;?$$

Use the formula for the area of a triangle to find the value of x:

$$A = \frac{bh}{2}$$
$$72 = \frac{(x)(x)}{2}$$
$$144 = x^2$$
$$x = 12$$

A 45–45–90 triangle's sides are always in the ratio $x:x:x\sqrt{2}$. Since the two legs are equal to 12, the hypotenuse, which is also the diameter of the circle, is $12\sqrt{2}$. Therefore, the radius is equal to $6\sqrt{2}$ and the area of the circle, πr^2, equals 72π. The area of the circle is $72\pi - 72$ square units larger than the area of triangle ABC.

5. **(C):** This is a Yes/No Data Sufficiency question. For xy to be negative, x and y need to have opposite signs.

On the number line shown, this would only happen if 0 falls between x and y. If 0 is to the left of x on the number line shown, both x and y would be positive, so $xy > 0$. If 0 is to the right of y on the number line shown, both x and y would be negative, so $xy > 0$. So the real question is: Does 0 fall between x and y on the number line?

(1) INSUFFICIENT: Test a couple of cases. If zero is to the left of y on the number line, zero could be between x and y. In that case, $xy < 0$ and the answer to the question is Yes. However, 0 could also be to the left of x. In that case, both x and y would be positive, so $xy > 0$ and the answer is No.

(2) INSUFFICIENT: The fact that xy and yz have opposite signs implies that one of the three variables has a different sign than the other two. If x, y, and z all have the same sign, xy and yz would have the same sign. Thus, this statement implies that 0 does not fall to the left of x (which would make all three variables, as well as xy and yz, positive) nor to the right of z (which would make all three variables negative and both xy and yz positive). The only two cases this statement allows are:

0 is between x and y: In this case, yz is positive and xy is negative, and the answer is Yes.

0 is between y and z: In this case, yz is negative and xy is positive, and the answer is No.

(1) AND (2) SUFFICIENT: Statement (1) restricts 0 to the left of y on the number line. This rules out one of the two cases allowed by statement (2), leaving only the case in which 0 is between x and y. Thus, xy is negative, and the answer is a definite Yes.

The correct answer is **(C)**: The two statements together are sufficient, but neither one works alone.

6. **(E):** This is a Yes/No Data Sufficiency question. The question "Does the shaded region represent more than 10 minutes on the timer?" is really asking about the area of a sector of a circle.

    Since 10 minutes is $\frac{1}{6}$ of the total 60 minutes, the question is asking whether the shaded region is equal to more than $\frac{1}{6}$ of the area of the circle.

    (1) INSUFFICIENT: The minute-hand is equal to the radius. If the radius is 10, the entire area of the circle is 100π. Is the area of the shaded region more than one-sixth of 100π? This statement doesn't provide any information about the size of the shaded region relative to the whole circle.

    (2) INSUFFICIENT: The area of the *sector* is more than 16π, but no information is given as to the area of the whole circle.

    (1) AND (2) INSUFFICIENT: The area of the entire circle is 100π, and the area of the sector is more than 16π. Is the area of the shaded region more than one-sixth of 100π? Find $\frac{1}{6}$ of 100π:

    $$\frac{100\pi}{6} = \frac{50\pi}{3} = 16.\overline{6}\pi$$

    Since $\frac{1}{6}$ of the area of the circle is actually $16.\overline{6}\pi$, knowing that the area of the sector is more than 16π is still insufficient—the area of the sector could be 16.1π or something much larger.

    The correct answer is **(E)**: Both statements together are still not sufficient.

7. **(D):** Both equilateral triangles and squares are **regular figures**. Regular figures (squares, equilaterals, circles, spheres, cubes, 45–45–90 triangles, 30–60–90 triangles, and others) are those for which you only need one measurement to know *every* measurement. For instance, if you have the radius of a circle, you can get the diameter, circumference, and area. If you have a 45–45–90 or 30–60–90 triangle, you only need *one* side to get all three. In this problem, if you have the side of an equilateral triangle, you could get the height, area, and perimeter. If you have the side of a square, you could get the diagonal, area, and perimeter.

    If you have *two* regular figures, as you do in this problem, and you know how they are related numerically (*the side of an equilateral triangle has the same length as the diagonal of a square*), then you can safely conclude that *any* measurement for *either* figure will give you *any* measurement for either figure.

    The question can be rephrased: What is the value of any part of either figure?

    (1) SUFFICIENT: This provides one length of the figure (the height of the triangle).

    (2) SUFFICIENT: The area of the triangle can be used to find the length of one side of the triangle.

    The correct answer is **(D)**: Each statement is sufficient by itself.

8. **(A):** This is a Yes/No question. Line L passes through three quadrants:

    1. Quadrant I, where x and y are both positive, so $xy > 0$ and the answer is Yes.

    2. Quadrant III, where x and y are both negative, so xy > 0 and the answer is Yes.

    3. Quadrant IV, where x is positive and y is negative, so $xy < 0$ and the answer is No.

If you can determine what quadrant point P is in, you will have sufficient information to answer the question. Also, Quadrant I or Quadrant III both return a Yes answer, so knowing that point P is in either of those two quadrants (even if you don't know which one) would be sufficient.

(1) SUFFICIENT: If $x > 4$, then point P is in Quadrant I. As a result, Yes, $xy > 0$.

(2) INSUFFICIENT: If $y > -5$, then point P could be in either Quadrant I ($xy > 0$) or Quadrant IV ($xy < 0$).

The correct answer is **(A)**: Statement (1) alone works, but statement (2) does not.

Lines and Angles

In This Chapter

- Intersecting Lines
- Parallel Lines Cut by a Transversal

In this chapter, you will learn the necessary fundamental properties of lines and angles, including for parallel lines.

CHAPTER 31 Lines and Angles

A straight line is the shortest distance between two points. As an angle, a line measures 180° as shown here:

Parallel lines are lines that lie in a plane and that never intersect. No matter how far you extend the lines, they never meet:

Perpendicular lines are lines that intersect at a 90° angle. Two perpendicular lines are shown below:

There are two major line–angle relationships to know for the GMAT. You'll learn about both in this chapter:

1. The angles formed by any intersecting lines

2. The angles formed by parallel lines cut by a transversal (a third line)

Intersecting Lines

Intersecting lines have three important properties.

First, the interior angles formed by intersecting lines form a circle, so the sum of these angles is 360°. In the figure: $a + b + c + d = 360$.

Second, interior angles that combine to form a line sum to 180°. For example, in the figure shown to the right, $a + b = 180$, because angles a and b form a line together. Other pairs of angles are $b + c = 180$, $c + d = 180$, and $d + a = 180$.

Third, when two lines intersect, angles found opposite each other are equal. These are called **vertical angles**. Thus, in the figure above, $a = c$, because these angles are opposite each other and are formed from the same two lines. Additionally, $b = d$ for the same reason.

These rules apply to more than two lines that intersect at a point, as shown in the figure to the right. Here, $a + b + c + d + e + f = 360$, because these angles combine to form a circle. In addition, $a + b + c = 180$, because these three angles combine to form a line. Finally, $a = d$, $b = e$, and $c = f$, because they are pairs of vertical angles.

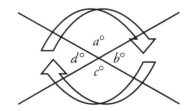

Parallel Lines Cut by a Transversal

The GMAT makes frequent use of figures that include parallel lines cut by a transversal.

Notice that there are eight angles formed by this construction, but there are only two *different* angle measures (*a* and *b*, as shown in the figure). All the **acute** angles (less than 90°) in this figure are equal. Likewise, all the **obtuse** angles (greater than 90° but less than 180°) are equal. Any acute angle plus any obtuse angle equals 180°.

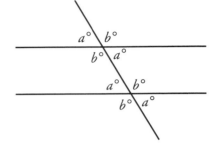

Thus, $a + b = 180$.

When you see a transversal cutting two lines that you know to be parallel, fill in all the *a* (acute) and *b* (obtuse) angles.

Sometimes the GMAT disguises the parallel lines and the transversal so that they are not readily apparent. In the first *Z* figure, the two horizontal lines are parallel and the angled line is the transversal, but the various angles created aren't fully apparent because the lines are truncated.

In these disguised cases, redraw the figure and extend the lines yourself so that you can more easily see all of the angles created, as shown in the second *Z* figure. You might also mark the parallel lines with arrows, as shown, in order to indicate that the two lines are parallel.

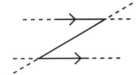

The GMAT uses the symbol ‖ to indicate in text that two lines or line segments are parallel. For example, if you see *MN* ‖ *OP* in a problem, you know that line segment *MN* is parallel to line segment *OP*.

Problem Set

Problems 1 and 2 refer to the given figure, where line *AB* is parallel to line *CD*.

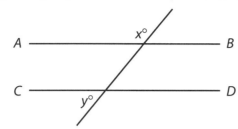

1. If $x - y = 10$, what is x ?

2. If $x + (x + y) = 320$, what is x ?

Problems 3–4 refer to the figure to the figure below.

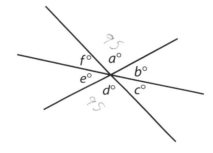

3. If a is 95, what is $b + d - e$?

4. If $c + f = 70$ and $d = 80$, what is b ?

Challenge! Problems 5–7 refer to the figure to the figure below.

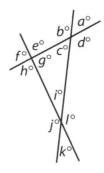

5. If $c + g = 140$, what is k ?

6. If $g = 90$, what is $a + k$?

7. If $f + k = 150$, what is b ?

Solutions

1. **95°:** The figure shows two parallel lines cut by a third, so $x + y = 180$. Add the two equations together to eliminate the y variable and solve for x:

$$
\begin{array}{r}
x + y = 180 \\
+ \quad x - y = 10 \\
\hline
2x = 190 \\
x = 95
\end{array}
$$

2. **140°:** The figure shows two parallel lines cut by a third, so $x + y = 180$. Substitute $x + y = 180$ into the given equation of $x + (x + y) = 320$ to solve for x:

$$
\begin{aligned}
x + 180 &= 320 \\
x &= 140
\end{aligned}
$$

   Alternatively, subtract the equation $x + y = 180$ from $2x + y = 320$ to eliminate y and solve for x:

$$
\begin{array}{r}
2x + y = 320 \\
-(x + y = 180) \\
\hline
x = 140
\end{array}
$$

3. **95°:** Because a and d are vertical angles, they have the same measure: $a = d = 95$. Likewise, since b and e are vertical angles, they have the same measure: $b = e$. Therefore, $b + d - e = b + d - b = d = 95$.

4. **65°:** Because c and f are vertical angles, they have the same measure: $c + f = 70$, so $c = f = 35$. Notice that b, c, and d form a straight line: $b + c + d = 180$. Substitute the known values of c and d into this equation:

$$
\begin{aligned}
b + 35 + 80 &= 180 \\
b + 115 &= 180 \\
b &= 65
\end{aligned}
$$

5. **40°:** If $c + g = 140$, then $i = 40$, because there are 180° in a triangle. Since k and i are vertical angles, k is also equal to 40.

6. **90°:** If $g = 90$, then the other two angles in the triangle, c and i, sum to 90. Since a and k are vertical angles to c and i, they sum to 90 as well.

7. **150°:** Angles f and k are vertical to angles g and i. The latter two angles, then, must also sum to 150. Therefore, the third angle in the triangle, c, must be $180 - 150$, so $c = 30$. Then, c and b create a straight line, or 180, so $30 + b = 180$, and $b = 150$.

Polygons

In This Chapter

In this chapter, you will learn about angle measures, perimeter, and area for certain two-dimensional shapes, including squares, rectangles, parallelograms, and trapezoids. You'll also learn about surface area and volume for certain three-dimensional shapes, including cubes and boxes.

CHAPTER 32 Polygons

A **polygon** is defined as a closed, two-dimensional shape formed by line segments. The polygons tested on the GMAT include the following:

- Three-sided shapes (triangles)
- Four-sided shapes (quadrilaterals)
- Other polygons with *n* sides (where *n* is five or more)

This section will focus on polygons of four or more sides. On the GMAT, the most commonly tested polygons of this category are squares and rectangles. Other shapes, such as trapezoids and parallelograms, can show up but are less common.

Quadrilaterals: An Overview

The most common polygon tested on the GMAT, aside from the triangle, is the **quadrilateral** (any four-sided polygon). Almost all GMAT polygon problems involve the special types of quadrilaterals shown below:

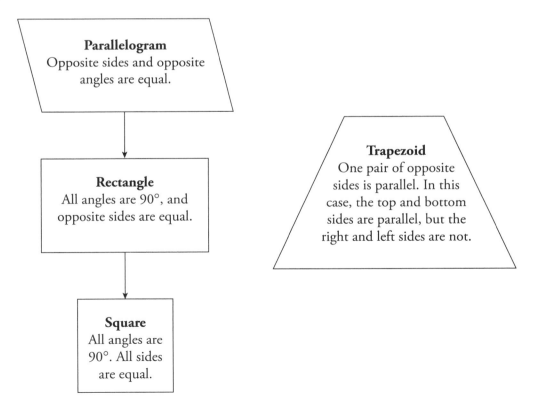

Parallelogram
Opposite sides and opposite angles are equal.

Rectangle
All angles are 90°, and opposite sides are equal.

Square
All angles are 90°. All sides are equal.

Trapezoid
One pair of opposite sides is parallel. In this case, the top and bottom sides are parallel, but the right and left sides are not.

Squares are a special subset of rectangles: They have all of the characteristics of rectangles plus the special additional characteristic that all sides are equal.

Likewise, rectangles are a special subset of parallelograms: They have all of the characteristics of parallelograms plus the special additional characteristic that all angles are 90°.

Polygons and Interior Angles

The sum of the interior angles of a given polygon depends only on the **number of sides in the polygon**. The following table displays the relationship between the type of polygon and the sum of its interior angles:

Polygon	# of Sides	Sum of Interior Angles
Triangle	3	180°
Quadrilateral	4	360°
Pentagon	5	540°
Hexagon	6	720°

This pattern can be expressed as the number of sides minus 2, multiplied by 180:

$$(n - 2) \times 180 = \text{Sum of Interior Angles of a Polygon}$$

Since this polygon has four sides, the sum of its interior angles is $(4 - 2)180 = 2(180) = 360°$. The interior angles of all four-sided polygons will always sum to 360°. This is true for squares, rectangles, trapezoids— anything with four sides.

Alternatively, a quadrilateral can be cut into two triangles by a line connecting opposite corners. Thus, the sum of the angles is $2(180) = 360°$.

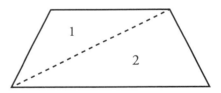

In the polygon with six sides, the sum of the interior angles is $(6 - 2)180 = 4(180) = 720°$.

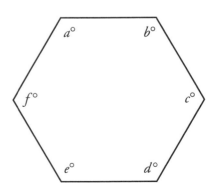

Alternatively, note that a hexagon can be cut into four triangles by three lines connecting corners:

Thus, the sum of the angles is $4(180) = 720°$.

By the way, the corners of polygons are also known as vertices (singular: vertex).

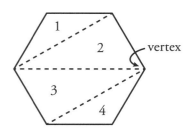

32

Polygons and Perimeter

The **perimeter** refers to the distance around a polygon, or the sum of the lengths of all the sides. The amount of fencing needed to surround a yard would be equivalent to the perimeter of that yard (the sum of all the sides).

The perimeter of the pentagon to the right is $9 + 7 + 4 + 6 + 5 = 31$.

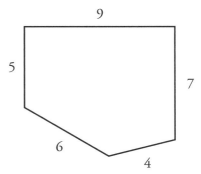

Polygons and Area

The area of a polygon refers to the space inside the polygon. Area is measured in square units, such as cm^2 (square centimeters), m^2 (square meters), or ft^2 (square feet). For example, the amount of space that a garden occupies is the area of that garden.

For the GMAT, definitely memorize the first two area formulas:

1. **Area of a Square = Side $\times$ Side = Side^2**

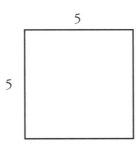

The side length of this square is 5. Therefore, the area is $5^2 = 25$.

2. **Area of a Rectangle = Length × Width**

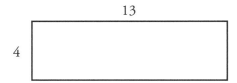

The length of this rectangle is 13 and the width is 4. Therefore, the area is 13 × 4 = 52.

The GMAT will occasionally ask you to find the area of a polygon more complex than a square or rectangle. The following formulas can be used to find the areas of other types of quadrilaterals. You may or may not see these shapes on the exam, so you'll need to decide whether you want to take the time to memorize the formulas.

3. **Area of a Trapezoid** $= \dfrac{(\textbf{Base}_1 \times \textbf{Base}_2)(\textbf{Height})}{2}$

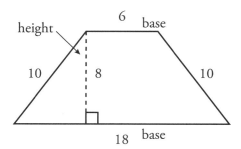

The bases are the two parallel lines. The height refers to a line perpendicular to the two bases. (You often have to draw in the height, as in this case.) In the trapezoid shown, $base_1 = 18$, $base_2 = 6$, and the height $= 8$. Another way to think about this formula is to take the *average* of the two bases and multiply it by the height: $\dfrac{(18 + 6)}{2}(8) = (12)(8) = 96$.

4. **Area of any Parallelogram = Base × Height**

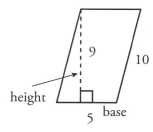

Note that the height refers to the line perpendicular to the base. (As with the trapezoid, you often have to draw in the height.) In the parallelogram shown, the base is 5 and the height is 9. Therefore, the area is 5 × 9 = 45.

Note that some more complex shapes can be divided into a combination of rectangles and right triangles. For example:

Solving in this way will take longer than using the real formula, but trapezoids are infrequent enough that you might be willing to take that risk in order to avoid having to memorize yet another formula.

Three Dimensions: Surface Area

You may see a problem involving either a rectangular solid or a cube. (Or you may not. Three-dimensional geometry is not all that common on the GMAT.)

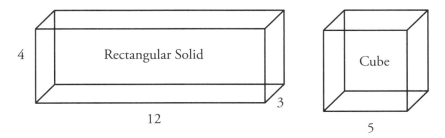

The surface area of a three-dimensional shape is the amount of space on the surface of that particular object. For example, the amount of paint that it would take to fully cover a rectangular box could be determined by finding the surface area of that box. As with simple area, surface area is measured in square units such as in^2 (square inches) or ft^2 (square feet).

   Surface Area = The *Sum* of the Areas of *All* of the Faces

Both a rectangular solid and a cube have six faces.

To determine the surface area of a rectangular solid, you'll need to find the area of each face—but you don't need to find six separate faces.

In a rectangular solid, the front and back faces have the same area, the top and bottom faces have the same area, and the two side faces have the same area. In the solid shown, the area of the front face is equal to $12 \times 4 = 48$. Thus, the back face also has an area of 48. The area of the bottom face is equal to $12 \times 3 = 36$, so the top face also has an area of 36. Finally, each side face has an area of $3 \times 4 = 12$. Therefore, the surface area, or the sum of the areas of all six faces, equals $48(2) + 36(2) + 12(2) = 192$.

To determine the surface area of a cube, you need the length of one side. First, find the area of one face: $5 \times 5 = 25$. Then, multiply by six to account for all of the faces: $6 \times 25 = 150$.

Three Dimensions: Volume

The **volume** of a three-dimensional shape is the amount of "stuff" it can hold. *Capacity* is another word for volume. For example, the amount of liquid that a rectangular milk carton holds can be determined by finding the volume of the carton. Volume is measured in cubic units such as in^3 (cubic inches), ft^3 (cubic feet), or m^3 (cubic meters).

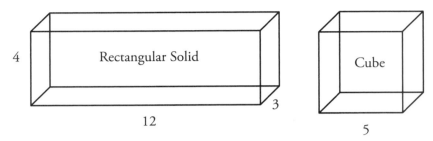

Volume = Length × Width × Height

The length of the rectangular solid shown above is 12, the width is 3, and the height is 4. Therefore, the volume is $12 \times 3 \times 4 = 144$.

In a cube, all three of the dimensions—length, width, and height—are identical. Therefore, knowing the measurement of just one side of the cube is sufficient to find the volume. In the cube above, the volume is $5 \times 5 \times 5 = 125$.

Beware of a GMAT volume trick, as in this example:

> How many books, each with a volume of 100 in^3, can be packed into a crate with a volume of 5,000 in^3 ?

It is tempting to answer "50 books" (since $50 \times 100 = 5,000$). However, this is incorrect, because you do not know the exact dimensions of each book! One book might be $5 \times 5 \times 4$, while another book might be $20 \times 5 \times 1$. Even though both have a volume of 100 in^3, they have different rectangular shapes. Without knowing the exact shapes of all the books, you cannot tell whether they would all fit into the crate or whether there would be empty space because the 50 books don't fill the crate perfectly.

When you are fitting three-dimensional objects into other three-dimensional objects, knowing the respective volumes is not enough. You must know the specific dimensions (length, width, and height) of each object to determine whether the objects can fit without leaving gaps.

Problem Set

Now that you've finished the chapter, try these problems.

1. If 40 percent of Andrea's living room floor is covered by a carpet that is 4 feet by 9 feet, what is the area of her living room floor?

2. A pentagon has three sides with length x and two sides with length $3x$. If x is $\frac{2}{3}$ of an inch, what is the perimeter of the pentagon?

3. Francis fences in three of the four sides of a rectangular yard. The unfenced side of the yard is 40 feet long. The yard has an area of 280 square feet. What is the length, in feet, of the fence that Francis installs?

4. In the figure shown, $ABCD$ is a quadrilateral, with AB parallel to DC. Point E is between D and C such that AE represents the height of $ABCD$ and E is the midpoint of DC. If AB is 4 inches long, AE is 5 inches long, and the area of triangle AED is 12.5 square inches, what is the area of $ABCD$? (Note: Figure not drawn to scale.)

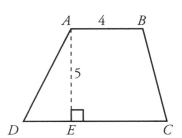

5. A rectangular solid has a square base, with each side of the base measuring 4 meters. If the volume of the solid is 48 cubic meters, what is the surface area of the solid?

6. If the perimeter of a rectangular flower bed is 30 feet, and its area is 44 square feet, what is the length of each of its shorter sides?

7. A rectangular swimming pool has a length of 30 meters, a width of 10 meters, and an average depth of 2 meters. If a hose can fill the pool at a rate of 0.5 cubic meters per minute, how many hours will it take the hose to fill the pool?

8. A rectangular tank needs to be coated with insulation. The tank has dimensions of 4 feet, 5 feet, and 2.5 feet. Each square foot of insulation costs $20. How much will it cost to cover the surface of the tank with insulation?

9. There is a rectangular parking lot with a length of $2x$ and a width of x. What is the ratio of the perimeter of the parking lot to the area of the parking lot, in terms of x ?

10. $ABCD$ is a square picture frame, as shown in the diagram. $EFGH$ is a square hole cut into the frame $ABCD$ as a space for a picture. The area of $EFGH$ (for the picture) is equal to the area of the picture frame (the area of $ABCD$ minus the area of $EFGH$). If $AB = 6$, what is the length of EF ?

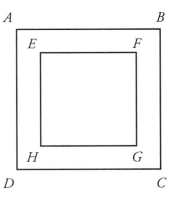

Solutions

1. **90 ft²:** The area of the carpet is equal to $l \times w$, or $4 \times 9 = 36$ ft². Set up a proportion to find the area of the whole living room floor. Use the simplified fraction for 40% to save time.

    $$\frac{2}{5} = \frac{36}{x}$$
    $$2x = 180 \qquad \text{Cross-multiply to solve.}$$
    $$x = 90 \, \text{ft}^2$$

2. **6 inches:** The perimeter of a pentagon is the sum of its five sides: $x + x + x + 3x + 3x = 9x$. If x is $\frac{2}{3}$ of an inch, the perimeter is $9\left(\frac{2}{3}\right)$, or 6 inches.

3. **54 feet:** In order to find the perimeter, you need the length and width of the yard. One side of the yard is 40 feet long; call this the length. The area of the yard is 280 square feet. Use this information to find the width of the yard:

    $$A = l \times w$$
    $$280 = 40w$$
    $$w = \frac{280}{40}$$
    $$= 7 \, \text{feet}$$

    Francis fences in the two 7-foot sides and one of the 40-foot sides. Thus, Francis needs $40 + 7 + 7 = 54$ feet of fencing.

4. **35 in²:** If E is the midpoint of DC, then $DE = EC = x$. Determine the length of x by using what you know about the area of triangle AED:

    $$A = \frac{b \times h}{2}$$
    $$12.5 = \frac{5x}{2}$$
    $$25 = 5x$$
    $$x = 5$$

    Therefore, the length of DC is $2x$, or 10.

    To find the area of the trapezoid, use the formula:

    $$A = \frac{b_1 + b_2}{2} \times h$$
    $$= \frac{4 + 10}{2} \times 5$$
    $$= 35 \, \text{in}^2$$

32

5. **80 m²:** The volume of a rectangular solid is equal to length × width × height. The length and width are both 4 meters long. Substitute values into the formulas as shown:

$$48 = 4 \times 4 \times h$$
$$h = 3$$

To find the surface area of a rectangular solid, sum the individual areas of all six faces:

	Area of One Face		Total Area of Identical Faces
Top and bottom:	$4 \times 4 = 16$	$\rightarrow$	$2 \times 16 = 32$
Four sides:	$4 \times 3 = 12$	$\rightarrow$	$4 \times 12 = 48$
	All 6 faces	$\rightarrow$	$32 + 48 = 80 \text{ m}^2$

6. **4 feet:** Set up equations to represent the area and perimeter of the flower bed:

$$A = l \times w \qquad\qquad P = 2(l + w)$$

Then, substitute the known values for the variables A and P:

$$44 = l \times w \qquad\qquad 30 = 2(l + w)$$

Solve the two equations using the substitution method:

$$l = \frac{44}{w}$$
$$30 = 2\left(\frac{44}{w} + w\right)$$
$$15w = 44 + w^2 \qquad \text{Multiply the entire equation by } \frac{w}{2}.$$
$$w^2 - 15w + 44 = 0 \qquad \text{Solving the quadratic equation yields two solutions:}$$
$$(w - 11)(w - 4) = 0 \qquad \text{4 and 11. Each represents a possible side length.}$$
$$w = \{4, 11\} \qquad \text{Since you were asked to find the length of the shorter side, the answer is 4.}$$

Alternatively, you can arrive at the correct solution by testing numbers. What length and width add up to 15 (half of the perimeter) and multiply to produce 44 (the area)? Some experimentation will demonstrate that the longer side must be 11 and the shorter side must be 4.

7. **20 hours:** The volume of the pool is length × width × height, or $30 \times 10 \times 2 = 600$ cubic meters. Use a standard work equation, $RT = W$, where W represents the total work of 600 m³:

$$0.5t = 600$$
$$t = 1,200 \text{ minutes}$$

Convert this time to hours by dividing by 60: $1,200 \div 60 = 20$ hours.

Alternatively, you could convert to the hourly rate first:

$$\frac{0.5 \text{ m}^3}{\text{min}} \times \frac{60 \text{ min}}{\text{hr}} = \frac{30 \text{ m}^3}{\text{hr}}$$

Next, use the standard work equation:

$$30t = 600$$
$$t = 20 \text{ hours}$$

8. **$1,700:** To find the surface area of a rectangular solid, sum the individual areas of all six faces:

	Area of One Face		Total Area of Identical Faces
Top and bottom:	$5 \times 4 = 20$	$\rightarrow$	$20 \times 2 = 40$
Side 1:	$5 \times 2.5 = 12.5$	$\rightarrow$	$12.5 \times 2 = 25$
Side 2:	$4 \times 2.5 = 10$	$\rightarrow$	$10 \times 2 = 20$
All 6 faces		$\rightarrow$	$40 + 25 + 20 = 85 \text{ ft}^2$

Thus, covering the entire tank will cost $85 \times \$20$, which equals $1,700.

9. $\dfrac{3}{x}$ **or 3 : x:** The length of the parking lot is $2x$ and the width is x. The perimeter is $2(2x + x)$ and the area is $(2x)(x)$. Set up a fraction to represent the ratio of the perimeter to the area:

$$\frac{\text{Perimeter}}{\text{Area}} = \frac{2(2x + x)}{(2x)(x)} = \frac{6x}{2x^2} = \frac{3}{x}$$

10. $\sqrt{18}$ **or $3\sqrt{2}$:** The area of the frame and the area of the picture sum to the total area of the image, which is 6^2, or 36. Therefore, the area of the frame and the picture are each equal to half of 36, or 18. Since $EFGH$ is a square, the length of EF is $\sqrt{18}$, or $3\sqrt{2}$.

Triangles and Diagonals

In This Chapter

- The Angles of a Triangle
- The Sides of a Triangle
- The Pythagorean Theorem
- Common Right Triangles
- Isosceles Triangles and the 45–45–90 Triangle
- Equilateral Triangles and the 30–60–90 Triangle
- Exterior Angles of a Triangle
- Triangles and Area
- Similar Triangles

In this chapter, you will learn all of the needed properties of triangles, including angle measures, perimeter, and area, as well as the rules for special triangles: isosceles, equilateral, and right. You'll also learn when and how to use the Pythagorean theorem.

CHAPTER 33 Triangles and Diagonals

The triangle is typically the most commonly tested polygon on the GMAT.

Right triangles (those with a 90° angle) require particular attention, because they have special properties that are useful for solving many GMAT geometry problems.

The most important property of a right triangle is the unique relationship of the three sides. Given the lengths of any two of the sides of a right triangle, you can determine the length of the third side using the Pythagorean theorem. There are even two special types of right triangles—the 30–60–90 triangle and the 45–45–90 triangle—for which you only need the length of *one* side to determine the lengths of the other two sides.

Finally, right triangles are essential for solving problems involving other polygons. For example, you might cut a square or rectangle into right triangles. Or, you might have a triangle inscribed in a circle or other shape.

The Angles of a Triangle

The angles in any given triangle have two key properties:

1. **The sum of the three angles of a triangle equals 180°.**

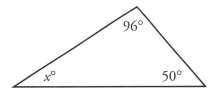

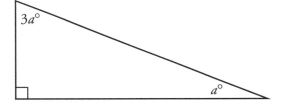

What is x? Since the sum of the three angles must be 180°, you can solve for x as follows:

$x = 180 - 96 - 50 = 34$

What is a? Since the sum of the three angles must be 180°, you can solve for a as follows:

$90 + 3a + a = 180 \rightarrow a = 22.5$

2. **Angles correspond to their opposite sides.** This means that the largest angle is opposite the longest side, while the smallest angle is opposite the shortest side. Additionally, **if two sides are equal, their opposite angles are also equal**.

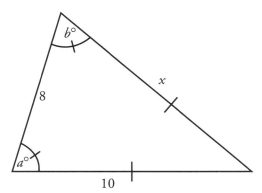

If $a = b$, what is the length of side x?

Since the side opposite angle b has a length of 10, the side opposite angle a must have the same length. Therefore, x is equal to 10.

Mark equal angles and equal sides with a slash, as shown. Also don't hesitate to redraw; if a figure is very different from the dimensions you were given, redraw the triangle closer to scale.

The Sides of a Triangle

Consider the following "impossible" triangle ABC and what it reveals about the relationship between the three sides of any triangle:

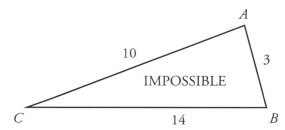

The triangle above could never be drawn with the given measurements. Why? Consider that the shortest distance between any two points is a straight line. According to the triangle shown, the direct straight line distance between point C and point B is 14; however, the indirect path from point C to B (the path that goes from C to A to B) is $10 + 3$, or 13, which is shorter than the direct path. This is impossible!

The example above leads to the following rule:

The sum of any two sides of a triangle must be greater than the third side.

If side CA is 10 and side AB is 3, then the maximum integer distance for side BC in the triangle above is 12. If the length of side BC is not restricted to integers, then this length is *less than* 13.

Any side must also be *greater than* the difference between the lengths of the other two sides. In this case, side BC must be longer than $10 - 3$, or 7.

Consider the following triangle and the proof that the given measurements are possible:

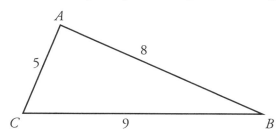

Test each combination of sides to prove that the measurements of this triangle are possible.

$8 + 5 > 9$	$8 - 5 < 9$
$9 + 5 > 8$	$9 - 5 < 8$
$9 + 8 > 5$	$9 - 8 < 5$

Note that the sum of two sides cannot be equal to the third side. The sum of two sides must always be *greater than* the third side. Likewise, the difference cannot be equal to the third side. The difference between two sides must be *less than* the third side.

If you are given two sides of a triangle, the length of the third side must lie between the difference and the sum of the two given sides. For example, if you are told that two sides are of lengths 3 and 4, then the length of the third side must be between $4 - 3 = 1$ and $4 + 3 = 7$, as shown here:

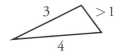 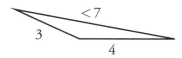

The Pythagorean Theorem

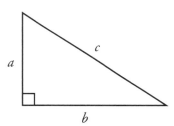

A **right triangle** is a triangle with one right angle (90°). Every right triangle is composed of two **legs** and a **hypotenuse**. The hypotenuse is the side opposite the largest angle (in this case, the right angle) and is often assigned the letter *c*. The two legs that form the right angle are often called *a* and *b* (it does not matter which leg is *a* and which leg is *b*).

Given the lengths of two sides of a right triangle, how can you determine the length of the third side? Use the Pythagorean theorem:

$$a^2 + b^2 = c^2$$

What is x?

$a^2 + b^2 = c^2$

$x^2 + 6^2 = 10^2$

$x^2 + 36 = 100$

$x^2 = 64$

$x = 8$

What is w?

$a^2 + b^2 = c^2$

$5^2 + 12^2 = w^2$

$25 + 144 = w^2$

$169 = w^2$

$13 = w$

Common Right Triangles

Certain right triangles appear over and over on the GMAT. It pays to memorize these common combinations in order to save time on the exam. Instead of using the Pythagorean theorem to solve for the lengths of the sides of these common right triangles, memorize the following Pythagorean triples:

Common Combinations	Key Multiples
3—4—5 The most popular of all right triangles $3^2 + 4^2 = 5^2$ $(9 + 16 = 25)$	6—8—10 9—12—15 12—16—20
5—12—13 Also quite popular on the GMAT $5^2 + 12^2 = 13^2$ $(25 + 144 = 169)$	10—24—26
8—15—17 Appears less frequently $8^2 + 15^2 = 17^2$ $(64 + 225 = 289)$	None

Watch out for impostor triangles! A non-right triangle with one side equal to 3 and another side equal to 4 does not have a third side of length 5. Likewise, if a right triangle has a side of 3 and a hypotenuse of 4, then the other leg is not 5; a leg can't be longer than the hypotenuse.

Isosceles Triangles and the 45—45—90 Triangle

An **isosceles triangle** is one in which two of the three sides are equal. The two angles opposite those two sides will also be equal. The most important isosceles triangle on the GMAT is the isosceles right triangle.

An isosceles right triangle has one 90° angle (opposite the hypotenuse) and two 45° angles (opposite the two equal legs). This triangle is called the 45—45—90 triangle.

The lengths of the legs of every 45–45–90 triangle have a set ratio; memorize this:

leg	leg	hypotenuse
$45°$	$45°$	$90°$
x	x	$x\sqrt{2}$

Try an example:

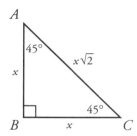

If the length of side *AB* is 5, what are the lengths of sides *BC* and *AC* ?

The question indicates that AB is 5, so $x = 5$. Use the ratio $x : x : x\sqrt{2}$ for sides $AB : BC : AC$ to determine that the sides of the triangle have lengths $5 : 5 : 5\sqrt{2}$. Therefore, the length of side $BC = 5$ and the length of side $AC = 5\sqrt{2}$. Try another example:

For a 45–45–90 triangle, if the length of side *AC* is $\sqrt{18}$, what are the lengths of sides *AB* and *BC* ?

Since the hypotenuse AC is $\sqrt{18}$:

$$x\sqrt{2} = \sqrt{18}$$
$$x = \frac{\sqrt{18}}{\sqrt{2}} = \sqrt{\frac{18}{2}}$$
$$x = \sqrt{9} = 3$$

Thus, the sides AB and BC are each equal to x, or 3.

Interestingly, the 45–45–90 triangle is exactly half of a square. That is, two 45–45–90 triangles put together make up a square. Thus, if you are given the diagonal of a square, you can use the 45–45–90 ratio to find the length of a side of the square:

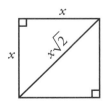

Equilateral Triangles and the 30–60–90 Triangle

An **equilateral triangle** is one in which all three sides (and all three angles) are equal. Each angle of an equilateral triangle is 60° (because all three angles must sum to 180°). A close relative of the equilateral triangle is the 30–60–90 triangle. Notice that two of these triangles, when put together, form an equilateral triangle:

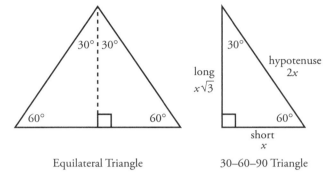

Equilateral Triangle   30–60–90 Triangle

The lengths of the legs of every 30–60–90 triangle have a set ratio; memorize this:

Leg	Leg	Hypotenuse
30°	60°	90°
x	$x\sqrt{3}$	$2x$

Try an example:

> If the short leg of a 30–60–90 triangle has a length of 6, what are the lengths of the long leg and the hypotenuse?

The question indicates that the short leg, which is opposite the 30° angle, is 6. Use the ratio $x : x\sqrt{3} : 2x$ to determine that the sides of the triangle have lengths 6 : $6\sqrt{3}$: 12. The long leg measures $6\sqrt{3}$ and the hypotenuse measures 12. Try another example:

> If an equilateral triangle has a side of length 10, what is its height?

The side of an equilateral triangle is the hypotenuse of a 30–60–90 triangle created when the height of the equilateral triangle is drawn (the dotted line in the equilateral triangle shown). Additionally, the height of an equilateral triangle is the same as the long leg of a 30–60–90 triangle. Since the hypotenuse is 10, use the ratio $x : x\sqrt{3} : 2x$ to set $2x = 10$ and determine that the value of x is 5. Therefore, the sides of the 30–60–90 triangle have lengths 5 : $5\sqrt{3}$: 10. The long leg has a length of $5\sqrt{3}$, which is the height of the equilateral triangle.

You may find it useful to estimate on some problems, in which case it will be good to know the approximate decimal forms for $\sqrt{2}$ and $\sqrt{3}$. If you're able to estimate aggressively, you can call either one 1.5. If you need to be more precise with your estimation, then $\sqrt{2} \approx 1.4$ and $\sqrt{3} \approx 1.7$. (A neat little mnemonic to help remember these: 2/14 is Valentine's Day and 3/17 is St. Patrick's Day.)

If you see a 45–45–90 triangle, use the ratio $x : x : x\sqrt{2}$. You can remember this ratio by always calling the smallest angle x (in this case, the two 45° angles) and then making the largest angle $x\sqrt{2}$ because there are two kinds of angles in this triangle, 45 and 90. (This isn't actually *why* the value is $\sqrt{2}$; it's just a way to remember the value.)

If you see a 30–60–90 triangle, use the ratio $x : x\sqrt{3} : 2x$. Remember this ratio by always calling the smallest angle x (in this case, the 30° angle) and the largest $2x$. The middle angle is $x\sqrt{3}$ because there are three kinds of angles in this triangle (30, 60, and 90).

If you get turned around on which side gets the 2 and which one gets the $\sqrt{3}$, compare the numbers: $\sqrt{3}$ is approximately 1.7. The value 2 is greater than 1.7, so 2 must go with the longest side.

Exterior Angles of a Triangle

An **exterior angle** of a triangle (x in the diagram shown) is equal in measure to the sum of the two non-adjacent (opposite) **interior angles** of the triangle (a and c in the diagram shown), as shown here:

$a + b + c = 180$ (sum of angles in a triangle).

$b + x = 180$ (form a straight line).

Therefore, $x = a + c$.

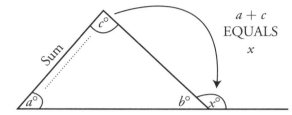

In particular, look for exterior angles within more complicated figures. You might even redraw the figure with certain lines removed to isolate the triangle and exterior angle you need:

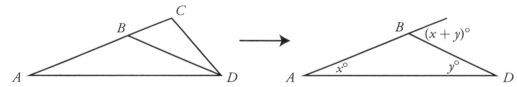

Triangles and Area

You are very likely to be asked to find the area of a triangle on the GMAT:

$$\text{Area of a Triangle} = \frac{\text{Base} \times \text{Height}}{2}$$

The **base** refers to the bottom side of the triangle. The **height** *always* refers to a line drawn from the opposite vertex to the base, creating a 90° angle.

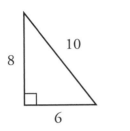

In the triangle on the left, the base is 6 and the height (perpendicular to the base) is 8. Therefore, the area is $(6 \times 8) \div 2 = 48 \div 2 = 24$.

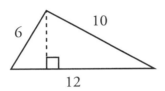

In this triangle, the base is 12, but the height is not shown. Neither of the other two sides of the triangle is perpendicular to the base. In order to find the area of this triangle, you would first need to determine the height, which is represented by the dotted line.

Although you may commonly think of the base of a triangle as whichever side is drawn horizontally or at the bottom, you can designate any side of a triangle as the base. For example, the following three figures show the same triangle, with each side in turn designated as the base:

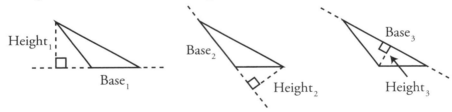

Since a triangle has only one area, the area must be the same regardless of the side chosen as the base. You can choose any pairing of height and base that you like, as long as the height is a perpendicular line drawn from the opposite vertex to the base that you've chosen.

Right triangles have three possible bases just as other triangles do, but they are special because their two legs are perpendicular. Therefore, if one of the legs is chosen as the base, then the other leg is the height. You can also choose the hypotenuse as the base, if that's easier for the problem.

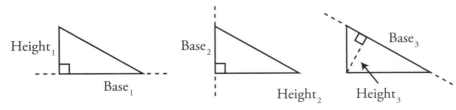

Similar Triangles

One final tool that you can use for GMAT triangle problems is the **similar triangle** strategy. Often, looking for similar triangles can help you solve complex problems.

In similar triangles, all of the **corresponding angles are equal** and the **corresponding sides are in proportion**, as in the triangles below:

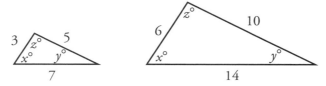

Once you find that two triangles have two pairs of equal (or congruent) angles, you know that the triangles are similar. If two sets of angles are congruent, then the third set of angles must be congruent, since the sum of the angles in any triangle is 180°.

Try an example:

What is the length of side *EF* ?

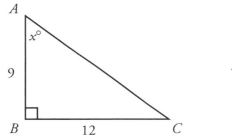 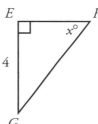

The two triangles above are similar because they have two angles in common (*x* and the right angle). Since they are similar triangles, their corresponding sides must be in proportion.

Side *BC* corresponds to side *EG* (since they both are opposite angle *x*). Because these sides are in the ratio of 12 : 4, you can determine that the large triangle is three times bigger than the smaller one. That is, the triangles are in the ratio of 3 : 1. Since side *AB* corresponds to side *EF*, and *AB* has a length of 9, you can conclude that side *EF* has a length of 3.

33

Problem Set

Now that you've finished the chapter, try these problems.

1. Two sides of a triangle have lengths 4 and 10. If the third side has a length of integer x, how many possible values are there for x?

2. In the figure shown, $AD = DB = DC$. If angle DCB is 60° and angle ACD is 20°, what is the value of x? (Note: Figure not drawn to scale.)

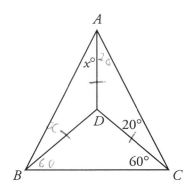

3. Beginning in Town A, Brogan rides a bike 10 miles west, 3 miles north, 5 miles east, and then 9 miles north, to Town B. What is the shortest distance between Town A and Town B? (Assume perfectly flat terrain.)

4. A square is bisected into two equal triangles, as shown in the figure. If the length of BD is $16\sqrt{2}$ inches, what is the area of the square?

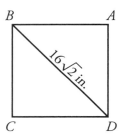

5. What is the value of x in the figure shown?

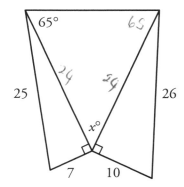

6. The size of a square computer screen is measured by the length of its diagonal. How much bigger is the visible area of a square 24-inch screen than the area of a square 20-inch screen?

Answers and explanations follow on the next page. ▶ ▶ ▶

Solutions

1. **Seven:** If two sides of a triangle are 4 and 10, the third side must be between $10 - 4$ and $10 + 4$. Therefore, the possible integer values for x are $\{7, 8, 9, 10, 11, 12,$ and $13\}$.

2. **$10°$:** If $AD = DB = DC$, then the three triangular regions in this figure are all isosceles triangles. Therefore, you can fill in some of the missing angle measurements as shown. Next, there are $180°$ in the large triangle ACB. Write the following equation for the three angles of the large triangle ACB:

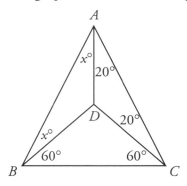

$$x + x + 20 + 20 + 60 + 60 = 180$$
$$2x + 160 = 180$$
$$x = 10$$

3. **13 miles:** Draw a rough sketch of the path Brogan takes, as shown. The direct distance from A to B forms the hypotenuse of a right triangle. The short leg (horizontal) is $10 - 5 = 5$ miles and the long leg (vertical) is $9 + 3 = 12$ miles. This is a common right triangle with dimensions 5–12–13. If you don't have that common triangle memorized, use the Pythagorean theorem to find the direct distance from A to B:

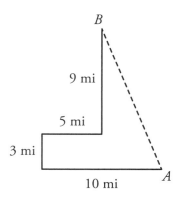

$$5^2 + 12^2 = c^2$$
$$25 + 144 = c^2$$
$$c^2 = 169$$
$$c = 13$$

4.   **256 in^2**: A square is formed from two 45–45–90 triangles. The diagonal of a square is $s\sqrt{2}$ and the given length of the diagonal in the problem is $16\sqrt{2}$. Therefore, the side length of square *ABCD* is $s = 16$ inches. The area of the square is s^2, or $16^2 = 256$.

5.   **50°**: Find the missing lengths of the two right triangles on the left and right sides of the figure. The right-hand triangle (10–*y*–26) is the 5–12–13 triangle multiplied by 2. The missing length, therefore, is $12 \times 2 = 24$. Use the Pythagorean theorem to find the value for the left-hand triangle:

$$7^2 + b^2 = 25^2$$
$$49 + b^2 = 625$$
$$b^2 = 576$$
$$b = 24$$

Since the two sides are the same length, the inner triangle is isosceles. Therefore, both angles opposite the equal sides measure 65°. Since there are 180° in a right triangle, $x = 180 - 2(65) = 50$.

6.   **88 in^2**: The diagonal of the larger screen is 24 inches. For a square, $d = s\sqrt{2}$, so:

$$24 = s\sqrt{2}$$
$$s = \frac{24}{\sqrt{2}}$$

You may have learned in school not to leave a root on the bottom of a fraction, but don't do anything about this yet. (In general, if you see annoying math, hold off on doing it as long as you can.) First, find the equivalent value for the smaller screen:

$$20 = s\sqrt{2}$$
$$s = \frac{20}{\sqrt{2}}$$

The area of a square is s^2, so do that math:

Large screen:

$$A = \frac{24}{\sqrt{2}} \times \frac{24}{\sqrt{2}}$$
$$= \frac{24 \times 24}{2}$$
$$= 24 \times 12$$
$$= 2 \times 12 \times 12$$
$$= 288$$

Small screen:

$$A = \frac{20}{\sqrt{2}} \times \frac{20}{\sqrt{2}}$$
$$= \frac{20 \times 20}{2}$$
$$= 20 \times 10$$
$$= 200$$

The square roots disappear on their own! The visible area of the larger screen is $288 - 200 = 88$ square inches bigger than the visible area of the smaller screen.

Circles and Cylinders

In This Chapter

- Radius, Diameter, Circumference, and Area

- Area of a Sector

- Inscribed vs. Central Angles

- Inscribed Triangles

- Cylinders and Volume

In this chapter, you will learn how to use the radius and diameter of a circle to find circumference and area, as well as how to find the area or circumference of just a portion of a circle. You'll also learn the difference between inscribed and central angles and how to use them. Finally, you'll learn about three-dimensional shapes related to circles, including cylinders and spheres.

CHAPTER 34 Circles and Cylinders

A **circle** is defined as the set of points in a plane that are equidistant from a fixed center point. A circle contains 360°.

Any line segment that connects the center point to a point on the circle is termed a **radius** of the circle. If point O is the center of the circle shown, then segment OC is a radius:

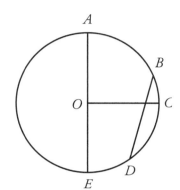

Any line segment that connects two points on a circle is called a **chord**, such as line BD. Any chord that passes through the center of the circle is called a **diameter**, such as line AE. The diameter is always two times the length of the radius.

The GMAT tests your ability to find the circumference and the area of whole and partial circles. In addition, some advanced problems may test **cylinders**, which are three-dimensional shapes made, in part, of circles. The GMAT may test your ability to find the volume of cylinders.

Radius, Diameter, Circumference, and Area

The relationships between the radius, diameter, circumference, and area remain constant for every circle. If you know any one of these values, you can find all of the rest.

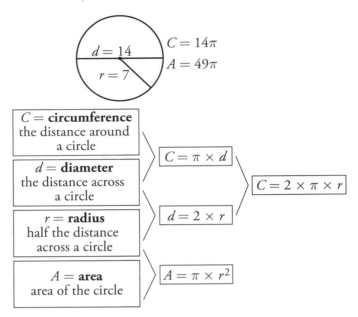

For Problem Solving questions, you will often need to use one of these values to solve for one of the other three. For Data Sufficiency questions, just knowing that you have one of these values is enough to know that you can find any of the others—so you may not have to do very much math at all.

The value of π is approximately 3.14. Most of the time, the GMAT will keep π in the answer, so you don't need to know what it is. Occasionally, you may need to estimate an answer; use 3 as the estimated value for π. Try an example:

> What is the area of a circle with a circumference of 16π?

In order to find the area of a circle, find the radius. The circumference of the circle is 16π and $C = 2\pi r$, so the radius must be 8. Plug this into the area formula:

$$A = \pi r^2 = \pi\left(8^2\right) = 64\pi$$

Area of a Sector

The GMAT may ask you to solve for the area of a sector of a circle instead of the area of the entire circle. You can find the area of a sector by determining the fraction of the entire area that the sector occupies. Try an example:

What is the area of sector *BCA* (the shaded region) in the figure?

First, find the area of the entire circle:

$$A = \pi r^2 = \pi \left(3^2\right) = 9\pi$$

Then, use the central angle to determine what fraction of the entire circle is represented by the sector. Since the sector is defined by the central angle of 60°, and the entire circle is 360°, the sector occupies $\dfrac{60^\circ}{360^\circ} = \dfrac{1}{6}$ of the area of the circle.

Therefore, the area of sector *BCA* is $\left(\dfrac{1}{6}\right)(9\pi) = 1.5\pi$.

Inscribed vs. Central Angles

The **central angle** is defined as an angle whose vertex lies at the center point of a circle. Another type of angle is termed an **inscribed angle**. An inscribed angle has its vertex on the circle itself.

The following figures illustrate the difference between a central angle and an inscribed angle:

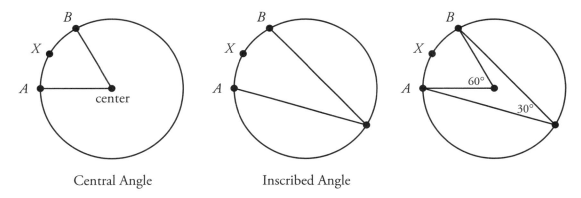

Central Angle   Inscribed Angle

In both cases, the angle defines both an arc (*AXB*, a portion of the circumference) and a sector (the pie-shaped wedge, a portion of the area).

In the circle at the far right, there is a central angle and an inscribed angle, both of which intercept arc *AXB*. The central angle for the arc is 60° (or one-sixth of the complete 360° circle). **An inscribed angle is equal to half of the equivalent central angle**, in degrees. In this case, the inscribed angle is 30°, which is half of 60°.

Inscribed Triangles

Related to this idea of an inscribed angle is that of an **inscribed triangle**. A triangle is said to be inscribed in a circle if all of the vertices of the triangle are points on the circle. The important rule to remember is this: **If one of the sides of an inscribed triangle is a *diameter* of the circle, then the triangle *must* be a right triangle.** Conversely, any right triangle inscribed in a circle must have the diameter of the circle as one of its sides (thereby splitting the circle in half).

In the second figure, triangle *ABC* must be a right triangle, since *AC* is a diameter of the circle.

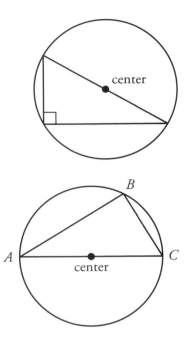

Cylinders and Volume

Cylinder questions are not especially common on the GMAT; you probably won't see any, but, if you do, you might not see more than one. If geometry is a weaker area for you, consider not studying this material and guessing immediately if you do see a cylinder problem on the exam.

The volume of a cylinder measures how much "stuff" it can hold inside. In order to find the volume of a cylinder, use the following formula:

$$V = \pi r^2 h \qquad V \text{ is the volume, } r \text{ is the radius, and } h \text{ is the height of the cylinder.}$$

Determining the volume of a cylinder requires two pieces of information: 1) the radius of the cylinder and 2) the height of the cylinder.

The figures below show that two cylinders can have the same volume but different shapes (and therefore each would fit differently inside a larger object):

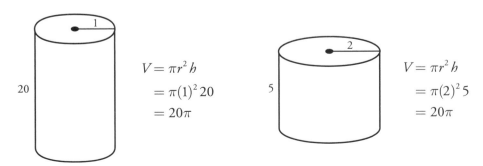

Problem Set

Now that you've finished the chapter, try these problems.

1. As shown in the figure, a circular lawn with a radius of 5 meters is surrounded by a circular walkway that is 4 meters wide. What is the area of the walkway, in square meters?

    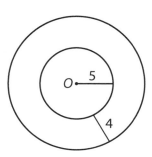

2. Ren can run π meters every 2 seconds. If a circular track has a radius of 75 meters, how many minutes does it take Ren to run twice around the track?

3. As shown in the figure, *BE* and *CD* are both diameters of a circle with center *A*. If the area of the circle is 180, what is the total area of the shaded regions?

    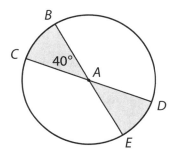

4. A cylindrical water tank has a diameter of 4 meters and a height of 20 meters. A water truck can fill π cubic meters of the tank every minute. How many minutes will it take the water truck to fill the water tank from empty to half full?

5. A Hydrogenator water gun has a cylindrical water tank, which is 30 centimeters long. A hose can fill the Hydrogenator with π cubic centimeters of water every second. If it takes 8 minutes to fill the tank with water, what is the diameter of the circular base of the gun's water tank, in centimeters?

Solutions

1. $56\pi \text{ m}^2$: The area of the walkway is the area of the entire image (walkway + lawn) minus the area of the lawn. Find the area of each circle and subtract:

    Large circle: $A = \pi r^2 = \pi(9)^2 = 81\pi$

    Small circle: $A = \pi r^2 = \pi(5)^2 = 25\pi$ Subtract: $81\pi - 25\pi = 56\pi \text{ m}^2$

2. **10 minutes:** The distance around the track is the circumference of the circle:

    $$C = 2\pi r$$
    $$C = 2\pi(75)$$
    $$C = 150\pi$$

    Running twice around the circle would equal a distance of 300π meters. At a rate of π meters every 2 seconds, Ren runs 30π meters every minute. Therefore, it will take Ren 10 minutes to run 300π meters.

3. **40:** The two central angles of the shaded sectors cover a total of $40° + 40° = 80°$. Figure out what fraction of the circle this represents, then use that fraction to solve for the portion of the area represented by the shaded regions:

    $$\frac{80}{360} = \frac{2}{9} \qquad\qquad \frac{2}{9} \text{ of 180 is 40.}$$

4. **40 minutes:** First, find the volume of the cylindrical tank:

    $$\begin{aligned} V &= \pi r^2 \times h \\ &= \pi(2)^2 \times 20 \\ &= 80\pi \end{aligned}$$

    If the water truck can fill π cubic meters of the tank every minute, it will take 80 minutes to fill the tank completely; therefore, it will take $80 \div 2 = 40$ minutes to fill the tank halfway.

5. **8 centimeters:** In 8 minutes, or 480 seconds, $480\pi \text{ cm}^3$ of water flows into the tank. Therefore, the volume of the tank is 480π. Use the height of 30 to solve for the radius:

    $$\begin{aligned} V &= \pi r^2 \times h \\ 480\pi &= 30\pi r^2 \\ r^2 &= 16 \\ r &= 4 \end{aligned}$$

    Therefore, the diameter of the tank's base is 8 centimeters.

Coordinate Plane

In This Chapter

- Positive and Negative Quadrants

- The Slope of a Line

- The Four Types of Slopes

- The Intercepts of a Line

- Slope-Intercept Equation: $y = mx + b$

- Horizontal and Vertical Lines

- The Distance Between Two Points

In this chapter, you will learn how to find the slope of a line and how to map a line onto a coordinate plane. You'll learn how to use the slope-intercept form of the equation of a line, as well as how to find the distance between any two points in a coordinate plane.

CHAPTER 35 Coordinate Plane

The **coordinate plane** is formed by a horizontal axis or reference line (the **x-axis**) and a vertical axis (the **y-axis**), as shown below. These axes are each marked off like a number line, with both positive and negative numbers. The axes cross at right angles at the number zero.

Points in the plane are identified by using an ordered pair of numbers, such as the point shown, which is written as $(2, -3)$. The first number in the ordered pair (2) is the **x-coordinate**, which corresponds to the point's horizontal location, as measured by the x-axis. The second number in the ordered pair (-3) is the **y-coordinate**, which corresponds to the point's vertical location, as indicated by the y-axis. The point $(0, 0)$, where the axes cross, is called the **origin**.

A line in the plane is formed by the connection of two or more points. Also, along the x-axis line, the y-coordinate is 0. Likewise, along the y-axis line, the x-coordinate is 0.

If the GMAT gives you coordinates with other variables, match them to x and y. For instance, if you have point (a, b), a is the x-coordinate and b is the y-coordinate.

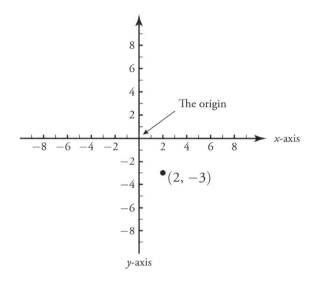

Positive and Negative Quadrants

There are four quadrants in the coordinate plane, as shown in the figure below. Start in the upper-right corner and move *counter*clockwise.

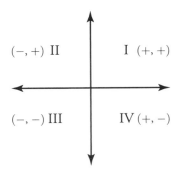

Quadrant I contains only those points with a **positive** *x*-coordinate and a **positive** *y*-coordinate.

Quadrant II contains only those points with a **negative** *x*-coordinate and a **positive** *y*-coordinate.

Quadrant III contains only those points with a **negative** *x*-coordinate and a **negative** *y*-coordinate.

Quadrant IV contains only those points with a **positive** *x*-coordinate and a **negative** *y*-coordinate.

The Slope of a Line

The **slope** of a line is defined as *rise over run*—that is, how much the line *rises* vertically divided by how much the line *runs* horizontally.

The slope of a line can be determined by taking any two points on the line and 1) determining the **rise**, or difference between their *y*-coordinates, and 2) determining the **run**, or difference between their *x*-coordinates. You can use the formula below to find a slope:

$$\text{Slope} = \frac{\text{Rise}}{\text{Run}}$$

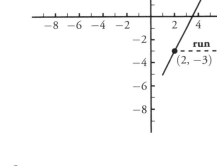

For example, in the graph shown, the line rises vertically from -3 to $+5$. To find the vertical distance, subtract the *y*-coordinates: $5 - (-3) = 8$. Thus, the line rises 8 units. The line also runs horizontally from 2 to 6. To find the horizontal distance, subtract the *x*-coordinates: $6 - 2 = 4$. Thus, the line runs 4 units.

Put the results together to find the slope of the line: $\frac{\text{Rise}}{\text{Run}} = \frac{8}{4} = 2$.

Two other points on the same line may have a different rise and run, but the slope will be the same. The rise over run will always be 2 because a line has a constant slope.

The slope of a line is equal to $\frac{y_2 - y_1}{x_2 - x_1}$.

For a different line, if you are given the two points $(2, 3)$ and $(4, -1)$, then you can find the slope:

$$\frac{-1 - 3}{4 - 2} = \frac{-4}{2} = -2$$

You can use the two points in either order, but make sure that y_2 and x_2 always come from the same point (and that y_1 and x_1 always come from the same point). Here's the slope for the same two points but used in reverse order, $(4, -1)$ and $(2, 3)$:

$$\frac{3 - (-1)}{2 - 4} = \frac{4}{-2} = -2$$

Either way, the slope is the same.

The Four Types of Slopes

A line can have one of four types of slopes:

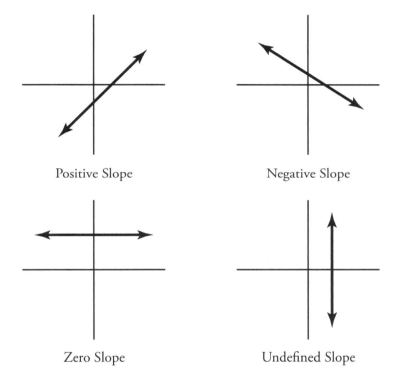

Positive Slope   Negative Slope

Zero Slope   Undefined Slope

A line with positive slope rises upward from left to right. A line with negative slope falls downward from left to right. A horizontal line has zero slope. A vertical line has undefined slope. Notice that the x-axis has zero slope, while the y-axis has undefined slope.

The Intercepts of a Line

A point where a line intersects a coordinate axis is called an **intercept**. There are two types of intercepts: the x-intercept, where the line intersects the x-axis, and the y-intercept, where the line intersects the y-axis.

The x-intercept is expressed using the ordered pair $(x, 0)$, where x is the point where the line intersects the x-axis. **The x-intercept is the point on the line at which $y = 0$.** In this graph, the x-intercept is -4, as expressed by the ordered pair $(-4, 0)$.

The y-intercept is expressed using the ordered pair $(0, y)$, where y is the point where the line intersects the y-axis. **The y-intercept is the point on the line at which $x = 0$.** In this graph, the y-intercept is 6, as expressed by the ordered pair $(0, 6)$.

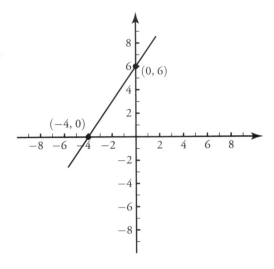

Slope-Intercept Equation: $y = mx + b$

35

Linear equations represent lines in the coordinate plane. Linear equations often look like this: $Ax + By = C$, where A, B, and C are numbers. For instance, $6x + 3y = 18$ is a linear equation. Linear equations never involve terms such as x^2, $\sqrt{x}$, or xy.

In coordinate plane problems, it can be useful to write linear equations in the slope-intercept form:

$$y = mx + b$$

In this equation, m represents the slope of the line and b represents the y-intercept of the line, or the point at which the line crosses the y-axis. When you want to graph a linear equation, rewrite the equation in the slope-intercept form. Try this example:

What is the slope-intercept form for a line with the equation $6x + 3y = 18$?

Rewrite the equation by solving for y as follows:

$$6x + 3y = 18$$
$$3y = 18 - 6x \qquad \text{Subtract } 6x \text{ from both sides.}$$
$$y = 6 - 2x \qquad \text{Divide both sides by 3.}$$
$$y = -2x + 6 \qquad \text{Rearrange. The } y\text{-intercept is } (0, 6), \text{ and the slope is } -2.$$

To graph this line, first put a point at $+6$ on the y-axis (because the y-intercept, b, equals 6).

Then, count down 2 units (because the slope is negative) and to the right 1 unit. Place another point.

Now, draw a line between the two points.

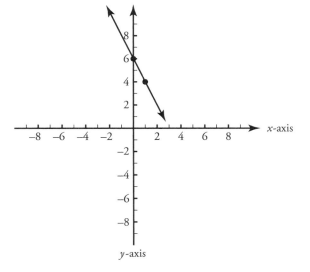

The GMAT sometimes asks you to determine which quadrants a given line passes through. For example:

Which quadrants does the line $2x + y = 5$ pass through?

First, rewrite the line in the form $y = mx + b$:

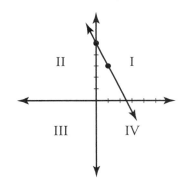

$$2x + y = 5$$
$$y = 5 - 2x$$
$$y = -2x + 5$$

Next, sketch the line. Since $b = 5$, the y-intercept is the point $(0, 5)$. The slope is -2, so the line slopes downward to the right from the y-intercept. A slope of -2 is the equivalent of $\frac{-2}{1}$. Count two places down from the intercept (the rise of a negative slope) and one place to the right (the run). Draw a second point, then connect the two points with a line. You can now see that the line passes through quadrants I, II, and IV.

Alternatively, find two points on the line by setting x and y equal to 0 in the original equation. In this way, you find the x- and y-intercepts:

$$x = 0$$
$$2x + y = 5$$
$$2(0) + y = 5$$
$$y = 5$$

$$y = 0$$
$$2x + y = 5$$
$$2x + (0) = 5$$
$$x = 2.5$$

The points $(0, 5)$ and $(2.5, 0)$ are both on the line.

Now, sketch the line using the points you have identified. If you plot $(0, 5)$ and $(2.5, 0)$ on the coordinate plane, you can connect them to see the position of the line. Again, the line passes through quadrants I, II, and IV.

Horizontal and Vertical Lines

Horizontal and vertical lines are not expressed in the $y = mx + b$ form. Instead, they are expressed as simpler one-variable equations.

Horizontal lines are expressed in the form:

$y = $ *some number*, such as $y = 2$ or $y = -7$

Vertical lines are expressed in the form:

$x = $ *some number*, such as $x = 3$ or $x = 5$

All the points on a vertical line have the same x-coordinate. This is why the equation of a vertical line is defined only by x. The y-axis itself corresponds to the equation $x = 0$. Likewise, all the points on a horizontal line have the same y-coordinate. This is why the equation of a horizontal line is defined only by y. The x-axis itself corresponds to the equation $y = 0$.

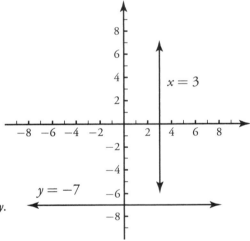

The Distance between Two Points

The distance between any two points in the coordinate plane can be calculated by using the Pythagorean theorem. For example:

What is the distance between the points $(1, 3)$ and $(7, -5)$?

Start by drawing a right triangle connecting the points, as shown here:

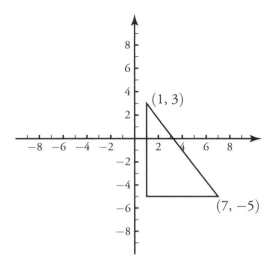

Next, find the lengths of the two legs of the triangle by calculating the rise and the run.

The *y*-coordinate changes from 3 to -5, a difference of 8 (the vertical leg).

The *x*-coordinate changes from 1 to 7, a difference of 6 (the horizontal leg).

Now, if you have a common right triangle, use what you've memorized. In this case, the triangle is a multiple of the common 3–4–5 triangle: 6–8–10. The hypotenuse of the triangle is 10, so the distance between the two points is 10 units.

Alternatively, use the Pythagorean theorem to calculate the length of the diagonal, which is the distance between the points:

$$6^2 + 8^2 = c^2$$
$$36 + 64 = c^2$$
$$100 = c^2$$
$$c = 10$$

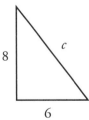

Advanced material for the Geometry unit can be found in Atlas, Manhattan Prep's online learning platform. Use the online material only if you feel that you have mastered everything in the Geometry unit of this strategy guide and only if you are aiming for a Quant section score of 48 or higher.

Problem Set

Now that you've finished the chapter, try these problems.

1. A line has the equation $y = 3x + 7$. At which point does this line intersect the y-axis?

2. A line has the equation $x = -2y + z$. If $(3, 2)$ is a point on the line, what is z ?

3. Which quadrants, if any, do NOT contain any points on the line represented by $x - y = 18$?

4. A line has a slope of $\frac{1}{6}$ and intersects the x-axis at $(-24, 0)$. At which point does this line intersect the y-axis?

5. A line has the equation $x = \frac{y}{80} - 20$. At which point does this line intersect the x-axis?

6. Which quadrants, if any, do NOT contain any points on the line represented by $x = 10y$?

7. Which quadrants, if any, contain points on the line represented by $x + 18 = 2y$?

8. A line has a slope of $\frac{3}{4}$ and intersects the point $(-12, -39)$. At which point does this line intersect the x-axis?

35

Answers and explanations follow on the next page. ▶ ▶ ▶

Solutions

1. **(0, 7):** A line intersects the y-axis at the y-intercept. Since this equation is written in slope-intercept form, $y = mx + b$, the y-intercept is the b portion of the equation: 7. Thus, the line intersects the y-axis at the point $(0, 7)$.

2. **7:** Substitute the coordinates $(3, 2)$ for x and y and solve for z:

    $$3 = -2(2) + z$$
    $$3 = -4 + z$$
    $$z = 7$$

3. **Quadrant II:** First, rewrite the line in slope-intercept form:

    $$y = x - 18$$

    Find the intercepts by setting x equal to 0 and y equal to 0:

    $$y = 0 - 18 \qquad\qquad 0 = x - 18$$
    $$y = -18 \qquad\qquad\quad x = 18$$

    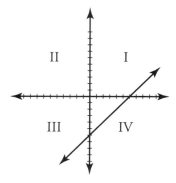

    Plot the points: $(0, -18)$ and $(18, 0)$. (In the diagram shown, each tick mark represents three units: 3, 6, 9, . . .) The line does not pass through quadrant II.

4. **(0, 4):** Plug the slope in for m. Then, use the given point to find the value of b:

    $$y = \frac{1}{6}x + b$$
    $$0 = \frac{1}{6}(-24) + b$$
    $$0 = -4 + b$$
    $$b = 4$$

    The variable b represents the y-intercept. Therefore, the line intersects the y-axis at $(0, 4)$.

5. **(−20, 0):** A line intersects the x-axis at the x-intercept or when the y-coordinate is equal to 0. Substitute 0 for y and solve for x:

    $$x = 0 - 20$$
    $$x = -20$$

    The line crosses the x-intercept at the point $(-20, 0)$.

6. **Quadrants II and IV:** First, rewrite the line in slope-intercept form: $y = \frac{x}{10}$

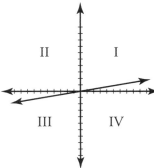

If you plug in 0 for either variable, the other variable will also equal 0. The line crosses the y-intercept at the origin $(0, 0)$. To find another point on the line, substitute any convenient number for x; given the equation, 10 would be a good number to choose:

$$y = \frac{10}{10} = 1 \qquad \text{The point } (10, 1) \text{ is on the line.}$$

Plot the points: $(0, 0)$ and $(10, 1)$. The line does not pass through quadrants II or IV.

7. **Quadrants I, II, and III:** First, rewrite the line in slope-intercept form: $y = \frac{x}{2} + 9$

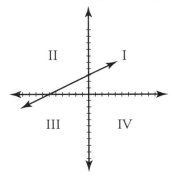

Find the intercepts by setting x equal to 0 and y equal to 0:

$$0 = \frac{x}{2} + 9 \qquad\qquad y = \frac{0}{2} + 9$$
$$x = -18 \qquad\qquad\qquad y = 9$$

Plot the points: $(-18, 0)$ and $(0, 9)$. (In the diagram shown, each tick mark represents three units: 3, 6, 9, ...) The line passes through quadrants I, II, and III.

8. **(40, 0):** First, plug the information given into the slope-intercept equation to find the value of b:

$$y = \frac{3}{4}x + b$$

$$-39 = \frac{3}{4}(-12) + b$$

$$-39 = -9 + b$$

$$b = -30$$

This allows you to write the equation of this line:

$$y = \frac{3}{4}x - 30$$

The line intersects the x-axis when $y = 0$. Set y equal to 0 and solve for x:

$$0 = \frac{3}{4}x - 30$$

$$\frac{3}{4}x = 30$$

$$x = 40$$

The line intersects the x-axis at $(40, 0)$.

35

Go beyond books.
Try us for free.

In Person

Find a GMAT course near you and attend the first session free, no strings attached.

**Find your city at
manhattanprep.com/gmat/classes**

Online

Enjoy the flexibility of prepping from home or the office with our online course.

**See the full schedule at
manhattanprep.com/gmat/classes**

On Demand

Prep where you are, when you want with GMAT Interact™— our on-demand course.

**Try 5 full lessons for free at
manhattanprep.com/gmat/interact**

Not sure which is right for you? Try all three! Or, give us a call, and we'll help you figure out which program fits you best.

Prep made personal.

Whether you want quick coaching in a particular GMAT subject area or a comprehensive study plan developed around your goals, we've got you covered. Our expert GMAT instructors can help you hit your top score.

CHECK OUT THESE REVIEWS FROM MANHATTAN PREP STUDENTS.

Contact us at 800-576-4628 or gmat@manhattanprep.com
for more information about your GMAT study options.